HISTORY OF LITERATURE SERIES

General Editor: A. NORMAN JEFFARES

HISTORY OF LITERATURE SERIES

General editor: A. Norman Jeffares

SIXTEENTH-CENTURY ENGLISH LITERATURE
Murray Roston

SEVENTEENTH-CENTURY ENGLISH LITERATURE
Bruce King

TWENTIETH-CENTURY ENGLISH LITERATURE
Harry Blamires

ANGLO-IRISH LITERATURE
A. Norman Jeffares

HISTORY OF LITERATURE SERIES

ANGLO-IRISH LITERATURE

A. Norman Jeffares

Schocken Books · New York

First American edition published by Schocken Books 1982

10 9 8 7 6 5 4 3 2 1   82 83 84 85

Published by agreement with The Macmillan Press Ltd., London

Typeset by
Cambrian Typesetters
Farnborough, Hants.

Printed in Hong Kong

ISBN 0-8052-3828-X

Contents

List of plates

Acknowledgements

Professor Eamonn Carrigan, Mr Douglas Mack, Dr Bo Sekine, Professor David Webb and Dr Robert Welch all aided me with helpful information and criticism.

The authors and publishers wish to acknowledge the following illustration sources.

Belfast Museum and Art Gallery 7; Bord Failte 14a; Camera Press Ltd/Gerald Karsh 9a; A.C. Cooper Ltd 5; C.P. Curran/Oxford University Press 15a; G.A. Duncan 14b; The Hon. Desmond Guinness 12; Illustrated London News 8; Isa MacNie 9b; National Gallery of Ireland 1, 3b; National Library of Ireland 3a, 4, 5b, 16a, 16b; Michael and Anne Yeats 10, 13.

The author and publishers also wish to thank the following who have kindly given permission for the use of copyright material:

Blackstaff Press Ltd for an extract from the poem 'Events in my Native Province' by John Hewitt; Faber and Faber Ltd for a verse from 'The Sunlight on the Garden' from *The Collected Poems of Louis Macneice*; Oliver D. Gogarty for extracts from his late father's poems 'Ringsend' and 'Fresh Fields' by Oliver St John Gogarty; Mrs Katherine B. Kavanagh for extracts from the late Patrick Kavanagh's poems 'To a Blackbird', 'The Great Hunger' and 'Who Killed James Joyce'; the Society of Authors as the Literary Representatives of the Estate of James Joyce for an extract from the poem 'Gas from a Burner' in *Pomes Penyeach*; A.P. Watt Ltd on behalf of Michael B. Yeats and Anne Yeats for extracts from the *Collected Poems of W.B. Yeats*.

Every effort has been made to trace all the copyright holders but if any have been inadvertently overlooked the publishers will be pleased to make the necessary arrangement at the first opportunity.

Editor's Preface

THE study of literature requires knowledge of contexts as well as of texts. What kind of person wrote the poem, the play, the novel, the essay? What forces acted upon them as they wrote? What was the historical, the political, the philosophical, the economic, the cultural background? Was the writer accepting or rejecting the literary conventions of the time, or developing them, or creating entirely new kinds of literary expression? Are there interactions between literature and the art, music or architecture of its period? Was the writer affected by contemporaries or isolated?

Such questions stress the need for students to go beyond the reading of set texts, to extend their knowledge by developing a sense of chronology, of action and reaction, and of the varying relationships between writers and society.

Histories of literature can encourage students to make comparisons, can aid in understanding the purposes of individual authors and in assessing the totality of their achievements. Their development can be better understood and appreciated with some knowledge of the background of their time. And histories of literature, apart from their valuable function as reference books, can demonstrate the great wealth of writing in English that is there to be enjoyed. They can guide the reader who wishes to explore it more fully and to gain in the process deeper insights into the rich diversity not only of literature but of human life itself.

A. NORMAN JEFFARES

TO JEANNE, BO AND MASARU

Introduction

ANGLO-IRISH literature is more than the work of some few outstanding recent writers — Shaw, Yeats and Joyce. Its history, extending from the medieval period, is composed of a body of literature in English which, though it is often subsumed into histories of English literature, is, generally speaking, intimately bound up with Ireland. To understand Anglo-Irish writing and the spirit of Janus-like attitudes it often expresses requires some knowledge of the Irish background: historical, political, economic, social and cultural. The historical tradition of the Anglo-Irish themselves extends over more than eight hundred years: it blends and contrasts with the very different Irish traditions which preceded it, which were themselves related to yet earlier traditions — for Ireland has layers of settlement going back into pre-history — and which continue to exist and to develop today.

The description 'Anglo-Irish' applied to literature is, to a certain extent, an increasingly accepted term of convenience in academic criticism: it does not exactly correspond to the historians' label, nor yet to the definition of it attributed to an exuberant Catholic Irish writer, 'a Protestant on a horse'. It has been called writing in English by Irish authors, and that is a reasonably broad working definition of it.

The need to justify removing Irish writing in English from histories of English literature in order to see it in its own terms as a continuous entity, a development of a particular literature, is now less pressing since the idea of separate Irish political identity has become accepted. And any history of English literature which failed to include, say, Swift or Farquhar or Goldsmith or Maria Edgeworth, or George Moore or Shaw, or Yeats or Joyce or Beckett, would hardly be representative of English literature. The fact that an Irish writer can appear in histories of literature that belong to two different kinds of culture, to, in effect, both traditions, those of two different islands separated by a very narrow strip of sea indeed, need not worry any reader unduly. The basic fact in most Anglo-Irish writers' lives has been this inheritance of two traditions, admittedly in varying degrees — education akin to that of writers in England but, above that, as with the Scots and the Welsh, an access to extra dimensions, and the fruitful, creative tensions created thereby. A companion, complementary history in this series by Dr Declan Kiberd deals with literature in the Irish language.

The strength of the achievement of the outstanding Anglo-Irish writers tends to obscure that of the lesser, who for various reasons are often left out of histories of English literature: and while the major authors are easily available and are continuously subjected to the minute attention of critics and scholars internationally, it is often surprisingly difficult to find texts of the minor writers.

How, then, is Yeats's phrase 'getting it all in order' to be applied to this corpus of literature, widely differing in range as in achievement? Some readers will wish for wide, sweeping literary—historical generalisations and categorisations, some for studies of genres, or themes, or periods, while some will opt for accounts of individual writers. The individual writer in Anglo-Irish literature tends to write in different forms and thus presents a problem if his work is to be considered as part of a genre: is Goldsmith, for instance, to be discussed as poet, as playwright, as novelist, as essayist, as populariser? Better probably to consider how this often difficult life shaped his easy versatility, the generous spirit his writings display.

Discussion of writers in earlier periods in the order of their dates of birth does provide a convenient guide to the chronological development of the literature and interrelations of authors: but by the end of the nineteenth century the increasing number of writers, and in the twentieth the development of the writing, make such an arrangement less useful, and accordingly modern writers are discussed under the headings of the genre in which their main reputations have been gained, though their writings in other forms are also discussed at the same time so that the reader's view of them is not fragmented. This arrangement also allows such things as themes and particular periods of writing as well as groups of writers — the Celtic Twilight, say, or the early Abbey dramatists — to be considered in close connection. This can, of course, lead to some apparent anomalies, to Beckett's work as a novelist (which he would probably consider himself primarily), for instance, being discussed along with his plays in the chapter dealing with twentieth-century drama. Similarly, while Yeats is obviously treated in the chapter on modern poetry, his dramatic writings and his prose are necessarily also included here to give a survey of the whole of his achievement. Within the three last chapters which deal with modern poetry, fiction and drama, writers are, as far as possible, kept in chronological order.

Writers can change and develop and express themselves in many ways and one of the aims of this history of Anglo-Irish literature is to convey a general sense of the scope of the writing of different individuals, to discuss — in as much detail as the format of this series permits — their diversity of ideas and interests, and to suggest how they use idiom or image inventively to illuminate their particular poetic, dramatic, narrative, fictional or contemplative vision of life.

Stirling   A. N. JEFFARES

1
The complex tradition

I Irish and Norman

CONTINUAL themes run through Anglo-Irish literature through which a complex cultural and political history is expressed. The literature records pleasures, pressures and tensions within an island of mixed races and religions where the instinct for survival — against local enemies, invaders, occupiers, poverty and climate — has resulted in the cult of the hero, in inventive wit and often black humour, in the acceptance of intuition and an awareness of the supernatural, in frequent assertion of nationalism against the domination of the neighbouring island, in praise of particular places and in a mixture of dreaming and often exaggerated talk that marks the influence of an oral culture, the test of which is a capacity to impress and to entertain.

One strain in such talk is ironic, full of self-mockery and mock-seriousness. It is present in the word-chasing of that early Irish scholar who loved his cat Pangur Bán:

> I and Pangur Bán my cat,
> 'Tis a like task we are at:
> Hunting mice is his delight,
> Hunting words I sit all night.

And it runs through written Anglo-Irish literature too, with Joyce hunting words, preoccupied with pushing English as far as it would go.

There are, however, many themes which occur and reoccur throughout Anglo-Irish literature in the work of both major and minor writers. This book seeks to trace some of them through the traditions and through the highly individual use made of English by Irish writers, from, if we consider some of the major writers, Swift to, say, Shaw, Yeats, Joyce and Beckett. The end of Anglo-Irish writing comes when the Irish

Free State was established in 1922 in the twenty-six counties and Northern Ireland in the remaining six. Writers born after 1922 can conveniently be considered as Irish rather than Anglo-Irish.

Can we then simply begin with Swift as the first major Anglo-Irish writer? The historical starting point properly comes earlier in 1169, the Irish equivalent of 1066, when the long tensions between the neighbouring islands began. In 1168 Dermot MacMorrough, the King of Leinster, driven out of his kingdom by the aggrieved husband of Devorgilla whom he had carried off some years earlier, appealed to Henry II for permission to recruit among his subjects. This granted, Dermot engaged the services of Richard Fitzgilbert de Clare, the earl of Pembroke in Wales, popularly known as Strongbow. Dermot offered him his daughter, Eva, in marriage (this marriage is the subject of a large symbolical canvas, opulent in the detail of its historicism, by the Irish painter Daniel Maclise (?1806/8–70) which is now in the National Gallery of Ireland) and the succession to his kingdom of Leinster. Other Normans were engaged, and in 1169 Maurice Prendergast and Robert Fitzstephen came to Ireland from Wales, with about two thousand men in all ('ninety heroes dressed in mail' according to an Irish account), and thus followed up the aid given two years earlier to Dermot by another Norman, Richard Fitzgodebert: they landed at Baginbun in Wexford and fortified the headland as a base. A traditional rhyme recorded this:

> At the creeke of Bagganbun
> Ireland was lost and wun.

Strongbow, who arrived in 1170, became King of Leinster on Dermot's death in 1171 and that year Henry II, no doubt not wishing Strongbow to become too powerful, crossed to Ireland and received the submission of the Irish kings and the Church, confirming Strongbow as ruler of the land of Leinster, as an appanage of his earldom of Pembroke.

The Anglo-Normans entered Ireland at the end of the monastic period of Gaelic poetry. Thus, in the largely Gaelic-speaking island, Norman French was added to the Latin of the monks, to the Norse established by earlier invaders in the trading cities along the east and south-east coasts, and to the English which was also spoken as a *lingua franca*, mainly in the towns. This linguistic mixture was ultimately to lead to a flexible use of language, the fusion to create a lively literature. As well as linguistic variety, however, there had come into Ireland lasting political and even racial tension. Two legal systems, English and Irish, existed side by side and this, as Sir John Davies perspicaciously realised in his *Discovery of Causes Why Ireland Was Never Subdued* (1612), created a lasting problem.

Two main areas existed, the one controlled by the Irish, and the other under the dominance of the Norman feudal lords. These lords were themselves ruled by a governor (called variously a Justiciar, Lord Deputy or Lord Lieutenant) appointed by the king in England, and aided by a council. In the thirteenth century a parliament was in existence in Dublin. The role of the English lordship (for the English king had been accepted as lord of Ireland since Henry II arrived in Ireland to make clear his feudal control over the Irish kings, and over Strongbow in particular), as it was carried out by the English officials and the parliament in Dublin, was to keep English law intact. This also included preserving English customs and speech in what was called the land of peace, the 'obedient shires', which made up the Pale or area controlled by them. And this purpose was clearly shown in the Statutes of Kilkenny (1366) which were designed to keep the English settlers in Ireland from adopting Irish ways of life: from intermarrying, from concubinage or from the fostering of children, from using the Irish language, from dressing, wearing their hair and riding horses in the Irish fashion, and from maintaining or entertaining Irish minstrels, poets or storytellers. The aim of keeping English and native Irish apart was, in modern terms, racialist. But it was vain in a time when Ireland was composed of a society run by individualistic leaders, whether Irish or feudal Normans, for intermarriage continued, the Irish language went on being used, and Irish poets flourished. And how could the 'King's Irish enemies' be loyal, when they were debarred from the benefits of English law?

Many of the Normans and the 'Old English' who followed them to Ireland had become, in effect, Irish during the twelfth and thirteenth centuries. Irish rather than English seems to have been used even in the Pale. And when the Statutes of Kilkenny were re-enacted in 1495 by Sir Edward Poynings (who had been sent by the Tudor monarchy to crush the power of the parliament in Dublin) the provisions banning the use of Irish were ignored. Indeed nearly a hundred years later the Lord Chancellor Gerarde was complaining in 1587 to Her Majesty's Commissioners that 'all English and the most part with delight speak Irish'; they were, he added, 'spotted in manners, habit and conditions with Irish stains' (*State Papers, Ireland, 1574–1585*). In *An Itinerary* (1617) the famous traveller Fynes Moryson (1566–1630) labelled the English in Ireland as 'degenerated'; they began, he wrote, 'to be enemies of the English . . . growne barberous by imbracing the tyrannical Lawes of the Irish . . . which caused them to take Irish names and to use their language and apparell.' Similar accounts of the 'Old English' in Ireland can be found in Sir John Davies, *A Discovery of the State of Ireland* (1631); he also called them degenerate, become 'meer Irish in their language . . . they not only forgot the English language but scorned the use of it.'

These comments suggest that Irish was freely used in the Pale well into the seventeenth century. Early on in their stay the Anglo-Normans had not only taken to the Irish language but also supported Irish poets, and under their patronage European chivalric poetry had influenced the course of Irish poetry. As can be seen in *Danta Gradha* (1916), Tomas O'Rathile's excellent collection of more than a hundred poems, Irish poets used old Irish forms of poetry to contain the new ideas of the troubadours: that love ennobled, that the beloved was exalted above the lover, indeed generally out of reach, and that love could never be satisfied. Adulterous, indeed heretical in its implications, this love poetry could take new directions in Ireland. Women were not so revered by the Irish poets, who could be highly ironic about jealousy and gossip. There was a balance between love and mockery, a goliardic spirit and, at times, a renunciation of women which reminds us that many poets ended up in monasteries. Gerald the Rhymer, the fourth earl of Desmond (*d.* 1398), represents the courtly element, but the historian Geoffrey Keating (*c.* 1570–*c.* 1650) the opposite tendency, especially in *A bhean làn do Stuaim* (a poem well translated by Patrick

Pearse, himself well-equipped to sympathise with Keating's single-mindedness).

The Ireland to which the Normans had come was an aristocratic civilisation in which traditions had been preserved orally by the poets and monks. Some of the few great manuscript books which have survived the period of the Danish invasions which occurred between 800 and 1014 and the turmoil caused by the subsequent Norman incursion were kept as prized possessions by individual families or religious communities. Dermot MacMorrough, for instance, who might on the face of it seem merely a thoroughly disliked and distrusted adulterous warlord, had kept *The Book of Leinster* in his palace at Ferns. These books contained a mixture of literary genres. *The Book of the Dun Cow*, the earliest of them, written by a scribe who died in 1106, is but a fragment of the original book, but contains romantic tales in prose, the voyage of Maeldun, and an imperfect version of the sagas of the Ulster Cycle including the *Tain-bo-Cualgne* (the *Cattle Raid of Cooley*) and an elegy on St Columkille. *The Book of Leinster*, written between 1155 and 1200, has nearly a thousand pieces of different kinds, genealogies, and the *Dindshenchas*, poems on places, as well as a full version of the *Tain*. Though it opens with the 'Book of Invasions', the invented history of Ireland from the Flood to St Patrick's coming, it also contains historical material. Other books, written in the fourteenth century, are the *Lebar Brecc*, the speckled *Book of MacEgan*, the *Book of Ballymote* and the *Yellow Book of Lecan*. From the fifteenth century come the *Book of Lecan* and the *Book of Fermoy*. Most of the *Lebar Brecc* was on religious topics; and the best known of the Irish books were, of course, copies of the gospels or scriptures, such as *The Book of Kells* (of the seventh or eighth century) with its elaborate and exuberant ornamentation and script, and the *Book of Armagh* (finished in 807) which contains a life and a confession of St Patrick.

II Early writings

The Norman invaders were affected, then, by the existing culture in Ireland and their energies at first seem to have been channelled along military lines so that, though there are some interesting Norman—French poems surviving — for instance 'The Song of Dermot and the Earl' in the Carew MSS in Lambeth Palace and the account of the fortification of a Wexford town, 'Rithmus Facture ville de Rosse', in Harley MS 913, the British Library — conditions in the twelfth and thirteenth centuries were not conducive to the writing of literature in English. By the fourteenth century life seems to have become sufficiently settled for some varied poetry to be written in the monasteries in English (no mere Irishman, *merus hibernicus*, could, by a law passed in Kilkenny, be a member of a religious order in the part of the country under the English Lordship). There were three famous monasteries in Kildare, Franciscan and Carmelite houses of Grey and White Friars, as well as St Brigit's double monastery of monks and nuns. It was probably in the Franciscan monastery of the Grey Friars that Friar Michael wrote 'Sweet Jesus'

> This world's love is gone away
> As dew on grass in summer's day
> Few there be well-a-way
> That love God his lore
> All we be iclung so clay [shrunk up like clay]
> We should rue that sore;
> Prince and King, what think they
> To live evermore?
> Leave your play, and cry aye
> Jesu Christ thine ore! [compassion]   (stanza 2)

> Alas, alas! Ye rich men,
> With muck why will ye fill your den?
> Think ye to bear it henne [hence]
> Nay, so may I thrive
> Ye shall see that all is fenne [dirt]
> The chattels of this life . . .   (from stanza 3)

> Poor was thine incoming
> So shall be thine outgoing;
> Thou shalt have not of all thy thing
> A penny bear to mould . . . .   (from stanza 5)

This poem is included in Harley MS 913 with four other pieces possibly by Friar Michael. This Franciscan manuscript also contains poems in the satiric, goliardic tradition, notably 'The Land of Cockaygne', an exuberant fantasy prompted by the proximity of the monks and nuns at the Cistercian Abbey in Inishloughnacht (*Inis* meaning land by a river; *leamhnacht*, fresh or sweet milk) outside Clonmel, where there had been some scandalous behaviour in the twelve-sixties. The poet had a realistic appreciation of comfortable living:

> The land is full of every good.
> There is no fly nor louse,
> In cloth, in farm, in bed, nor house;
> There is no thunder, sleet, nor hail,
> Neither a vile worm nor snail,
> Nor no storm, rain, or wind,
> There is no man nor woman blind,
> But all is sport, joy and glee,
> Lucky's he who there may be.   (1136—44)

He also exhibited a quality of wonder at the rich profusion of this imagined land:

> Of the streams all the mould
> Stones precious and gold.
> There is sapphire and uniune,
> Carbuncle and astiune,
> Smaragde, lugre, and prassiune,
> Beryl, onyx and topasiune,
> Amethyst and chrysolite,
> Chalcedony and epitite.   (1187—94)

But he was lyrical indeed when he envisioned the nuns of the Abbey of Inishloughnacht upon the river:

> Another abbey is thereby,
> Forsooth a great fair nunnery,
> Upon a river of sweet milk
> Where is plenty great of silk.
> When the summer day is hot
> The young nuns take a boat
> And do them forth in that river
> Both with oars and with stere. [rudder]
> When they be far from the abbey
> They make them naked for to play,
> And leap down into the brim
> And do them slyly for to swim.   (147—59)

There is a habit of irreverence at work in another poem, a

sense of fun, of satire aimed at every kind of person, and a touch of amused self-consciousness in that satire:

> Hail Saint Christopher with thy long stake!
> Thou bearest our Lord Jesus Christ over the broad lake,
> Many great congers swim about thy feet.
> How many herrings for a penny at Westcheap in London?
>> This verse is of holy writ,
>> It comes of noble wit.   (stanza 2)

> Hail be ye brewsters with your gallons,
> Pottles and quarts over all the towns.
> Your thumbs bear much away, shame have the guile;
> Beware of the cucking-stool, the lake is deep and filthy.
>> Sikerlich he was a clerk
>> That so slyly wrought this work.   (stanza 17)

Another theme, to crop up later in Irish writing, appears in part of a lyric recorded in the *Red Book of Ossory*, among other vernacular fragments prefixed to the Latin hymns recorded by Richard de Ledrede, Bishop of Ossory (*c*. 1316–60): this is the lament of a young girl married to an old man:

> Alas how shold y syng?
> Yloren is my playng
> How shold y with that olde man
> To leven and [let?] my leman
> Swettist of al thingye.

A rude ballad exists in Harley 913 on the death of Peter de Bermingham, who died in 1308, a notorious hater of Irishmen:

> . . . Ever he rode about
> With strength to hunt them out
> As hunter doth the hare.   (from stanza 9)

> For when they thought best
> In the wilderness to have rest,
> That no man should them see,
> Then he would drive a quest
> Anon to their nest
> In the place where they would be.   (stanza 10)

This ballad also tells of his treacherous murder of the O'Conors Faly at a feast in 1305. There has been argument about the provenance of a better-known fourteenth-century poem, which W. B. Yeats was to adapt in 'I am of Ireland'; it runs thus:

> Icham of Irlaunde
> Aut of the holy lande of Irlande
> Gode sir pray ich ye
> For of saynte Charite
> Come ant daunce wyt me
> In Irlande.

On the same folio is 'The Maid of the Moor', full of effective repetition as its four stanzas describe the maid, her food, drink and bower. It begins

> Maiden in the mor lay,
> In the mor lay,
> Sevenighte fulle,
> Sevenighte fulle,
> Maiden in the mor lay
> In the mor lay
> Sevenighte fulle and a day.

Constant unrest comes through in two poems, written in Waterford in the fifteenth century, and included in the Hanmer papers, (*State Papers, Ireland 1601–03*), one by the mayor, and one by Patrick Strong. More interesting is an interlined translation of an Irish poem, also in the *State Papers, Ireland 1601–3*:

> You and I will go to Finegall.
> You and I will eat such meats as we find there.
> You and I will steal such beef as we find fat
> I shall be hanged and you shall be hanged
> What shall our children do?
> When teeth do grow unto themselves as their
> fathers did before?

The two Irishmen were planning their theft in Finegall, or Fingal, north of Dublin, which was in the Pale and had its own dialect, as did the inhabitants of the baronies of Bargy and Forth in Wexford. Their dialect was described in the seventeenth century as 'the dregs of the ancient Chaucer English' by Richard Stanihurst who preserved the story of a gentleman telling them he was learning some Gaelic from them, when they were in fact speaking their variety of English.

From the sixteenth century comes a poem of sixteen lines on the Templars and their master Jacques de Molay, contained in the vellum *Book of Howth*. The work of many poets must, of course, have disappeared. Some, of whom no other trace exists, are later listed by Sir James Ware and Richard Stanihurst.

In prose there are Latin writings of some interest, for instance the long account (in Harley MS 641) of the troubles Richard de Ledrede caused himself by prosecuting Dame Alice Kyteler and her associates for witchcraft. And that redoubtable opponent of the mendicant orders, Richard Fitzralph, Archbishop of Armagh, wrote *De Pauperie Salvatoris* between 1350 and 1356, and Jofroi (*d.* 1300) of Waterford translated the *Secreta Secretorum* and works of Dares Phrygius and Eutropius into French. Jofroi's French version of the *Secreta Secretorum* was in turn translated by James Yonge, a Dublin notary, who wrote up the pilgrimage made by the Hungarian Lawrence Rathold de Pasztho to St Patrick's Purgatory between 1411 and 1412: this is one of the most fascinating of several early documents about the place and the pilgrimage. About 1425 a translation of the *Expugnatio Hibernica*, an account of Henry II's conquest of Ireland by Giraldus Cambrensis (*c.* 1147–1223), was made.

An early movement of Irish literary material into English occurs in *The Book of Howth* (published in the *Calendar of the Carew Manuscripts*, London, 1871, v, 1–260) which contained material from the Fenian cycle of Irish literature: there is a genealogy and an account of how the Fenians were defeated by the kings of Ireland. This includes the account of St Patrick's rather clumsy baptism of Finn's son Ossian:

> St Patrick having a croyge or bahell in his hand, wherein was a long prick of iron, and in saying his service at that baptism, he thought that he strake the bayghell down on the ground, and by chance he strake it through Osseyn's foot, which suffered it patiently, and after service done, a great deal of blood appeared on the ground. St Patrick asked Osseyn why he did not complain when he felt himself hurt. He said that he thought it was part of the baptism. He was of the age of seven score and eight years at the time.

The saint is elsewhere described as impaling one of the feet of a king of Munster in similar fashion. *The Book of Howth* also tells a story of Gorre's son Here killing his father, going mad and dying when he fights the sea — material obviously linked to the Ulster, Red Branch cycle's story of Cuchulain fighting the sea.

In general, drama was not to be expected in Irish culture, which was local and rural, though there was a tradition of miming at wakes and weddings and there was some mumming which came from English folk tradition. In the cities in the fourteenth century some plays were acted in Latin at Easter; and what seems to have been the earliest morality play in English, *The Pride of Life*, exists in the account rolls of the canons of the Priory of the Holy Trinity (later Christ Church) Dublin; this was copied out in the first half of the fifteenth century. A miracle play, *The Play of the Sacrament*, exists in a late-fifteenth-century version. There are references to pageants at that time and to Christmas plays being given on Hoggin Green in Dublin in 1528.

Up to the sixteenth century some of the great Norman families, often intermarried with the Irish, had long carried out what the historian Edmund Curtis (1881–1943) called 'aristocratic home rule'; but, however blurred distinctions between the races could become in some regions, the Tudors in their desire to centralise power attempted to raise barriers, to separate. Thus Henry VIII reintroduced measures against the Irish language and Irish culture. In 1536 Lord Grey's parliament echoed the Kilkenny prohibitions about keeping Irish minstrels, 'rymours' and bards. Its main purpose, however, was to force through Reformation, which was strongly resisted by the Irish and the Anglo-Irish. There had long been the issue of the ownership of land between the Irish and the incomers from England and to this was now added the bitterness of religious difference. In 1556 an area approximately that of Leix and Offaly, confiscated under Edward VI, was thrown open to planters, to 'English subjects born either in England or Ireland'. The plantation of Munster which took place in 1586 — when the earl of Desmond's estates were turned over to 'undertakers' who undertook to colonise the land — greatly increased Irish resentment at the attempted imposition of Protestantism.

The situation had become complicated because the older settlers in Ireland — the 'Old English' — also felt resentment

against the intrusion of officials and fresh settlers from
England. The 'Old English' were loyal to the English sovereign
but they had a sense that they, 'the English of Ireland', were
too much at the mercy of their mother country. They shared
the native Irish reaction against the aggressive English policy
of planting colonies of Protestants (other plantations followed
the seizure of Munster — that of Ulster under James I, 1603–
25, and Cromwell's 'planting' of all Ireland except for
Connacht and Clare, 1652–4) in Ireland. They were very
close indeed to the Irish. In *A Literary History of Ireland*
(1899) Douglas Hyde (1860–1949) remarked that

> After a few generations the Anglo-Normans had completely forgotten
> Norman-French, and as they never, with few exceptions, learned
> English, they identified themselves completely with the Irish past, so
> that among the Irish poets we find numbers of Nugents, Englishes,
> Condons, Cusacks, Keatings, Comyns and other names.

But the ability of earlier great Norman families — Fitzgeralds,
for instance — to form friendships with Irish rulers, to support
Gaelic learning and literature, had now gone. The attitude of
the Elizabethan English to Irish bards was stern: they were
regarded as keeping resistance alive through their songs and
stories. Acts were directed against them and the penalties
were severe. O'Brien, earl of Thomond, for instance, was
forced to hang three distinguished Gaelic poets. Edmund
Spenser recorded in his *View of the Present State of Ireland*
(1596) how he had caused

> dyverse of them to bee translated unto me, that I might understand
> them, and surelie they savored of sweete witt and good invencion,
> but skilled not of the goodlie ornamentes of Poetrie yett were they
> sprinckled woth some prettie flowers of theire owne naturall devise,
> which gave good grace and Comelynesse unto them, The which it is
> greate pyttee to see so abused to the gracinge of wickednes and vice,
> which would with good usaige serve to bewtyfie and adorne vertue.

The trouble was that the Irish bards threatened English rule
by keeping alive the traditions, history and identity of a
largely aristocratic Irish civilisation. Spenser, who came to
Ireland in 1580 as secretary to Lord Grey de Wilton and had
received his own large share of the confiscated Desmond
lands in Munster in 1586, regarded their poems as expressing

a dangerous desire 'to maintain their own lewde libertie, they being most desirous there-of'. And he thought they should be put to death. But this Irish liberty was largely lost at the Battle of Kinsale (1601). Indeed the aristocratic Irish civilisation was virtually extinguished at the Flight of the Earls (1607); this abandonment by the last powerful Irish lords of the struggle with England meant that most poets throughout Ireland lost their often munificent patrons, and the Irish literary tradition became submerged.

Before this happened, however, there was a flaring up of talent in the first half of the seventeenth century. There are the thirty poems in what is called the Contention of the Bards, 'literary zeal and genealogical fury' in the words of Douglas Hyde, who thought the poems prompted by a desire to rouse the ardour of their respective chiefs. In prose there were the writings of Geoffrey Keating (*c.* 1570—*c.* 1650) who studied at Bordeaux, became known as a popular preacher in Tipperary but offended a local lady by a forthright sermon on adultery, and had to hide as an outlaw in the glen of Aherlow for some years. There he began his *Foras feasa an Eirinn*, his *History of Ireland*, about 1620; it was based on his study of ancient vellum books and manuscripts. Keating belonged, he tells us, to the Old Galls or the Anglo-Norman race, and he wrote his book as a defence of Ireland against the unfair attitudes of such authors as Giraldus Cambrensis and Edmund Spenser. This was an extremely popular work, and is a completed narrative unlike the *Annals of the Four Masters*, which dealt mainly with facts as far as they could be established. The *Annals*, begun in 1632 and finished in 1636, were based on the travels of Michael O'Clery (*c.* 1580 —1643) throughout the ecclesiastical houses of Ireland in search of material for a collection of lives of the Irish saints. O'Clery was helped by three others, Farfassa O'Mulchrony, Peregrine O'Clery and Peregrine O'Duigenan in completing the *Annals*. They were written by learned men for a learned audience, and little read after the seventeenth century.

2
Colonial and Ascendancy

I The early eighteenth century

AN application of Renaissance — and Protestant — attitudes
to education in Ireland marked the foundation of the University of Dublin in 1591. Before that Irishmen had, perforce,
gone overseas to study. Some went to England. The first
sixteenth-century writer in English of any note was Richard
Stanihurst (1547—1618) who attended University College,
Oxford, then read law at Lincoln's Inn. He had been educated
at the school in Kilkenny run by Peter White, a Waterford
man who had himself been a Fellow of Oriel College, Oxford.
Stanihurst returned to Ireland with Edmund Campion as his
tutor. Using the library of his pupil's father, John Stanihurst,
the Recorder of Dublin and Speaker of the Irish House of
Commons, Campion wrote a *History of Ireland* in ten weeks
in 1571. Stanihurst revised this superficial piece and it was
published with his own *Treatise containing a Plaine and
Perfect Description of Ireland* in *Holinshed's Chronicles* (1577).
Stanihurst was not very sympathetic to Ireland; Geoffrey
Keating listed him among those who strove 'to vilify and
calumniate both Anglo-Irish colonists and the Gaelic natives'.
Stanihurst may have been an intellectual snob, as his own
epistle 'Dedicatory to Lord Dunsany' suggests in its attack on
contemporary poets who had not had the *sine qua non* of a
classical education. He regarded them as

> diverse skavingers of draftye poetrye in this oure age that bast theyre
> papers with smearie larde savoring all too geather of thee frynig pan.
> Good God what a frye of such *wooden rythmours* doth swarme in
> stacioners shops who neauer enstructed in any grammar schoole, not
> atayning too thee paringes of thee Latin or Greeke tongue yeet lyke
> blynd bayards rush on forward, fostring theyre vayne concertes
> wyth such over-weeing silly follyes as they reck not too bee con-
> demned of the learned for ignorant, so they bee commended of thee
> ignorant for learned.

He himself had written love poems inspired by a girl 'in body fine fashioned, a brave Brounette' but as she and her mother wished for a match he rapidly curbed his 'affection with discretion'. He did, however, marry later; on the death of his wife in 1579 he left for Leyden where he published a very rough translation of Virgil.

More promising was the poetic talent of Gerald, Baron of Offaly; but he died at the age of twenty-one in 1581, repenting his gambling in 'A Penitent Sonnet':

> ... Therefore take example by me,
> That curse the luckless time
> That ever dice mine eyes did see,
> Which bred in me this crime ... .

While the Irish tradition preserved by the poets and scribes was largely oral in character, not much writing in English has survived from the sixteenth century for the reasons that precluded earlier literature both in Irish and English from preservation. The state of fairly constant warfare, coupled with the closure of the monasteries, had meant the destruction or dispersion of manuscripts; printed material was not produced in Ireland until Humphrey Powell set up his printing press in Dublin in 1550. When the new university was founded its charter described the college as providing for the education, training and instruction of youths and students so that they could be assisted in studying the liberal arts and in cultivating virtue and religion. It would also, no doubt, counteract the Irish language described as 'free denizoned in the English pale', and complained of as a canker that 'took deep root'. In the Queen's own words it would provide 'knowledge and civilité', – both were virtues that many Irishmen had long sought in continental as well as English universities at, say, Bologna or Padua, at Montpellier or Paris, at Louvain or Salamanca. And now that many of these foreign universities were dominated by the counter reformation – Geoffrey Keating, for instance, had been educated at Salamanca, and Michael O'Clery at Louvain – the new university in Dublin would serve as a protective bastion of Protestantism for young Irishmen.

Michael O'Clery's near-contemporary James Ussher (1581–1656), one of the first three students admitted to

Trinity College, at the age of thirteen, demonstrated in his subsequent career that the college in Dublin developed from its beginnings a capacity to generate solid learning and to become quickly respected for it in England and Europe. Ussher was widely known for his textual scholarship which, though it never eventuated in the edition of the Bible for which his contemporaries hoped, did reveal his sceptical side in Patristic studies, for example his sharp arguments about the spuriousness of some of the Ignatian letters were borne out by subsequent factual discoveries. He also had a deep knowledge of the movement from Celtic monasticism to diocesan episcopy in the Irish Church. He was not concerned to create personal renown so much as to lay a good foundation for the work of others by generously and energetically building up the library of the college. He made several visits to England, became friendly with the other great book collectors of the time, Camden, Selden, Cotton and Bodley, and even employed a clergyman, Thomas David, to buy books in Aleppo for the college. He is best known — by the superficial — for his affirmation that 4,004 years elapsed from the Creation to the birth of Christ; it is perhaps as well to offset this by remembering Gibbon's tribute to Ussher's 'copious statement' in *Ecclesiastical Antiques of the British Churches* (1639) 'of all that learning could extract from the rubbish of the dark ages'.

Scholars do not always fit into the blueprints of prejudiced politicians: in the early days of the college there was a lively interest in the Irish language. Within ten years of its foundation, the Book of Common Prayer had been translated into and printed in Irish; there were Irish services in the chapel during Provost Bedell's days, and Irish versions of Old and New Testaments were attempted (the former was not published till the end of the century). In the tenure of the Provostship by Robert Ussher (1629–34) a chapter of the Irish Testaments was read aloud at dinner, and in that of Narcissus Marsh (1678–9) a monthly sermon was preached in Irish. Interest in Irish lapsed, however, until the end of the eighteenth century, and was not to flower fully until the work of its distinguished graduate Douglas Hyde yet a century later. No creative work occurred, but the interest of Sir James Ware (1594–1666) in Irish matters, influenced by Ussher's example, eventuated in the publication of his *Antiquities of Ireland*, followed by his *Lives of the Irish Bishops* and, his best-known work, *De Scriptoribus Hiberniae* (1639) — the *Writers of Ireland*. Ware wrote briefly and accurately in Latin, his work being later translated and revised in 1700 by his grandson-in-law Walter Harris in *The Whole Works of Sir James Ware* (1739—64). Ware listed five authors, of whose works nothing is known beyond his description of them as writers of carols, ballads and sonnets.

The wars of the seventeenth century were probably responsible for a rapid decline in cultural rapport between the communities. In general the irruption of Cromwellian settlers into Ireland (Cromwell, like Augustus earlier, no doubt saw the political advantages of getting an army back on to the land and away from his capital as well as holding Ireland more securely) meant that there was to be little nurturing of the dying Irish culture. Frank O'Connor (1903—66) has summed it up in *The Backward Look* (1967) by remarking that the Irish and the Old English shared a cultural nationality: 'they remained distinguished up to Cromwellian times, but when they wrote, when they sang and when they built they were practically indistinguishable.' He thought that this cultural nationality was partly destroyed because the Cromwellians came from the English lower and middle classes and were 'townsfolk who could not understand a cultural nationality that belonged to a landed gentry with feudal and royalist ideas.' The new settlers, he argued, were not at all likely to harbour bards and rhymers in their homes, and this is probably true of their early years in Ireland.

During the seventeenth century there was a fairly Puritan attitude in Trinity College. The majority of the undergraduates were Protestants: those who wished to become authors had several choices open to them. Whereas Irish was still used by a very large part of the population, in the second half of the century its literature was lingering on in hedge-schools (open-air schools common from the seventeenth to the nineteenth centuries during the ban on Catholic education) but it became a shadow, an echo of its earlier aristocratic self in the hands of itinerant poets and storytellers whose auditors had become the country folk. English was, then, the language of government, of trade, and of commerce with the world

outside. And, of course, Irish writers in English formed part
of the contemporary culture of an English world. They were
born or brought up in Ireland; they had a wide outlook; they
often left for England and ultimately their larger audience
was there. The image of 'the garrison' has its merits, for the
analogies explain many of the Anglo-Irish attitudes. J. C.
Beckett has pointed out in *The Anglo-Irish Tradition* (1976)
that the Anglo-Irish, because of their ambivalent attitudes,
rarely wrote on Irish topics, except on those directly concerned
with political, religious or economic controversy, when they
confidently regarded themselves as representatives of a
distinct nation and firmly asserted the constitutional rights of
Ireland. It was only after the Union of 1800, he maintains,
when the ideas of a separate political unity appeared to have
vanished, that they sought themes for literature in Irish
history, society and scenery.

Anglo-Irish writing in the seventeenth century certainly
had little to mark it as written in Ireland. Roger Boyle, first
earl of Orrery (1621–79), was educated at Trinity College,
Dublin, and wrote heroic drama, after the French fashion of
rhymed plays, tragedies and comedies, as well as *Parthenissa*
(1654–69), a long unfinished heroic romance, and a *Treatise
of the Art of War* (1677). His lifeless plays were, surprisingly,
successful on the London stage; he produced *The General*
himself in Dublin under the title *Altermara* in 1662. His
brother Robert Boyle (1627–91), author of *The Sceptical
Chymist* (1661) and of many scientific essays, left Ireland
for Eton at the age of four and returned on only a few
occasions. Wentworth Dillon, fourth earl of Roscommon
(1633–84), wrote poems, but is known for his *Essay on
Translated Verse* (1684). All four of them were writing in
the current classical stream of English fashion, as were those
writers listed in E. R. McClintock Dix's *Catalogue of Early
Printed Dublin Books 1600–1700* (1898–1912) as authors
of panegyrics, odes, elegies, poems of welcome on Arrivals
and good wishes for Departures. And what could be a more
English poem than *Cooper's Hill* (1642)? Yet its author, Sir
John Denham (1615–69), was also born in Ireland, of mixed
English and Irish stock. His tragedy *The Sophy* (1642)
obviously drew its inspiration from outside either island, and
the fact that he translated the *Aeneid* reminds us that polite

literature was generally based upon knowledge of the classics, which induced a wider, generalising attitude. Thus *Cooper's Hill* finds its way into histories of literature for its neo-classic virtues, of balance and rational control, rather than its celebration of a particular place.

The exuberance and exaggeration of what was known of Irish mythology were not likely to appeal to the emerging neo-classical spirit, and certainly were not treated with great respect by James Farewell, who modelled himself upon Samuel Butler's earlier and cruder form of satire. In *The Irish Hudibras, or Fingallian Prince. Taken from the Sixth Book of Virgil's Aeneids and Adapted to the Present Times* (1689), he has Nees enter Hell via Patrick's Purgatory in Lough Derg and meet there various heroes of Irish legend, who are treated with jocose contempt:

> And here was that prodigious Tooll
> That monstrous geant Finn MacHeugle,
> Whose carcass bury'd in the meadows,
> Took up nine acres of Pottadoes.

This is Hudibrastic certainly, but vigorous too; its vigour is matched by that of a surviving piece of popular writing, a racy comment on the death of the duke of Grafton, a son of Charles II, who was mortally wounded during the siege of Cork in 1690:

> Here fell Henry Duke of Grafton
> As good a Blade as e'er had haft on
> Or e'er made a Pass
> At a lad or lass;
> But a bullet of Cork
> Soon finished his work
> Pox rot him
> That shot him;
> A son of a whore
> That got him.
> I'll say no more,
> But here fell Henry Duke of Grafton.

Most Anglo-Irish writing in the seventeenth century, then, did not necessarily possess particularly Irish qualities. Take, for example, the eloquent questions that shaped a sermon (included in *Miscellanies in Prose*, ed. Andrew Carpenter,

1972) by Anthony Dopping (1643–97), elected a Fellow of Trinity College at the age of nineteen, and Bishop of Meath for the last fifteen years of his life:

> Doe not all the usurers and merchants, all the labourers and trades-men under the sun, toyle and care, labor and contrive, venter and complot for a little mony, which few get, and scarce any man desires so much as to cover five acres of ground with? And is this pitiful scume, this so poore a limited heepe of dirt, the reward of all the labor, and the end of all the care, the designe of all the malice and the recompense of all the wars in the world?
>
> And can it bee Imagined that life it selfe, a long, happy, and aeternall one, a perfect and glorious Kingdome that shall never have an end, nor its joys abated with fears or jealousys, with care and sorrow, — that such a life and such a kingdome, should not be worth a few houres of seriousnesse?

Here Dopping, as Archbishop Ussher before him, is writing within the established guidelines of his chosen career in the Church, and his sermon has a universal quality about it.

On the other hand, Dopping's friend William King (1650–1729), who held various offices in the Irish Church before being appointed Archbishop of Dublin in 1703, was a Williamite in his political views, and his lively attack upon the administration of Tyrconnell, James II's Lord Lieutenant in Ireland, entitled *The State of the Protestants of Ireland under the late King James's Reign* (1691), gives the reader an idea why he was unpopular in England, for this is a vigorous asser-tion of a particular Irish point of view. King, however, is seen to best advantage in his letters: his correspondence with Dean Swift is well known. He had as strong views as Swift about the role of the Church of Ireland, but was more politic in expressing them. A letter written to William Smyth, about his marriage to 'a sweet tempered girl and of very good sense', is full of good advice, and conveys something of King's realistic wisdom:

> I have observed that the things which cause coldness between marryed people are commonly trifles, for in greater matters their interest joins them, & therefore I would intreat y^u to consider of what value the matter is that disgusts you, & lay it in the scale with the pleasure & satisfaction of your life which depends on your being well with your wife, & be sure not to lose that for a humour or fancy, or a

trifle. Advise & be advised by her, & tell her in kindness if y^u observe anything that is uneasy to y^u in her conduct, but not at the time y^u are disgusted, but rather wait the softest & most pleasant intervall.

King had strong views that Irish claims, particularly in matters of the Church, should count most in Irish appointments. These views were shared by Jonathan Swift (1667–1745), whose relationship with King was an uneasy one. Swift respected King's intellect; but he did not always like the politic advice he received from him. Temperamentally they were poles apart, yet their alliance could be powerful – as can be seen from their correspondence. This shared feeling of Anglo-Irish identity, based upon deep loyalty to the Protestant Church of Ireland, was given its first full literary expression by Swift, who asked in fine rhetorical form:

Were not the people of Ireland born as *Free* as those of *England*? How have they forfeited their Freedom? Is not their *Parliament* as fair a *Representative* of the *People* as that of *England*? And hath not their Privy Council as great or a greater share in the Administration of Publick Affairs? Are they not Subjects of the same King? Does not the same *Sun* shine on them? Have they not the same *God* for their Protector? Am I a *Free-Man* in *England*, and do I become a *Slave* in six Hours by crossing the Channel?

Swift regarded himself as belonging to the true English people of Ireland. He did not regard Ireland as a depending kingdom. He deeply disliked being a colonial, the more so for having had his heady experience of political power in England. But the original crossing the Channel from Ireland to England must have been an eye-opening experience for many Irish writers. Swift, like Congreve and indeed most of the Fellows and undergraduates of Trinity College, fled from Ireland when James II's Lord Deputy, Tyrconnell, pursued a policy of giving power to Catholics and undoing the Reformation. The King's troops occupied the college as a garrison in 1689. After experiencing the transition several times, Dublin seemed 'wretched' to Swift and Ireland 'miserable'. The scale of English wealth, the variety of intellectual life, and the lack of provincialism were to be admired, and then envied, upon his disappointed return to Ireland, to take up his appointment as Dean of St Patrick's Cathedral, a return to what he ironically called his 'banishment'.

Swift's education at Trinity College had laid the foundations for what we might now regard as equivalent to a long, indeed vast doctoral and post-doctoral course of reading balanced by the simultaneous acquisition of social and political polish at Moor Park, Sir William Temple's ordered home near Farnham. Here, as dependant and amanuensis, he first came into contact with Sir William's great world of courts and diplomacy, of the making of peace, of the writing of elegant essays and the laying-out of gardens. He met the King, he was promised preferment, he read and practised his own prose.

The *Battle of the Books* (1704) was a mock-heroic praising the ancients. Swift was no lover of the new science which had so reformed English style through the insistence of the members of the Royal Society upon close, naked speech. He thought English prose had been at its best in 'the peaceable part of King Charles the First's Reign'. In the *Battle of the Books* there is wit in plenty, the free play of an imaginative mind, and a very lively imaginative style. But it is nothing like *A Tale of a Tub* (1704) which overflows with his copious reading and consequently exhibits, as Dr Johnson remarked, 'so much more thinking, more knowledge, more power, more colour' than any of his other works. In part it parodies the writings of others; but it is richly endowed with his own distinguishing flair for irony, his intellectual energy and his ruthless integrity.

Armed with this weaponry, this capacity for ridicule, wit, irony, paradox and surprise, all of them reinforced by a strong emotional intensity, Swift emerged from thirty years of preparation for life. In the process he left his rich, complex literary style behind. As a priest in the Church of Ireland he had to preach; and then as a political writer in London and Dublin he had to persuade. The prose was no longer self-indulgent, the self-expression of a superb and playful intellect; now it was written with a sharp consciousness of its audience, and out of a compulsive desire to influence that audience's thoughts and actions. What writer before Swift entered into such a position of political power by influencing the decisions of the Tory ministry; or helped to stop a war by his writings in the *Examiner*; or brought political journalism to such an efficient awareness of how to hit the target with exactly the right weight of explosive satire?

When Swift returned to Dublin, to become Dean of St Patrick's Cathedral, sent, he said, 'to die like a poisoned rat in a hole', he was virtually forced into becoming an Irish patriot. The misery and poverty he saw round him seemed to be caused not only by the parliament in Westminster, but also by the failure of the Irish to help themselves. He became so seized by the need to transmit his ideas simply and effectively that he had the proof sheets of Faulkner's Dublin edition of his works read aloud not only to himself but also to two manservants whose understanding of his writing had to be clear before he would pass the proofs. He had moved back into a land where oral communication counted: back, he felt, to live a country life in town.

Though he had good friends in Ireland, he missed being at what he considered the centre; he missed the intellectual stimulus and the gaiety of the Scriblerians in England; but he continued to indulge in the kind of mystery they enjoyed. Take, for instance, his frequent concealment of his authorship. *A Tale of a Tub* had ruined his hopes of a bishopric or deanery in England: he had learned a bitter lesson from this. Thus his friend Charles Ford was given elaborate instructions about how the manuscript of *Some Free Thoughts upon the Present State of Affairs* (1741) was to reach the printer. It was to be sent

> by an unknown hand . . . Do not send it by the Penny post, nor your Man, but by a Porter when you are not at your Lodgings. Get some Friend to copy out the little Paper, and send it inclosed with the rest, and let the same Hand direct it, and seal it with an unknown seal.

This was partly a love of mystery for its own sake. The printer Benjamin Motte had told Pope that he did not know whence or from whom he had received the manuscript of *Gulliver's Travels* which was 'dropped at his house in the dark, from a hackney coach'.

Gulliver's Travels (1726) appeals to readers on many levels: its profundity and its pessimism have been emphasised incessantly; but its invention, its fun, and its sheer entertainment have made it his best-known and most highly praised work. Fortunate are those who read it first in childhood. The four voyages of Gulliver are in the well-established, successful genre of the traveller's tale and parodies of it, such as those

of Lucian, Sir Thomas More, Rabelais and Cyrano de Bergerac.
Defoe's *Robinson Crusoe* had used the traveller's tale seven
years earlier, and Swift was also parodying William Dampier's
accounts of his voyages.

Humanity is regarded from four different points of view;
we see Gulliver, gigantic among the Lilliputians, then dwarfed
by the Brobdingnagians, next commonsensical in the mad
world of Laputa where scientific invention has run riot, and
finally among the brutish manlike Yahoos and the elegant,
coolly rational horses, the Houyhnhnms, who regard him as
irrational. This all adds up to an attack upon human pride.
Gulliver is as much an object as an instrument of satire: we
need to remember that he is not Swift. He is not always
admirable; his naïve attitude to the Lilliputians unfolds a
picture of cruelty and treachery; though the Brobdingnagians
are insensitive, their King is horrified by Gulliver's account of
the recent history of European politics: he cannot but con-
clude, he tells Gulliver, that 'the Bulk of your Natives, to be
the most pernicious Race of little odious Vermin that Nature
ever suffered to crawl upon the Surface of the Earth.' The
King rejects Gulliver's offer to build cannons for him, being
amazed that 'so impotent and groveling an Insect . . . could
entertain such inhuman Ideas, and in so familiar a manner as
to appear wholly unmoved at all the Scenes of Blood and
Desolation, which I had painted as the Common Effect of
those destructive Machines, whereof he said, some evil Genius,
Enemy to Mankind, must have been the first Contriver.' The
third book attacks the progressive projectors, scientists and
linguists, as well as providing political allegory. The fourth
book has upset many critics who, thinking Swift hated man,
have perhaps been over-confident in their ability to interpret
it, underestimating Swift's ironic complexity − and his
humour seen, for instance, when Gulliver is described by his
friends as trotting like a horse and is ridiculed for falling into
the voice and manner of the Houyhnhnms − and his view
that man, though capable of reason, was not a rational
creature. Gulliver, as we realise in the last chapter, suffers
from the pride he attacks in others: over-simplistic, he is
absurd in his misanthropy and misogyny:

> As soon as I entered the House, my Wife took me in her Arms, and
> kissed me; at which, having not been used to the Touch of that

odious Animal for so many Years, I fell in a Swoon for almost an Hour. At the Time I am writing, it is five Years since my last Return to *England*: During the first Year I could not endure my Wife or Children in my Presence, the very Smell of them was intolerable; much less could I suffer them to eat in the same Room. To this Hour they dare not presume to touch my Bread, or drink out of the same Cup; neither was I ever able to let one of them take me by the Hand.

Swift wrote *Gulliver's Travels* between 1721 and 1725 while he was engaged in his pamphleteering on behalf of Irish economic freedom. There were very real dangers which accompanied the writing and publishing of political pamphlets. In 1720 Government had prosecuted the printer of Swift's *Proposals for Universal Use of Irish Manufactures* (1720). It was written out of his sympathy for the Dublin weavers, a feeling earlier expressed in *The Story of the Injured Lady*, a piece written in 1707 but not published until after his death; this described the effects of English legislation on the Irish wool trade, and regretted that Ireland had not been treated as Scotland had in the Act of Union of 1707. Swift took up a position like that of William Molyneux (1656–98), a Dublin MP and one of the founders of the Dublin Philosophical Society in 1683, who had published *The Case of Ireland being bound by Acts of Parliament in England, Stated* (1698). Molyneux's view was that Ireland had its own parliament in Dublin and owed allegiance to the King, but not to the parliament at Westminster. He argued that though the two countries had the same head of state they were distinct and separate in their several jurisdictions, and he rejected any idea of colonial status for Ireland in an excited passage:

> Have not Multitudes of Acts of Parliament both in *England* and *Ireland* declared *Ireland* a *compleat Kingdom*? Is not Ireland stiled in them all, the *Kingdom* or *Realm* of Ireland? Do these *Names* agree to a *Colony*? Have we not a Parliament and Courts of Judicature? Do these *things* agree with a *Colony*?

Swift seized on two points: one political, the other economic. He attacked the appointment of Englishmen to key offices in Ireland, as in 'a libel on Doctor Delaney' where he described the English Viceroy's task:

> And what condition can be worse?
> He comes to *drain* a *Beggar's Purse*:
> He comes to *tye* our Chains on faster,
> And shew us *England* is our Master.

This matter of political appointments was always a sore point with the Anglo-Irish: and Swift was also convinced that Ireland should be able to export her goods where she liked.

In 1722 both Swift and his printer risked severe punishment. The occasion was the granting of a patent to William Wood, an English ironmaster, which would allow him to coin copper money for Ireland. Both Houses of Parliament in Dublin, the Irish Privy Council, the Lords Justice and Commissioners of Revenue were all against the measure, but it was Swift's *Drapier's Letters* which destroyed any credibility the proposed coinage might have had, and the patent was finally withdrawn in 1725. Swift obviously enjoyed adopting a persona, and he chose to write the series of letters attacking Wood's proposed coinage as though he were a Dublin shop-keeper. The first letter was addressed to 'the Shop-Keepers, Tradesmen, Farmers and Common-People of Ireland', the fourth to 'the Whole People of Ireland'. Here Swift's sense of the absurd kept breaking through, notably where he contemplates one of the likely effects, if Wood's halfpence were in circulation, upon Squire Conolly who was said to have Sixteen Thousand Pounds a Year:

> if he sends for his *Rent* to Town, *as it is likely he does*, he must have Two *Hundred and Forty Horses* to bring up his *Half Years Rent*, and two or Three great Cellars in his House for Stowage.

After Wood's project was killed Swift attained fame as a popular patriot in Ireland, and bonfires were lit to welcome 'the Drapier' home. All this popularity was decidedly ironic in view of his ambivalent attitude to Ireland.

Swift was ahead of his age in his fastidiousness and awareness of hygiene — and the lack of it around him. His cloacal poems, which so shocked Victorian taste and still surprise many modern readers, express his fascinated horror of filth. He probably tried to exorcise this disgust by facing it and writing about it, and hence the bedroom poems (for instance, 'The Lady's Dressing Room', 'A Beautiful Young Nymph Going to Bed' or 'Strephon and Chloe', which parody the falsities of love poetry), as well as that excellent poem on a London street, the 'Description of a City Shower', and many others in a similarly realistic vein. He often used the couplets Butler had made effective in *Hudibras*; he avoided the more 'serious' formal approach of Pope, and his best-known poem, the 'Verses on the Death of Dr Swift', is typical of his use of light and witty verse to convey a serious apologia:

> My female Friends, whose tender Hearts
> Have better learn'd to act their Parts,
> Receive the News in *doleful Dumps*,
> 'The Dean is dead, (*and what is Trumps?*)
> 'Then Lord have Mercy on his Soul.
> '(Ladies I'll venture for the *Vole*.)
> 'Six Deans they say must bear the Pall.
> '(I wish I knew what *King* to call.)
> 'Madam, your Husband will attend
> 'The Funeral of so good a Friend.
> 'No Madam, 'tis a shocking Sight,
> 'And he's engag'd To-morrow Night!
> 'My Lady *Club* wou'd take it ill,
> 'If he shou'd fail her at *Quadrill*.
> 'He lov'd the Dean. (*I lead a Heart*.)
> 'But dearest Friends, they say, must part.
> 'His Time was come, he ran his Race;
> 'We hope he's in a better Place.' . . .
>
> 'He gave the little Wealth he had,
> 'To build a House for Fools and Mad:
> 'And shew'd by one satyric Touch,
> 'No Nation wanted it so much:
> 'That Kingdom he hath left his Debtor,
> 'I wish it soon may have a Better.'

Swift was equally disgusted by poverty, by its lack of order, its deep misery. And satire was one remedy for it: satire could cut through the corruption, channel the rubbish out of sight, sweeten its smell, diminish the cant, and expose the stupidities for what they were. Human life was absurd, irrational, untidy, unjust. He lashed vice and he certainly could use ridicule devastatingly. His poem 'The Legion Club' shows a Juvenalian rage at the failings of Ireland's great men. His deep pessimism about public affairs emerged clearly in such pieces as *A Short View of the State of Ireland* (1727–8). Then came the three years of bad harvest which resulted in severe distress — 'every place strowed with beggars' he wrote to Pope. Swift's response to the situation was his most effectively horrifying satire *A Modest Proposal for Preventing the Children of of the Poor in Ireland from being Burdensome, and for making them Beneficial* (1729). This creates an effect on the reader which is the more disturbing for Swift's seeming detachment: he puts forward his proposal as if he were some kind of social economist, giving a matter-of-fact air to his outrageous solution by providing statistics and apparently arguing the case dispassionately:

> I have been assured by a very knowing *American* of my Acquaintance in *London*; that a young healthy Child; well nursed, is at a Year old, a most delicious, nourishing and wholesome Food: whether *Stewed, Roasted, Baked* or *Boiled*; and, I make no doubt, that it will equally serve in a *Fricasie* or *Ragoust*.

The calculations have been careful. Out of the proposer's computation of a total of 120,000 children, 20,000 could be reserved for breeding, the remaining 100,000 sold 'at a year old to *Persons* of *Quality* and *Fortune*, through the Kingdom; always advising the Mothers to let them suck plentifully in the last Month, so as to render them plump and fat for a good Table.' The *Modest Proposal* is the ultimate statement of Swift's *saeva indignatio*; 'I grant', remarks his proposer, 'this food will be somewhat dear, and therefore very *proper for Landlords*; who, as they have already devoured most of the parents, seem to have the best title to the children.'

Swift was representative of his age in his attitude to nature. On the one hand, he disliked its wilder, more savage aspects, as his Latin poem on Carbery Rocks in County Cork indicates. On the other, he had a typically eighteenth-century appreciation of nature methodised, as is shown in his letters to Stella from London. It was probably when he entered Sir William Temple's household at Moor Park, in Farnham in 1689 that Swift, then twenty-two, had first met Esther Johnson, a protégée of Sir William's, who was then about eight. It isn't certain when he first called her Stella, but he used the name in a birthday poem to her in 1719. He directed her reading, and she became his closest friend. When Sir William Temple died he left her some land in Ireland, and she and her friend Rebecca Dingley moved there in 1701. Swift wrote frequently to the ladies from London between 1710 and 1717. These playful, forthright, indeed happy letters, collected as the *Journal to Stella*, not only give a fascinating picture of his personal life in London but also convey, like the poems he wrote to her, something of his deep affection for her. He told her in a poem that he

> . . . gladly would your sufferings share
> or give my scrap of life to you,
> And think it far beneath your due;
> You to whose care so oft I owe
> That I'm alive to tell you so.

When, after an enigmatic relationship of thirty or more years, she died in January 1728, Swift, in the Deanery, sat down to write an account of 'the truest, most virtuous and valuable friend that I or perhaps any other person ever was blessed with.' This is a haunting piece, the more so for the heartbroken restraint underlying his careful description of Stella, who was

> sickly from her childhood until about the age of fifteen; but then grew into perfect health, and was looked upon as one of the most beautiful, graceful, and agreeable young women in London, only a little too fat. Her hair was blacker than a raven, and every feature of her face in perfection.

He was ill on the night of her burial in the Cathedral; he moved into another apartment in his Deanery 'that I may not see the light in the church which is just over against the window of my bed-chamber.' He himself was buried at the foot of the next pillar to her grave: he wrote not only her epitaph, telling how she was 'celebrated under the name of Stella in the poems of Jonathan Swift, dean of this Cathedral', but also his own, the Latin of which has been so nobly Englished by Yeats:

> Swift has sailed into his rest;
> Savage indignation there
> Cannot lacerate his breast.
> Imitate him if you dare,
> World-besotted traveller; he
> Served human liberty.

In the *Journal to Stella* the playful nature of their friendship (the spirit of 'Vive la Bagatelle' informed much of the attractive side of his character) emerges in his queries about the state of his improvements to his glebe at Laracor in County Meath. He was anxious for news about the fruit trees he had planted, about the canal he had dug, and he wondered how his trout were faring. Laracor was his retreat, his Sabine farm, where he got the exercise and air in which he delighted. The prospect of wandering in dressing gown through his Irish garden had seemed very attractive to the negotiator in London, the more so in 1712 when Swift opened the equivalent of a modern letter bomb addressed to Harley, the Lord Treasurer. This event produced the following prose squib:

A GREAT PLOT!

The second part of St. Paul's screw-plot
or Mine arse in a Ban-Box!

Prick up year Ears all ye Citizens — Attend O ye Citizens' Wives — be Amaz'd and Confounded ye Milliners, Ye Abigails and all the Tribe of Ban-Box Carriers — a Plot is lately broken forth, a dismal, deep, horrid, fanatical, unheard of Plot! Found out by Parson Swift in a Ban-Box — Parson Sw—t found it there, and he swears it is a Plot, a curs'd, damned, fanaticall Plot, — for tho' He has peeped in many a Ban-Box — Yet he never found such a Plot before — a Pistol and a Couple of Inck-horns to shoot my Lord — O Villains, to shoot My Lord Treasurer — to shoot — him with Inckhorns — O Grub-Street Plotters! . . .

While this country clergyman was exercising political power in London through his pen, and by his writing helping to bring a European war to an end, he was at the same time delighting in the company of men and women who shared his delight in the bagatelle. The Scriblerus Club had provided him with friends in England who seemed as inventive and witty as he; among them he could give vent to his imaginative power, he could be merry, he could be himself. And he could be particularly Anglo-Irish in laughing at himself. There are many poems in this vein which range from the wry treatment of himself in *Cadenus and Vanessa*, that enigmatic account of his risky, eventually damaging friendship with Esther Vanhomrigh, to the 'Verses on the Death of Dr Swift', when his humour was a buffer against tedium, when he missed his friends. Throughout his life there was a hatred of being dull; he wrote that his

method of Reforming
Is by laughing, not by Storming.

In *An Argument to prove, That the Abolishing of Christianity in ENGLAND, May, as Things now Stand, be attended with some Inconveniences, and, perhaps not produce those many good Effects proposed thereby* (1717) there is an excellent example of Swift's ability to jest in the midst of being profoundly serious, for he obviously cared deeply about Christianity and the Church, but did not curb his ironic wit in defending them — just as *Gulliver's Travels* later arose out of his deeply ironic awareness of human contradictions: reason and passion made man

> A mingled Mass of Good and Bad
> The worst and best that could be had.

Swift could indulge his fantasy, his word play and his irresistible sense of parody because of his proud, fiery independence, his desire to be used like a lord, and his assumption of a position of power and prestige not unlike that achieved by Gaelic poets over the centuries before. His residence in both islands, his crossings of the Irish sea, had given him an extra assurance. Those Anglo-Irish who lived only in Ireland could, after all, hardly risk incurring the odium of their fellows in Ireland by impairing in any way the stabilisation achieved by the Williamite victory. But he had seen the larger issues of Europe and had affected their course; he had indeed been at the centre. Thus he could attack the Westminster government's treatment of its colony out of a proud assertion of equality which he compressed into the Drapier's exploring, explosive question: 'Am I a *Free-Man* in *England*, and do I become a *Slave* in Six Hours by crossing the Channel?' And his efforts were increasingly appreciated as Anglo-Irish disillusion with the English government under Walpole developed. His point about slavery was echoed by Rev. William Dunkin whose poem 'On the Drapier' praised the Drapier's reason thundering through the land, expressing a true public spirit:

> Undone by Fools at home, abroad by Knaves
> The Isle of Saints became the land of Slaves.

A friend and protégé of Swift's, Thomas Parnell (1679–1718), who was ordained in 1700, frequently visited London where by 1711 he was on friendly terms with Pope and was one of the original members of the Scriblerus Club. He helped Pope with his translation of the *Iliad* and wrote an Introductory Essay for it. After the death of his wife in 1711 he became melancholic, lived in retirement in Ireland from 1715 to 1718, and died in Chester after visiting his old friends in London in 1718. Pope edited his varied *Poems on Several Occasions* in 1722. Parnell is an attractive and often neatly witty minor poet; to his two best-known anthology pieces 'The Hermit' and 'A Night Piece on Death' should be added a charming lyric 'My days have been so wondrous free'.

Another to be aided by Swift was Laetitia Pilkington (1712–50) who married a poor parson for whom Swift obtained a post in 1731; the marriage broke up and Mrs Pilkington tried her hand unsuccessfully at running a bookshop in London before returning to Dublin. Her racy *Memoirs* (1748) give a picture of Swift's last days.

A gentler spirit than Swift's breathed through the writings of George Berkeley (1685–1753), Bishop of Cloyne, who went to Kilkenny College a little after him: at the age of seventeen he entered Trinity College, coming into a more settled atmosphere than that prevailing in Swift's undergraduate days. Berkeley took his BA in 1704, and became a Fellow of the College three years later. Apart from Latin, Greek, Hebrew and French, he read mathematics and knew his Newton well. And, of course, there was Locke's *Essay Concerning Human Understanding* (1690) to discuss. In 1707 Berkeley began his famous notebooks (they have been called *Philosophical Commentaries* by A. A. Luce in his edition of 1942). Some of the entries in them were designed for later book publication, probably on a larger scale than he achieved in *An Essay towards a New Theory of Vision* (1709) and the *Principles of Human Knowledge* (1710), others being terse, lively comments (what Yeats called his 'snorts of defiance') on the work of mathematicians, theologians and philosophers. This item (numbered 696 by Luce) shows us his aim, of warning the reader against the fallacy of words, against being cheated into absurdities by plausible, empty talk:

Let him not regard my Words any otherwise than as occasions of bringing into his mind determin'd significations so far as they fail of this they are Gibberish, Jargon & deserve not the name of Language. I desire & warn him not to expect to find truth in my Book or any where but in his own Mind. W^{t}ever I see my self tis impossible I can paint it out in words.

Berkeley had formed his belief in immaterialism before he began putting his thought into the notebooks; in item 279 he remarked 'I wonder not at my sagacity in discovering the obvious tho' amazing truth, I rather wonder at my stupid inadvertancy in not finding it out before. 'tis no witchcraft to see.' Then he wrote and erased a line which the editors think ran 'We know nothing but our own thoughts or wt these think'. He commented that if we could discover 'the nature and meaning and import' of existence we could see the only way the world must be constructed. This he thought wholly new; it marked him off from the sceptics; and the discovery was that existence is either to be perceived or to perceive, God exists, and there are only 'spirits' and 'ideas'. He thought much learning was made obscurer than it need be, and that common sense was on his side. He was opposing what he thought the falseness of the speculative sciences and he was demonstrating the existence and attributes of God, the immortality of the soul, as well as reconciling God's foreknowledge with the freedom of men. And so he writes his *Principles of Human Knowledge* with a directness, elegant simplicity and confidence.

> Ideas imprinted on the senses are real things, or do really exist; this we do not deny, but we deny they can subsist without the minds which perceive them, or that they are resemblances of any archetypes existing without the mind: since the very being of a sensation or idea consists in being perceived and an idea can be like nothing but an idea. Again, the things perceived by sense may be termed *external*, with regard to their origin, in that they are not generated from within, by the mind its-self, but imprinted by a spirit distinct from that which perceives them. Sensible objects may likewise be said to be without the mind, in another sense, namely when they exist in some other mind. Thus when I shut my eyes, the things I saw may still exist, but it must be in another mind.

He wrote *Alciphron, or the Minute Philosopher* (1732) when he was at Newport, Rhode Island, waiting for news of his projected college in Bermuda. This dialogue obviously owes a lot to Plato, the stream of its anti-deism or anti-free-thinking carries much learning, and yet it is eminently readable. This is good, clear and fluent eighteenth-century prose, and Berkeley's description of the card-playing splenetic English rakes, the 'minute philosophers' as he called them, provides a good example of his fluent, easy style;

> CRITO: I readily comprehend that no man upon earth ought to prize anodynes for the spleen more than a man of fashion and pleasure . . . Something there is in our climate and complexion that makes idleness nowhere so much its own punishment as in England, where an uneducated fine gentleman pays for his momentary pleasures with long and cruel intervals of spleen; for relief of which he is driven into sensual excesses, that produce a proportionable depression of spirits, which, as it createth a greater want of pleasures, so it lessens the ability to enjoy them. There is a cast of thought in the complexion of an Englishman which renders him the most unsuccessful rake in the world. He is (as Aristotle expresseth it) at variance with himself. He is neither brute enough to enjoy his appetites, nor man enough to govern them. He knows and feels that what he pursues is not his true good; his reflexion serving only to shew him that misery which his habitual sloth and indolence will not suffer him to remedy. . . .

> EUPHRANOR: . . . But pray tell me, do these gentlemen set up for minute philosophers?

> CRITO: That sect, you must know, contains two sorts of philosophers, the wet and the dry. . . . The dry philosopher passeth his time but dryly. He has the honour of pimping for the vices of more sprightly men, who in return offer some small incense to his vanity. Upon this encouragement, and to make his own mind easy when it is past being pleased, he employs himself in justifying those excesses he cannot partake in. But, to return to your question, those miserable folk are mighty men for the minute philosophy.

The run of the last sentence is pure Dublinese and reminds us that Berkeley wrote happily to his friend Percival from Leghorn in 1713/14 to say that 'Ireland is certainly one of the finest countries and Dublin one of the finest cities in the world.' His letters resemble his philosophical prose; he was not self-consciously literary. His letter to Tom Prior from Turin describes his travels with that same dislike of wild nature Swift had shown in his poem on Carbery Rocks:

> . . . On New Year's Day we passed Mount Cenis, one of the most difficult and formidable parts of the Alps which is ever passed over

by mortal men. We were carried in open chairs by men used to scale these rocks and precipices, which in this season are more slippery and dangerous than at other times, and at the best are high, craggy, and steep enough to cause the heart of the most valiant man to melt within him. My life often depended on a single step. No one will think that I exaggerate, who considers what it is to pass the Alps on New Year's Day. . . .

While the Alps have their 'most horrible precipices' he advises Pope to come to Italy, arguing that 'to enable a man to describe rocks and precipices, it is absolutely necessary that he pass the Alps.' Later he described the scenery of Rhode Island enthusiastically:

The face of the country is pleasantly laid out in hills vales woods and rising grounds, watered with several rivulets. Here are also in some parts very amusing rocky scenes, and fine landscapes and islands.

Significantly, however, he broke off, perhaps with some self-mockery, for he had a good sense of humour, 'But I forebear for fear of being thought Romantic.'

His concern for his financial affairs appears in his letters to Tom Prior, notably 'the great expence' which he would incur on entering into a small bishopric; and his ill-health at Cloyne no doubt emphasised a situation which seemed 'cut off from the ways of men and sequestered from the rest of the world'. He occupied himself with medicine, notably his belief in the efficacy of tar-water, so cogently put forward in *Siris* (1744); but what haunts the reader most of all and perhaps conveys best Berkeley's nature is the sad letter he wrote on the death of his young son:

My dear Lord,

I was a man retired from the amusement of politics, visits, and what the world calls pleasure. I had a little friend, educated always under mine own eye, whose painting delighted me, whose music ravished me, and whose lively gay spirit was a continual feast. It has pleased God to take him hence. God, I say, in mercy hath deprived me of this pretty gay plaything. His parts and person, his innocence and piety, his particularly uncommon affection for me, had gained too much upon me. Not content to be fond of him, I was vain of him. I had set my heart too much upon him — more perhaps than I ought to have done upon anything in this world.

Thus much suffer me, in the overflowings of my soul, to say to your Lordship, who, though distant in place, are much nearer my heart than any of my neighbours.

Adieu, my dear Lord, and believe me, with the utmost esteem and affection,

Your faithful, humble, Servant,

G. CLOYNE

Berkeley was not discontented with living in Ireland; he regarded himself as Irish; he had not been unsettled, as Swift had been, by being poor and by seeing the wealth of England when he was a dependant; and so he wrote in his *Philosophical Commentaries*:

There are men who say there are insensible extensions, there are others who say the wall is not white, the fire is not hot &c. We Irish men cannot attain to these truths.

The Mathematicians think there are insensible lines, about these they harangue, these cut in a point, at all angles these are divisible ad infinitum. We Irish men can conceive no such lines.

The Mathematicians talk of w^t they call a point, this they say is not altogether nothing nor is it downright somthing, now we Irish men are apt to think something & nothing are next neighbours.

Berkeley, however, had had his experience of social and intellectual success among his neighbours. This began with his first visit to England in 1713, when he became a friend of Arbuthnot, Pope, Addison and Steele (for whom he wrote three *Guardian* Essays) as well as Bishop Atterbury, the earl of Pembroke and Bolingbroke. He records political events in 1715 with inner knowledge; and then he himself was swept into his project for the college in Bermuda. He experienced the apprehension of several that a college there might alienate America from England, he realised the gulf between those who tried to plan a colony's future and those who were interested only in the financial returns from one. And he experienced the inevitably frustrating administrative delays in getting matters settled. Despite all the idealism and hope for another Golden Age expressed in his poem 'On America' he was to find that the coolness of the English ministry at a distance caused the failure of his scheme, and it may be that these experiences prompted his cry in *The Querist* (1735): 'Whether, if there was a Wall of Brass a thousand Cubits high, round this Kingdom, our Natives might not nevertheless live cleanly and comfortably, till the land, and reap the Fruits of it?' In *The Querist* Berkeley's views resemble the desires of Molyneux and Swift for fair economic treatment of Ireland by England; these were shared by the fourteen men who met in Trinity College in 1731 to form the Dublin Society (still flourishing as the Royal Dublin Society, responsible *inter alia* for the annual Horse Show) 'for improving Husbandry Manufactures and other useful arts'.

Berkeley also realised, like Swift, that self-help was necessary. His queries began with 'Whether there ever was, is, or will be an industrious Nation poor, or an idle rich?' One query as to whether an academy would cost the public more than £200 a year expressed the need for establishment of a school of art to train artists and artisans. The Dublin Society took over an art school, begun by Robert West, sometime after 1739 (a school of architects was set up about 1765 and one of modelling in 1811) and this supplied a stream of painters, in whom the citizens of Dublin took increasing pride.

Many of the Anglo-Irish, however, who moved out of Ireland into England were concerned not so much about the state of the country they had left behind as with the need to further their own careers in England. This is exemplified clearly in the case of those dramatists who found their audiences in London. Secular drama in Ireland began to be performed later than in England. It seems to have commenced with visits of strolling players from London from 1589 onwards, with the Queen's Players and the earl of Essex's players giving performances in Dublin and Youghal. Then an amateur interest developed: in the last three years of Elizabeth's reign the gentlemen in Dublin Castle acted in plays; the Dublin tradesmen's guilds put on plays, and so did the undergraduates in Trinity College and the apprentice lawyers. Under Strafford's regime plays were performed by his retinue, and John Ogilby (1600–76) came with a company from London, then dangerous with the plague raging in 1636 and 1637. A 'pretty little theatre' was opened in Werburgh Street in Dublin in 1635 and Ogilby was appointed Master of the Revels in Ireland. James Shirley, a refugee from the London plague, wrote four plays first staged in Dublin, among them *St Patrick for Ireland* (1639), the first play to deal with an Irish subject. By 1662 the Smock Alley Theatre was also in existence in Dublin, though the drama suffered a temporary set-back with a new Viceroy who disapproved of it between 1669–71. The Smock Alley players made a successful tour to Oxford in 1677 and to Scotland in 1681. Drama in Dublin advanced considerably under the care of Joseph Astbury (1638–1720), who proved a lively Master of Revels.

Despite the existence of two theatres in Dublin Anglo-Irish writers preferred the larger audiences of London. Congreve was by no means the earliest writer to move from Ireland into a whirl of theatrical successes there. Though Lo (or Lod, or Lodwick, or Ludowick) Barry (? *b.* 1591–?), who was probably the second son of Lord Barry and born in County Cork, had a London success in 1610 with a comedy *Ram Alley or Merry Tricks* which seems to be the first play by an Irish dramatist, the first professional writer of repute to find a ready and appreciative audience in London was Nahum Tate (1652–1715). He was the son of 'Faithful Teate', a clergyman who had lost three children in the 1641 rebellion, moved to England and then returned to the parish of St Werburgh in Dublin. Nahum studied at Trinity College and published his *Poems* in 1677. They consisted of translations of Tibullus, Catullus, Propertius and Virgil's *Eclogues*, as well as his own pastorals, which were full of fashionable Ardelias, Daphnes, Julias, and various swains who, once they were shot through by Love's darts, wandered mournfully in shady groves. He first saw a play staged in London in 1678, and then wrote several plays himself, the first being *Brutus of Alba: or the Enchanted Lovers* (1678), founded upon the story of Dido and Aeneas (Tate wrote (1689) the libretto in Purcell's opera of this name) and dedicated to his patron, the earl of Dorset. This is rather a heavy-going, uninspired drama, like *The Loyal General* (1680). He dealt with riskier material in *The Sicilian Usurper* (1687), using *Richard II* as a base for it. This play was dropped after its third performance, and he took to the politically safer, more profitable activity of improving Shakespeare, with a successful — indeed skilful —

version of *King Lear* (1687), notorious for its happy ending. He copied John Marston's *Eastward Ho* (1605) in *Cuckold's Haven*, performed in 1685; he echoed Fletcher in the *Island Princess*, performed two years later, and Webster in *Injured Love*, which was never acted; and he wrote a second part for Dryden's *Absalom and Achitophel* (1682). He defended farce strongly in the second edition (1693) of *A Duke and No Duke* (1685), his adaptation of Aston Cokayne's *Trappolin Supposed a Prince* (1633): this play was still running successfully in the nineteenth century.

Ten years later he became Poet Laureate and then found his true *métier* in composing with Nicholas Brady, a fellow Irishman originally from Cork, a metrical version of the Psalms (1696), which he followed with an *Essay on Psalmody* (1710). His best-known work was *Panacea — a Poem on Tea* (1700), and 'While Shepherds watched their Flocks by Night' is also attributed to him. His adaptation and metrical version of the Psalms continued to be popular; some are included in modern hymnals, as for instance 'As Pants the Hart for Cooling Streams', Psalm 62. He himself, however, seems to have had his financial difficulties, being reported on one occasion as hiding from his creditors in the Mint at Southwark.

The long career of Thomas Southerne (1660–1746) had some parallels with that of Tate. He too went to Trinity College before crossing to the Middle Temple in London. In 1692 Southerne finished *Cleomenes* for Dryden, who had written the prologue and epilogue for his first play, a tragedy called *The Loyal Brother: The Persian Prince* (1682). *Isabella, or The Fatal Marriage* (1694) and *Oroonoko* (1695), both tragedies, are now his best-known plays, both based on novels by Mrs Behn. The former has a considerable comic part in a sub-plot, the language is striking, and the construction finely planned. The latter is adapted from Mrs Behn's novel about the grandson and heir of an African King, trapped into slavery and brought to Surinam where he meets Imoinda, sold into slavery when the African King, himself enamoured of her, had discovered that she and Oroonoko were in love with each other. Southerne introduced some comic elements into the sub-plot of this play also, and added a further complication — of the deputy Governor, Byam, also falling in love with Imoinda. The play was very successful for many years. A later play, *The Fate of Capua* (1700), was in the stoic mode, and has some interesting character portraits.

Southerne also wrote several comedies, beginning with *The Disappointment; or, The Mother in Fashion* (1684). *Sir Anthony Love* (1690) was notable for its breeches part written for the actress Mrs Mountford; this *risqué* play, full of farcical action, moves at a spanking pace and was very popular. An unsuccessful play in its own time, *The Wife's Excuse: or, Cuckolds Make Themselves* (1692) now interests us because it gives psychological reasons for marital discords, for adultery, in a savagely satiric way that was obviously based upon Southerne's knowledge of fashionable society. A contemporary description of him stresses this inside knowledge as well as his shrewd observation:

> his Gallantry is natural and after the real manner of the Town; his acquaintance with the best Company entered him into the Secrets of their Intrigues, and no Man knew better the Way and Disposition of Mankind.

Professor Sutherland has drawn attention to the behaviour of Mrs Friendall in this play as she reflects upon the public insult given to her cowardly husband:

> Whatever I think of him, I must not let him fall into the Contempt of the Town. Every little Fellow, I know, will be censoriously inquisitive and maliciously witty upon another Man's Cowardice, out of the pleasure of finding as great a Rascal as himself.

The Maid's Last Prayer: or, Any rather than Fail (1693) was a more effective comedy for the stage; its sprightly conversation, its more direct exploration of near-farcical comedy made for its success.

Southerne handled his financial affairs much more efficiently than did Nahum Tate, and he seems to have made far more money from his plays than was common — one of them, he told Dryden, had brought him in £700 — and Pope described him as

> Tom, whom Heaven sent down to raise
> The price of prologues and of plays.

Unduly neglected by modern criticism and worth reviving, Southerne was at times an original as well as a highly popular dramatist, the blend of sharp dialogue and lively farce in his comedies explaining his contemporary success.

Just as Swift's enjoyment of irony at his own expense seems a trait more indulged in Ireland than in England, so a tendency to push farce as far as possible is also noticeable in Irish humour; it has provoked adverse criticism at times from English critics. An earlier Irish dramatist, Thomas Duffet (*fl.* 1676) who composed some elegant songs, was representative of this tendency; he wrote several burlesques, *The Empress of Morocco*, *The Mock-Tempest* and *Psyche Debauch'd*, which contained a good deal of mockery of Dryden, Shadwell and Settle.

Like many of her countrymen, Susannah Centlivre (1670—1723) saw London as her goal, and ran away from home, getting lifts, walking and meeting on the way a Cambridge undergraduate who dressed her in boy's clothes and kept her at Cambridge until he could afford to send her on to London. She married at sixteen, was twice widowed by twenty, and took to writing as well as acting for a living. *The Beau's Duel* (1702) was a lively comedy. She gave up her stage career after marrying Joseph Centlivre in 1706, and then wrote her very successful if slight plays of intrigue, *The Busybody* (1709) and *A Bold Stroke for a Wife* (1718). Perhaps her own adventures led her to write *The Wonder! A Woman Keeps a Secret* (1714) which retails the adventures of Isabella who, when her father plans to marry her off to Don Guzman and locks her up, jumps out of a window into the arms of a conveniently passing Captain Briton whom she eventually marries.

To a certain extent Susannah Centlivre was writing these plays in the new vein of comedy which had succeeded the Restoration comedy of manners. That genre, effectively attacked by Jeremy Collier in 1698, had reached its height in Congreve's *The Way of the World* (1700).

Whether William Congreve (1670—1729) should properly be considered part of Anglo-Irish literary tradition is a moot point. After he was born in Bardsey, a village in Yorkshire, his father moved to Ireland, and William, like Swift, was educated at Kilkenny College and then at Trinity College, Dublin, where St George Ashe was his tutor, as he was Swift's. Like Swift, Congreve had left Ireland in 1688 because of the current dangers to Protestants under the aggressively Catholic policies of the Viceroy, Tyrconnel. In England there was a significant difference between the positions of the two young men: whereas Swift had had to occupy a dependant's position in Sir William Temple's household, Congreve's father could afford to send his son to the Middle Temple in 1691 when he himself returned to Ireland as agent for Richard Boyle, earl of Cork, after the Williamite victory. Congreve's knowledge of the classics was good; it impressed Dryden, whom he met on arriving in London from a family property in Stafford-shire. Dryden included him among the contributors to a volume of translations of Juvenal and Persius, and also included his translations of Homer in a later volume. In 1692 Congreve published his novel *Incognita*, which he may have written at Trinity College. The novel imitates dramatic techniques: it has a double plot, with two pairs of lovers. Mistaken identities and family feuds are straightened out in a finely controlled, sophisticated and elegant story. Congreve now seemed well-launched into literary life, but it was the theatre which attracted him most of all. He had subject matter in plenty in London.

There must have been an exciting show passing before his erstwhile provincial eyes in the capital; there was the talk of the wits at Will's Coffee House; there was his study of the law to remind him of the economic aspects of marriage. Indeed in his, as in most of the contemporary comedies of manners, the finances are carefully sorted out by the end of the play. He had shown Dryden the manuscript of his first play, *The Old Batchelour* (1693), the first draft of which he had written in Staffordshire. Dryden had never seen such a first play in his life, he remarked, but as Congreve was not well acquainted with the stage when he came to London he himself helped the young man to polish it: 'the stuff was rich indeed, it wanted only the fashionable cutt of the town.' Congreve got help from Thomas Southerne also, and he had actor friends, among them several who had acted at the Smock Alley Theatre in Dublin: Barton Booth ('Jubilee Dicky'), Henry Norris and Robert Wilks (*c.* 1665–1732) whose career is well told in Daniel O'Bryan's *Authentic Memoirs: or the Life and Character of . . . Mr Robert Wilks* (1732).

The Double Dealer (1694) was a sombre, complicated but

powerful play which was not a success. His next comedy, *Love for Love* (1695), was Congreve's best stage play; a conflict between youth and age in the orthodox traditions of the genre, it has traces of older traditions, for Foresight is a Jonsonian figure in his devotion to astrology, and so Tattle and Scandal can make a thorough fool of him, just as Angelica mocks the elderly Sir Sampson Legend for acting the part of a heroic lover. Sir Sampson is an enraged father, forerunner of Sheridan's Sir Anthony Absolute. Here, in Act II, he abuses his son Valentine:

> . . . Impudence! Why, sirrah, mayn't I do what I please? Are not you my slave? Did not I beget you? And might not I have chosen whether I would have begot you or no? Ouns, who are you? Whence came you? What brought you into the world? How came you here, sir? Here, to stand here, upon those two legs, and look erect with that audacious face, hah? Answer me that? Did you come a volunteer into the world? Or did I beat up for you with the lawful authority of a parent, and press you to the service?

The play abounds in wit and irony, but behind it there seems to be some idealism, disillusioned perhaps, but none the less exhibiting an awareness that man has a better side. 'Men are generally hypocrites and infidels,' remarks Angelica to Scandal, 'They pretend to worship but have neither zeal nor faith.' She is, however, unlike the other women in the play, aptly named Mrs Foresight and Mrs Frail. She and Valentine, who wins her, depart from the orthodox conventions and conversations of Restoration comedy just as Millament and Mirabel in *The Way of the World* (1700), his last play, show a similar, more elegant desire for a lasting marriage depending upon mutual freedom, upon mutual respect for each other:

> MILLAMENT: . . . And d'ye hear, I won't be call'd Names after I'm Marry'd; positively I won't be call'd Names.
>
> MIRABEL: Names!
>
> MILLAMENT: Ay as Wife, Spouse, my Dear, Joy, Jewel, Love, Sweetheart, and the rest of that Nauseous Cant, in which Men and their Wives are so fulsomely familiar — I shall never bear that, — Good Mirabel don't let us be familiar or fond, nor kiss before Folks, like my Lady Fadler and Sir Francis: Nor go to Hyde-Park together the first Sunday in a new Chariot, to provoke Eyes and Whispers; And then never to be seen there together again; as if we

were proud of one another the first Week, and asham'd of one another ever after. Let us never Visit together, nor go to a Play together, but let us be very strange and well bred: Let us be as strange as if we had been marry'd a great while; and as well bred as if we were not marry'd at all.

The Way of the World, as Congreve admitted in his Dedication, did not suit the general taste. Manners had become too much of a mask; the balance between the extravagance of heroic tragedy (Congreve tried his hand at the heroic play with *The Mourning Bride*, 1697) and the realism of the sceptical libertine satire of comedy had come to an end. The audience was changing: the theatre had become tired of the tradition of the court wits, tired of deceiving, posturing and shallow levity. Ultimately this comedy turned into a laughter of despair, which had originally mocked puritanism but now became a shield against over-serious thought, probably a defence against the implications of the new science and rationalism. Genuine emotion, however, kept breaking out here and there, and when Congreve wrote *The Way of the World* he was trying to bring order out of the complexity of life, to show how deceptive are its appearances, how tragedy can lurk under the polished surfaces. But the day of that particular kind of wit in the theatre was clearly over; *The Way of the World* was perhaps the supreme achievement of the genre, and too refined for its age at that.

George Farquhar (*c*. 1677–1707) was to show the theatre a way out of what had become a cul-de-sac, once he had expressed his own ebullient youth in the lively, exuberant characters of Roebuck in *Love and a Bottle* (1698) and Sir Harry Wildair in *The Constant Couple, or a Trip to the Jubilee* (1699), a racy comedy and an extremely successful one, being performed fifty times in five months. *Sir Harry Wildair* (1701) was a weaker play, but after it came *The Twin-Rivals* (1702), an experimental comedy, both harsh and moral. Farquhar moved the action of his most successful plays, *The Recruiting Officer* (1706) and *The Beaux' Stratagem* (1707), out of London. The fresh spirit of these sparkling comedies is far removed from the smart drawing rooms, coffee houses and taverns of the metropolis. Here in *The Recruiting Officer* are country bumpkins, a farmer's children, country gentlemen, the constable, the poacher and his mistress, justices of the peace, and, suddenly arrived among this rustic community, the recruiting officer and his sergeant, who explains himself clearly:

> KITE: Yes, sir, I understand my business, I will say it. You must know, sir, I was born a gypsy and bred among that crew till I was ten year old. There I learned canting and lying. I was bought from my mother, Cleopatra, by a certain nobleman for three pistoles, who, liking my beauty, made me his page. There I learned impudence and pimping. I was turned off for wearing my lord's linen and drinking my lady's brandy, and then turned bailiff's follower. There I learned bullying and swearing. I at last got into the army, and there I learned whoring and drinking. So that if your worship pleases to cast up the whole sum, *viz*., canting, lying, impudence, pimping, bullying, swearing, whoring, drinking, and a halberd, you will find the sum total will amount to a recruiting sergeant.

> WORTHY: And pray, what induced you to turn soldier?

> KITE: Hunger and ambition. The fears of starving and hopes of a truncheon led me along to a gentleman with a fair tongue and fair periwig who loaded me with promises, but I gad 'twas the lightest load that I ever felt in my life. He promised to advance me, and indeed he did so, to a garret in the Savoy. I asked him why he put me in prison; he called me lying dog and said I was in garrison, indeed 'tis a garrison that may hold out till doomsday before I should desire to take it again.

Farquhar presented his characters with sympathy. Captain Plume is like his earlier character Sir Harry Wildair; he is a man of refined sensibility beneath his military mask, and the heroine Silvia has a lively time disguised as a young man. The lovers care for each other; there is no straining after wit, though the speeches and situations provide ample amusement for any audience. Indeed the play has had a well-deserved history of success; it was never omitted from a season in its first seventy years, and was selected as the fourth production of the new National Theatre in London in 1963.

The Beaux' Stratagem is also set in the country: in it Farquhar was drawing on his experiences in Lichfield on his own recruiting tour there in 1705. The characters were based upon local people, while Foigard the disguised Irish priest surely derives from Farquhar's upbringing in Ireland — he is reputed to have fought at the Battle of the Boyne at the age of thirteen. Into this local milieu come two young men from London, cynically seeking wealthy marriages to repair their fortunes. But the play centres upon Mrs Sullen, and while there is a benevolent scepticism present in the ending, with Aimwell succeeding to his brother's title and estate, and Archer about to win Mrs Sullen as a divorce is arranged, there is no mockery, none of, say, Wycherley's earlier urban attitudes to country characters. What Farquhar brought to these plays was an Irish quality, neither wit, nor yet humour, but something best described as fun, an effervescing quality to be repeated most effectively in Goldsmith's comedies.

William Philips (d. 1734), son of the Governor of Derry, had a more tragic bent, exemplified in The Revengeful Queen (1698) and Hibernia Freed (1722); in his St Stephen's Green: or, the Generous Lovers (1699/1700) he had an English servant observe

> that none Despise Ireland so much as those who thrive best in it. And none are so severe in their Reflections upon it as those who owe their Birth and Fortune to it; I have known many of them when they come first to London, think there is no way so ready to purchase the title of a wit as to Ridicule their own Country.

Another Irishman, though perhaps not often thought of as such, Sir Richard Steele (1672–1729), who came to England at the age of thirteen and later, by enlisting as a private in the Coldstream Guards, lost the succession 'to a very good estate in the county of Wexford from the same humour which he has preserved ever since, of preferring the state of his mind to that of his fortune', did not possess much of this sense of fun. His humour was, however, combined with an Irish dislike of pretension in his comedy The Funeral: or Grief à la Mode (1701). This play, while it echoed the morality of The Christian Hero (1701; this book made him decidedly unpopular with his fellow officers when he became an Ensign), was light and lively, notably in its satiric treatment of undertaking. The Lying Lover (1704) and The Tender Husband (1705) were less successful, rather in the vein of Susannah Centlivre's didactic but successful play about a reformed gambler, The Gamester (1705); The Lying Lover was, in Steele's own words, 'damn'd for its piety' and The Tender Husband had an over-sentimental ending.

Steele, however, developed his particular dramatic ability to the full in *The Conscious Lovers* (1722). This was a sentimental drama which marked the full arrival and acceptance of refinement in the theatre. The play's sententious wisdom does not entirely kill its comic vein though it comes near to doing so, and the play earned over £2,500 in its first season, more than the company had ever made by a single play. It matched the taste of the new kind of middle-class audience, and the arrangement of a marriage between the children of landowning aristocrat and city merchant is symbolic of a shift in social values. No longer does the dramatist portray the wits' ridicule of the 'cit' or citizen, but Steele even puts in the mouth of Mr Sealand, the merchant, a somewhat smug speech of self-praise which would have been inconceivable on the stage twenty years before:

> . . . we merchants are a species of gentry that have grown into the world this last century, and are as honourable, and almost as useful, as you landed folks, that have always thought youselves so much above us.

The merchants were symptomatic of an increasing audience, which Anglo-Irish writers were not only entertaining skilfully in the theatre, but also manipulating at deeper levels. While dramatists such as Colley Cibber had realised that there was a change in public sensibility, it was Steele who effectively refined sentimental comedy; but this was probably because he had been deeply involved in the popular, educative and civilising work of the periodicals. The *Tatler* first appeared in 1709 and Steele wrote the first seventeen numbers himself. The *Spectator* which succeeded it probably owed its success to Steele as much as Addison with whom the journal is usually associated, since Addison, when he revived the journal a year and a half after it had ceased (with its fifty-fifth number), tended to preach without entertaining. And so its revival did not last long. Steele realised the need to avoid priggishness, and demonstrated this in his later journals, the *Guardian* and *The Englishman*. There is some irony in the fact that Anglo-Irishmen such as Swift and Steele had been forming public taste in the hub of the larger nation which dominated their native country. The effect of these journals in Queen Anne's day was considerable. Not only did they affect standards of taste in an age when there was an expanding middle class and a country audience wanting to know about the topics of the day, the social attitudes of the metropolis, but also they influenced politics in a very striking way.

II The later eighteenth century

In the latter half of the eighteenth century English influence was continuously felt in Ireland. Minor eighteenth-century Anglo-Irish poetry, for example, was obviously affected by English models in style, but given an Irish turn. Laurence Whyte (*d.* 1754), for instance, in his *Original Poems on Various Subjects, Serious and Diverting* (1740) liked octosyllabics:

> Thy aid O Butler! help me Swift!
> Here give your Bard a gentle lift,
> Wh' admires your Measure short and sweet,
> Which moves along with nimble feet,
> And travels further in good Rhyme
> Than stately Blank in twice the time.

And he applied them firmly to Absentee landlords:

> our gentry all run wild
> And never can be reconcil'd
> To live at home upon their Rent
> With any Pleasure and Content.

Samuel Whyte (1733–1811), the famous Dublin school-master, effectively echoed the fashionable night poetry of the graveyard school:

> Tis Night, dead Night; and o'er the Plain
> Darkness extends her Ebon Ray
> While wide along the gloomy scene
> Deep silence holds her solemn sway.

He included in *The Shamrock* (1772) a poem attributed to William King which has the exuberance of some of Swift's verse:

> Mountown! thou sweet retreat from Dublin cares,
> Be famous long for Apples and for Pears;
> For Turnips, Carrots, Lettuce, Beans and Peas,

> For Peggy's Butter and for Peggy's Cheese.
> May fat geese gaggle round thy cramm'd Barn Door,
> Nor e'er want Apple Sauce and Mustard Store
> Ducks in thy Ponds and Chickens in thy Penns,
> And be thy Turkies numerous as thy Henns.

A touch of the same mock naïvety marks the hearty narrative of a poem by the Dublin actor Thomas Mozeen (or Mozen, *d.* 1768), 'The Kilruddery Hunt', included in *A Collection of Miscellaneous Essays* (1762):

> In seventeen hundred and forty four
> The fifth of December — I think 'twas no more;
> At five in the morning by most of the clocks
> We rode from Kilruddery to try for a fox.
> Ten minutes past nine was the time of the day,
> When Reynard unkennelled, and this was his play.
> Bray Common he passed, leaped Lord Anglesea's wall
> And seemed to say 'Little I value you all'.

The fashionable cult of sentimentality reappeared, notably in *The Fool of Quality* (1766) a novel by Henry Brooke (1703–83) that is vibrant with sentiment, yet remains eminently readable. Brooke translated Tasso and wrote several tragedies, notably the bombastic *Gustavus Vasa* (1739) as well as a second novel *Juliet Grenville* (1774). He married a girl of fourteen, had a large family, among them his daughter Charlotte whose *Reliques of Irish Poetry* (1789) was to be so influential. Brooke himself wrote a poem 'Comrade' which purported to be a fragment of a saga; his *Universal Beauty* (1735) anticipates Erasmus Darwin, and was highly praised in the eighteenth century for its treatment of science. After his wife's death Brooke shut himself away from society, being himself a man of tender sensibilities. But the novel's supreme practitioner of sensibility was, of course, Laurence Sterne (1713–68). Born in Clonmel where his mother had relatives, he was brought to York for a time when his father's regiment was broken, then to Dublin; thence to Exeter and back to Derrylossary, near Annamoe in Wicklow, where he is reputed to have had that wonderful escape in falling through the millrace whilst the mill was going, and of being taken up unhurt. 'The story', he wrote, 'is incredible, but known for truth in all that part of Ireland — where hundreds of the Common People flocked to see one.'

Sterne's father Roger, unsuccessful Ensign, brought his family to Dublin, and next settled in Carrickfergus; then Laurence was sent to school in England, never to return to Ireland. What he had gained from growing up in Ireland was the common heritage of many Anglo-Irish writers; genteel poverty, rich relatives, and talk as the cheapest means of entertainment. Mock-seriousness, serious mockery: the strain runs from Swift to Shaw, from Sterne to Joyce: even gentle Goldsmith shared this capacity for self-mockery. And the English reader is often surprised at the way so many of them failed to allude to their mothers, or to do so in respectful terms. Perhaps they felt that their mothers had failed, in choosing as husbands those who in turn failed to provide adequately for their developing families, thus handing on a virtual duty of ambition to their sons.

Sterne's career was the Church, but by 1759 he found preferment 'long coming (& for aught I know I may not be preferr'd till the Resurrection of the Just) and am all that time in labour how must I bear my Pains?' This particularly Anglo-Irish problem, of how ambition was to overcome genteel poverty, was perennial. Sterne's query runs as leitmotiv through the history of Anglo-Irish literature. Predecessors in Sterne's predicament include Swift, Farquhar and Goldsmith, and Sterne himself anticipated Shaw who said in the Preface [1921] to his first novel *Immaturity* that but for the accident of a lucrative talent he would have been poorer than Spinoza 'for at least he knew how to grind lenses, whereas I could not afford to learn any art. Luckily, Nature taught me one'. And Sterne too had his art: 'the air and originality' of *Tristram Shandy*, he wrote, must resemble the author.

So Sterne wrote, in his own special way, about everything he found laughable or moving, struck his very successful bargain with the publisher, Dodsley, and launched the stream of consciousness on the world, 'finding it very hard in writing such a book as *Tristram Shandy* to mutilate everything in it down to the prudish humour of every particular' (Letter to Warburton, 19 June 1760). And thus in *The Life and Opinions of Tristram Shandy, Gentleman* (1759–67) plot was seemingly abandoned, innovation established, and Sterne, always experimenting, never heavy, observed characters in their private worlds, produced by the association of ideas which have no connection in nature. And yet the novel has an underlying chronology, for time runs at different speeds in it as in life. Sterne controlled the novel's progress skilfully through the long time of its publication, sharing through eight years the experience of its gloriously idiosyncratic humour with his reader, sometimes imagined as a man, or often as a woman, for Sterne almost lived upon the stimulus of flirtation, leaving blanks and asterisks as a challenge to the reader's response.

Sterne's sentimentality was imparted to his reader in a conversational tone; he responded to any and almost every emotional stimulus; he could create kindly tenderness as well as coarse bawdy, and, ultimately, he had a fine sense of the absurdity of human behaviour. Thus there are such jokes as the hot chestnuts, the request made by Mrs Shandy at the moment of Tristram's procreation as to whether Mr Shandy had remembered to wind the clock, of Uncle Toby's encounter with the widow Wadman: and they are balanced by pedantry and a mockery of it, and indeed by Mrs Shandy's complete inability to fathom her husband's intellectualising theories. Sterne had plundered Swift too — witness his development of Swift's sermon 'The Difficulty of Knowing One's-self' in his sermon on 'Self Knowledge', a comparison which has been made by Lansing Van der Heyden Hammond in *Laurence Sterne's 'Sermons of Mr Yorick'* (1948). The search for self-knowledge was a fundamental, continuous process in Sterne's mind. *Voilà un persiflage!* cries one of his characters in *A Sentimental Journey through France and Italy* (1768) and his own attitude to life in *Tristram Shandy* does not seem, in the English sense, serious:

> — My good friend, quoth I — as sure as I am I — and you are you — And who are you? said he. — Don't puzzle me; said I.   (VII, XXXIII)

And so he can tell us in *Tristram Shandy* that he begins with writing the first sentence and trusts to Almighty God for the second. This extreme variation, then, runs between a reflective amble and the giddy gallop of instant reaction, instant recording of emotions (both the slow and the speedy so noticeable in the action of his novels). As readers we are brought very near both the deliberate and the spontaneous; the result is a virtually unique immediacy.

Sterne's investigation of his own individuality, his own identity, is to be found at its most intense in his *Journal to Eliza* (published as *Yorick to Eliza*, 1775). This, modelled upon Swift's *Journal to Stella* is, however, very different in tone and reminds us that Sterne's temperament must have reflected his tubercular physical condition. He met Eliza Draper in London in 1767; within two months she sailed back to her husband in Bombay. Sterne, who had found in her 'a bewitching sort of nameless excellence', poured out for her all his heightened feelings, 'poor sick-headed, sick-hearted Yorick' that he was: ill, feverish in his hectic imagination yet able to make high comedy out of his treatment for what he argues was only apparently venereal disease.

His sense of humour pervades *A Sentimental Journey through France and Italy*. Its beginning is memorable — 'They order said I, this matter better in France.' In the episodes, the vignettes, of the *Journey*, Sterne's control over his material is more obvious than in *Tristram Shandy*; his last book was short, consistent, and often surprising in its sudden narrative, its dashes, and its author's ability to leave an incident in the air. Sterne's sentimentality asks the reader to share the writer's capacity not only to feel emotion but also to appreciate the emotions of others. Thus we have the famous incident of the man lamenting his dead ass, and thus, too, the incident of the grisette and the gloves, or, indeed, in the memorable conclusion, the supreme example of Sterne's teasing, the account of the author's sharing a bedroom with a lady from Piedmont and the terms of their treaty:

> . . . You have broken the treaty, monsieur, said the lady, who had not more sleep than myself. I begged a thousand pardons; but insisted it was no more than an ejaculation. . . . She maintained 'twas an entire infraction of the treaty . . . I maintained it was provided for in the clause of the third article . . .

> . . . Upon my word and honour, madame, said I, stretching my arm out of bed by way of asseveration — (I was going to have added, that I would not have trespassed against the remotest idea of decorum for the world) —
> — But the *fille de chambre*, hearing there were words between us, and fearing that hostilities would ensue in course, had crept silently out of her closet, and, it being totally dark, had stolen so close to our beds that she had got herself into the narrow passage which

separated them, and had advanced so far up as to be in a line between her mistress and me; —

So that, when I stretched out my hand, I caught hold of the *fille de chambre's* ——

Sterne is never dull: there is nice if somewhat sly self-mockery at work here, mixed in with and indeed alleviating the sentimentality.

Such fine humour did not always grace the work of those Anglo-Irish dramatists who made their careers in writing for the London stage. There was, however, some subtlety in the way in which Charles Macklin (1697/9—1797) blurred the distinctions between life and drama. To him the borderline must have been tenuous for though he began work in a public house, and ended up owning a tavern and coffee house in Covent Garden, he was a highly successful actor for sixty-five years. He accidentally killed another actor in a green-room quarrel, but escaped punishment; his autobiographical writings are vigorous and lively. They convey something of what he contributed to the English stage in the eighteenth century, for he was probably second only to Garrick in his dramatic energy, his acting ability unquenched at the age of eighty. As an author he could produce convincing dramatic dialogue. He met an Irish officer in the Prussian service in a tavern near Covent Garden and based on his idiosyncrasies the character of Sir Callaghan O'Brallaghan in *Love à la Mode* (1784; produced 1759). Sir Callaghan is contrasted with a Scot, Sir Archibald MacSarcasm, and given some lively speeches:

. . . . it rebuts a man of honour to be talking to ladies of battles, and sieges, and skrimages — it looks like gasconading and making the fanfaron. Besides, madam, I give you my honour, there is no such thing in nature as making a true description of a battle.

CHARLOTTE: How so, sir?

SIR CALLAGHAN: Why, madam, there is much doing everywhere; for every man has his own part to look after, which is as much as he can do, without minding what other people are about. Then, Madam, there is such drumming and trumpeting, firing and smoking, fighting and rattling everywhere; and such an uproar of courage and slaughter in every man's mind; and such a delightful confusion altogether that you can no more give an account of it than you can of the stars in the sky.

The True-Born Irishman: or, The Irish Fine Lady, produced in 1762 and rewritten as *The Irish Fine Lady* in 1767, shows Macklin's ability to write realistically, while in *The Man of the World* (1781) he extracted a good deal of humour out of the stock plot of youth versus age, for his hero marries the daughter of a poor officer rather than the wealthy lady his father, Sir Pertinax MacSycophant, had chosen for him. This is a play attacking political corruption, the self-exposure of the self-interest of Sir Pertinax being extremely effective.

Other Anglo-Irish authors included Arthur Murphy (1727–1805), Dr Johnson's friend, who wrote some successful tragedies, comedies and farces after he became disgusted with the law. *The Way to Keep Him* (1760; revised in 1761 in five-act form) is in the classical tradition of the comedy of manners and proved popular over a long period; the pace Murphy achieved in this play – as in *The School for Guardians* (1767), based on Molière – was matched by the smart tempo of his farces, such as *The Apprentice* (1756), *The Upholsterer; or, What News?* (1758) and *What We Must All Come To* (1764; rewritten as *Three Weeks after Marriage*, 1776). Murphy also wrote biographies of Fielding, Johnson and Garrick, as well as the *Gray's Inn Journal*.

A pioneer in creating English comic opera, Isaac Bickerstaffe (*c*. 1733–?1808/12) was born in Dublin and acted as page to Lord Chesterfield, the Lord Lieutenant, before being commissioned as an Ensign in 1745: he was a Second Lieutanant from 1746–55 and 1758–63. His *Love in a Village* (1761) with music by Thomas Arne was most popular; like his other work, it was not very original, being based on Wycherley's *The Gentleman Dancing-Master* (1673) and Charles Johnson's *The Village Opera*. Though taxed with plagiarism, Bickerstaffe's wit and satiric touch, his capacity to match words to music made his operas most successful. After *The Maid of the Mill* (1765), he collaborated with Charles Dibdin as composer in *Love in the City* (1767). They combined forces several times, notably in *Lionel and Clarissa* (1768), and *The Padlock* (1768), a farce. They also created Italianate short operas, *The Ephesian Matron* (1769) and *The Recruiting Serjeant* (1770), which were performed at Ranelagh House. Bickerstaffe's career ended in 1772 when he left England to avoid being arrested as a homosexual.

Like Murphy, a friend of Johnson and a member of the
Club, Edmund Malone (1741—1812) was taught by Charles
Macklin before going to Trinity College, Dublin in 1756. He
is probably the first distinguished Anglo-Irish literary critic,
and his edition of Shakespeare has considerable merit. John
O'Keefe (1747—1833), who was an actor at the Smock Alley
Theatre in Dublin (1762—74), wrote a comic opera *The
Son-in-Law* (Dublin, 1783), moved to London after its
triumph at the Haymarket in 1779, and wrote in all about
fifty plays. He called some of them operas and interlarded
their action frequently with songs. Among them are a lively
farce, *The She-Gallant: or Square Toes Outwitted* (1767),
The Prisoner at Large (1788), a serious attack on absentee
landlordism, and *The Wicklow Gold Mines, or, the Lady of
the Hill* (1796) with its Irish setting for comic opera. Two of
his plays were very successful in their day, *The Agreeable
Surprise* (1781) and *Wild Oats* (1792). The latter, revived by
the Royal Shakespeare Company in 1976, is an obvious reaction against sentimental comedy; the plot uses stock devices,
but the main character, Rover, is a striking player who can
quote appositely in emergencies. James Kenney (1780—
1849) adapted many French plays, but in his farce *Raising
the Wind* (1803) created a fresh and lasting type in Jeremy
Diddler.

A virtual high priest of sentimental comedy appeared in
Hugh Kelly (1739—77) who left Dublin for London, began
work at his trade of stay-maker, turned journalist and wrote a
novel, *Memoirs of a Magdalen; or, The History of Louisa
Mildmay* (1767). His theatrical poem *Thespis* annoyed a lot
of people, but it led to his first comedy, *False Delicacy* (described by Johnson as 'totally void of character'), being
produced at Drury Lane in 1768. Kelly entered the Middle
Temple in 1769, and wrote *A Word to the Wise* (1770). This
comedy was suspected of being written for government pay,
and attacked until the management withdrew it. His tragedy,
Clementina (1771) was not successful, but his next comedy,
A School for Wives (1774), was staged under Addington's
name, its real authorship being revealed after the ninth night.
It had considerable success, though *The Romance of an Hour*
(1774) which followed it was a failure. *The Man of Reason*
lasted for only one performance in 1776. This led Kelly to

abandon writing drama and take up the law seriously.

When Kelly's *False Delicacy* was staged at Drury Lane in 1768 it outplayed Oliver Goldsmith's first comedy *The Good Natur'd Man* at Covent Garden. This was a very different kind of play, for Goldsmith (1728–74) considered sentimental comedy a bastard form of tragedy; he thought that the sentimental comedy of his day caused the neglect of genuine tragedy as well as harming the humour of true comedy. He put his views in an essay of 1773, *On Sentimental Comedy*, and his two comedies, *The Good Natur'd Man* (1768) and *She Stoops to Conquer* (1773), show how he translated his ideas into practice.

When Goldsmith turned to the theatre he had been living by his pen for some years. After graduating from Trinity College, Dublin in 1749, he had attended medical lectures in Edinburgh in 1752 and 1754 and then spent nearly a year at the University of Leiden before leaving on his great year of philosophic vagabondage 'with a guinea in his pocket, one shirt to his back, and a flute in his hand'. He walked through Flanders, France, Switzerland and Italy, probably returning through Germany. He learned a great deal about European thought in the process, and when he arrived in London in 1756 he found — after a few false starts — his true craft. He could write with ease, elegantly yet unaffectedly, wearing his knowledge lightly, and indulging in some ironical gaiety in his 'Chinese Letters', through the pretended ignorance of a Chinese observer of English ways of life. These letters have an ironic detachment about them characteristic of Anglo-Irish views of England. To Goldsmith, as to many another Irish writer, England with all its wealth, the authority of its great men, was both admired and resented:

> The English are a people of good sense; and I am the more surprised to find them swayed in their opinions by men who often from their very education are incompetent judges. Men who, being always bred in affluence, see the world only on one side, are surely improper judges of human nature: they may indeed describe a ceremony, a pageant, or a ball; but how can they pretend to dive into the secrets of the human heart, who have been nursed up only in forms, and daily behold nothing but the same insipid adulation smiling upon every face. Few of them have been bred in that best of schools, the school of adversity; and by what I can learn, fewer still have been bred in any school at all.   (Letter LVII)

The professional writer, however pleasing his works, or profound his knowledge, lost prestige because of his poverty. Goldsmith was yet another Irish writer who knew this situation well:

> As soon as a piece therefore is published, the first questions are, Who is the author? Does he keep a coach?   (Letter LVII)

By the early seventeen-sixties he had become a friend of Dr Johnson, Sir Joshua Reynolds and other members of the famous Club founded in 1763. Johnson recognised Goldsmith's merits and praised them unselfishly, selling his novel *The Vicar of Wakefield* (1766) for him, and persuading him to finish his poem *The Traveller* (1764) which was the first work to be published under his own name. In *The Traveller* Goldsmith contrives to break through eighteenth-century restraints, giving generalised reflections great strength and dignity. He sought what he called true declamation, 'a plain, open and loose style'. His words are often plain, but they are persuasive and, because he was an emotional man, they are powerful too. *The Traveller* is a meditation upon loneliness, upon the attraction of home for the wanderer whose varying moods are skilfully indicated in the midst of the traveller's descriptions of people and places, his felicitous statement of 'known truths'.

The Deserted Village (1770), his second longer poem, deals with depopulation. In it he gives us vignettes irradiated by gentle humour, character sketches in miniature, of the smith, the village schoolmaster, and the preacher, who was 'passing rich on forty pounds a year'. We get the erstwhile life of the village scaled down in such a way that its apparently assured continuity of life is conveyed. The repetition of 'How often' adds to this effect:

> How often have I paused on every charm,
> The sheltered cot, the cultivated farm,
> The never failing brook, the busy mill,
> The decent church that topt the neighbouring hill,
> The hawthorn bush, with seats beneath the shade,
> For talking age and whispering lovers made!
> How often have I blest the coming day,
> When toil remitting lent its turn to play
> And all the village train from labour free
> Led up their sports beneath the spreading tree . . . .

These simple memories attain poignancy when the contrast between their succession, the former homely contentment, and the subsequent empty, depopulated countryside is drawn; a pensive note pervades the poem's counterpointing of past and present. Goldsmith is, in part, telling us of his own memories of the Irish midlands (though much of his description in the poem is obviously of an idealised English village) and of the hopes he once had of returning to 'these humble bowers':

> I still had hopes, for pride attends us still,
> Amidst the swains to show my book-learn'd skill,
> Around my fire an evening group to draw,
> And tell of all I felt, and all I saw;
> And, as a hare, whom hounds and horns pursue,
> Pants to the place from whence at first she flew,
> I still had hopes, my long vexations past,
> Here to return — and die at home at last.

Goldsmith is also expressing the perennial nostalgia of the exile: it is no whit less powerful for being more restrained than subsequent laments of exiles in the nineteenth century. Goldsmith worked hard to create an air of spontaneity in his poetry, often drafting it in prose; he shrugged off solemnity when he could, as in the 'Elegy on the Death of a Mad Dog' or in his last poem, 'Retaliation', that generous response to his friends' teasing. He achieved an easy elegance in the 'Stanzas on Woman':

> When lovely woman stoops to folly,
> And finds too late that men betray,
> What charm can soothe her melancholy,
> What art can wash her guilt away?

How well he could use conventional forms for original observation and expression emerges when he is contrasted with his contemporaries. John Cunningham, for instance, (1729–73) who was educated at Drogheda and became a strolling player on the strength of his farce *Love in a Mist* (1747), was encouraged by Shenstone to write poetry. Even though his 'Day — a Pastoral' has some merit, he was typically fashionable; his praise of Newcastle ale rings far truer than his traditional love songs to various ladies and his completely conventional pastoral poetry.

Goldsmith was also successful in fiction, where he portrayed an orderly Christian life. In his novel *The Vicar of Wakefield* (1766) there is an effective miniaturisation at work, which allows the novelist to recount a series of appalling misfortunes which disrupt the contented life of the Vicar's family; here Goldsmith uses an approximation to the Gaelic present habitual tense in establishing the pastoral contentment which is so rudely shattered:

> The little republic to which I gave laws was regulated in the following manner: by sunrise we all assembled in our common apartment, the fire being previously kindled by the servant; after we had saluted each other with proper ceremony, for I always thought fit to keep up some mechanical forms of good breeding, without which freedom ever destroys friendship, we all bent in gratitude to that Being who gave us another day. This duty being performed, my son and I went to pursue our usual industry abroad, while my wife and daughters employed themselves in providing breakfast, which was always ready at a certain time. I allowed half an hour for this meal, and an hour for dinner; which time was taken up in innocent mirth between my wife and daughters, and in philosophical arguments between my son and me.

The Vicar of Wakefield is remarkable for its creation of a likeable character in the person of the Vicar. Throughout the novel, Goldsmith's gentle irony is at work:

> It must be owned, that my wife laid a thousand schemes to entrap him; or, to speak it more tenderly, used every art to magnify the merit of her daughter. If the cakes at tea ate short and crisp, they were made by Olivia; if the gooseberry-wine was well knit, the gooseberries were of her gathering; it was her fingers which gave the pickles their peculiar green; and in the composition of a pudding it was her judgement that mixed the ingredients. Then the poor woman would sometimes tell the squire, that she thought him and Olivia extremely of a size, and would bid both to stand up to see which was the tallest.

As well as his humane reflections upon the lessons he had learned in his own pilgrimage through life Goldsmith amuses his readers with a story full of fun, of anticlimax, of absurdity. When the Vicar remarks that he isn't sure 'whether we had more wit among us now than usual' but is certain that 'we had more laughing, which answered the end as well', we are in touch once again with fun, which is certainly not wit, nor perhaps even humour.

Whatever it is, it makes for good stage comedy. When Goldsmith wrote *The Good Natur'd Man* he lacked a command of stagecraft, and he did not maintain a comic pace sufficiently throughout the play's action. He could create character convincingly. No doubt his hero, Honeywood, had elements of self-portraiture. Like Goldsmith, he had no harm in him: he trusted everyone; he was filled with the universal benevolence Goldsmith had seen in his own unworldly clergyman father, who had, he remarked, wound his children up to be mere machines of pity. Goldsmith was always a good touch for the mass of needy writers — and Irish people — who surrounded him when he was in funds. The story of his giving his bedding to a poor woman when he was an undergraduate in Dublin is typical of his own good nature. His generosity led him to know what debt was: for he often overspent in his generosity, and then overworked to catch up again. Thus the situation in the play where Honeywood pretends to Miss Richland that the bailiffs in his house are visiting acquaintances is convincing: but, funny though it is, it did not please the audience at Covent Garden. The situations, the dialogue, the crosspurposes of the plot are amusing, the characters (notably Lofty who pretends to know and to be able to wield influence with the great) are novel; and yet the play is not all of a piece, perhaps because Goldsmith had not written sufficiently out of his own experiences.

When he did exploit a reputed experience of his schooldays — an occasion when he had lost his way, and was directed by a practical joker to a local squire's house which he then proceeded to treat in ignorance as an inn — and when he created in one of his characters a shyness with ladies of quality but familiarity with barmaids, he had the ingredients of a plot which allowed him to develop his sense of fun — and farce — hilariously. *She Stoops to Conquer* has a timelessness about it, and Tony Lumpkin, the irascible Squire Hardcastle's stepson who likes the appreciation of a loutish audience, surely goes back to Goldsmith's own youth in the Irish midlands, to those days on which he looked back and about which he wrote so nostalgically to his friend Bob Bryanston.

Goldsmith succeeded in this attempt to make people laugh; he let the audience see the ironies of the situation; and his tolerant amusement irradiates the activities of the characters as the play dashes along, its mixture of absurdity and anti-climax welded together by farce, comic contrivance and a classical pruning of excess.

This particular comic vein was quickly continued in Sheridan's comedies, *The Rivals* being produced in 1775, two years after *She Stoops to Conquer*. Like Goldsmith, Richard Brinsley Sheridan (1751–1816) feared the effect on the theatre of sentimental comedy, and attacked it in a prologue written for the play's second appearance (as well as expressing his dislike more thoroughly in *The Critic* (1779), where Sir Fretful Plagiary is a mockery of Cumberland, the author of many sentimental plays). Liveliness of action characterises *The Rivals*, the complications of the plot being skilfully devised. The conflict between youth and age is there, and a varied range of characters: Sir Anthony Absolute is an autocratic father; Mrs Malaprop, a vulgarian aiming at London standards, achieves immortality through the rich confusion of speech with which Sheridan enclosed her; Lydia Languish is a headlong romantic, her silliness caused by reading light novels from the circulating library; Bob Acres, unlike the elegant Anthony Absolute, is clumsily countrified; Faulkland shows us jealousy in its eighteenth-century fashion; Julia is a foil to Lydia; and the vitality of Sir Lucius O'Trigger, a fiery Irishman (possibly founded upon Charles Macklin's Sir Callaghan O'Brallaghan), emerges throughout the play. In it Sheridan is poking fun at the society he saw in Bath. Goldsmith's *Life of Richard Nash* (1762) tells us how Nash, in his role of Master of Ceremonies there, had established the tone of the fashionable society which centred upon the Spa and the Assembly Rooms.

Whereas Goldsmith's sense of comedy ultimately may have derived from the Elizabethans and was akin to that of Farquhar, both Macklin and Sheridan modelled themselves upon the classical Restoration comedies of wit and intrigue, though they contrived to be funny without being coarse or cynically amoral. Sheridan grew up with knowledge of the practical side of the theatre. His father Thomas Sheridan (1719–88), son of the famous Thomas Sheridan, Swift's witty schoolmaster friend, was an actor who played at the Smock Alley Theatre in Dublin and at Covent Garden and Drury Lane. He became manager of the Theatre Royal, Dublin, in 1746 and held the post successfully for eight years. Though· he wrote several books on reading and the English language, he also wrote tragedies and a farce, *Captain O'Blunder* (1754), with a somewhat gullible stage Irish hero. His wife Frances Sheridan (1724–66) also wrote effectively. Her *Memoirs of Miss Sidney Biddulph extracted from her own Journal* (1761) had a reputation in her lifetime though now it seems slow in action, something which cannot be said of her comedy *The Discovery* (1763), a lively, cleverly constructed play, highly approved by David Garrick. She also wrote *The Dupe* (1763), another comedy, and her unacted play of 1765, *The Trip to Bath*, unpublished in her lifetime, was supposed to have been used by her son in writing *The Rivals*. Frances Sheridan's comedies owed much to Restoration vivaciousness and they move rapidly, with good dialogue.

The difference between appearance and reality, so often utilised by Restoration dramatists, particularly interested her son, and so he put well-tried ingredients into his best-known comedy, *The School for Scandal* (1777): mistaken identity; lovers kept apart, to be finally rewarded; mockery of the country girl in town life; above all, the exposure of hypocrisy.

Satire of the polite world, mockery of current scandal-mongering and journalism, would not alone have ensured this play's continuing success; in it Sheridan presented enjoyable ridicule and yet transcended it, his dramatic sense providing suspense and the unexpected reversal, his dialogue being witty, indeed sparkling. The true natures of the Surface brothers are shown and Lady Sneerwell exposed. And so all has not been what it appeared to be; the ironies have merged with the ludicrous, the screen tumbles and with it comes revelation. Audiences still enjoy the effects of the working out of this skilful plot, 'the modish ritual, and the elaborate and decorative clothes', the elegance of what was already becoming virtually part of a past age as Sheridan wrote his play.

Sheridan's fame as a dramatist has lasted; the plays are there, they are performed. But what of his own performance as an orator? It is always difficult for later readers to appreciate past oratory, designed to be heard, suited to its occasion, depending not a little upon emotional responses from the speaker's audience. We know, however, how Sheridan's contemporaries viewed his achievement. Burke valued, indeed had infinite confidence in his capacities, and persuaded him to join in the attack on Warren Hastings: the result was Sheridan's first speech, of five and a half hours, on the motion of impeachment in the House of Commons in 1787 (where he had taken his seat in 1780) which was a complete triumph. And Sheridan repeated it in his second oration, his acting ability reinforcing the highflown sentiments which gave his long account of Indian affairs such an effective, emotive force.

There was a flowering of oratory among the Anglo-Irish in the latter part of the eighteenth century. While Sheridan's parliamentary career is inevitably linked with India, Edmund Burke's embraced, as well as India, the American colonies, Ireland and France. He brought to Westminster a legal training and frustrated literary ambition.

Burke (1729—97) graduated at Trinity College in 1748, then crossed to London to study law at the Middle Temple in 1750, intending to return to Dublin to practise. By 1757 he had changed his mind and offended his father in so doing — in 1756 he had befriended the American Joseph Emin and told him that his name was 'Edmund Burke, at your service. I am a runaway son from my father, as you are', and it was in 1756 that Dodsley had published Burke's first book *A Vindication of Natural Society or, A View of the Miseries and Evils arising to Mankind from every species of Artificial Society*. This put forward his belief that there should be deference in society; imagination run riot would ruin any respect for inherited wisdom; and anarchy would ensue. His deeply ironic treatise pleads for natural society, and for natural reason, against atheists, divines and politicians. Here were Bolingbroke's earlier arguments against Christianity treated with irony and shown to be ultimately disruptive of society. And here was prose as eloquent as Bolingbroke's, fully armed against the warfare Burke had found everywhere in his vast reading.

The success of *A Vindication* led to the publication in the same year of Burke's *Philosophical Enquiry into the Origin of our Ideas of the Sublime and Beautiful* (1756) which he had begun when he was nineteen. In this he went beyond Locke's emphasis upon rationality: he recognised the power of emotion; he was deeply interested in the psychological effects of grandeur, darkness and mystery. He distinguished between sublimity and the beautiful, the one founded upon delight (which could include horror) and the other upon love. In effect he was bridging the gap between Augustanism's insistence upon reason and the full-blooded emotional innovation of the self- and nature-regarding Romantics. It is not completely satisfactory, however, to label him — as often happens — as a neo-classicist. Perhaps his unease with his age hindered his ambition of having a literary career. Despite these early successes he left his projected history of England unfinished as well as his *Hints for an Essay on the Drama*, and his *Tract on the Popery Laws in Ireland*. He edited the *Annual Register* for Dodsley from 1759 onwards — not a role he admitted to, and it brought in only £100 a year; then in 1765 he launched himself upon his proper career. He was elected an MP in December of that year at the age of thirty-seven, and by the following spring had established his reputation as a speaker. He had turned to politics 'not at all as a place of preferment, but of refuge'. He wrote to Charles O'Hara about his entry into politics: 'I was pushed into it and I must have been a Member, and that too with some Eclat or be a little worse than nothing.'

Burke's halfway position between classicism and romanticism emerges clearly in his political writings. He had high ideals, but he tempered them pragmatically. Thus, as Robert A. Murray has pointed out in his *Edmund Burke: A Biography* (1931), he was closely akin to Swift in his attitude to truth. Swift held that violent zeal for truth 'has a hundred to one odds to be either petulancy, ambition or pride' and Burke, in his remarks upon those clergy, doctors and lawyers who petitioned to be relieved from subscribing to the Thirty-Nine Articles, preferred peace:

> Perhaps truth may be far better. But as we have scarcely even the same certainty in the one that we have in the other, I would, unless the truth were evident indeed, hold fast to peace, which has in her company charity the highest of the virtues.

In *The Suspecting Glance* (1972) Conor Cruise O'Brien also considers Burke's writings close to those of Swift. Though Burke, he says, came out of the nation of defeated, Gaelic,

Catholic Ireland, Swift was of the Protestant nation and of English origin:

> What they shared was not a national characteristic but a social experience of a kind that leaves a deep mark — the experience of an underside, of a wilder and more dangerous world, and one in which assumptions current in the more comfortable society come up against limits. The language in which both men wrote was formed by the ruling- and middle-classes of the dominant society. Their experience on this fringe was such as to make their imaginations stretch and test the comfortable language in some ways, and prune and discipline it in others.

Just as Swift sought the simplest language to achieve his political ends so Burke's language was equally rational and persuasive. Swift also occupied a middle position between two literary periods: his early prose was complex, in the seventeenth-century manner, before he learned the need to appeal to an apparently rationalising eighteenth-century audience and, more important, to reach a wide section of that audience. Both men probably used irony because of not completely accepting the assumptions of the ages in which they lived. Irony provided a sophisticated, double way of seeing things: and both Anglo-Irishmen obviously needed this extra intellectual scope.

Burke's irony could burst out in the midst of his most persuasive prose. The *Reflections on the Revolution in France* (1790) show how he wanted peace above all; he never liked

> this continual talk of resistance and revolution, or the practice of making the extreme medicine of the constitution its daily bread. It renders the habit of society dangerously valetudinarian; it is taking periodical dozes of mercury sublimate, and swallowing down repeated provocatives of cantharides to our love of liberty.

Burke's inclinations, as he put them in his speech on Conciliation with America, were to see all government, every human benefit and enjoyment founded upon compromise and barter. He thought that the sovereign authority of the English government should be kept as a sanctuary of liberty, but that if the Westminster government became one thing, the colonists' privileges another, that if the two things existed without any mutual relation then 'the cement is gone; the cohesion is loosened; and everything hastens to decay and dissolution.' His view of parliament was at times idealistic: it was not, he declared,

> a *congress* of ambassadors from different and hostile interests; which interests each must maintain as an agent and advocate, against other agents and advocates; but parliament is a *deliberative* assembly of *one* nation, with *one* interest that of the whole; where, not local purposes, ought to guide, but the General good, resulting from the general reason of the whole.

Such a reasonable view was inevitably opposed to revolution; balanced against it were Burke's gradualism, his awareness of the need to make law certain, his knowledge that the condition of the criminal code was abominable, that it must be reformed, and by his idea that society was a contract, a continuity. He could state such ideas with measured, stately eloquence in his *Reflections on the Revolution in France*; what gives a particular force to these views is the emotional engagement which strikes through the prose. This is very obvious in his *Thoughts on the Prospect of a Regicide Peace in a series of letters* (1796) where he adapts a famous image of Swift's and gives it new form. In his *Letter . . . concerning the sacramental Test* (1709) Swift wrote that the Church was more menaced by Dissenters than by Roman Catholics:

> It is agreed among Naturalists, that a *Lyon* is a larger, a stronger and more dangerous enemy than a *Cat*; yet if a Man were to have his choice, either a *Lyon* at his Foot, bound fast with three or four Chains, his Teeth drawn out, and his Claws pared to the Quick, or an angry *Cat* in full liberty at his Throat; he would take no long Time to determine.

Burke attacks those gentlemen who drew a parallel between Algiers and France, remarking, with a dash of *realpolitik*, that different conduct should be held with regard to an evil at an immense distance and when it is at the door:

> I certainly should dread more from a wild cat in my bed-chamber, than from all the lions that roar in the deserts behind Algiers. But in this parallel it is the cat that is at a distance, and the lions and tigers that are in our ante-chambers and our lobbies. Algiers is not near; Algiers is not powerful, Algiers is not our neighbour; Algiers is not infectious. Algiers, whatever it may be, is an old creation; and we

have good data to calculate all the mischief to be apprehended from
it. When I find Algiers transferred to Calais, I will tell you what I
think of that point.

Burke's response to the bloodiness of the revolution, his
prophesying its increasing savagery, was founded not only
upon his reading in history but also on his innate Irish knowledge of what the revolutionary cycle brought with it:
political passion turned into recurrent revenge, reprisal and
repression. Only Dickens, perhaps, could match Burke's
instinctive horror of the anarchy, with his own intense loathing of revolutionary mobs so graphically given life in *A Tale
of Two Cities*.

This instinctive, emotional response to violence underlay
Burke's writings, and his use of irony increased as his dis-
appointments multiplied. There was the excitement of the
constitution granted to Ireland in 1782, in part a tribute
to Lord Charlemont and the strength of the Irish volunteer
movement; there was the hope that the two islands might
draw closer; mutual affections could do more than any
artificial ties for mutual help and mutual advantage. He wrote
encouragingly to Charlemont about the new development;
but upon the promise of Grattan's parliament there followed
a reality of both public and private despair. Burke's son
Richard had died in August 1794, and public events seemed
menacing. The French had been in the Low Countries, and
Burke thought there was a dangerous threat from radical
agitators in England, while Ireland was deeply discontented.
But he considered that the Irish Catholics were conservative
by nature and should therefore be emancipated. He wanted
through such a measure to create support for an anti-Jacobinical
stance in Ireland. He wanted, he wrote in a revealing letter of
26 May 1795 to Sir Hercules Langrishe, a measure which
would tend to promote the concord of the citizens:

> The worst of the matter is this: you are partly leading, partly driving
> into Jacobinism that description of your people whose religious
> principles — church polity, and habitual discipline — might make
> them an invincible dyke against that inundation.

Burke showed, ironically, how Catholics desiring seats and
places were told that this was only a pretext '(though Protes-

tants might suppose it just *possible* for men to like good places and snug boroughs for their own merits) for them to strip Protestants of their poverty.' If you treat men as robbers, Burke commented, 'why robbers, sooner or later, they will become.'

Inflexibility, however, was the policy of the Irish administration. Apart from a natural self-interest in keeping their powerful, financially rewarding positions, men such as Fitzgibbon the Lord Chancellor, Beresford the Revenue Commissioner, and Forster the Speaker feared the results of conciliation: the change was too great to contemplate. But the appointment of Lord Fitzwilliam as Lord Lieutenant in 1794 seemed to promise a new era in England's treatment of Ireland. Grattan made a speech which indicated that a new Catholic relief bill would admit Catholics to parliament, which attacked France and strengthened the armed forces. But by March Fitzwilliam had left Ireland, convinced that his cabinet colleagues in England had been disloyal to the conciliatory measures he had begun to implement. Burke realised the harm done. Though long resident in England, he knew his Ireland and wrote to Grattan, sadly recording the complacency, 'the profound security' of everyone in England.

Events were well and truly in train for the tragedy of 1798. Burke himself, however, was to live only till 1797. And in 1796 he wrote his *Letter to a Noble Lord*. This reply to the duke of Bedford, who had complained at Burke's receiving a pension of £1,200 a year, produced some sweeping, swinge-ing prose. Burke was not 'like his Grace of Bedford, swaddled and rocked, and dandled into a legislator.' He defended his life, explained his policies, his services in strengthening the constitution and, in a bitter, Swiftian passage which deserves to be remembered as much as the famous panegyric, 'the delightful vision' of the Queen of France whom Burke had seen at Versailles, he described the emptiness of life after his son had died:

I greatly deceive myself, if in this hard season I would give a peck of refuse wheat for all that is called fame and honour in the world . . . I live in an inverted order. They who ought to have succeeded me are gone before me. They who should have been to me as posterity are in the place of ancestors. I owe it to the dearest relation (which ever must subsist in memory) that act of piety, which he would have performed to me; I owe it to him to show that he was not descended as the Duke of Bedford would have it, from an unworthy parent.

While Burke had advocated in England the cause of the Irish Catholics in Ireland, Henry Grattan (1746—1820) had continued in Dublin to put the political arguments of Molyneux and Swift. Like them he refused to grant England any right to regard Ireland as a subordinate kingdom. The parliament at Westminster, he claimed, should not attempt to make laws for Ireland. Behind the declaration of Irish rights, formulated in a speech of 19 April 1780, had loomed the economic attitudes of Swift: 'The same power which took away the export of woollens and the export of glass may take them away again.' He knew Molyneux's arguments well and referred to 'the compact of Henry', the 'charter of John' — and to the passions of the people. He reminded his audience that in 1778 a commission had gone to America and the commissioners had offered to all or any of the American states 'the total surrender of the legislative authority of the British Parliament'.

Grattan had realised that the Ascendancy must change itself, and in his speech of 20 February 1782 got to the essential point: the question of whether the Irish parliament should grant Roman Catholics the power of enjoying estates. He asked his audience

. . . whether we shall be a Protestant settlement or an Irish nation? Whether we shall throw open the gates of the temple of liberty to all our countrymen, or whether we shall confine them in bondage by penal laws? So long as the penal code remains we can never be a great nation. The penal code is the shell in which the Protestant power has been hatched, and now it has become a bird, it must burst the shell or perish in it.

Later in 1782, on 16 April, Grattan carried repeal of the Declaratory Statute, George I, the Perpetual Mutiny Bill, and abolition of the Privy Council's unconstitutional powers. This famous Declaration of Independence was a triumphant piece of political oratory, and it acknowledged handsomely the inspiration of Molyneux and Swift.

I am now to address a free people: ages have passed away, and this is the first moment in which you could be distinguished by that appellation . . .

> I found Ireland on her knees, I watched over her with a paternal solicitude; I have traced her progress from injuries to arms, and from arms to liberty. Spirit of Swift! spirit of Molyneux! your genius has prevailed. Ireland is now a nation . . .
>
> She is no longer a wretched colony, returning thanks to her governor for his rapine, and to her king for his oppression; nor is she now a squabbling, fretful sectary, perplexing her little wits, and firing her furious statutes with bigotry, sophistry, disabilities, and death, to transmit to posterity insignificance and war . . . .
>
> You, with difficulties innumerable, with dangers not a few, have done what your ancestors wished, but could not accomplish; and what your posterity may preserve, but will never equal: you have moulded the jarring elements of your country into a nation.

Grattan's parliament marked the final flowering of the Anglo-Irish Ascendancy: visible signs of its confidence can be seen in big houses here and there in the countryside, though the main witnesses to its good taste are the buildings of Dublin erected in the last thirty years of the eighteenth century. James Gandon's (1743–1824) elegant Custom House, begun in 1781, and his majestic legal building, the Four Courts, begun in 1786, give distinction to the Liffey's quays. There were such great houses as Powerscourt House (1771), Belvedere House (1786), Clonmell House (1778) and Alborough House (1792), while in Fitzwilliam, Mountjoy and Merrion Square speculative builders provided for the professional classes of Dublin civilised town houses in warm-toned brick with subtle proportions in their dignified granite-surrounded front doors and elegant fan lights. In these houses as well as in the big houses in the countryside was to be found, Sir Jonah Barrington thought, 'that glow of well-bred — and cordial vinous conviviality' which was 'peculiar to high society in Ireland'. This society encouraged the work of the Irish silversmiths, the lively chasing and curving lines of whose cutlery lent grace to its tables; it encouraged itself with whiskey and claret, poured from and into the sparkle of Waterford glass; it enjoyed the sumptuous tooled leather of the bookbinders, and its furniture, often blackened to resemble bog oak, was exuberant in its carving until the influence of Sheraton was felt in the late eighteen-seventies. The plaster work moved from the vigorous rococo introduced by the Francini brothers (whose ceiling at Carton for the earl of Kildare is superb) to a flowering in the work of the stuccoers, Robert West and Michael Stapleton, before reaching a restrained classicism.

In Dublin the Theatre Royal was built in Aungier Street and rivalled the Smock Alley Theatre; another theatre was opened in Crow Street in 1759. Theatres were built in the provinces. A malt house had been converted into a theatre in Cork in 1713, and this was followed by the Theatre Royal in 1736, rebuilt in 1797, and by another theatre for the Cork Company of Comedians in the seventeen-forties. In 1761 Spranger Barry, the manager of the Dublin Crow Street theatre, opened his theatre in Cork and the construction of another Cork theatre in Henry Street followed in 1779. In Galway, Robert Owenson, Lady Morgan's father, played in the theatre in Kirwan's Lane in 1782, though by 1795 this was used only by amateurs. Other theatres were built in Ennis, Limerick and Waterford. At Kilkenny and Derry the Tholsel and Town Hall were used for performances; later a theatre was built in Derry in 1774, and a new theatre in 1789. Belfast, which had a playhouse before 1730, had several theatres built between 1768 and 1794.

Painting developed rapidly in the latter half of the eighteenth century. Hugh Douglas Hamilton, one of the early pupils of the Dublin Art School, was very successful as a portrait painter. He spent some time in Italy and then returned to Dublin to paint many memorable pictures, notably a *Cupid and Psyche*. In his brief career Robert Healy (*d.* 1771) produced some delightful, original paintings, notably those of the Conollys at Castletown House (see *Plate 12*). Nathaniel Hone (1718–84) trained in Dublin and later was a founder member of the Royal Academy. A superb painter of children, he based himself on Dutch examples; his self-portraits are powerful images of a man of aggressive temperament. Thomas Hickey (1756–1816), like many another Irish artist, did not find enough work in Dublin after several years there and moved to India and Portugal. A nice link between painting and literature is provided by James Barry (1741–1806), a Cork builder's son who began painting there, studied for some months in the Dublin Society's schools and became friendly with Edmund Burke, who introduced him to Reynolds. He left for the Continent in 1765, financed by Burke. Some years after his return to England (in 1771) he painted Burke and himself as *Ulysses and his companions escaping from Polyphemus*, a neat neo-classical joke. He painted Shakespearean subjects successfully, then embarked on the impressive series of murals, *The Progress of Human Culture*, in the Royal Society of Arts in the Adelphi. He was the great master of the neo-classic style, and his *Self Portrait* of 1803 remains his most striking work.

Another artist upon whom Burke exerted an influence was the romantic landscapist George Barret (?1728/32–84), another founder member of the Royal Academy, whom Burke described as 'a wonderful observer of the accidents of nature': his skies are particularly good, as are those of a minor painter Jonathan Fisher (*d*. 1809). Another painter, Thomas Roberts (1749–78), was perhaps the most successful interpreter of landscapes in a nostalgic, serene manner. Apart from some sensitive landscapes Nathaniel Grogan (?1740–1807), another painter from Cork, exhibited a lively touch of satire in his portrayal of peasants. There is a distinctly Dutch influence about his dark cottage interiors.

Exteriors of fine public buildings were to grace the Irish scene during the latter part of the eighteenth century. In Dublin, for instance, there was the Parliament House in College Green with its magnificent portico designed by Edward Lovett Pearce; it was adapted for the Bank of Ireland after the Union by Francis Johnston (1761–1809), whose work included the Viceregal Lodge in Phoenix Park and St George's Church in Hardwicke Place. Palladian seems now to have been the most successful style in eighteenth-century Irish buildings (there were often stables or cowsheds behind the facades, since the classical house developed from the castle and was built with an eye to emergencies); but Greek revival and neo-classical were perhaps ultimately too restrained for Ireland and gave way to Gothic. But of all the eighteenth-century buildings the most graceful is the superb neo-classical Casino at Malahide designed by Sir William Chambers for the earl of Charlemont. Chambers was also responsible for the Chapel and the Examination Hall in Trinity College: their classical balance and restraint, their clear outlines and organised rhythms, occur in the earlier great Palladian West Front (1755–9) of the college opposite the Bank of Ireland. There is a dignity, an authority, and a sureness of purpose about these buildings.

Sureness of purpose marked Grattan's efforts too: he had a

statesman's vision, but his vision of Irish independence was not shared by his audience in the Dublin parliament. His liberal views on what made a nation, especially his realisation of the need for Catholic emancipation, were too advanced for his parliamentary colleagues. While he asserted the triumph of Swift's ideas that claimed political independence for Ireland, these were not ideas which had envisaged Catholics advancing to power. Swift had wanted neither Presbyterian nor Catholic in any position of influence. And Grattan's own parliamentary idealism about emancipation was not put to the test: it was overtaken by the revolutionary pressures which Burke feared so strongly, by the desire of Wolfe Tone and his friends for a united Irish republic, to be created out of a union between Catholic and Episcopalians and Presbyterians. The bloody insurrection of 1798 was followed by the Act of Union of 1800. This abolished the parliament in Dublin, and with its abolition the political *raison d'être* of the Protestant concept of the Irish nation evaporated. And, ironically, Grattan had to sound the knell for his own dreams.

The views of Castlereagh and Pitt had prevailed and, despite the emotive eloquence of Robert Emmet's (1778–1803) speech from the dock after the failure of his rising in 1803, the Union was to offer during the nineteenth century the concept of belonging to a larger imperial community which very many Anglo-Irish found acceptable. But Anglo-Irish literature was inseparably bound with both the dreams and the realities of politics: writers naturally tended to become involved in both, perhaps because of the size of the community. The expression of their attitudes took on many forms, notably that of oratory, Irish rhetoric stemming from a characteristic mixture of oral tradition and an inborn sense of the dramatic (already seen in Sheridan's easy transition from successful dramatist to equally successful parliamentary orator), a constructive fusion of classical cohesion and an enlivening Irish exuberance.

Towards the end of the eighteenth century there was much eloquence to be heard in the Dublin parliament and courts. Henry Hood (1732–91), for instance, had a lawyer's precision of phrase, the exact arguments of logic constantly at his command; Walter Hussey Burgh (1742–83) achieved fame

with a speech on Free Trade with a peroration which heralded
his resignation from the office of Prime Sergeant:

> Talk not to me of peace, Ireland is not at peace. It is smothered war.
> England has sown her laws as dragon's teeth, and they have sprung
> up as armed men.

And John Philpot Curran (1750—1817) blended with the
rhetoric of the Bar an intensity of utterance and an obvious
fiery patriotism — notably exhibited in his defence of Archibald Hamilton Rowan on 29 January 1794 — which led
Thomas Davis to characterise him as possessing a deep-sea
mind.

The revolutionary leaders of the United Irishmen, however,
contributed literature of a more nationalistic kind. The
Journals of Wolfe Tone (1763—98) convey a wide range of
experience. The early accounts of pleasurable picnics by the
Dublin seaside are in ironic contrast to the situation of Tone
in his cabin aboard the *Indomptable* when the French ships
tossed in an easterly gale in Bantry Bay in December 1796.
He had impressed Carnot in Paris, become an adjutant general
in the French army, and argued that an invasion force of at
least 20,000 French soldiers was necessary in Ireland. Tone's
account of the mismanaged expedition is moving in its detachment, its absence of bravado as he lay in his hammock
expecting the *Indomptable* to sink in the storm turned
hurricane that scattered this fleet: 'If we are taken my fate
will not be a mild one; the best I can expect is to be shot as
an *emigre rentre* unless I have the good fortune to be killed in
the action.'

His *Journal* is written with a sharp eye for detail as his
account of his meetings with Napoleon reveals Tone's quizzical
nature: he recorded how he argued the desire of the refugee
United Irishmen in Paris to take part in a landing in Ireland
and went on:

> We have now seen the greatest man in Europe three times, and I am
> astonished to think how little I have to record about him. I am sure
> I wrote ten times as much about my first interview with Charles de
> la Croix, but then I was a greenhorn; I am now a little used to see
> great men, and great statesmen, and great generals, and that has, in
> some degree, broke down my admiration. Yet, after all, it is a droll
> thing that I should become acquainted with Buonaparte. This time

twelve months I arrived in Brest from my expedition to Bantry Bay. Well, the third time, they say, is the charm. My next chance, I hope, will be with the *Armee d'Angleterre*. — *Allons!   Vive la Republique!*

The optimism, the mercurial buoyancy of this passage turned to a sombre tone when he was captured in October 1798. This was after a desperate battle, when he had manned one of the *Hoche*'s batteries to the end, and well knew what to expect: at his court martial his speech was direct and dignified:

What I have done has been clearly from principle and the fullest conviction of its rectitude. I wish not for mercy — I hope I am not an object of pity. I anticipate the consequence of my caption [capture], and I am prepared for the event. The favourite object of my life has been the independence of my country, and to that object I have made every sacrifice.

He had earlier written in his diary that he hated the name of England. He hated her before his exile and would hate her always. At his trial he attacked England as the bane of Ireland; he had sought help from France because Ireland was too weak to achieve her freedom alone; he had followed Washington's example: he had done his duty: 'And I have no doubt the Court will do their's — I have only to add, that a man who has thought and acted as I have done, should be armed against the fear of death.'

Robert Emmet was more eloquent in his famous speech from the dock; he too explained his reasons for seeking French aid; he too had wished to follow Washington's example; and he too faced death, offering his life for the principles of morality and patriotism:

Let no man write my epitaph; for as no man who knows my motives dare now vindicate them, let not prejudice or ignorance asperse them. Let them and me rest in obscurity and peace; and my tomb remain uninscribed, and my memory in oblivion, until other times and other men can do justice to my character. When my country takes her place among the nations of the earth, *then* and *not till then*, let my epitaph be written. I have done.

3
The nineteenth century

I From the Act of Union to the fall of Parnell 1800—91

RELATIONS between Ireland and England in the nineteenth century were affected by land tenure, religion and a desire for self-government. Emmet's forlorn rebellion took place in 1903 and, according to the historian Edmund Curtis, there were only four or five years of normal government between 1796 and 1823. It was a period of Coercion Acts and agrarian discontent, particularly when prices slumped after the Napoleonic Wars, and landlords gained greater power to eject tenants for non-payment of rent.

Four factors altered the nature of Irish life during the century. Firstly, O'Connell in gaining Catholic emancipation brought English-style politics into operation, and urged the Irish-speaking part of the population to use English. Secondly, the establishment of national schools in 1831 where English was the sole medium of education also spread knowledge of English. Thirdly, the great Potato Famine which began in 1845 and lasted until 1848 left the country deeply changed, since the population of Ireland decreased from about eight million to six and a half, through starvation, disease and emigration. The Famine left a legacy of bitter distrust of English administration and not least in the large Irish section of the American population. And fourthly, perhaps the most significant change of all was brought about by legislation in Westminister, the series of Land Acts, beginning with Gladstone's of 1870 and culminating in the Wyndham Land Act of 1903. In effect these acts bought out the landlords and turned Ireland into a land of small farmers.

The eighteen-thirties were occupied with the Tithe Wars, but the problem created by the established church was not solved until the disestablishment of the Church of Ireland in 1869. In the forties O'Connell attempted to repeal the Act of

Union. He virtually abandoned this aim when he cancelled a vast meeting planned to take place at Clontarf in 1843 once this was proscribed by the government. But the Young Ireland movement had come into being in 1842, and put forward a case for Independence based upon a sense of cultural nationalism, advocated strongly in *The Nation*. The abortive rising of 1848 marked the end of the Young Ireland movement. It was succeeded by the formation of the Irish Republican Brotherhood, and the badly organised Fenian rising of 1867, strongly supported by Irish-American funds. This was a movement for political independence going back to the traditions of 1798 which was to continue to attract many Irishmen. A Home Rule Association with more limited aims was founded in 1854 and had fifty-nine MPs in Westminster by 1874; it was given more fire and strength in 1878 when Charles Stewart Parnell, elected in 1875, became the leader of this Irish party. It began to be very powerful in Westminster. The Land League was set up in 1879 and forced various reforms — the Land Acts of 1881, 1887 and 1891. Parnell's party numbered eighty-six in 1885 and Gladstone began his efforts to introduce Home Rule. This split public opinion in England, while in Ireland, Ulster prepared to resist it. But the Irish party split upon Parnell's involvement in the O'Shea divorce proceedings in 1890. After his death in 1891, in the political lull that followed, the movement known as the Irish Literary Revival was launched.

During the earlier nineteenth century tillage flourished; a great part of the population lived upon potatoes, using their grain crops to pay their rents; the repeal of the Corn Laws and the disappearance of many families who had leased very small amounts of land meant that larger holdings were used for cattle and sheep. Industry developed rapidly in Belfast, the city's population increasing as its industries — shipbuilding and linen — increased in strength. The construction of railways led to a development in trade and the progressive movement of cattle from western areas to eastern and eventually to English markets. This is a period when Dublin gained some excellent architecture in the four main-line railway stations: Broadstone (1841–50), Amiens Street (1844–6), Kingsbridge (1845–50) and Harcourt Street (1859).

There was a general increase in domestic housing, particularly in Dublin and Cork — Mount Pleasant Square of 1830, for instance, demonstrates the development of Dublin outwards — a process later accelerated by the two railway lines which opened up the southern coast line and its hinterland.

There had been a rapid multiplication of lawyers in Dublin after the Union. Despite the steady development of trade and commerce in the nineteenth century (Jacob's biscuits, the Guinness brewery) Dublin had some of the worst urban slums in Europe, with people crammed in tenement buildings often with no more than one outside tap and one lavatory shared between eighty or more people. Something of this bleak squalor has been captured in the paintings of Walter Fredrick Osborne (1859–1903), notably in *Saint Patrick's Close, Dublin.*

National schools were followed by new universities. Non-denominational Queen's Colleges were founded at Dublin, Belfast, Cork and Galway in 1845; they were denounced by the Catholic bishops. When Newman was put in charge of a Catholic university in Dublin in 1854 it was not successful. There followed the creation of the Royal University of Ireland, an examining, degree-granting university, which was to become the National University of Ireland in 1908, a federal system composed of the University Colleges of Dublin, Cork and Galway and St Patrick's College, Maynooth.

During the nineteenth century Ireland had vastly altered in population, in its way of farming, and in its system of land tenure. The Catholic population had been emancipated and gradually developed a new middle class in the cities and country towns; as a result of the Famine, the new educational system and a great involvement in political life, English became the language of the vast majority of the population, the old Irish traditions and language shrinking to areas of Munster, Connacht and Donegal and some other sea-board counties; and conflict between those who wanted to be ruled from Dublin and those who ruled from London simmered sometimes above, sometimes below the surface, erupting in virtually every generation. To a certain extent emigration to England and America provided a safety valve, but with the result that there was strong anti-English feeling in the United States on the part of the Irish-Americans, who nursed a sense of grievance and blamed the English government for the circumstances that had forced them to leave Ireland. It was a century in which the Anglo-Irish finally lost the remains of their political power as the effect of the Land Acts and the premature death of Parnell. But they were to achieve a lasting power over the written, spoken and acted word.

II The first quarter

1800, the year of the Act of Union, marks a turning point in Anglo-Irish literature. That was the year *Castle Rackrent* was published. What difference did this novel make? In it Maria Edgeworth (1767—1849) produced a new genre, opening up new ideas for exploration. *Castle Rackrent*, the first regional novel, describes the 'facts' and 'manners of the Irish Squires, before the year 1782'. Here is autocratic eccentricity, here is a liveliness of life echoed in the vitality of this story by the old stewart Thady Quirk. The tale has several innovations: it is an account of four generations of the one family. The decline and fall of the Rackrents, the results of their feckless extravagance and reckless generosity are told through one point of view, that of Thady. And a third novelty is the use of the English spoken in Ireland. In Appendices the Irish words are glossed and comment on Irish customs is provided. We are left wondering just how artless Thady the narrator is: but the artfulness of his son Jason, who finally takes over the estate, is not in doubt at all. Maria Edgeworth filled the story with irony and anti-climax.

At the end of the tale we are told that it is laid before the English reader as a specimen of manners and characters which are perhaps unknown in England. Indeed Maria Edgeworth is echoing Swift's sixth Drapier's letter with its complaint that England entertained only the grossest superstitions about its neighbour, that till within a few years the domestic habits of no nation in Europe were less known to the English than those of their sister country. She regards Arthur Young's *Tour of Ireland* (1780) as the first faithful portrait of its inhabitants, she prophesies that the few gentlemen of education residing in Ireland will resort to England, and she asserts that whether the Union will hasten or retard the amelioration of

Ireland is difficult to decide. Her remedy for what she saw as 'A mixture of quickness, simplicity, cunning, carelessness, dissipation, disinterestedness, shrewdness and blunder' is education, and her moral, didactic vein emerges in the *Tales of Fashionable Life* where the two Irish tales, *Ennui* in the first series (1809) and *The Absentee* in the second series (1812), stand out from the rest. They take on extra colour and energy when the action occurs in Ireland.

Ennui is the study of Lord Glenthorn, a bored young man who returns to his estates in Ireland where he is stirred into a more active life and final redemption as a person. He becomes interested in his tenants, has to deal with contrasting land agents, one a rascal, the other full of commonsense — an Edgeworthian virtue — and combats a rebel conspiracy. The tensions underlying Irish life are echoed here, and Anglo-Irish answers to the problem of Ireland are given: equality with England rather than colonial status, prosperity rather than poverty, and education for the peasantry. What is needed, above all, is a genuine knowledge and understanding of Ireland on the part of the English. Here Lady Geraldine, as Anglo-Irish as her name (for the Geraldines and Fitzgeralds had been great families in earlier Irish history), has nothing but contempt for the English Lord Craglethorpe who prides himself that he understands Ireland. Lord Glenthorn is a useful figure, since his reactions to travel on Irish roads, his experiences in returning to his castle at night, allow Maria to present Ireland dramatically.

She develops this technique very effectively in *The Absentee*, a story in which the printed dialogue benefited from being originally planned for the stage and then written at high speed, since her tendency to didacticism is kept in check despite the story's strong moral and political purpose. It examines the effects of the Union upon Irish life, and portrays Dublin after the Irish parliament in College Green had been abolished and Irish members absorbed into Westminster. This novel provides a penetrating analysis of the decline, the deterioration of life, once political power had disappeared and the former capital had become merely a provincial city.

Lord Colambre, the hero, arrives incognito in Ireland and we see various aspects of Irish life through his eyes: the pretentious vulgarity of Dublin's suburban milieu, its *nouveau riche* characters offset by Count O'Halloran, a former Irish officer in the Austrian service, now a representative, in his castle, of the old Gaelic aristocracy. This satire of Dublin life balances the earlier picture of Colambre's mother, Lady Clonbrony, who has vainly struggled to become accepted in fashionable English society. Her resulting affectation is exposed. This is a view of English life expressed by Anglo-Irish writers earlier. Swift, too, had been harsh on Irish ladies who copied English fashion and did not use local materials; Charles Macklin in *The True-Born Irishman* (1762) had pilloried Irish ladies who returned from visiting England with various English affectations; his hero was a virtuous landlord of Swiftian economic views who persuades his wife not to waste money on imported luxuries. The impression of Dublin is followed by scenes in the west of Ireland, where Colambre sees miserable poverty and the corruption caused by bad agents, by the absence of the landlords. The novel's contrasts, between polite society and the life of the peasantry, sharply reinforce its social criticism.

Ormond (1817) is another pioneering novel; its scope and pace effectively hold the reader's attention; and its narration shows Maria's capacity to tell a story at its best. She wrote *Ormond* at high speed in order to be able to read it to her father, who was severely ill, on his eighty-third birthday. He, lively as ever despite his illness, had written parts of the novel and its preface in which he bade the indulgent reader 'farewell for ever'. Maria tells how he 'corrected the whole by having it read it over to him *many* times, often working at it in his bed for hours together — once at the end, for six hours, between the intervals of sickness and exquisite pain.' In this impressive novel she shows us how the hero, Harry Ormond, is affected not only by his surroundings but also by his reading. As a result he wants to become an Irish Tom Jones, runs the risk of becoming a blackguard, but reforms after reading Richardson's *Sir Charles Grandison*. He skips the heavier passages, at first dislikes Sir Charles, and then decides to emulate him, seeing that he not only possesses the generous attitudes of Tom Jones but also is useful and respected 'by the highest and most accomplished of the sex'. Harry experiences two forms of Irish life: firstly the orthodox Anglo-

Irish society of Castle Hermitage, the showiness of Sir Ulick O'Shane's hospitality where the bottle passes frequently among the men and the ladies chatter over the tea table; then, contrasted with this, the dominion of Cornelius O'Shane, self-styled 'King Corny', in the Black Isles, a practical place where hunting, shooting and a life of lawless freedom prevail. Sir Ulick is a jobber with good prospects, but Corny is an original who values his independence and enjoyment. There follows a period in Paris, and Harry returns to Ireland, eventually to marry Florence Annaly, whose family is an admirable one: generous, but just, and all for responsible improvement. Harry has learned from his mistakes and he settles down to be an improving landlord himself.

Harry Ormond is a warmhearted, lively, likeable young man, and King Corny a development of Count O'Halloran. Maria Edgeworth founded him upon an eccentric character, James Corry, and modelled Sir Ulick upon Sir John de Blacquiere and Admiral Thomas Pakenham, a neighbour of the Edgeworths. She often created characters by drawing directly upon her knowledge and impressions of people she had met or her father described. Thus her novel *Patronage* (1814), an excellent study of professional life which deals with the problem of making one's way in the world, contains many of these figures in a disguised form, among them Charles Kendal Bushe, the Primate of Ireland, the Bishop of Meath, and the famous bluestocking Lydia White. The novel was generally regarded as a *roman a clef*, though whether the Edgeworth family's role in it was recognised by the public is doubtful. Maria's father was the source for Mr Percy, her brother Richard for Mr Percy's eldest son, and her stepsister Honor for the heroine Caroline while she herself was a model for Rosamund.

She wrote better when she could base her work upon real characters and events — so much the better, thought Byron, 'being *life*'. And her attention to the detail of Irish speech is confirmed not only by the *Essay on Irish Bulls* (1802), particularly in the chapter on 'Irish Wit and Eloquence', which she wrote with her father, but also by notes in various commonplace books. Here, for instance, is some of an extract which Maria sent to Sir Walter Scott:

LANGAN'S DEFEAT

A gentleman who passed through Bridge Street Dublin on the 12th of June last after the news of Langan the boxer's defeat had reached Dublin saw a crowd of people assembled, listening to a woman who stood with one arm akimbo and with her stick in the other hand struck the ground exclaiming:

'Oh Langan! Langan! Langan! Where are you now! You're be't! you're be't! — Be't by an English buck! — Well be't so ye are and kicked — Och! that ever I should see this day! — That Paddy's land should ever see this day! — To see the shamrock trodden under *fut* [foot] by an English buck! — But the devil mend ye! —

Oh Donolly Donolly! Sweet Dan Donolly! It's you that could fight your way like a jantleman, so you could — You never was be't, but you came home with your victories to die dacent in Paddy's land. My *darlant* [darling] you was ! — I'll drink you health as long as I live so I will — and who dares say I wont . . .

. . . Langan I'll tell you what . . . and I'm sure all here will agree, will acquiesce with me . . . you ought to cut your throat or hang yourself like Lord Castlereagh sooner than ever come again to Paddy's land —

Don't come Langan! — Don't come Langan for if you do I'll kick you Langan — I'll knock you down — and kick you for falling —

If you do come itself you must cross the *say* [sea] — and if you do cross the sea you must come in some sort of a ship & if you do get into a ship I'll curse that ship, and it shall never reach Paddy's land! —

Having said this the woman thumped her stick upon the flag with great emphasis — then walked off in a leisurely dignified manner — A little chimney sweeper met her — as she passed along she looked calmly at him and said 'Get out of my way my little flour merchant' — and so walked on.

Such an enjoyment of the lively vigour and inventiveness of Irish versions of English, often mimicked and stylised, has long been an element in Anglo-Irish life. In sending this story to Scott, Maria showed her respect for her original: 'There are some things I think [I] could have made better — But even in my infinite conceit I respect the truth of nature & leave it all to your Honor's honor.' This delight in Irish imaginative use of English occurs from Swift onwards to, say, Somerville and Ross and Synge, to Yeats and Lady Gregory. Maria Edgeworth does not, however, deploy it much in her

letters, lively though these can be. Here and there among
them are hints of the powder keg of the seventeen-nineties;
for instance, she wrote to her aunt Mrs Ruxton in 1796:

> All that I crave for my own part is, that if I am to have my throat
> cut, it may not be by a man with his face blackened with charcoal. I
> shall look at every person that comes here very closely, to see if
> there be any marks of charcoal upon their visages. Old wrinkled
> offenders I should suppose would never be able to wash out their
> stains; but in others a *very* clean face will in my mind be a strong
> symptom of guilt — clean hands proof positive, and clean nails ought
> to hang a man.

There are crisp accounts of the dramatic events of the
1798 rising in Longford in her letters to Mrs Ruxton and
Sophy Ruxton; these are matter of factly told, and can be
matched by the direct and clear account in Chapters X–XII
of the second volume of *Memoirs of Richard Lovell Edgeworth, begun by himself and concluded by his daughter
Maria Edgeworth* (1820). These *Memoirs* give us an excellent
insight into the character of Maria's father; he was outgoing,
lively and more sensitive than is commonly thought, and his
effect on Maria was one of enthusiastic yet critical encouragement. He was an inventor, an improver, an honest landlord, a
civilised man, outspoken and warmhearted. His *Memoirs*
should be contrasted with Sir Jonah Barrington's *Personal
Sketches of his Own Times* (2 vols, 1827; 3rd vol., 1833).
These were perhaps the first presentation — as George A.
Birmingham argued — of the rollicking Irishman of later
literary tradition, and are filled with the ethos of the anonymous '*The Rakes of Mallow*':

> Beauing, belling, dancing, drinking,
> Breaking windows, damning, sinking,
> Ever raking, never thinking,
>   Live the rakes of Mallow.
>
> Spending faster than it comes,
> Beating waiters, baliffs, duns,
> Bacchus' true-begotten sons,
>   Live the rakes of Mallow.
>
> One time naught but claret drinking,
> Then like politicians thinking
> To raise the sinking-funds when sinking,
>   Live the rakes of Mallow.

When at home with dadda dying
Still for Mallow water crying;
But where there's good claret plying,
   Live the rakes of Mallow.

Living short but merry lives;
Going where the devil drives;
Having sweethearts but no wives.
   Live the rakes of Mallow.

Racking tenants, stewards teasing,
Swiftly spending, slowly raising,
Wishing to spend all their lives in
   Raking as in Mallow.

Then to end this raking life,
They get sober, take a wife,
Ever after live in strife,
   And wish again for Mallow.

Here is the hard-riding, hard-drinking and duelling society
some of whose members, probably influenced by London
mores, had formed the Dublin Hell Fire Club at the Eagle
Tavern on Cork Hill in the seventeen-thirties. Swift had
attributed the leadership of the new fashions to the English
painter James Worsdale and another painter, by name Lens.
Worsdale painted members of the Hell Fire Club, drinking at
a table, and he also painted for Edward Croker the Limerick
Hell Fire Club, the squires and their lady member Mrs Blenner-
hassett whose revels are described in the *Eclogues* of Daniel
Hayes:

But if in endless Drinking you delight
Croker will ply you till you sink outright
Croker for swilling floods of wine renowned
Whose matchless Board with various plenty crowned
Eternal Scenes of Riot, Mirth and Noise
With all the thunder of the Nenagh Boys
We laugh we roar, the ceaseless Bumpers fly
Till the sun purples o'er the Morning sky
And if unruly Passions chance to rise
A willing Wench the Firgrove still supplies.

This society, perhaps surprisingly, also produced gentlemen
capable of designing its Palladian mansions, commissioning its
fine furniture, bookbindings and silverware, liking broad
streets and graceful public buildings. Barrington's *Recollections* are *sui generis*, however much echoes of the Rackrent

family sound in them: read, for instance, the fifth chapter on 'Irish Dissipation in 1778' with its account of how the gentlemen, the 'hardgoers', indulged in their 'shut-up pilgrimage' supported by claret, collops, chickens and piping, next day's cockfighting, the final dance and a 'raking pot of tea'.

Beneath the energetic gaiety there was a sensibility which emerges here and there in the *Recollections*. And they convey the tensions of the times very clearly indeed, notably when Barrington describes the dinner party in April 1798 in Wexford where he realised how deeply committed his relatives and friends were to the United Irishmen. He was 'in the midst of absolute though unavowed conspirators' and decided that he must quit Bagenal Harvey's house, Bargy Castle, or else turn the conversation: he tried the latter

> Now, my dear Keogh, it is quite clear that you and I in this famous rebellion shall be on different sides of the question, and, of course, one or the other of us must necessarily be hanged at or before its termination — I upon a lamp-iron in Dublin or you on the bridge at Wexford. Now, we'll make a bargain! — if we beat you, upon my honour I'll do all I can to save your neck, and if your folks beat us, you'll save me from the honour of the lamp-iron!

The bargain caused much merriment; but on his next visit to Wexford Barrington was to see the heads of his host, Keogh and another guest, Colclough, on spikes over the Court House door in Wexford.

Maria Edgeworth's first novel, *Castle Rackrent*, had appeared two years after 1798. And it dealt — as the preface insists and many critics have failed to understand — with an altogether earlier period of Irish life. In 1820 Maria's father wanted her to bring the story up to date by adding another generation — 'anecdotes of Jason McQuirk's family since 1782' — and to redress the picture of Ireland given in *Castle Rackrent*. In the *Essay on Irish Bulls* he and she had given their specimens of speech which were collected carefully, and were accurate, 'verbatim' or 'fact' being used to describe similar phrases and speeches in the *Irish Tales*. But they were interested now in the present, and in preferring it to the work of historians of the past they had no fear 'of giving offence to any but rusty antiquaries'.

This preference was understandable in terms of the Edge-worthian desire for economic improvement, for education, and for equality with the English. Though, in effect, she had written national novels, politically she was — in both intellectual and emotional terms — pre-nationalist, indeed pre-romantic, perhaps because of her father's influence on her, perhaps because of the Anglo-Irish concept of an Irish nation represented by themselves. With this she obviously agreed. But she was not provincial; she thought the Anglo-Irish should not abuse their power, and that the English should understand Ireland better; she wrote in the 'Editor's Note' at the end of *Castle Rackrent* that 'the domestic habits of no nation were less known to the English than those of her sister country, till within these few years.' She followed Swift too, with a realisation of the need for self-help on the part of the Irish themselves. Despite her original optimism, her liberal belief in improvement, she became disillusioned. It seemed impossible to her, writing in 1834:

> to draw Ireland as she now is in a book of fiction — realities are too strong, party passions too violent to bear to see, or care to look at their faces in the looking glass, and curse the fool who held the mirror up to nature — distorted nature, in a fever. We are in too perilous a case to laugh, humour would be out of season, worse than bad taste.

What had happened? Why could she not now write about Ireland? Apart from more obvious reasons — the political changes, the rise of Daniel O'Connell's demagoguery — part of the answer, at least, lies in that dismissal of antiquarianism in *Irish Bulls*, for this marks a failure to understand the oral traditions of Gaelic Ireland. They reached back into the far-off past and, because they were oral, without the distancing of print, of history, they presented and still present a traditional past as immediate as yesterday.

Interest in the past of Ireland had developed in the latter part of the eighteenth century. This followed English and Scottish interests: Bishop Percy's *Reliques of Ancient English Poetry* (1765) was one sign of the times, emphasising the richness of ballad poetry, and Thomas Gray's interest in Celtic and Norse literature another, while James MacPherson, who published his *Fragments of Ancient Poetry Collected in the Highlands of Scotland and Translated from the Gaelic or*

Erse language in 1761, produced *The Poems of Ossian* in 1765, and, spurious though these were, they suited their time; there was a ready audience for them. In Ireland similar sensibilities were at work investigating the now nearly vanished Gaelic past. There were several histories of Ireland, by Fernando Warner, by J. H. Winne, and by Sylvester O'Halloran (1728–1807) whose *A General History of Ireland* (1774) was to have a profound effect on Standish O'Grady in the next century. Charles Henry Wilson published *Poems translated from the Irish Language into the English* (?1782); Joseph Cooper Walker produced his *Historical Memoirs of the Irish Bards* in 1786. Charlotte Brooke (1740–93) published her translations with the original Irish in her *Reliques of Irish Poetry* in 1789. Her renderings of the Red Branch and Fenian (she was the first to use the word) material had an immense influence, as had the earlier translation of Geoffrey Keating's very popular *History of Ireland* by Dermot O'Connor. Keating was also translated by Peter Walsh, Michael Kearney, Theophilus O'Flanagan, Humphrey and Thomas Moynihan, and Michael Comyn, though the version by Dermot O'Connor was the only one read till 1723. There were other editions in 1726, 1738, 1809, 1841 and 1857. *A General Collection of the Ancient Music of Ireland* appeared in three collections made by Edward Bunting in 1796, 1809 and 1840. He was a music teacher in Belfast, whose interest in Irish music had been greatly stimulated by the famous gathering of nearly a dozen Irish harpers — one of them ninety-seven years old and blind — at Belfast in 1792. These are among the obvious, most influential books. Apart from the early interest in Irish in Trinity College various works of translation had been undertaken. The Dublin Philosophical Society with which Molyneux is associated (it was founded in 1683, lasted till 1688 but was refounded in 1707) eventually led to the Royal Irish Academy of 1786, which has encouraged work on Irish literature ever since. Hugh McCurtin (1680–1755) compiled an English-Irish dictionary in 1732; he had earlier written a *Brief Discourse of the Antiquity of Ireland* (1717). There was Swift's version of 'Plearaca na Ruarcach', the 'Description of an Irish Feast' originally composed by Hugh MacGauran. A translation of the Deirdre legend by Theophilus O'Flanagan (1762–1814) was published in the *Transactions of the Gaelic Society* in 1808, and a version of Roderic O'Flaherty's *Ogygia* by James Hely appeared in 1793.

The antiquarian movement was developing strongly by the close of the eighteenth century in what was virtually a rediscovery of the language, customs and culture of Gaelic Ireland. Its existence argued that there was no longer a fear of the Gaelic civilisation, that none of Spenser's apprehensions about the infective dangers of its culture remained, since its political power had vanished long since. And yet, paradoxically perhaps, this antiquarian movement soon became patriotic. The transition can be seen clearly in Lady Morgan's writings. Born Sydney Owenson (?1776/?83—1859), the sprightly and gifted daughter of the actor-manager associated with the theatre at Galway, who sent her to a Huguenot School at Clontarf, she turned governess after her father lost his money and became a strolling actor. When he had his theatrical headquarters at Sligo, Sydney, who had a highly romantic temperament, indulged in sentimental flirtations and correspondences with army officers. A typical Anglo-Irish situation occurred when the family were staying there. Sydney's sister Olive came in from a walk to find Sydney sitting in the parlour with two officers, Captain White Benson and Captain Earle, all talking high sentiment and all the three shedding tears. Molly the maid came in to set the table, thought the officers had stayed long enough and said 'Come, be off with yiz — an the master will be coming in to his dinner, and what will he say to find you fandangoing with Miss Sydney!' Olive, who loathed sentiment, fell on them with her stick and pelted them with apples she had collected on her walk. Sydney, sensibility overcome by comedy, collapsed in laughter. Somewhat to her father's displeasure White Benson continued to write to her, but he kept within the platonic limits of friendship she had laid down in addressing 'the sister' of his heart. Sydney endorsed a letter of his written from York in June 1798 in his high strain with the cool comment that this elegant-minded and highly gifted young man had drowned himself near York some months after she received this letter.

Platonic friendship dominated her first novel *St Clair: or the heiress of Desmond* (1804); she wrote this in Sligo, her father encouraging her to finish it. The novel's narrator, a young Englishman, writes from Connaught 'where you find the character, the manner, the language and the music of the ancient Irish in all their primitive originality.' He hopes to find in Connaught the literary traditions which illustrate the history and character of every country which has managed to preserve them. He discovers the local heiress Olivia Desmond who, like Sydney Owenson herself, sings and plays the harp. Her grandfather, the 'true type of the old Irish Chieftan' is the only gentleman in the locality to cultivate Gaelic literature: he has a ruined castle, a druidical cromlech, an Irish harper and Gaelic manuscripts. The hero reads *Ossian*, and the heroine lends him *Werter*. The novel's new material — the scenery of the west of Ireland and Irish cultural history — takes second place, however, to its romantic context. The introspective intensity and the self-pitying sensibility of the youthful love affair are given fashionable highly strung expression. This kind of writing informed Sydney Owenson's second novel, *The Novice of St Dominick* (1805), which adds pedantry to sensibility with a dash of nature *à la* Mrs Radcliffe thrown in.

The Wild Irish Girl (1806) established Sydney Owenson's fame. This romantic, sentimental novel was designed to present Ireland to English readers, but whereas Maria Edgeworth's *Ennui* (written in 1804) used the same device (probably influenced by English travellers' accounts of Ireland, notably Arthur Young's), of propelling a stranger into Ireland and recording his reactions to the Irish scene, the aims of the two novelists were very different. Maria's hero, Lord Glenthorne, had been born in Ireland but left Ireland at the age of two; a faded sophisticate, he had to be redeemed from his boredom so that he could demonstrate that his understanding had been cultivated, that he could be active, rich and happy. In the process we see Ireland through his eyes. But Horatio Mortimer, the hero of *The Wild Irish Girl*, had to be instructed about the past civilisation of Ireland, the present injustice under which it laboured, as well as coming under the spell of the western scenery and members of the old Gaelic civilisation still living there.

He is sent to Ireland to recover from 'vitiated dissipation' and takes notes of the scenery, seeing it in terms of Salvator Rosa:

If the glowing fancy of Claude Lorrain would have dwelt enraptured on the paradisial charms of English landscape, the superior genius of Salvator Rosa would have reposed its eagle wing amidst those scenes of mysterious sublimity with which the wildly magnificent landscape of Ireland abounds.

Irish scenery had to conform to Italian vision — the 'stupendous heights' of cloud-capped mountains, the 'impervious glooms' of deep embosomed glens, the 'savage desolation' of uncultivated heaths and boundless bogs, the 'rich ruins' of a picturesque champagne, all have to be appreciated by Horatio. He also begins to learn about the hardships of Irish peasant life, has a meal in a cottage, hears the Cualin sung, and sees the company join in a jig played by a piper; and he realises that he had been prejudiced against the character of peasants. Here endeth his first anthropological lesson; his next is economico-political when he listens to a steward inveighing against the peasantry, then hears from others of the steward's own exactions. He is now ready for the novel's real lesson: that Ireland had in its old Gaelic way of life a genuine culture.

He meets the Prince of Inismore, Father John his chaplain, and the Lady Glorvina, his daughter (probably founded on Elizabeth, daughter of Sir Malby Crofton, as well as on Sydney's own life) who knows Irish as well as Greek and Latin, cures the sick within twenty miles, is too proud to visit the quality, but talks to the poor in smoky cabins. She sings, plays the harp and has 'an effulgency of countenance.' Horatio is attracted by her, but asks himself what has he to expect from 'the unpolished manners, the confined ideas of this Wild Irish Girl'?

He soon finds out as she gives him a disquisition on the Irish harp (some pages of the novel provide about twenty-two or twenty-three lines of footnotes to two or three lines of text!) and follows this with lessons in Irish, on Irish poetry (Sydney's father was described in an obituary as 'the best Irish scholar of his day and perhaps the last Irish musician'), on virtually everything Irish as, for instance, when she imparts information in return to a query on how the Irish could procure so expensive an article as saffron for dying clothes:

'I have heard Father John say' she returned, 'that saffron, as an article of importation, would never have been at any time cheap enough for general use. And I believe formerly, as *now*, they communicated this bright yellow tinge with indigenous plants, with which this country abounds.

'See', she added. springing lightly forward, and culling a plant which grew from the mountain's side — 'see this little blossom, which they call here, "yellow lady's bed straw", and which you, as a botanist, will better recognise as the *Galicens borum*; it communicates a beautiful yellow; as does the *Lichen juniperinus*, or 'cypress moss' which you brought me yesterday; and I think the *resida luteola* or 'yellow weed' surpasses them all.

The lessons continue; there is even a southern view of the northern character; a mild echo of Swift's sharp view of the Presbyterian cat — somewhat domesticated now — but still highly critical:

Here the ardour of the Irish constitution seems abated, if not chilled. Here the *cead mile failta* of Irish cordiality seldom lends its welcome home to the stranger's heart. The bright beams which illumine the gay images of Milesian fancy are extinguished; the convivial pleasures dear to the Milesian heart, scared at the prudential maxims of calculating interest, take flight to the warmer regions of the South.

The novel ends with a plea for the blending of differences between Catholic and Protestant, Irish and English, when Horatio finally marries Glorvina — though not before a melodramatic, positively Elizabethan clearing of apparent corpses takes place in the ruined chapel of the castle.

This mixture of Ossianic elements, mingled with Nature according to Mrs Radcliffe and Salvator Rosa, with its vision of Ireland's past glories and its plea for Catholic emancipation, for alleviation of Ireland's present plight, was highly successful. It provided readers with a new subject; writing it turned Sydney Owenson's attention to patriotic politics and its reception gave her a social success. In 1812 she married the Viceroy's doctor, Charles Morgan; as a wedding present, the Viceroy, the marquess of Abercorn, had knighted him. Lady Morgan's salon in Kildare Street subsequently provided a focus for literary and political life in Dublin.

Lady Morgan was not content, however, to rest on her laurels. She wrote three more novels as well as lively travel books and an enthusiastic if verbose biography of Salvator

Rosa. The novels were *O'Donnel* (1814), in part an historical exploration, in part a picture of a Catholic Irish gentleman descended from Red Hugh O'Donnel, the Elizabethan earl of Tyrconnel. This slow-moving novel provides informative descriptions of the Giant's Causeway, and the slighted governess turned duchess. The hero's gentlemanly virtues are over-stressed somewhat defensively throughout, his difference from the English characters continuously emphasised. *Florence MacCarthy* (1818) was an investigation of the attitudes of those members of the Ascendancy who so frequently came from big houses to lead nationalist movements. The satire was political, and the novel contains an attack on John Wilson Croker (1780–1857) in the character of councillor Con Crawley. Croker, a Galway man who was called to the Irish Bar in 1802, first won fame by his verse satire *On the Present State of the Irish Stage* (1804) and his prose satire on Dublin, *Intercepted Letters from Canton*, was published the same year. Croker, who was secretary to the Admiralty for twenty-two years, is best known for his conservative and often savage criticism – particularly of Lady Morgan – in the *Quarterly Review* with which he was associated from its foundation in 1809.

The O'Briens and the O'Flahertys (1827), Lady Morgan's best novel, embraced, in her words, events which prepared the Rebellion and accomplished the Union. The novel explores the effect of the Penal Laws. It gives an amusing picture of a review of troops in the Phoenix Park, with the slapstick comedy of Lady Knocklofty's runaway carriage. There are good passages on the Volunteers; and Lady Morgan's penchant for the Gothic came alive in her description of Dublin's 'lanes and alleys, cribs and dens' drawn in all the squalors of 1770, but to be changed, she wrote, from 1782 onwards into a metropolitan city worthy of praise for its spacious streets and beautiful quays. There was an awakening of spirit, as the Penal Code's effects were ameliorated and the Anglo-Irish entered upon that all too brief period of their independence. Lady Morgan describes Trinity College, and the role of the College Historical Society, realising the effect on young patriotic minds of Grattan's heroes:

Swift and Molyneux were again read with avidity, Locke was not yet banished from the course of collegiate instruction. Curran, Yelverton,

Grattan, Flood, Burgh and Ponsonby, had but recently come from the meditation of their philosophical hardy and convincing pages, and were already shedding a glory, which effaced the memory of that dullness that had expelled the creator of Gulliver and had rejected the poet of Auburn.

The spirit of the people was awakened, she wrote; it was an echo of Grattan's idealism which breathed through her novel: republicanism and aristocracy are both made attractive in this story of Murrough O'Brien, a young patriot who becomes a volunteer and a United Irishman, leaves Ireland after 1798, and reaches the rank of General in the French army.

While the movement of Irishmen to the Continent generally resulted from such defeats as those of the Williamite war when Patrick Sarsfield and so many others became 'wild geese', serving with distinction in French and other European forces, or else from rebellions that failed, there had also been a movement in the opposite direction, of Huguenot refugees into Ireland – among them the ancestors of Charles Robert Maturin (1782–1824). Maturin's father, a well-to-do functionary until he was apparently wrongfully dismissed from his post in 1809 (he was later given another position), sent Charles to Trinity College, where he shone in the debates of the College Historical Society but did not find academic work attractive, if we are to judge by the comments of Ormsby Bethel in his second novel *The Wild Irish Boy* (1808). Maturin obtained a Foundation Scholarship, however, in 1798. He does not seem to have been involved in political activities at all, but rather to have envisaged a literary career. None the less, like most Anglo-Irish, he was not entirely enamoured of the English; and *The Wild Irish Boy* exhibits some hostility to the Union.

Maturin, however, is chiefly occupied with the effect of nature upon his hero, although his first novel, *Fatal Revenge: or, the Family of Montorio* (1807), had gone to the heart of a future Anglo-Irish dilemma: the clash between English neo-classical, cosmopolitan culture and the Irish folk tradition, which was closer to nature.

So Maturin draws upon Rousseau and Wordsworth, and brings a new attitude to Anglo-Irish writing in *The Wild Irish Boy*. He modelled this novel, obviously, upon Lady Morgan's *The Wild Irish Girl*, but in it his whole attitude to scenery is different from hers, for he regards nature as mentally and physically beneficial to his hero, who lives three years of 'romantic intoxication' in the Lake District, where he becomes an 'incurable visionary'. He reads *Ossian* and blends this, and his Wordsworthianism, with Irish nationalism in a direct and somewhat odd way, dressing up the usual Irish remarks about the differences between the Irish and English character.

Maturin takes over the idea used by Maria Edgeworth and Lady Morgan, of introducing a sophisticated stranger into romantic Irish surroundings, but he hurls him into a love affair more passionate than anything Maria would have written; he also draws a ruined Irish castle and its chieftain complete with chaplain, and provides anthropological lore about the Irish. The chieftain attacks the English bitterly:

Is it for those who have desolated the country, and razed every mark of power or of resistance from the face of it, to demand where is the proof of power, or of resistance, and after beating down with the savageness of conquerors, the monuments of our strength and greatness, to ask with the insolence of conquerors, what monuments of strength and greatness are left to us?

The chieftain's attitude, however, is rooted in the past, as, to a certain extent, Maturin was himself. For as well as finding Wordsworthian romanticism attractive he was deeply read in Gothic romance. Indeed in some respects he stands midway between the Gothic and the Romantic genres, though he is generally regarded — perhaps by those who have only read *Melmoth the Wanderer,* the only one of his works in print in this century — as being a Gothic novelist alone. He was experimenting with various approaches as his deliberate exercises in Edgeworthian style, his treatment of the English speech of the peasants in *The Wild Irish Boy* clearly indicate. His third novel *The Milesian Chief* (1812), while it founders as a novel because of its absurd reliance upon coincidence and the artificial containment of the action within a small group, does exhibit an interest in the question of why an intelligent young Irishman would consider rebellion against English rule, and supplies reasons why any such attempt was bound to fail without adequate aid from continental Europe. *The Milesian Chief,* however, remains in the mind chiefly because in it Maturin made clearer than before that the basic partition of Ireland is between east and west, with the Shannon as the natural boundary. To the west lay adventure and romance for the Anglo-Irish writer; crossing the Shannon meant entering a new scene, an older if poverty-stricken civilisation.

Maturin used this western scenery for a tragic backdrop: doom-laden despair swept symbolically over his characters as the rain and wind beat in on ruins, solitary islands, barren mountains and the flat boglands of the west. When he was a curate in Loughrea he had disliked the flatness west of the Shannon: he was obviously more at home in the scenery of the Dublin and Wicklow mountains in which he had himself grown up, as his next novel, *Women; or Pour et Contre* (1818) clearly demonstrates. It contains rhapsodic descriptions of the tranquillity washed in by the waves of Dublin Bay towards Killiney Hill, and of the sombre storm which sweeps in from the sea over Bray Head, towards Luggelaw in County Wicklow, to delight one of the heroines, Zaira, who goes into raptures over the beauties of nature while the lightning of this summer storm flashes around her elegant equestrian picnic. Maturin uses the different reactions of two heroines to thunder to show the nature of their personalities, and thus to reveal the hero's reactions to them; this is part of the psychological approach which occupies a good deal of the character-analysis in *Women*.

This novel contains other original ideas — it is the first study of an intense undergraduate love affair, and it applies Gothic techniques to an urban setting. But Maturin's real penchant for Gothic horrors emerged in *Melmoth the Wanderer* (1820) which has been called the apogee of the genre. An emotional response to suspense, mystery and the supernatural was sought, and so Maturin sets the beginning of the story in an eerie country house in Wicklow:

The weather was cold and gloomy; heavy clouds betokened a long and dreary continuance of autumnal rains; cloud after cloud came sweeping on like the dark banners of an approaching host, whose march is for desolation. As Melmoth leaned against the window, whose dismantled frame, and pierced and shattered panes, shook with every gust of wind, his eye encountered nothing but that cheerless of all prospects, a miser's garden — walls broken down,

grass-grown walks whose grass was not even green, dwarfish, dod-
dered, leafless trees, and a luxuriant crop of nettles and weeds
rearing their unlovely heads where there had once been flowers, all
waving and bending in capricious and unsightly forms, as the wind
sighed over them. It was the verdure of the church-yard, the garden
of death.

This realism leads to the unfolding of the Chinese-box-like
plot, a continuity of storytelling which increases the suspense
and yet keeps the story rooted in a kind of credibility through
the peasant characters. Melmoth has sold his soul to the devil,
he is doomed, and yet Maturin invests him with sympathy,
and creates a tragedy out of a predominantly religious theme.
In *The Albigenses* (1824), which owed its inception to the
success of Scott's historical novels, Maturin was transferring
Irish material to another place and time, as had Lady Morgan
in her novel of Provence, *The Novice of St Dominick* (1805).
Maturin's novels have always proved popular in France;
indeed Balzac was moved to write a sequel to *Melmoth* in
Melmoth réconcilié.

Fascinating though his novels can be, they abound with
flaws: excessive use of complication, coincidence, sentimentality and melodrama. What then of his attempts at drama
itself? He wrote *Bertram, or the Castle of St Aldobrand*, a
tragedy (1816); *Manuel, a tragedy* (1817) and another
tragedy *Fredolfo* (1817). His friendship with Scott, and the
interest Byron took in the play, led to *Bertram* being staged
at Drury Lane in 1816. Its success spurred Maturin into
writing his other plays, but they were not successful, and
the blasphemy in *Bertram* was stupidly attributed to Maturin
himself. His career in the Church, like Swift's earlier, was
harmed by his writing being misunderstood.

Despite his faults Maturin wrote most compellingly, his
capacity for intensity and his deep interest in emotion,
sanctioned indeed by Burke's essay *On the Sublime*, evoked
and can still evoke imaginative responses from his readers;
he was interested in the role of the artist in a society apparently over-ready to polarise between race and race, or
between religion and religion, or between religion and free
thought. He was deeply interested in the problem of guilt,
and so his heroes and villains are often caught up in a struggle
between conventional orthodoxy and advanced thought.

Maturin obviously enjoyed speculation; and conversation held such threats for his writing that he sealed his lips with a wafer so that he should not be tempted into talking instead of writing: indeed he is reputed to have worn a red cockade as a sign he was not to be disturbed when working. Maturin was a social man, and when he became curate of St Peter's, then a fashionable Dublin church, he liked talking to intelligent women, he enjoyed dancing and found the pull from study to drawing room almost overpoweringly strong.

Another who found his spiritual home in drawing rooms, albeit those of London, was Tom Moore (1779–1852), a year older than Maturin, who was also an undergraduate at Trinity College. Unlike Maturin he was not detached in his attitude to political events. Many of his friends were members of the United Irishmen. One of them, Edward Hudson, influenced Moore's political sentiments and shared an interest in music with him. A good flautist, Hudson had collected old Irish airs, and the two young men had a copy of the airs which Edward Bunting had set down as they were played at the famous festival of harpers held in Belfast in 1792.

Moore cared deeply for his country, and played his part in giving its spirit expression, though nationalists have grudged him recognition. This is probably because he chose to leave Ireland, because he realised clearly, like Shaw later, that if he were to make his way he needed a larger stage for his talents than Dublin could provide. Like Maturin he was sociable, but unlike Maturin he was able to use his flow of language successfully once he allied his singing to the writing of lyrics. Like Maturin he disliked the Trinity College syllabus, but he turned to translating Anacreon, and this volume came out in 1800, followed the next year by *The Poetical Works of the Late Thos. Little, Esq.* and, after his experiences in the West Indies and America, by his *Epistles, Odes and Other Poems* (1806). His metrical ability was sure even in his innovations, he created a flowing ease reminiscent of the seventeenth-century cavalier poets and, like them, he was not intellectually difficult, but turned his verses with a touch of *risqué* wit. His immorality seemed to Jeffrey, pontificating in the *Edinburgh Review*, to be more 'insidious and malignant' than that of Rochester and Dryden. Tenderness seemed to be combined with vile and vulgar sensuality, but there was a 'singular sweetness and melody of versification'. These poems set Byron — fifteen years old when he knew them by heart — to write poetry, eventually to beat Moore — and Scott — out of their respective fields. Scott took to the novel, but Moore found himself at home in writing the *Irish Melodies*. William and James Power suggested that Sir John Stevenson should write the music for lyrics to be collected from Irish poets. Moore knew no Gaelic, but he sang beautifully. He altered some of the airs because he had to, realising that they were unsuited to singing because they had been taken down by Bunting from harpers' versions; it is surprising, however, how little he did alter; he was interested in making popular songs, not in preserving Irish music (which, after all, was Bunting's ambition) and his achievement is remarkable.

Moore has suffered at the hands of the critics. Hazlitt, for instance, thought the case of Ireland was hopeless if Moore's national airs 'do indeed express the soul of impassioned feeling in his countrymen'. But then Moore was not writing what Hazlitt thought he ought to write. He was writing, says Terence de Vere White (in *Tom Moore, the Irish poet*, 1977), to charm, and it was a considerable achievement to have brought Ireland's story into those London lives. And he adds, very correctly, that 'we are at seas as to the impression made by the words unless we can imagine Moore singing them', reminding us that Moore wanted the music to be printed with his words.

The quality that remains in the mind, in the ear, is that of plangency allied to the necessary limpidity of the lyrics. 'At the mid hour of night' captures it, and perhaps an even more obvious example is 'Oft in the stilly night'. Moore's experience and skill as a singer taught him the values of assonance; he used open vowels freely and employed consonants for accentuation; his sound and rhythm were at the service of his dramatic sense, for he wanted singers to come as near speaking his words as possible, paying as little attention as possible to the rhythm or time in singing them. He thought he was writing songs of feeling and delicacy, he wished to preserve the 'swell and sweetness of intonation' and a mechanical observance of time would, he thought, completely destroy 'all those pauses, lingerings, and abruptness which the expression of passion and tenderness requires'.

The first volume of *The Irish Melodies* was published in 1807, the last in 1834. In 1815 his *National Airs* included what is probably the best of his songs:

> Oft, in the stilly night,
>   Ere Slumber's chain has bound me,
> Fond Memory brings the light
>   Of other days around me;
>   The smiles, the tears,
>   Of boyhood's years,
>   The words of love then spoken;
>   The eyes that shone,
>   Now dimm'd and gone,
>   The cheerful hearts now broken!
> Thus, in the stilly night,
>   Ere Slumber's chain hath bound me,
> Sad Memory brings the light
>   Of other days around me.
>
> When I remember all
>   The friends, so link'd together,
> I've seen all around me fall,
>   Like leaves in wintry weather;
>   I feel like one
>   Who treads alone
>   Some banquet-hall deserted,
>   Whose lights are fled,
>   Whose garlands dead,
>   And all but he departed! . . .

Lalla Rookh (1817) was founded upon vast reading about the Orient. Moore had been busy writing it since 1811, but despite the work he put into it, and despite its popularity at the time (Longmans paid him 3,000 guineas for it!) only bits of it survive — and the songs at that. Moore himself now foretold that the Melodies, 'those little ponies, would beat the mare *Lalla Rookh* hollow.' And so he combined an insouciant variety and fluent control (we find it in some of Goldsmith's songs, too, such as 'When lovely woman stoops to folly') which has a superb lightness of touch:

> The time I've lost in wooing,
> In watching and pursuing
>   The light that lies
>   In Woman's eyes,

Has been my heart's undoing.
Though Wisdom oft has sought me,
I scorn'd the love she brought me,
  My only books
  Were Woman's looks,
And folly's all they've taught me. ....

The sombre side, the melancholia, appeared in Moore's
tribute to his friend Robert Emmet, 'O breathe not his
name', his response to the request that no epitaph be written
for him until his country had taken her place among the
nations of the earth, though his song on Sarah Curran,
Emmet's love, is far better:

She is far from the land where her young hero sleeps,
  And lovers are round her, sighing;
But coldly she turns from their gaze, and weeps,
  For her heart in his grave is lying.

She sings the wild song of her dear native plains,
  Every note which he loved awaking; —
Ah! little they think, who delight in her strains,
  How the heart of the Minstrel is breaking!

He had liv'd for his love, for his country he died,
  They were all that to life had entwin'd him, —
Nor soon shall the tears of his country be dried,
  Nor long will his love stay behind him.

Oh! make her a grave where the sunbeams rest,
  When they promise a glorious morrow;
They'll shine o'er her sleep like a smile from the West,
  From her own lov'd Island of Sorrow!

Moore was fluent and emotive but there was a price to be
paid in the sentimentality which emerges in 'As slow our
ship', 'The Last Rose of Summer', and especially in 'Believe
me if all those endearing young charms'. But what Moore did
succeed in conveying so convincingly, so effectively, was not
only emotion vibrantly ranging from sorrow to joy but also
an awareness of the evocative, plangent power of names.
There is, for instance, 'The Song of Fionnuala', where Moore
was probably drawing on the translations of Theophilus
O'Flanagan:

> Silent, oh Moyle, be the roar of thy water,
>   Break not, ye breezes, your chain of repose,
> While, murmuring mournfully, Lir's lonely daughter
>   Tells to the night-star her tale of woes.
> When shall the swan, her death-note singing,
>   Sleep, with wings in darkness furl'd?
> When will heaven, its sweet bells ringing,
>   Call my spirit from this stormy world?
>
> Sadly, oh Moyle, to thy winter-wave weeping,
>   Fate bids me languish long ages away;
> Yet still in her darkness doth Erin lie sleeping,
>   Still doth the pure light its dawning delay.
> When will that day-star, mildly springing,
>   Warm our isle with peace and love?
> When will heaven, its sweet bells ringing,
>   Call my spirit to the fields above?

Moore dwelt on names repetitively: 'Tis Innisfail — 'tis Innisfail'. He apostrophised them: 'Sweet Inisfallen, fare thee well'; 'Glendalough, thy gloomy wave/Soon was gentle Kathleen's grave'; 'Oh Arranmore, lov'd Arranmore/How oft I dream of thee'. He ranged 'from Dinis' green isle to Glena's wooded shore'; he celebrated 'the sweet vale of Avoca' as well as 'Tara's halls'. And historical events were linked with place:

> Tho' lost to Mononia, and cold in the grave,
> He returns to Kinkora no more.

He touched on a perennial problem in 'As vanquish'd Erin':

> As vanquish'd Erin wept beside
> The Boyne's ill-fated river
> She saw where Discord, in the tide,
> Had dropp'd his loaded quiver.

And, like Lady Morgan, Moore could patriotically link places in the present with even older past Irish history, as in 'Let Erin Remember the Days of Old':

> On Lough Neagh's bank as the fisherman strays,
> When the clear cold eve's declining
> He sees the round towers of other days,
> In the wave beneath him shining . . . .

The Memoirs of Captain Rock (1824) is neglected by most Irish critics, probably because the general Irish disparagement of Moore's patriotism — his being attacked as 'the darling of the London Drawing Rooms' puts them off reading it, just as later Charles Lever was attacked for his earlier novels by Irish critics who surely could not have read his later work. But *The Memoirs of Captain Rock* give an honest reaction to what Moore found in Ireland in 1818. He was depressed by Dublin, 'the seat of wrangle and illiberal contention'. He loved Ireland but hated Dublin; he regarded its inhabitants as a 'low, illiberal, puddle-headed, and gross-hearted herd'. What he saw in his tour outside Dublin left him appalled by the evidence of misrule, and he originally planned *The Memoirs of Captain Rock* as a factual account before giving it fictional form. As a result it carries a great deal of history: the light touch, the near flippancy of its beginnings sugars the ironic pill of its attack on British policy in Ireland.

As a biographer he wrote well and perceptively; his lives of Sheridan (1825) and Lord Edward Fitzgerald (1831) exhibit a natural sympathy, while his own friendship with Byron meant that his biography, despite avoidance of direct discussion of some aspects of Byron's life, still has a certain authority, and conveys contemporary feeling for Byron. Reading Moore's own *Journal* in the full modern version (ed. Peter Quennell, 1964) ought to alter superficial views of his character and achievement. His lasting service to his country was also to literature in general.

While Moore had made the impact of Ireland felt beyond the Irish Sea a few other poets had been exploring Irish material in English. John Philpot Curran (1750—1817), for instance, used a Gaelic metre very effectively in that haunting bravado of 'The Deserter's Meditation:

> If sadly thinking, with spirits sinking,
> Could more than drinking my cares compose,
> A cure for sorrow from sighs I'd borrow,
> And hope to-morrow would end my woes.
> But as in wailing there's naught availing,
> And Death unfailing will strike the blow,
> Then for that reason, and for a season,
> Let us be merry before we go.

It was Curran's able defence that got an acquittal for William
Drennan (1754–1820), a Belfast doctor tried with Hamilton
Rowan for issuing the Address of the United Irishmen to the
Volunteers. Drennan was probably the first, in a rhetorical
poem 'When Erin first rose', to christen Ireland the 'Emerald
Isle'; he wrote a tougher poem, 'The Wake of William Orr', on
the hanging of William Orr, a moderate United Irishman. Orr
was unsuccessfully defended by Curran in 1797 on a charge
of administering an unlawful oath, a charge he denied.

The metre Curran used in 'The Deserter's Meditation' was
employed by Richard Milliken (1767–1815) in a particularly
Anglo-Irish way. This, as Geoffrey Taylor remarked in his
anthology, *Irish Poets of the Nineteenth Century* (1951),
captured the grandiloquence of the hedge-schoolmasters: displays of learning, fine words used for effect — if not always
in the correct sense — and a generally insouciant inconse-
quence. The last quality can be seen in the last stanza of 'The
Groves of Blarney':

> There's statues gracing
> This noble place in —
> All heathen gods
>   And nymphs so fair;
>
> Bold Neptune; Plutarch,
> And Nicodemus,
> All standing naked
>   In the open air!
>
> So now to finish
> This brave narration
> Which my poor genii
>   Could not entwine;
>
> But were I Homer,
> Or Nebuchadnezzar,
> 'Tis in every feature
>   I would make it shine.

Milliken wrote this burlesque poem in an endeavour to
surpass in absurdity a poem on Castle Hyde by an itinerant
poet. A final stanza was added to 'The Groves of Blarney' by
'Father Prout', Francis Sylvester Mahoney (1804–66), a
sociable priest turned literary journalist in London and Paris:

There is a stone there
That whoever kisses
Oh! he never misses
 To grow eloquent;
'Tis he may clamber
To a lady's chamber
Or become a member
 Of parliament.
A clever spouter
He'll soon turn out, or
An out-and-outer
 To be let alone.
Don't hope to hinder him,
Or to bewilder him,
Sure he's a pilgrim
 From the Blarney Stone!

Mahoney, whose *The Reliques of Father Prout* (1836) are still amusing to read, gave this kind of poetry fresh sophistication in 'The Bells of Shandon'. Another of his poems (his poems and Milliken's are the better for being heard when they are sung late at night in a Cork accent at a party), 'The attractions of a Fashionable Irish Watering-Place', developed his delight in mock-naïve burlesque rhyming:

The town of Passage
Is both large and spacious
and situated
 Upon the say.
'Tis nate and dacent
And quite adjacent
To come from Cork
 On a summer's day.
There you may slip in
To take a dipping
Fornent the shipping
 That at anchor ride,
Or in a wherry
Come o'er the ferry
To Carrigaloe
 On the other side . . . .

Northern dialect was aimed at by James Orr (1770–1816) in the 'Death and Burial of an Irish Cottier'; but he was sentimental, particularly in the 'Song of an Exile'. A Wexford man and anti-Unionist MP for that country, George Ogle (1739–1814), who wrote light pastorals and drinking songs, showed an interest in Irish in his charmingly limpid and highly successful 'Mailligh Mo Stor' which also demands to be sung:

> As down by Banna's banks I strayed
>   One evening in May
> The little birds in blithest notes,
>   Made vocal every spray;
> They sung their little notes of love,
>   They sung them o'er and o'er.
> Ah! gradh mo chroide, mo cailin og,
>   'Si Mailligh mo stor.

Another Wexford poet, Thomas Furlong (1794—1827), developed an interest in the words of Irish poetry; he translated 'Mary dear', 'Mary Maguire' and 'Roisin Dubh' from the Irish; his 'John O'Dwyer of the Glen' refers to the Elizabethan English felling woods which contained Irish hiding places. Every fourth line counterpoints the smoothly flowing rhythm, producing a short, stabbing impression. Furlong's translations of O'Carolan have a particularly successful swiftness about them.

The first really effective translations of Irish poetry, however, were made by Jeremiah Joseph Callanan (1795—1829), who studied at both Maynooth and Trinity College, joined the army when short of money but was bought out, like Coleridge, by his friends. He became a schoolmaster in Cork, and collected ballads and legends in Munster, then succumbed to tuberculosis, spending his last two years in Portugal. Aided by William Maginn, in whose father's school he taught, he published his early translations in *Blackwood's Magazine*. His longest poem is *The Recluse of Inchidony* (1830) written in Spenserian stanzas, which contain good descriptive passages of a Byronic kind. 'The Outlaw of Loch Lene', his best-known work, is probably a translation of a folk poem:

> Oh, many a day have I made good ale in the glen,
> That came not of stream, or malt, like the brewing of men;
> My bed was the ground; my roof the greenwood above,
> And the wealth that I sought — one far kind glance from my love.

The lyrical gift he displays in this poem is also striking in his 'Gougane Barra' of 1826. *Poems* (1861) clearly demonstrates Callanan's innovatory role as a translator from the Irish, for he caught not only the rhythm but also the emotional intensity of his originals.

More orthodox poetry was written by Edward Lysaght (1763–?1810/11), barrister and wit, known as 'Pleasant Ned' whose 'Kate of Garnyvillo' has echoes of Henry Carey's 'O happy Myrtillo' and to whom 'Kitty of Coleraine' has been attributed. The best of this nineteenth-century minor poetry written in the English manner was in a Wordsworthian mode, and here Sir Aubrey De Vere (1788–1846), himself the father of a better poet, demonstrated his topographical interests in such poems as 'Kilmallock' with its ruined shades of feudal pomp. His poem 'The Rock of Cashel' reverts to an eighteenth-century melancholia, while in his cheerier 'Castle Connell' the faint ruins of De Burgo's towers are offset by the songs of birds:

> While cottage smoke goes drifting on the breeze;
> And sunny clouds are floating overall.

Though De Vere's descriptive verse was mostly inspired by Wordsworth, he also portrayed his Irish patriotism in sonnets such as 'Lismore', 'The Shannon' and 'The Soldiers of Sarsfield'. His longer work seems self-indulgent to a modern reader; but he does convey an obvious delight in the actual scenery of Ireland. This delight was matched by a gentle, heartfelt 'Sonnet written during his residence in [Trinity] College' by Charles Wolfe (1791–1823):

> My spirit's on the mountains, where the birds
> In wild and sportive freedom wing the air,
> Amidst the heath-flowers and the browsing herds,
> Where Nature's altar is, my spirit's there.
> It is my joy to tread the pathless hills,
> Though but in fancy — for my mind is free,
> And walks in sedgy ways and trickling rills,
> While I'm forbid the use of liberty.
> This is delusion but it is so sweet
> That I could live deluded. Let me be
> Persuaded that my springing soul may meet
> The eagle on the hills — and I am free.
> Who'd not be flatter'd by a fate like this?
> To fancy is to feel our happiness.

Wolfe's reputation, of course, rests upon a single poem 'The Burial of Sir John Moore' with its repeated echoing negatives, 'Not a drum was heard, not a funeral note', culminating in

> We carved not a line and we raised not a stone —
> But we left him alone with glory.

A virtual contemporary of Wolfe's, William Maginn (1794–1842) was educated at Trinity and taught, like his friend Callanan, in his father's school, before becoming a successful London journalist. Vastly popular in his lifetime, his verses — which appeared in *Noctes Ambrosianae* (5 vols, 1863–5) — have a slick fluency which makes some of them still amusing to read.

George Darley (1795–1846) the mathematician, whose *Errors of Ecstasie* appeared in 1822, was another minor poet, but he possessed considerable power. The poems in his *Nepenthe* (1835) have a rush of imagery enhanced by strictly controlled metre and an intensity of vision. His 'Dirge' from *The Sea Bride* is often anthologised and has a swing to it which implants its imperatives in the mind:

> Wash him bloodless, smooth him fair,
> Stretch his limbs and sleek his hair:
> Dingle-dong, the dead bells go!
> Mermen swing them to and fro.

'Siren Chorus' has the same touch of sureness about it, the same balance and control. Darley's choice of adjectives is excellent, but the movement of his verse is kept up by his effective use of verbs, so that he usually impresses by his energy. Despite his harking back to Elizabethan and Jacobean models, he is worth more attention than he usually gets, and this, to a limited extent, is also true of Aubrey De Vere (1814–1902) who wrote some elegant poems on classical subjects in a Landoresque way. His *Dirges* are, however, un-English; they are contained in his *Innisfail, a Lyrical Chronicle of Ireland* (1862) which treats episodes in Irish legend and history, seeking to 'embody the *essence* of a nation's history'. This contains a melancholia prophetic of the later Twilight poets, and anticipates Yeats in using the traditional rose symbol for Ireland in a mystic way:

> The little black rose shall be red at last
> What made it black but the east wind dry?
> And the tear of the widow that fell on it fast?
> It shall redden the hills when June is nigh.

> The silk of the kine shall rest at last!
> What drove her forth but the dragon-fly?
> In the golden vale she shall feed full fast
> With her mild gold horn, and her slow dark eye.

He wrote religious poetry and, after his conversion to Roman Catholicism, many hymns. His lyric quality, which is sometimes reminiscent of Shelley's, appears to good effect in *In Ruin reconciled*, his religious feeling in 'Dei Genetrix'.

The early decades of the nineteenth century had seen the matter of Ireland put before English and continental readers, not only through Charlotte Brook's *Reliques of Ancient Irish Poetry* and *Moore's Melodies*, Maria Edgeworth's novels, Lady Morgan's romances and Maturin's Gothicism; there were lesser prose writers at work as well. Mary Leadbeater (1758—1826), for instance, whose *Poems* appeared in 1808, to be followed by *The Cottage Dialogues* (1811), which earned her Maria Edgeworth's friendship, *The Landlord's Friend* (1813), *Tales for Cottagers* (1814) and *Cottage Biographies* (1822). She also wrote *Memoirs of Richard and Elizabeth Shackleton* (1822) and *The Pedlar, a Tale* (1824). She was the daughter of a Quaker family, her grandfather, Abraham Shackleton, having taught Edmund Burke who formed his closest friendship with Shackleton's son Richard, Mary's father. She married a local landowner of Huguenot descent, kept the village post-office and recorded events in her Kildare village from 1766 to 1824 in *The Annals of Ballytore*, published as *The Leadbeater Papers* (1862). She wrote with simple effectiveness and many passages are most moving in their often gruesome account of the 1798 rebellion as it passed though Ballitore:

> As my friend and I walked out to see a sick neighbour, we looked with fearful curiosity over a wall inside of which we saw lying the youthful form of the murdered Richard Yeates. There he had been thrown after his death, his clothes undisturbed, but his bosom all bloody. For many days after I thought my food tasted of blood, and at night was frequently awakened by my feeling of horror, and stretched forth my hand to feel if my husband was safe at my side.

III The second quarter

From 1825 onwards a new kind of vigour marked developments in the novel. Maria Edgeworth, Lady Morgan and

Maturin had been of the landlord or professional classes. Now there emerged writers who knew the life of the Irish country-side from the point of view of the cabin and small farm: the Banim brothers, Gerald Griffin and William Carleton. The younger of the Banim brothers, John (1798—1842), was educated at Kilkenny College and the drawing academy of the Royal Dublin Society. He moved to Dublin to recover from the death of his fiancée in 1820, and after the success of his *Damon and Pythias* in 1821 at Covent Garden suggested to his brother Michael (1796—1874), who was looking after the family shop and farm in Kilkenny, that they should produce a series of national tales on the lines of Scott's fiction. They wrote these as *Tales by the O'Hara Family*, the first series of which was published in 1825 and proved very popular. *Croohore of the Bill Hook* (1825) was by Michael, who wrote about nineteen of their twenty-four works. This novel, like *The Ghost Hunter and His Family* (1831), cont-tained a characteristic mixture of Irish folklore, attitudes of other-worldliness and realistic details. Realism marked the Banims' accounts of rural life before the Famine; they dealt with violent crime and its effects in a decidedly sombre manner, and did so with an often humourless melodramatic Gothic gusto. *The Nowlans* (1826) is a good example of this. Their sense of patriotism emerges in their treatment of politico-historical themes, in, for instance, *The Boyne Water* (1826), based on the Siege of Limerick, *The Croppy* (1828), set in the Penal period, and *The Denounced* (1830), an account of the 1798 rebellion.

In 1823 John Banim was visited in London by Gerald Griffin (1803—40) who had gone there to make a literary career. Banim tried to help him by introducing him to editors and literary people, but Griffin, by nature proud and touchy, rejected his aid. Failing to interest the Irish actor, William Charles Macready (1792—1873 — whose father, originally a Smock Alley actor, acted at Covent Garden and wrote three plays) — in his tragedy *Aguire*, Griffin supported himself by hack journalism, sometimes providing material on Irish customs and Irish usages in English. During three years of this work he managed to write *Holland-Tide; or, Munster Popular Tales* (1827), his first collection of Irish stories. These are uneven, over-explanatory, with too many self-consciously humorous scenes interposed in the all too often improbable action. At this time he generally wrote a clumsy circumlocutory prose, though the speech he gave to his country folk was as lively and vital as the supposedly genteel dialogue was stilted and stereotyped. Griffin hankered for the effect of drama. In his second collection, *Tales of the Munster Festivals* (1827), he adds a note to 'The Half-Sir' to say that the plot of the tale is that of a two-act drama.

Griffin was trying to see Ireland detachedly. In 'The Half-Sir' he created in Eugene Hammond a character like himself, solitary and over-sensitive to the point of morbidity, 'a sort of gentleman' ill at ease in a society of extremes. There is also a comic, indeed classic portrayal of a 'downstart', Mr O'Neil, the shabbiest and poorest of his family who has 'relations that wouldn't know me in the street! Simple as I sit here, there's not one o' my family that wouldn't be ashamed to be seen speaking to me in any public place.'

Griffin wrote his first and best novel, *The Collegians* (1829), at high speed, responding daily to the printer's messenger who arrived after breakfast to demand more copy. He based this novel on the actual murder of a young girl for which the son of a country family and his boatman were hanged in 1820.

The Collegians provides a mixed cross-section of Irish provincial life, from boatmen, horse-traders, servants and peasants through the new expanding middle class of Catholic middlemen, portrayed in the Daly family, to the props of the Ascendancy: the magistrates, the doctor and the commandant of militia. And there are the 'half sirs', the duelling, drinking squireens, Connollys and Creaghs who visit the aristocratic Chutes of Castle Chute. There are four main characters, two young men and two young women; in this Griffin was probably following Scott's example, just as he often echoes the way Scott's narrative prose falls into blank verse. Hardress Cregen secretly marries Eily O'Connor, the daughter of a rope-maker, in a Wordsworthian appreciation of simplicity, then becomes disenchanted with her brogue and untutored ways; his ambitious mother presses him to marry Anne Chute. Kyrle Daly, cool and controlled, provides a counterbalance to Hardress, described by his creator as 'his mother's spoiled pet, ruined by indulgence'. The exploration of Hardress's

character carries the novel compellingly along its melodramatic path to the murder of Eily by Danny the servant,
who later informs on Hardress. Griffin well understood his
character's inability to come to terms with the world, and
Hardress Cregen is, surprisingly, equally credible in both his
arrogant, energetic violence and his passionate pathetic
repentance.

Griffin's next novels, published together in three volumes
in 1829, were *The Rivals* and *Tracy's Ambition*. The first has
for subject a melodramatic rivalry between Francis Riordan,
a rebel, and Richard Lacy, of the police, for the hand of
Esther Wilderming; its main interest, however, centres in the
incidentals: a hedge-school, shebeens, evictions and death-
bed scenes. It is a general attack upon politicians and corruption. *Tracy's Ambition* is a more effective story, told by Abel
Tracy, an ambitious man who sacrifices his happiness for
promises of preferment put to him by Dalton, a repressive
magistrate. Himself a Protestant, Tracy has married a Catholic
and been, until associated with Dalton, received well by the
local people. They turn against him, his wife is murdered by
terrorists, and he then reacts against Dalton, whose son is also
murdered. Tracy eventually lapses into a peaceful life. Griffin
was too concerned not only to show the ill effects of excessive
ambition but also to illustrate the actual miseries of Irish life,
which could, he thought, be removed if the poverty of the
peasantry were alleviated and the landlords' attitudes altered.

There followed *The Christian Psychologist* (1830), an ineffective group of moral tales. For his next historical novel,
The Invasion (1832), Griffin read deeply; but he did not
digest his reading (later editions contained notes by Eugene
O'Curry correcting Griffin's mistakes); his opening is slow
and over-informative. This is a picture of an island of heroes,
saints and scholars, but it rapidly turns into another exploration of the differences between two characters: Kenric the
proud solitary, the doomed Northumbrian, and Elim, the
Ithean or Milesian hero.

Tales of my Neighbourhood (1835) provides in 'The Great
House' a naïve view of life in a big house told in the lively
speech of a village shopkeeper, and in 'The Blackbirds and
the Yellow Hammers' an aspect of rural Irish life not often
dealt with, a faction fight. *The Duke of Monmouth* (1836)

was a mistaken attempt at another historical novel. Griffin's energies were flagging; he felt he was pursuing frivolity and entered the Christian Brothers' teaching order, giving up writing altogether. His posthumous work included *Talis Qualis or Tales of the Jury Room* (1842), with some good comedy, and *Gisippus* (1842), which Macready produced, a study of a Griffin-like character, 'a fellow of exquisite susceptibility'.

Of a very different stamp from the Banims and Griffin was William Carleton (1794–1869). Bilingual, he grew up in County Tyrone near the Monaghan border, an area where Orangemen and Ribbonmen carried on an intermittent but persistent internecine struggle. His father was a farmer who passed on old stories and traditions to his family, and his mother sang songs in Irish. As is recorded in David J. O'Donoghue's *The Life of William Carleton* (1896), he grew up in a magnificent mixture of learning and idleness:

> No dance missed me. I was perpetually leaping [He once leaped the river at Clogher Karry, and the place was known afterwards as Carleton's Leap], and throwing the stone and the sledge. No football match was without me. I have gone five miles to wakes and dances. We had not only what were known as common dances in those days, but we had what were politely called balls. The difference between a ball and a common dance was this. At the ball we had whisky . . . .

He had been taught by a hedge-schoolmaster, Pat Frayne, and, after his father died, went south to Munster as a poor scholar, theoretically to become a priest. He returned home, read voraciously, imbibed *Gil Blas* and then set off east. He passed bodies in gibbets (the germ of his 'Wildgoose Lodge' in *Traits and Stories of the Irish Peasantry*) tutored, tried being a hedge-schoolmaster, and fetched up in Dublin. There, wanting to marry after two years' random teaching, he became a clerk in the Sunday School Society. He met the Rev. Caesar Otway, a Protestant clergyman, the author of *Sketches in Ireland*, notable for its description of Lough Derg as a place of degraded superstition. In a conversation with Otway, Carleton, who had made the pilgrimage there, described the religious ceremonies that, he wrote afterwards, detached him from the Roman Catholic Church and prevented him from being a priest. At Otway's instigation he wrote 'The Lough Derg

Pilgrim', and Otway published it (signed 'W') in the *Christian Examiner* (which he edited) in April and May 1828. This paper was strongly anti-Catholic and Carleton had adapted himself to its line. The main point about the story is that it was written out of a full personal undersanding of aspects of Irish life which had not before been effectively put into print. Self-educated as he virtually was Carleton had no suitable tradition within which to work, yet he experimented away continuously. And he wrote with a vigour that matched his physical energy. He contributed to the *Christian Examiner* for several years, and the first series of his *Traits and Stories of the Irish Peasantry* was published in two volumes in 1830. These stories deal with particular topics such as wakes, funerals, fights, hedge-schools, religious observations, weddings and fairy tales.

What emerges from Carleton's writings is the sheer vitality of life in Ireland before the Famine. Take 'The Party Fight and Funeral', for instance; here after an epic single combat between two leaders, which ends with one of them getting a fractured skull, a grim battle is joined between Ribbonmen and Orangemen:

> It absolutely resembled a military engagement, for the number of combatants amounted to at least two thousand. In many places the street was covered with small pools and clots of blood which flowed from those who lay insensible; while others were borne away bleeding, groaning, or staggering, having been battered into a total unconsciousness of the scene about them.

In the second series the violence spills out in 'Wildgoose Lodge', originally the 'Confessions of a Reformed Ribbonman' when first published in the *Dublin Literary Gazetter* in 1833, where its truth was stressed. The story — based upon an actual incident, the burning alive of the inhabitants of Wildgoose Lodge in reprisal for its owner's having informed on men who had raided the house earlier — is made more powerful by its first person narrative and by its melodramatic hysteria.

'Tubber Derg, or the Red Well' (originally 'The Landlord and Tenant' in the *National Magazine*, 1831) tells of an industrious tenant ruined by a careless landlord and bad agent. The tenant, Owen M'Carthy, is one of the few characters with dignity and self-respect in the *Traits and Stories*; he is matched by Jemmy M'Evoy in 'The Poor Scholar' whose simplicity and developing strength of character have a true nobility. This story is humane; indeed, it is moving in its account of the young man who battles to become a priest and thus to restore his father's fortunes. His aim was realistic: entering the priesthood was the one way out of unending and unrewarding toil; and the story, which later deals with the spiritual aspects, relates to Carleton's strong feelings about the tenure of the land, the landlords' lack of knowledge of their tenants and the evil of unscrupulous land agents. This is Maria Edgeworth's *The Absentee* presented from the tenants' point of view; but Carleton also saw that there were idle and poltically motivated tenants — he abhorred the Ribbonmen.

The obverse side of the quarrelling, the faction fighting, and the abductions is to be found in 'Phelim O'Toole's Courtship', which captures the energetic trickery of a rogue hero, yet another of Carleton's stories which gives a sense of the pulsating vitality of the Irish country people before the Famine. The ending, however, is sombre, for Phelim is transported for Ribbonism.

Carleton wrote the English he heard in the countryside and he occasionally brought in Irish, notably where strong emotions are involved; here is an example from his *Traits and Stories* (2nd series, II, 1833):

> 'I will speak to her', said Jemmy, 'in Irish, it will go directly to her heart: — *mhair, avourneen, tha ma laht, arish!* — Mother, my darling, I am with you at last.
> 'Shamus, aroon, avick ma chree, whil thu lhum? wuil thus lhum?* — Jeremy, my beloved, son of my heart, are you with me? — are you — are you with me?
> 'Ish maheen a tha in, a vair dheelish machree* — It is I who am with you, beloved mother of my heart!'

Most interesting is his use of swearing, and 'An Essay on Irish Swearing' is extremely useful, for in it he explains many of the oaths, imprecations and ejaculations so constantly used by his characters. This essay should be read against Maria Edgeworth's one on Irish bulls, which she defends as clear in sense and common to other languages. Carleton, however, values Irish swearing for its unique quality. He praises terms of affection, he sees the poetic invention in the curses, and emphasises the great difference between English and Irish swearing, the latter being religious in origin.

> If the Englishman were pugnacious and in the habit of appealing to the body of his opponent when angry, as Paddy is, it would not be singular in him, in order to fill up the measure of his resentment, to damn that part of his enemy which he cannot reach. But Paddy, who takes signal vengeance on the body, is not satisfied with this; he must also send the soul to punishment.

Carleton's sense of comic humour, based upon a delight in individual idiosyncracy, was most evident in the *Traits and Stories* (the final version of which appeared in the 1843 edition); they echoed oral storytelling with most of its emphasis on character rather than construction. As he moved into longer fiction — his novel *Fardorougha the Miser* with its savage yet sympathetic picture of a peasant miser and his steadfast wife, first published in the *Dublin University Magazine*, appeared separately in 1839 — he was over-inclined to didacticism. Like Burns he wrote in two ways, naturally and stiffly, and in his self-conscious style seems to have been aiming at an audience which did not know the nature of life outside the towns in Ireland. His novels are not as successful as the *Traits and Stories* because he stood outside their action; he could not manipulate his plots, and his genuine sense of the ghastly or the sensational could often become over-Gothic. But his own inner division probably reflected the divided state of Ireland in the eighteen-thirties — ('realities too strong, party passions too violent' in Maria Edgeworth's phrase of 1830.) His novels are correspondingly dark and gloomy. *Valentine M'Clutchy* (1845) is propaganda, a denunciation of landlords and agents, the whole system of land tenure. He drew a darker picture still in *The Black Prophet* (1847), published serially in the *Dublin University Magazine* in 1846, as a warning, after the potato crop had failed for two years in succession. Carleton knew what famine was like from his own experiences of lesser famines in 1817 and 1822; he returned to this theme again in lurid manner in *The Black Baronet* (1852) and *The Squanders of Castle Squander* (1852), where Lady Squander visits a grave-yard to discover it covered with half-eaten human limbs and with a dog gnawing a human head.

In general Carleton's picture of Ireland shows his love of landscape, which appears in some of his poems, notably those dealing with Ulster scenery. Here is an example:

> As the white low mist the meadows kissed
> In the summer twilight's glow,
> And the otter splashed and the wild duck dashed
> In the sedgy lake below,
> 'Twas sweet to hear the silver bell
> For the flocks of high Dunroe:
> From the rail's hoarse throat the ceaseless note
> Would flit, now far, now high,
> And the quavering hum of the snipe would come
> Quick shooting from the sky.

He also conveyed his hatred of extortion of all kinds — Darby Skinadre in *The Black Prophet* embodies most of them. He had the capacity to convey the teeming life and lawlessness of an overcrowded, poverty-stricken countryside. And in this collection of *Tales and Sketches, Illustrating the Character, Usages, Tradition, Sports and Pastimes of the Irish Peasantry* (1845) he stressed the genuineness of his material; his people and place, though 'unpretending', were, in a literary sense, real. His posthumous, unfinished *Autobiography*, published in 1896 with his letters, tells the story of his youth in much more effective prose than he used in his fiction. Carleton, despite all his obvious faults, remains a perhaps surprisingly powerful writer, and he was the first to voice with full effectiveness the language and the emotional vitality of peasant Ireland before the Famine.

Another novelist, William Hamilton Maxwell (1792–1850), who became rector of Balla, County Mayo after serving in the British Army, was also writing of the life of the Irish countryside in his best-known work, the lively *Wild Sports of the West of Ireland* (1832). The mixed contents of this book contain good narrative as well as descriptions and advice. It is much more readable than his novels *The Fortunes of Hector O'Halloran And His Man Mark Antony O'Toole* (n.d.), or *Brian O'Linn; or Luck is Everything* (1848). Maxwell and Charles Lever (1806–72) became friends. Lever trained as a doctor and had an adventurous time in North America. He returned to Ireland, dealt with a cholera epidemic in Clare in 1832, then moved to be a dispensary doctor at

Portrush, and after that left Ireland again to practise in Brussels. The first item of *The Confessions of Harry Lorrequer,* influenced by Maxwell's work, was published in the *Dublin University Magazine* in 1837, the last in 1840; and this light-hearted series of episodes in the life of an English subaltern who delighted in Irish life became highly popular. Lever followed it with *Charles O'Malley, the Irish Dragoon* (also anonymous) with its vivid pictures of abundant Anglo-Irish hospitality, and he has been judged by Irish critics largely on these two rattling stories ever since. They are amusing and lively; they avoid the sombre side of life that Carleton was portraying. And they suited English readers: indeed there was a wide acceptance of Lever's early rollicking view of Ireland: in Harry Lorrequer's words, it was ' a round of dining, drinking, dancing, riding, steeple chasing, pigeon shooting and tandem driving . . . late breakfasts, formal dinners, Garrison Balls and plays'. He was accused of portraying stage Irishmen, and indeed he echoed the farce of restoration and eighteenth-century Irish dramatists; but those who accuse him of stage-Irishry and leave it at that have apparently failed to read the novels of his middle and late period.

Lever, incidentally, is often associated with another writer accused of perpetuating the stage Irishman, Samuel Lover (1797–1868), originally a marine painter and miniaturist. He illustrated his first book *Legends and Stories of Ireland* (1831), settled in London in 1835, and published his novel *Rory O'More* (originally written as a ballad, later as a play) in 1837, following it with *Handy Andy* (1842) which was extremely successful. Lever wrote literally hundreds of songs — among them 'The Low-backed Car' — but he is still remembered for his humorous, admittedly stage-Irish, creation of Handy Andy, a willing but witless larger-then-life lout.

Lover had been one of the founders of the *Dublin University Magazine,* which Charles Lever returned to Dublin to edit in 1842. He stayed three years in Dublin entertaining hospitably, as he did everywhere, notably in Florence in the late eighteen-forties when he lived high, finding it impossible to retrench, 'sipping champagne on a tight rope'. He became vice-consul at La Spezia in 1852, then consul at Trieste where he died in 1872.

The founding of the *Dublin University Magazine* in 1833

by Lover, Isaac Butt (later the creator of the Home Rule party) and others demonstrated that the intellectual vitality of Dublin — the lack of which in the post-Union period Maria Edgeworth had shown in *The Absentee* (1812) and Charles Lever was to make even clearer in *Barrington* (1862) — was reviving. Though the policies of its founders were Tory, Unionist and, in reaction to Catholic emancipation in 1829, strongly Protestant, the magazine provided for Gaelic literature in translation, for studies of the history, cultural background and antiquities of Ireland. There was an expansion of the scope of Irish writing in English, spurred on by a desire for a fuller expression of Irish life and traditions. Thus, for instance, the magazine included contributions by Carleton.

The pleasures of Dublin's social life between 1842 and 1845, however, did not compensate Lever for the attacks made on him by nationalists during his editorship of the *Dublin University Magazine*. Carleton, in an unsigned review of *Jack Hinton* in 1843, was particularly vicious, and so were Daniel O'Connell and Thomas Davis. The paradox was that Carleton himself was unpopular and seen as a detractor of Ireland until his *Valentine M'Clutchy*, and that Lever, with his *Jack Hinton* (1843), had begun the criticism of English rule in and attitudes to Ireland, which continued throughout those succeeding novels of his which dealt with Irish subject matter. He complained that the English — and how often is this view expressed in the course of Anglo-Irish literature! — simply did not realise how different the Irish were from them.

Thus there followed many novels by Lever which treated Ireland in a more complex, varied way. The hero of *Tom Bourke of 'Ours'* (1844) vows hatred against the enemies of his country, sympathising with the sufferings of the peasantry; he leads a mob on the night of the voting for the Union, and finally becomes a soldier in the French army, 'rebellion enough to make Dan [O'Connell] recant his judgement of me', remarked Lever. His next novel, *The O'Donoghue* (1845), criticised the system of land tenure: it is set in the period of 1798, and attacks many aspects of the Ascendancy as well as the ignorance of the English about Ireland. Lever was assailed from all sides for these two novels. In *St Patrick's Eve* (1845) he sympathised more deeply with the Irish poor, while in *The Knight of Gwynne* (1847) he dwelt on the intrigues which brought about the Union despite many who resisted 'offers and temptations'. He realised that the reckless extravagance of the gentry created their downfall, and in *Roland Cashel* (1848) satirised Castle circles in Dublin affectedly aping English fashion as well as the new emergent middle class in all its suburban showy vulgarity. *Con Cregan* (1849) depicted decline in Dublin under Castle rule; *Maurice Tiernay* (1850) included the French landings at Killala and Castlebar in 1798; and *Sir Jasper Carew* (1852) went back to the Cromwellian period before reaching the time of the Ascendancy.

A visit to Ireland in 1854, the year *The Dodd Family Abroad* appeared, gave Lever a fresh feeling of exasperation with English rule in Ireland, and though the introduction to *The Martins of Cro' Martin* (1854) expressed a hope for greater generosity, he had begun to despair of politics — and of the Anglo-Irish for not providing adequate leadership for the Irish people. Their example of 'duelling of a morning and drinking overnight' was, at the least, out of date. The new Catholic middle class was successfully reaching for and grasping political power. Lever's growing cynicism about politics — well expressed in *Davenport Dunn* (1857) — was developed differently in *Barrington* (1862) which showed the folly of romanticising the Ascendancy past. Indeed in *Luttrell of Arran* (1863) the main character withdraws from an uncongenial Irish society. *Sir Brook Fossbrooke* (1865) also analyses the Anglo-Irish decline and the misrule of Ireland by England, a theme treated impressively in Lever's last novel *Lord Kilgobbin* (1872).

This is the novel by which Lever should be judged. It is a despairing picture, of a decaying and discontented Anglo-Irish Ascendancy at the mercy of political unrest, angry terrorism and that English ineptitude, swinging between repression and appeasement, which he could not venerate. He had come a long way from his early insouciant indifference to face the pressing problems of political life. He had learned, in Balzac's manner, to fill a wide canvas with varied characters, to move from picaresque farce to a carefully contrived comedy of human errors, rooted in ignorance and indifference to the Irish reality that he himself observed with an elegaic sense of its perennial tragedy.

Lever's career covered thirty-five years in a century which had begun with Maria Edgeworth's successful attempt in *Castle Rackrent* (1800) to show English readers what life in Ireland was like. This story had begun the regional novel; the subsequent popularity of novelists such as the Banims, Griffin, Carleton, Maxwell and Lover shows that there was a large audience, in Ireland as well as England, interested in Irish life. The antiquarianism which had informed the work of the early-nineteenth century Irish novelists, Lady Morgan and Maturin, was followed by an increasing curiosity about the folklore of Ireland. And the popularity of Crofton Croker's work in the eighteen-twenties helped to develop this audience. Thomas Crofton Croker (1798—1854) travelled widely in the south, collecting material for his *Researches in the South of Ireland* (1824) and *Fairy Legends and Traditions of the South of Ireland* (1825). The latter was the first collection of oral legends to be made in the British Isles; it was so successful (the Grimm brothers translated it into German, a French version was soon issued and the work itself was reprinted frequently in English) that Croker followed it with two more volumes in 1828. (He wrote other books later but none of them approached the popularity of *Fairy Legends and Traditions*.) He turned the oral legends into carefully constructed literary narratives possessing a light and witty style, but he also supplied notes about his sources, the local legends and customs, and the irrational and superstitious element in them which he strongly deprecated.

Croker was followed by many collectors. Samuel Lover, for instance, had issued his *Legends and Stories of Ireland* in book form in 1831; most collectors, however, published their material in journals. The earlier work of Ogle, Furlong and Callanan in translating from the Irish was developed in the eighteen-thirties and forties. James Hardiman (1790—1855), an active member of the Royal Irish Academy, sub-commissioner in the Records Office in Dublin, and later librarian of Queen's College, Galway, issued *Irish Minstrelsy, or the Bardic Remains of Ireland* (1831), with the Gaelic text balanced by English translation. He added notes, a selection of Turlough O'Carolan's poetry, and an account of the Irish bards from early times to the eighteenth century. The translations appealed to contemporary readers, as they were meant to, for Hardiman wanted to make a case for Irish poetry and therefore sought to write in a currently fashionable style.

Edward Walsh (1805–50) conveyed the liveliness of oral tradition in his *Reliques of Irish Jacobite Poetry* (1844) and *Irish Popular Songs* (1847). But of all the earlier-nineteenth century translators and adapters of Irish material the poet James Clarence Mangan (1803–49) was the most idiosyncratic and inventive. In his teens and early twenties he contributed verses to Dublin almanacks, using various *noms de plume*. Lonely, introspective, nervously depressed, and becoming addicted to alcohol, he joined the Comet Club, and wrote extravaganzas for its journal.

Though Mangan's early poetry poured out in impressive if anonymous profusion for the periodicals, it did not lack craftsmanship. He gave up scrivening and tried to earn a living by translating from the German; one of his most successful adaptations is 'Gone in the Wind', after Rückert, a powerful piece 'full of rhetorical inversions and interrogations'. He also wrote translations of Spanish and Islamic material. He fell in love but his love was not returned. He took to opium and became more eccentric; his life and work afford many parallels to those of Edgar Allen Poe. After being employed in the Ordnance Survey from 1832 until the Office closed in 1842, Mangan worked in the Library in Trinity College, Dublin. During this period he developed nationalist sympathies; his patriotic interest in Irish poetry and folklore stemmed from his work and contacts in the Ordnance Survey. He began by versifying crude translations by others, probably in prose, and it is debatable whether he worked from the originals later. But, whether he knew Irish himself or not, he invested his Irish poems with a nervous force and vigour virtually unique in the period. His 'Dark Rosaleen', for instance, with its easy flow of words, intricate rhyme scheme, and lilting quality, has a strength emphasised by repetition:

> I could scale the blue air,
> I could plough the high hills,
> Oh, I could kneel all night in prayer,
> To heal your many ills!
> And one . . . beamy smile from you
> Would float like light between

> My toils and me, my own, my true,
> My Dark Rosaleen!
> My fond Rosaleen!
> Would give me life and soul anew,
> A second life, a soul anew,
> My Dark Rosaleen!

'O'Hussey's Ode to the Maguire' exhibits a wild passion in its singing stanzas:

> Though he were even a wolf ranging the round
>   green woods,
> Though he were even a pleasant salmon in the
>   unchainable sea,
> Though he were a wild mountain eagle, he could
>   scarce bear, he
> This sharp sore sleet, these howling floods.

Mangan was indeed an impressive poet; he could write with moving, haunting simplicity in 'Siberia':

> In Siberia's wastes
> No tears are shed,
> For they freeze within the brain:
> Nought is felt but dullest pain
> Pain acute, yet dead . . . .

This self-styled 'tortured torturer of reluctant rhymes' produced a paradoxical metrical insouciance in 'Twenty Golden Years Ago' or 'The Time of the Barmecides' while 'The Nameless One' conveys a clear picture of his own despair:

> And he fell far through that pit abysmal
> The gulf and grave of Maginn and Burns
> And pawned his soul for the devil's dismal
> Stock of returns . . . .

Mangan's prose included an *Autobiography* (ed. James Kilroy, 1967), and his troubled life, cut short by cholera, inspired both Yeats and Joyce by its romantic achievement and intensity.

Mangan had owed his post in the Ordnance Survey to the antiquarian, musician and artist George Petrie (1790–1866), who was educated at Samuel Whyte's famous school in Dublin and at the art school of the Dublin Society. Here he made friends with the Wexford-born Francis Danby (1793?—

1861) and James Arthur O'Connor (1792–1841); the three went to London in 1813. Danby decided to stay on and become 'an English artist' and his romanticism was attributed to his Irish origin, though this is hard to substantiate — probably only one or at most two of his pictures being inspired by an Irish theme. Petrie, however, returned to Ireland. His illustrations of Irish buildings, contributed to many guide books, were drawn with meticulous accuracy and elegance. He was also interested in music and collected many airs during his travelling, which he published as *The Ancient Music of Ireland* (1855). His antiquarian interests appeared in many articles for the *Dublin Penny Journal*; (he himself edited the *Irish Penny Journal* during its first year of life in 1842). His most famous work was probably his *Essay on the Round Towers of Ireland* (1845), later included in his *Ecclesiastical Architecture of Ireland* (1845). Petrie's work at the Ordnance Survey to which he was attached from 1833 to 1839 was imaginative in its scope; he collected many collaborators who shared his interest in the past of Ireland. Petrie's assistants at the Ordnance Survey included Eugene O'Curry (1796–1862), who catalogued, transcribed, and translated Irish manuscripts, his *Lectures on the Manuscript Materials of Ancient Irish History* being published in 1861, and John O'Donovan (1809–61) the scholar and topographer who edited and translated *The Annals of the Four Masters* (1848–51). The line of scholars and antiquarians running through the nineteenth century was a strong one. It includes John O'Daly (1800–78); Patrick Kennedy (1801–73) whose contributions to the *Dublin University Magazine* were published in several books, the best known being *Legendary Fictions of the Irish* (1866); James Henthorn Todd (1805–69); Edward Walsh (1805–51); Sir William Wilde (1815–76), the famous occultist and father of Oscar, who in addition to his medical writings combined descriptions of scenery and antiquities in *The Beauties of the Boyne and the Blackwater* (1849) and *Lough Corrib and Lough Mask* (1867). Brian O'Looney (1827–1901) was another useful translator, and Whitley Stokes (1830–1909), who spent twenty years in India, published, with John Strachan, a *Thesaurus Paleohibernicus* (1901–10), a collection of Old Irish glosses, and edited many other Irish texts and glosses. Another doctor and scientist who collected and translated Irish poetry was George Sigerson (1836–1925), one of the founders of the Feis Ceoil, whose *The Poets and Poetry of Munster* (1860) was followed by his best-known work, a collection of translations called *Bards of the Gael and Gall* (1897). Sigerson became an active senator of the Irish Free State at a ripe age in 1922.

To return to the earlier nineteenth century, it is clear that the magazines provided a very useful role. Both Mangan and Sir Samuel Ferguson (1810–86), for instance, contributed to the *Dublin University Magazine*. Ferguson was probably its most characteristic author. Born in Belfast, he disliked nationalism, indeed was perturbed by his view of Ireland's future: but the Irish Protestant, 'deserted by the Tories, insulted by the Whigs, threatened by the Radicals, hated by the Papists, and envied by the Dissenters', could contribute, as he put it in 'A Dialogue between the Head and Heart of an Irish protestant' in the November 1833 issue, could perhaps even survive, by being aware of 'the Irish history of centuries'. He argued that the Anglo-Irish did not fully understand their Catholic fellow-citizens, and that they must begin to do so. His own contribution was impressive. He applied himself to the Gaelic epic, the heroic pagan age of the legends and sagas, particularly to the Red Branch, Ulster cycle, and the twenty-two translations he published in the *Dublin Magazine* in 1834 are good lively poetry.

Ferguson differed greatly from Mangan, who tended to be swept along by the emotions of his verse. There is a controlled, vigorous, masculine, marching quality in Ferguson's lines, a certain lack of the sensuous, which meant that his translations, though more accurate and more effective as verse than earlier work, such as that of James Hardiman, did not achieve popularity. Ferguson was not good at creating character; he may, as Padraic Colum suggested, have been unduly desirous of making his Celtic heroes dignified Victorians. But he did match the toughness of his originals effectively at least once, in 'The Welshmen of Tirawley', a narrative poem which tells of the choice offered to the Welshmen of Tirawley in Connaught who, on being offered the choice of being blinded or castrated, chose blindness.

Lays of the Western Gael (1865) was followed by a long

poem, *Congal* (1872), based on the bardic romance of 'The Battle of Moyra', which is marred by excessively obvious technique: decoration, inversion, and over-intricate prosody. Despite this there is a rugged strength in some passages, such as Aidan the bard's song about Ulster:

> . . . from where tumultuous Moyne
> Heaves at Benmore's foot-fettering rocks with
>   ceaseless surging toil.

Ferguson can be very impressive in some of his short poems, such as the 'Lament for the Death of Thomas Davis' with its energy and the fresh Keatsian-like compound adjectives he frequently created so effectively. His version of an Old Irish song, 'The Fair Hills of Ireland,' and 'Ceann Dubh Deelish' (for which Charlotte Brooke had earlier despaired of finding English words) with its simple repetition was memorable. He also used repetition effectively in 'Deirdre's Lament for the Sons of Usnach' with its rhetorical rhythm:

> Woe is me! by fraud and wrong —
> Traitors false and tyrants strong —
> Fell Clan Usnach, bought and sold,
> For Barach's feast and Conor's gold.
>
> Woe to Eman, roof and wall! —
> Woe to Red Branch, hearth and hall! —
> Tenfold woe and black dishonour
> To the false and foul Clan Conor!
>
> Dig the grave both wide and deep,
> Sick am I, and fain would sleep!
> Dig the grave and make it ready,
> Lay me on my true love's body.

Two of Ferguson's poems, 'The Loyal Orangeman' (which should be read aloud in a strong Ulster accent) and 'At the Polo ground', on the Phoenix Park murders of 1882, may surprise the reader who sees Ferguson through the anthologists' eyes as very much the President of the Royal Irish Academy (which he became in 1882 two years after the appearance of his *Poems*). His ballad of Anna Grace, 'The Fairy Thorn', and his translations of the love songs of 'men in outlawry and misery' may ultimately be regarded as his best work and as having most influence on later poets, several of whom saw 'Anna Grace' as the real starting point of the later literary revival.

Very different from the *Dublin University Magazine* (which ran from 1838 to 1877; it was succeeded, to a certain extent, by the *Dublin University Review* founded in 1885) was *The Nation*, founded in 1842 by Sir Charles Gavan Duffy (1816– 1903), John Blake Dillon (1816–66) and Thomas Davis (1814–45). This weekly newspaper, which developed the audience for which the *Dublin* and *Irish Penny Magazines* of the eighteen-thirties had catered, was strongly nationalist and influential; it ran until 1848, the year of the abortive rising led by William Smith O'Brien. It was revived in 1849 and then ran till 1896. The Young Ireland movement, as Davis and his colleagues were known, moved away from Daniel O'Connell's constitutionalism; not only did they encourage extreme nationalism but also they sought to combine with it an interest in Irish culture. Mangan, for instance, though he had contributed to the *Dublin University Magazine*, found a congenial home for his patriotic poetry, his translations and adaptations of Gaelic originals in *The Nation*. It also published Davis's own very rhetorical poetry. His ballads 'A Nation once again' and 'The West's asleep' are characteristic of his intensely emotional, sometimes overblown style, often little more than crude — and effective — political propaganda. He was a highly influential journalist.

John Mitchel (1815–75), who wrote for *The Nation*, was too bitter for Gavan Duffy, and so he left to found another journal called, after Wolfe Tone's movement, *The United Irishman*: his policy was to encourage farmers to adopt passive resistance, but he was ready to incite more active measures. He was sentenced to fourteen years' transportation for his part in the 1848 uprising, and was the only Young Irelander to produce a genuinely literary work in his *Jail Journal* (1854), which is a graphic, at times moving and forthright account of his experience as a prisoner in Bermuda and Tasmania and of his escape to America in 1853. He gave a sharper edge to the earlier revolutionary nationalism of Wolfe Tone. His satire can be Swiftian when he focuses on the failure of the English bureaucrats to fathom the extent of the catastrophe of the Famine — 'The almighty indeed', he remarked, 'sent the potato blight, but the English created the famine.' His caustic rage surges through this description:

> There, in the esplanade before the 'Royal Barracks', was erected the national model soup-kitchen, gaily bedizened, laurelled, and bannered, and fair to see; and in and out, and all around, sauntered parties of our supercilious second-hand 'better classes' of the castle-offices, fed in superior rations at the people's expense, and bevies of fair dames, and military officers, braided with public braid, and padded with public padding; and there, too, were the pale and piteous ranks of model-paupers, broken tradesmen, ruined farmers, destitute semp-stresses, ranged at a respectful distance till the genteel persons had duly inspected the arrangements — and then marched by policemen to the place allotted to them, where they were to feed on the meagre diet with chained spoons — to show the 'gentry' how pauper spirit can be broken, and pauper appetite can gulp down its bitter bread and its bitter shame and wrath together; — and all this time the genteel persons chatted and simpered as pleasantly as if the clothes they wore, and the carriages they drove in, were their own — as if 'Royal Barracks', castle, and soup-kitchen, were to last forever.

IV After the Famine

The history of the novel in Ireland tends to move by fits and starts. The didactic element in Maria Edgeworth's novels was echoed by Mrs S. C. Hall (1800—81), who wrote copiously of Irish peasant life, but her didacticism was so intrusive it spoils the general effect of her work for modern readers. But the achievement of Sheridan Le Fanu (1814—73) was very different indeed and still commands our attention by its emotive force and often macabre, sinister effects. He de-veloped the Gothic strain of Maturin to considerable effect but, like other novelists of his time, he was more strongly affected by the political turmoil of the nineteenth century. As faction fighting in the countryside was replaced by the Tithe war, his father, the Dean of Emly, rector of Ardnagechy and Abington, lost most of his income, and the son grew up very conscious that the power of the Ascendancy, and the role of the established and Tory Church of Ireland, were in decline. His experience of agrarian and sectarian strife in the Limerick countryside underlay the sensational, the Gothic atmosphere of his major novels, no doubt reinforced by the effects of the Famine.

Le Fanu's novels include *The Cock and Anchor, being A*

Chronicle of Old Dublin City (1845), based on his dislike of politics and distrust of the Whigs; *The Fortunes of Colonel Torlogh O'Brien* (1847), another historical novel; *The House by the Churchyard* (1863), a murder story with an over-complicated but none the less effective plot, set in Chapelizod (then a village outside Dublin) of 1767; and *Uncle Silas: A Tale of Bartram-Haugh* (1864) where Le Fanu's treatment of the transcendental implications of landscape and his Swedenborgianism combine in a story where Uncle Silas is, as is argued by Le Fanu's biographer, W. J. McCormack, the dead soul of Austin Ruthyn. This story is convincingly told by the girl whom Uncle Silas seeks to control and destroy; her sense of horror, the emotional intensity achieved, matches any writing in this genre.

Le Fanu's first fiction had appeared in the *Dublin University Magazine* between 1838–40, a series of stories collected as *The Purcell Papers* (1880), where he adopted the persona of an eighteenth-century Catholic priest. Here the characteristics of his fiction were soon established, notably a skilful use of a narrator, an awareness of the supernatural, a concentration on the characters' awareness of the coming of death, a preoccupation (in which he seems to continue Maria Edgeworth's themes) with the fates of owners of big houses, a deliberate use of atmospheric landscape, and an underlying parallelism between the politics of the past and present.

Le Fanu bought three Dublin newspapers and formed the *Evening Mail* out of them; he also acquired the *Dublin University Magazine* in 1861 and sold it eight years later; he had detached himself from politics, in which his early attitudes had see-sawed; he was in turn anti-O'Connell, pro-Repeal of the Union, a supporter of Young Ireland, an unsuccessful seeker of a Tory seat. Out of his political interests had come his popular patriotic ballads 'Shamus O'Brien' and 'Pauding Crohoore'; but after his wife's death in 1858 he became 'the invisible prince', virtually a recluse in his Merrion Square house. He continued to write: his religious doubts — and those of his wife — had pervaded his thinking in the eighteen-fifties and some of the sixties. The stresses and strains of this period emerge clearly in *Seventy Years of Irish Life* (1893) by Sheridan's brother, William Richard Le Fanu. Though Sheridan Le Fanu wrote new novels and rewrote old ones, he found himself more at ease in the short story in his last years; these stories express an anticipation of eternal rest. Under the influence of his friend Patrick Kennedy, Le Fanu was using traditional folktale materials while Isaac Butt's Home Goverment Association was providing a fresh political atmosphere in Dublin.

Le Fanu did not take the Fenian rising of 1867 very seriously, but another younger novelist, Charles James Kickham (1828–82), served four years of a fourteen-year sentence for his part in it, having edited *The Irish People*, the Fenian newspaper that had built up the Fenian movement with reports of strong Irish-American support for its aims. He wrote *Sally Kavanagh* (1869) in prison, but is now remembered for *Knocknagow; or the Homes of Tipperary* (1879), a nostalgic novel with a typically complex nineteenth-century plot. It was extremely popular in its day as country people recognised something of their own life in its pages. It had a large number of characters and some effective if sentimental scenes.

A successful career of writing for American journals, and cutting a dash in New. York's literary bohemia, was abbreviated when Michael Fitzjames O'Brien (1828–62) died of a wound received in the American Civil War; he had written various stories, such as 'The Diamond Lens', out of a lurid imagination which ranged over magic microscopy and mesmerism as well as five plays, of which *A Gentleman from Ireland*, first produced in 1854, was the best known.

Sensationalism and sentimentality coloured *Hurrish* (1886) by Emily Lawless (1845–1913), a violent story of the Land League period set in the Burren, the wild limestone country of County Clare:

> The evening was closing in, the sun sinking like a red-hot cannon-ball into the grey, cool breast of the Atlantic. . . . The western sky was clear, and almost colourless, but upon the other side, beyond the interesting Burren hills, it was a mass of finely graduated colour. A multitude of arrowy flames, like the *disjecta* of some aerial volcano, were shooting their fiery prints, one after the other, in a continuous flight across the zenith . . . .

'Red as the devil! red as the devil!' exclaims one of the characters, and there is a sudden awareness of impending trouble. This stark scenery provides a sinister background to the agrarian violence which is about to erupt again and overwhelm Hurrish and his family; the general theme is the relationship of the Irish tenant to English law; and though the melodramatic action can be over-crude the drawing of the simplistic characters makes the novel both moving and memorable. Of her other nine novels, Emily Lawless showed originality in placing *Grania* (1892), a romantic tale, in the very realistically described ambience of the Aran islands. She showed the ravages of war in *Maelcho* (1894), which deals with the Desmond rebellion, and in *With Essex in Ireland* (1890) a work purporting to be a contemporary document. Two poems, 'After Aughrim' and 'Clare Coast', included in *With the Wild Geese* (1902), her collection of lyrics and ballads, are striking. She obviously found her best inspiration in the bare, even barren places of the west, and in the people who fought for a living there or were forced to emigrate:

> See, cold island, we stand
> Here tonight on your shore,
> Tonight, but never again;
> Lingering a moment more.
> See, beneath us our boat
> Tugs at its tightening chain,
> Holds out its sail to the breeze,
> Pants to be gone again.
> Off then with shouts and mirth,
> Off with laughter and jests,
> Mirth and song on our lips,
> Hearts like lead in our breasts.

Many hearts have beaten faster when reading *Dracula*, the novel by Bram (Abraham) Stoker (1847–1912), a Dubliner who after a distinguished career at Trinity was called to the Bar and entered the civil service. His love of the theatre, however, led him to act as secretary and general factotum to Sir Henry Irving from 1878 on. He wrote several novels, *The Snake's Pass* (1891) being set in Mayo, but *Dracula* (1897) is the novel for which he will remain known, with its macabre ghoulishness, the melodramatic doings of Count Dracula, the vampire, in London and in his castle set in the romantic Transylvanian scenery. *Dracula* was influenced, obviously, by Sheridan Le Fanu's vampire story *Carmilla*, and the genre in

Ireland probably goes back to Maturin's *Melmoth the Wanderer*.

The violence of life in the west of Ireland which Emily Lawless had interpreted in fiction was given expression in verse by William Allingham (1824–89), who treated it with searching realism and sympathetic understanding in his *Laurence Bloomfield in Ireland* (1864), a Crabbe-like picture, and in 2,300 heroic couplets too, of a young, liberal Irish landlord in England, a hated land agent who is murdered, and a peasant who joins the Ribbonmen. There are police and bailiffs, poverty and evictions, for this is indeed the life of the cot 'as truth will paint it and as bards will not'. And yet Allingham is best known for his anthology pieces, 'The Fairies', for instance with its light touch:

> Up the airy mountain
> Down the rushy glen
> We daren't go a-hunting
> For fear of little men;
> Wee folk, good folk
> Trooping all together;
> Green jacket, red cap
> And white owl's feather.

In 'The Winding Banks of Erne: or, the Emigrant's adieu to Ballyshannon' he wrote lovingly of Ballyshannon (where he grew up and for some years worked as a customs officer). In this poem he transmits his affection through the names of the local places

> The music of the waterfall, the mirror of the tide,
> When all the green-hill'd harbour is full from side to side —
> From Portnasun to Bulliebawns, and round the Abbey Bay,
> From rocky Inis Saimer to Coolnargit sandhills grey . . .

Though he did not fully fit into Victorian life in England Allingham had Victorian tastes; when he moved to England he virtually worshipped Tennyson, who was often boorishly rude to him, as *William Allingham, a Diary* (1907) clearly shows in its modestly charming way. His shorter poems exhibit an effective capacity for creating atmosphere, as in 'Ruins at Sunset', 'The Ruined Chapel', and 'After Sunset'; while his strong visual sense is memorable in 'A Mill':

> Two leaps the water from its race
> Made to the brook below,
> The first leap it was curving glass
> The second bounding snow . . . .

The attractive nature of this very Victorian man emerges in the innocent simplicity of 'Four Ducks on a Pond':

> Four ducks on a pond,
> A grass-bank beyond,
> A blue sky of spring
> White clouds on the wing;
> What a little thing
> To remember for years —
> To remember with tears!

Thomas Caulfield Irwin (1823—92) was also influenced by Tennyson; his poetry is decidedly uneven, but well worth sifting for occasional brilliant passages of description, neo-logistic and effective forcing of language to respond to his needs, and some flowing runs of magical verse.

John Francis O'Donnell (1837—74) wrote with too great facility; in his work the effect of Tennyson produced some glibness, though his capacity for close observation can be rewarding:

> Soft sleeps the village in the maze
> Of dreamy elm and sycamore
> Soft slides the river's rosy tide
> Through blossomed edges by the shore,
> Rushes, and pendent willows hoar.
> The little boat moored in the cove
> Takes no pulsation from the stream,
> But shadowed on the water lies
> The lovely image of a dream.

Many of these nineteenth-century minor poets had tended, naturally enough, to be swept along in the current of English romantic verse. There had been even more reason for drama-tists to seek an audience in England. Richard Lawlor Shiel (1791—1851), for instance, who turned to writing plays while waiting for briefs, had followed up the success of *Adelaide, or the Emigrants* in Dublin in 1814 with three plays that were to London's liking. These were *The Apostate* (1817), *Bellamira* (1818) and *Evadne* (1819). But despite writing two more plays, his practice at the Bar (his *Sketches of the Irish Bar* (1854) seem livelier now than his drama) and politics ended a literary career which was largely of contemporary interest. James Sheridan Knowles (1784–1862) achieved a greater success, with more melodramatic exuberance, in *Virginia* (1820), *William Tell* (1825), *The Hunchback* (1832) and *The Love Chase* (1837).

Melodrama, however, reached its peak in the nineteenth century with Dion Boucicault (1820–90), whose *London Assurance* (1841) was a comedy which achieved outstanding success. Boucicault was the natural child of a Dr Dionysius Lardner and George Darley's sister (who separated from her husband Samuel Boursiquot in 1819). Born in Dublin, he lived in France for some years, then returned to England, to leave for the United States in the early eighteen-fifties. There he developed an ability to present a current situation melodramatically and usually with a startling climax — as with the famous heroine tied to the railway track.

He moved to more pathetic Irish subject matter in *The Colleen Bawn or, The Brides of Garryowen* (1860) which later became an operetta, *The Lily of Killarney* (1867), and he followed this with such successes as *Arrah-na-Pogue; or, The Wicklow Wedding* (1864) and *The Shaughraun* (1881). Boucicault toured with his own company; he managed other touring companies at the same time; and he made a great deal of money through his activities. In all he probably wrote, adapted or translated about one hundred and fifty plays. His productions were lavish and efficiently mounted; he captivated vast audiences, and had a considerable influence as actor-manager. But after he returned to New York in 1872 his fortunes and his influence had declined. His own plays, however, sometimes sentimental as well as melodramatic, were full of lively, often witty, dialogue (his own remarks could be amusing: 'None but the brave deserve the fair, and none but the brave can live with some of them') and their characters have a certain charm. They are still played upon occasion, and their vitality, their lively and vigorous dialogue demonstrate how Boucicault was able to reverse the role of the stage Irishman so successfully, making him no longer an inevitable butt. Despite some boasting and addiction to alcohol, he can now also appear as an able as well as an amusing character.

The theatrical as well as the literary world appealed to the Cork-born painter Daniel Maclise (?1806/8–70) whose work included many Shakespearian subjects as well as an excellent portrait of his friend Charles Dickens. His narrative paintings were skilfully executed on a large scale and remain worthy of admiration. As Bruce Arnold has pointed out, there was great variety in the work of Irish artists in the latter half of the nineteenth century, in landscape, historical and genre painting. Like Maclise, the genre painter William Mulready (1786–1863) lived mainly in England; he produced some of the finest Victorian nudes (which were, incidentally, highly admired by Queen Victoria); these were delicately voluptuous, executed with an admirable balance between outline and shading. During the period John Henry Foley (1818–74) created some of Ireland's best sculpture. His statues of Burke and Goldsmith, particularly the latter, outside Trinity College, and his Daniel O'Connell, manage to be both intimate and impressive.

V Ends and beginnings

Several writers whose genius was not immediately recognised began to be published in the eighteen-eighties: George Moore (1852–1933), Oscar Wilde (1854–1900), George Bernard Shaw (1856–1950), and William Butler Yeats (1865–1939). Moore was to learn the beginnings of his novelist's craft from the French naturalists, Flaubert and Zola, to try out his attitudes to Ireland as a subject for fiction in *A Drama in Muslin* in 1886. Then, after having established himself as a highly successful writer with *Esther Waters* (1894), he returned to Ireland for the first years of the twentieth century to join in the literary movement, the literary renaissance begun and dominated by Yeats in the nineties. Moore strongly sympathised with Douglas Hyde's (1860–1949) contemporaneous efforts to revive and preserve Irish, expressed through the founding of the Gaelic League in 1893. Wilde and Shaw were to continue in the line of those eighteenth-century Anglo-Irish dramatists who had sought their audiences in London; like them they were to exploit the conventions of the comedy of manners but more self-consciously, at times almost paradoxically inverting them. But while Shaw could write within that tradition he was also experimenting, using the theatre as a means of expressing his own deeply serious views out of a basic puritanism and as a means of educating his audiences into a new self-awareness. Yeats and Hyde sought to create an awareness of the richness of Irish tradition, Hyde of the wealth of Irish literature, available in both oral and written Irish, and Yeats of the traditions expressed in fairy and folk tales, in legends and in the mythological material he found in translations of Irish literature into English.

The full strength of Moore, Shaw, Hyde and Yeats became clear in the eighteen-nineties, but their effect upon the twentieth century marks them out as modern writers and they will subsequently be considered as such, while Wilde, who represents virtually the final fling of Anglo-Irish writing in the genre of the comedy of manners, is obviously a man of the late nineteenth century, particularly in its aesthetic phase. He was the son of Sir William Wilde and 'Speranza' (Lady Wilde, née Jane Francesca Elgee, 1826–96) who, apart from publishing ardent nationalist verse and prose under this pen name in *The Nation* which included many poems by women – her *Poems* appeared in 1864 – had also written several works on folklore, notably *Ancient Legends of Ireland* (1887). When he was an undergraduate at Trinity College, Dublin, he was reputedly told by the formidable wit and scholar John Pentland Mahaffy, a Fellow and later Provost of the College, that he had better go to Oxford, on the grounds that he was not clever enough for them at Trinity College, Dublin. Wilde followed this advice and became an aesthete, rebelling à la Walter Pater and the American painter Whistler, on the lines begun and established by the Pre-Raphaelites, against conventional tastes in art, letters and morality. From Oxford, where he won the Newdigate Prize at the climax of a highly successful career, he proceeded to conquer the world of London society. Clad in velvet knee-breeches, silk stockings, and a flowing bow tie, he became known as a witty, iconoclastic conversationalist, amazing society with unconventional quips and eipgrams. He was one of the first Anglo-Irish writers to venture into America, using to advantage his artificial, stylised skills as a speaker.

His first play was not a success, but after *Lord Arthur*

Savile's Crime (1887) and the superb children's fairy tales of *The Happy Prince and Other Tales* (1888) Wilde became recognised in the nineties for his brilliance: he crammed into five years his dialogues on *The Critic as Artist* (included in *Intentions*, 1891); his sinister novel *The Picture of Dorian Gray* (1891, originally published in *Lippincott's Monthly Magazine* in 1890); the comedy of *Lady Windermere's Fan*, produced in 1892, and the erotic tragedy *Salomé* (1893); this was refused a licence in the United Kingdom, and produced in Paris in 1896; it was translated by Lord Alfred Douglas in 1894; the comedy *A Woman of No Importance* (staged 1893; published 1894); *The Sphinx* (1894), a long lyric; and the two comedies staged in 1895, *An Ideal Husband* and *The Importance of Being Earnest*.

Wilde's trial at the Old Bailey toppled him from Fortune's wheel in 1895; his essay on Shakespeare's Sonnets, 'The Portrait of Mr W. H.', had been a sign of his growing interest in sexual inversion. His friendship with Lord Alfred Douglas was ill-fated, and he had become reckless in his homosexuality. He was sentenced to two years' hard labour, ostracised from society, and died in Paris in 1900 at the age of forty-six. *The Ballad of Reading Gaol* (1898) is moving and direct in its account of a prison execution:

> We tore the tarry ropes to shreds
> With blunt and bleeding nails;
> We rubbed the doors, and scrubbed the floors,
> And cleaned the shining rails:
> And, rank by rank, we soaped the plank,
> And clattered with the pails.
>
> We sewed the sacks, we broke the stones,
> We turned the dusty drill;
> We banged the tins, and bawled the hymns,
> And sweated on the mill:
> But in the heart of every man
> Terror was lying still.

Elsewhere Wilde wrote with feeling that

> Prison life makes one see people and things as they are. That is why it turns one to stone. It is the people outside who are deceived by the illusions of life in constant motion. They revolve with life and contribute to its unreality. We who are immobile both see and know.

De Profundis (1905), part of a long letter written to Lord Alfred Douglas from prison in 1897, reveals more of Wilde's grandiose but poignant artificiality:

> Society, as we have constituted it, will have no place for me, has none to offer; but Nature, whose sweet rains fall on unjust and just alike, will have clefts in the rocks where I may hide, and secret valleys in whose silence I may feel undisturbed.

Wilde was the maker of epigrams *par excellence*: to love oneself, he wrote, is the beginning of a life-long romance; and the characters in his comedies very obviously delight in presenting themselves wittily. His own phrase 'Nothing that actually occurs is of the slightest importance' could be applied to them, but then, like preceding Anglo-Irish dramatists from the Restoration onwards, like Farquhar, Goldsmith and Sheridan, Wilde wanted to amuse. And, like them, he probably found much of his comedy of manners in English society. Indeed Yeats recognised that England was a strange land to this Irishman, claiming that to Wilde the aristocrats of England 'were as the nobles of Baghdad'. He chose to create amusement by reversing the orthodoxies, by surprising the audience:

> LADY BRACKNELL: I had some crumpets with Lady Harbury, who seems to me to be living entirely for pleasure now.
>
> ALGERNON: I hear her hair has turned quite gold from grief.

His plays are beautifully constructed. He put his genius, he said, into his life, his talent into his work; he was a sophisticated craftsman, and careful, hard work underlay the brilliant finish of his work. *The Importance of Being Earnest* is, quite simply, a classic comedy of manners.

4
Modern poetry

I Twilight to twentieth century

YEATS vastly overshadows other Anglo-Irish poets: indeed
the award of the Nobel Prize in 1923 may remind us of his
international standing, his achievement as one of the great
poets who have written in English. That achievement was
intimately linked with his desire to be an Irish poet, to reshape his country's intellectual attitudes by giving its mythology expression in an Irish literature in English which would
be equal to the best literature produced by European civilisation. Yeats wanted to get Irish literature away from the
propaganda, the patriotic stereotypes of young Ireland, to de-
Davisise it, in John Eglinton's phrase. And in his youth he
wished to create a popular movement, particularly through
drama, which would give Ireland a noble vision of national
culture, while at the same time expressing his own search for
belief through his magical, mystic and occult studies. 'To
Ireland in the Coming Times' claims that he is part of the
patriotic tradition, but with a difference:

> Nor may I less be counted one
> With Davis, Mangan, Ferguson,
> Because, to him who ponders well,
> My rhymes more than their rhyming tell
> Of things discovered in the deep,
> Where only body's laid asleep.

After the exciting days of his popularity in the initial
stages of the literary revival in the nineties when, often
influenced by him, many poets and poetesses wrote in
Twilight mood, he came up against an opposing force. This
had a different recipe for Ireland's regeneration — the Irish-
Ireland movement — which ehoed Davis's ideas that Irish was
essential for the preservation and regeneration of Ireland.

Hyde's *Love Songs of Connacht* which, like Charlotte Brooke's *Reliques* earlier, gave the originals as well as translations from the Irish, had appeared in 1893, the year the Gaelic League was founded, and they acted as a catalyst for the growth of this cultural nationalism. Its extreme aims were put in *The Leader*, founded by D. P. Moran in 1900, and in his book *The Philosophy of Irish Ireland* (1905). Out of the intellectual ferment which followed the death of Parnell came, as F. S. L. Lyons has pointed out so cogently in *Culture and Anarchy in Ireland 1890–1939* (1980), the quarrel between an Irish Ireland 'which insisted that all who were not with it were against it', and an Anglo–Irish Ireland, which fought desperately to establish a common ground between the Gaelic and the English cultures and to call that common ground simply 'Irish'. And out of the quarrel came Yeats's middle period of disillusion when, his anger stimulated by the attack made in the Abbey by extreme, puritanical nationalists on Synge's plays and by the reception given to Sir Hugh Lane's offer of his pictures to Dublin, he reacted against his own earlier poetry of escape, of nostalgic longing and wistful idealism. He began to train his new direct poetry on to public targets. Alienated by the attitudes of the new middle-class Ireland he moved to an appreciation of aristocracy and its ability to provide enlightened patronage for art. Later, his dreams of reconciling two cultures in 'this blind bitter land' virtually over, even though he was later to become a senator in the Irish Free State and to put down roots in Galway and Dublin, he was to discover his particular intellectual ancestry in eighteenth-century Anglo-Irish writers.

In them he sought sanction for his desire to see Ireland using its able men, moulding its system upon them. Out of the period from his marriage in 1917 to his death in 1939 came the great poetry, supremely personal in its treatment of its subjects: love, the threat to civilisation, his vision of history and personality, his hatred of old age, his ennobling regard for his friends, his assessment of his art and of himself. His poetry, written over a long period from his seventeenth to his seventy-third year, increased in vitality: as he grew older his muse did indeed grow younger; and this vast creative energy made emulation difficult, virtually impossible for younger, lesser poets. Yeats himself had found a way to escape

from under the spreading tree of English Victorian poetry by
turning to Irish folklore, legend and mythology. But none of
those who were of his age or followed him in Ireland could
approach, let alone match the rare achievement of his particular genius in exploring and exploiting this heritage of Irish
tradition. Thus when the poets of the Twilight period are
surveyed — T. W. Rolleston, Jane Barlow, Katharine Tynan,
Alice Milligan, Rose Kavanagh, Ethna Carbery, Nora Hooper
and Seumas O'Sullivan, to name but a few of them — there
seems ample reason for Yeats's very human raging by 1914 at
'the fools' who wore 'as though they'd wrought it' the coat
that he had since 1889:

> . . . covered with embroideries
> Out of old mythologies
> From heel to throat . . . .

Of Yeats's contemporaries AE, George Russell (1867–
1935), two years younger, who had seemed likely to rival
him when his first volume, *Homeward: Songs by the way* was
published in 1894, failed to develop his visionary sense in
succeeding volumes, and his *Collected Poems* (1913) remind
us that poetry was but one of AE's many modes of expression. Though he was to publish four other single volumes (in
some of which his pacific nature opposed itself to the violence
of war and civil war) and a volume of *Selected Poems* by
1935, the year he died, he remains, despite one or two very
good poems, a minor poet.

Several poets born about the beginning of the eighteen-
eighties and therefore about fifteen years younger than Yeats
— Joseph Campbell, Padraic Colum, and James Stephens —
left Ireland (in 1924, 1914 and 1924 respectively) and to a
certain extent their poetic powers decreased or disappeared
once they left: a reason why, perhaps, the decade after the
Irish Free State was established is not particularly notable for
poetry other than that of Yeats. Patrick Pearse was of the
same generation as these three poets, and demonstrated an
interesting talent in his poems, his Irish ones being better
than his English, but his career, like that of other promising
poets — Thomas MacDonagh and Joseph Mary Plunkett —
was cut short by a firing squad in 1916, while a younger poet
of considerable ability, Francis Ledwidge, was killed in

France in 1917. Gogarty, a year older than Campbell and Pearse, revealed himself in the nineteen-twenties and, despite critical over-reaction to Yeats's over-praising him in his Introduction to the *Oxford Book of Modern Verse 1892–1935*, his poetry is attractive and polished in its classical manner.

Approximately fifteen years younger than these poets were Austin Clarke and F. R. Higgins. Clarke exemplifies the overshadowing effect of Yeats, for he did not come into his own until well after the older poet's death, being decidedly conscious of Yeats's masterly achievement. Higgins, like Gogarty, was encouraged by Yeats, who enjoyed their Rabelaisian, outrageous conversation, but whereas Gogarty exhibited an insouciantly classical control in his poetry Higgins overflowed exuberantly. His first three most interesting volumes, published in the twenties, went beyond Campbell, Pearse, Colum and Stephens in an enthusiasm for the folk. Though born in Mayo, Higgins grew up in Meath, and thus provides yet another example of an eastern Protestant finding in the Irish-speaking Catholic west of Ireland a strange, richly sensuous source of intense vitality: he idealised the peasantry, but by the thirties he seems to have lost interest in the subject, turning instead to a more intellectual symbolic and eventually superficial mode.

The list of Anglo-Irish poets Yeats included in the *Oxford Book of Modern Verse 1892–1935* is significant. Of the older writers we find Lady Gregory, Yeats himself, and AE; of the next generation Gogarty, Campbell, Colum and Joyce; of poets born in the nineties MacGreevy and F. R. Higgins (but *not* Austin Clarke), and then, of those born in the twentieth century, Frank O'Connor, whose excellent work in translating from Irish poetry Yeats had encouraged, Cecil Day-Lewis and Louis MacNeice. Both Day-Lewis and MacNeice became conscious of their Anglo-Irish heritage, MacNeice earlier in his career than Day-Lewis: though their poetry is largely centred upon English life, to a certain extent upon politics in the thirties but later upon much more personal, individualistic attitudes to life, they both were affected by their Irish backgrounds, MacNiece particularly so. While English intellectual life with all its post-war disillusionment and foreboding for the future influenced both of them, different forces acted upon Thomas McGreevy and Denis Devlin and, later, their friend Brian Coffey. Continental (particularly French) ideas, as well as those of Eliot and Pound, can be clearly detected in their work written in the nineteen-thirties and forties. Mac-Neice's contemporary John Hewitt concentrated upon northern Irish themes until he moved to England for a time, while the work of poets two years younger, Padraic Fallon and Bryan Guinness, is typical of much modern writing in its variety of subject and technical ability.

Technical ability was also the dominant aspect of Austin Clarke's early work; but the complexity of the models afforded by Irish poetry demanded too much of him and his readers in his early work, despite the favourable reception given to his first volume *The Vengeance of Fionn* of 1917. He was probably too late for success in his retelling of the Irish legends, no matter how accomplished his technique could be; by this time Yeats was 'walking naked', and Austin Clarke was to exploit in the conflict of body and spirit material more suitable to his needs; he placed this conflict in the world of medieval Ireland, basing it upon Irish satire of the medieval Church. Clarke's *Collected Poems* appeared in 1936; he returned to Ireland from London in 1937 and became preoccupied with verse drama. It was not until 1955, when *Ancient Lights* was published, that it was revealed how effective his sense of moral outrage could be. He matched a correct length of poetic exposure to the subject of contemporary Irish life in many of the poems he poured out in such profusion in the nineteen-fifties and sixties, their satire marked by conscious craftsmanship.

Craftsmanship sometimes seems lacking in the middle work of Patrick Kavanagh, but he thought deeply about the nature of poetry, and his early poems in *The Ploughman* (1936) reflect this. *The Great Hunger* (1942), however, marks the same kind of impulse that motivated Austin Clarke's later poetry. Whereas Clarke found the smug assumptions of modern urban middle-class Ireland sadly wanting, so Kavanagh dispelled up any vestiges of Twilight mistiness that might still have clung to Irish rural life.

Whereas Joyce had chosen silence, exile and cunning as his defence against a clerically controlled society, both Clarke and Kavanagh spoke out at home, and though their cunning sometimes did not prevent them going on too long, their careful attention to words makes much of their poetry memorable. *The Great Hunger* recounts the failure of Kavanagh's small farmer, Maguire, to escape from the prison of poverty, the norms of piety and routine, and the suppression of sensuality, from the sheer, stark barrenness of his life.

Kavanagh, however, having developed the satiric ferocity of 'The Paddiad' in 1949, an attack on the mediocrity of contemporary Irish poets, and indulged in other satiric outbursts, changed, after a lung operation, into a poet of reflective wisdom. His use of the sonnet form now gives the firm control his previous poems often lacked. The simplicity of these poems contains originality, a personal comment, and a sense of freedom. *Come dance with Kitty Stobling and other poems* (1960) is a good example of how poetry had become emancipated from the past modes of the Irish renaissance, just as Clarke's later work was to focus freely upon the actuality of the present, though he lacked the intellectual toughness and the ultimate aesthetic coherence of Yeats.

II William Butler Yeats

To Yeats life itself was perennially intertwined with Ireland and its literature. He was sharply aware as a child of the differences between Irish and English life, not only through living both in the west of Ireland in Sligo, with his Pollexfen grandparents, and in London, and by going to school both in Hammersmith and in Dublin, but also as a result of hearing these differences frequently discussed by his father. John Butler Yeats (1839–1922), who comes alive in all his complexity in William M. Murphy's *Prodigal Father, The Life of John Butler Yeats* (1978), was an inveterate and lively conversationalist, a stimulating letter-writer and an artist the merits of whose paintings are not universally recognised, though the virtues of his sensitive pencil drawings are increasingly admired. He brought his son up with the idea that a gentleman is not concerned with 'getting on'. He also stimulated his interest in poetry, reciting it aloud to him and discussing it incessantly.

When Yeats decided that he would become a poet he wanted, out of a fierce love of the place, to write about Sligo as Allingham had about Ballyshannon. Out of sympathy with English 'mental images' as a schoolboy in England, Yeats discovered instead the excitement of Gaelic mythology and literature which he read in the translations of earlier scholars, lent to him by John O'Leary, an old Fenian leader who had returned to Dublin from exile in 1885. O'Leary's *Recollections of Fenians and Fenianism* (1896) conveys something of this dignity and detachment, and explains something of his influence over the youthful Yeats who, steeped in Irish folklore, was also deeply affected by the writings of Standish James O'Grady (1846–1928). O'Grady's own interest had been stimulated by reading Sylvester O'Halloran's *A General History of Ireland*. Eugene O'Curry's *Manners and Customs of the Ancient Irish* (1873) also had a considerable effect on him. O'Grady's own *History of Ireland: Heroic Period* (1878; 1880) contained versions of Irish mythological tales and those of the Ulster Red Branch cycle: then came his *History of Ireland: Critical and Philosophical* (1880). Next he turned to writing novels about Ireland's history and mythology: *Red Hugh's Captivity* (1889), *Finn and His Companions* (1892), *In the Wake of King James* (1896), and *The Flight of the Eagle* (1897). He dealt somewhat stiffly with Cuchulain in a trilogy (1894, 1901, 1920) and wrote boys' adventure stories as well as editing a journal, *The All-Ireland Review* (1900–7). His writing excited younger writers, not so much by its quality — for it is often verbose (Yeats called it a 'kind of blazing torch light'); he tended to emasculate the original material and foist morality upon it — but by the sense of excitement he conveyed in discovering Gaelic Ireland's literary and cultural heritage. He did this to such an extent that he was called by some the father of the Irish literary revival.

He is not, incidentally, to be confused with his cousin, Standish Hayes O'Grady (1832–1915), who was a friend of O'Curry and O'Donovan when he was at Trinity College: after thirty years as an engineer in the United States he translated tales from old Irish manuscripts in *Silva Gadelica* (1892) and he also compiled a *Catalogue of Irish Manuscripts in the British Museum* which was completed after his death by Robin Flower (1881–1946), who was himself the author of *The Western Island; or, The Great Blasket* (1944), an appreciative account of island life, as well as an eminently readable posthumous book *The Irish Tradition* (1947), and of two excellent volumes of translations, *Love's Bitter-Sweet* (1925) and *Poems and Translations* (1931).

Another influence on Yeats was the work of Sir Samuel Ferguson. Yeats's first published prose was an enthusiastic review of Ferguson's poetry in October 1886; and in another longer article on him in the *Dublin University Review* he began by attacking Irish critics for their indifference to Irish writers, ending with an appeal to Irish readers to study the legends of their own country, addressing himself to those young men whom the emotion of patriotism 'has lifted into that world of selfless passion in which heroic deeds are possible and heroic poetry credible'. As well as discovering James Clarence Mangan, Yeats read deeply in translations from the Gaelic by scholars such as O'Curry, O'Donovan, and Brian O'Looney.

Yeats's own *Mosada*, a verse play, was published in pamphlet form in 1886. His early gentle wistful poetry at first echoed the arcadianism of Spenser, but in describing places in Sligo he expressed his own personality and interests, especially when he wrote of the supernatural. There, in the Sligo described in his novel *John Sherman* (1891), he busied himself collecting folktales and tales of fairy belief, some of which appeared in his *Fairy and Folk Tales of the Irish Peasantry* (1888) and *Irish Fairy Tales* (1892). In 1889 came *The Wanderings of Oisin*, a poem in three parts, recounting the adventures of the human hero Oisin who followed the immortal Niamh to three islands, of Living, of Victories, and of Forgetfulness. This poetry with its apparently vague symbolism marks Yeats's clear emergence with a distinctive voice: it is rich in imagery, preoccupied with the passing of time, a tapestry which converts the Gaelic story which Yeats read in various translations into a cloudy dreamy delicacy, apart from the hero's final raging at his return in old age to a far feebler civilisation.

In 1889, when he was twenty-three, Yeats fell deeply in love with Maud Gonne, the daughter of an English colonel, who was a fervent Irish nationalist. He wrote his play *The Countess Kathleen* (1892; later spelt as *Cathleen*) for her, trying to fuse Christian and pagan traditions, and to convey his own feelings in the person of the poet Kevin (later Aleel) who stresses the claims of subjective life. He poured out love poems to her; they were devoted but defeatist, as in 'He wishes for the Cloths of Heaven':

> Had I the heavens' embroidered cloths,
> Enwrought with golden and silver light,
> The blue and the dim and the dark cloths
> Of night and light and the half-light,
> I would spread the cloths under your feet:
> But I, being poor, have only my dreams;
> I have spread my dreams under your feet;
> Tread softly because you tread on my dreams.

Despite his poverty he proposed to her in 1891, and continued to do so at intervals; she always refused him but wished him to remain a close friend. He shared with her his hopes of creating an Irish order of mysteries. He continued to want to combine Christian and pagan material in his writing, as the prose of *The Celtic Twilight* (1893) and the complex imagery of a poem such as *The Secret Rose* show. The rose in his poems of the eighteen-nineties, in *The Countess Kathleen and various legends and lyrics* (1892), *The Secret Rose* (1897) and *The Wind Among the Reeds* (1899), for instance, stood for Ireland — as in the work of earlier Irish poets — but also as a symbol of the four-petalled rose that went with the Cross of the Rosicrucian system; it also symbolised spiritual beauty, and Maud Gonne. Apart from its mixture of Christian and pagan elements when the pagan King Conchobar dies of frenzy incurred by his druid telling him that Jesus Christ was being crucified by the Jews, 'The Secret Rose' contained elements of Yeats's continuous attempts to find a personal belief. From his teens on he explored Buddhism, mystic writings, Theosophy, magic, Rosicrucianism, and the Kabbala; he edited Blake, and he joined the magical order of the Golden Dawn. But he had a powerfully sceptical cast to his mind as well, and was torn between contrarieties, so at first he allowed his mystical ideas into his poetry with caution. Yeats was equally excited by Gaelic mythology. Many characters from it — for instance Fergus and Maeve, Deirdre and King Conor of Ulster, and, particularly, the hero Cuchulain — people his poems, and the poetry increasingly became more complex, indeed esoteric in its symbolism as he incorporated into it the results of his wide and deep reading in both Gaelic mythology and the occult tradition.

In the eighteen-nineties Yeats was influenced by the English poets of the Rhymers' Club, by Lionel Johnson and Ernest Dowson, and particularly by his friend Arthur Symons through whom he learned about the French symbolists. After the split in the Irish parliamentary party and Parnell's death in 1891 Yeats founded literary societies in Dublin and London, thinking the lull in politics would permit a literary movement to develop effectively, that a cultural renaissance could be created to reshape Irish minds. English art was jaded, Irish art could draw upon an old mythology with fresh energy. He was determined to be an Irish poet and saw himself following Davis, Mangan and Ferguson; but he had also to create an audience and to encourage others to write. His literary journalism, his propaganda, his editing work of the nineties was large in scope (as the two volumes of his *Uncollected Prose* and his *Letters* clearly demonstrate); he himself became involved in revolutionary politics, only to be disillusioned by the Jubilee riots of 1897 in Dublin (which he described graphically in 'The Stirring of the Bones' in his *Autobiographies*), and even more so by Maud Gonne's unexpected marriage in 1903 to John MacBride, an extreme nationalist who had fought against the British in South Africa.

The poems in *The Wind Among the Reeds* had pushed his ideas of restricting poetry to beauty, to essences, to what was, in effect, a suggestive, a deliberately esoteric symbolism, as far as was possible. This was a poetry concerned with beauty, excluding the ugly, the contemporary from its melancholic shadows. It was an adjectival poetry: grey, misty, dim, piteous, lonely ... His much revised play *The Shadowy Waters* (1900) was an equally symbolic drama of escape, of the heroic gesture, the union of hearts, and love of superhuman kind. His prose, too, had become elaborate: the style of the stories of *The Secret Rose* (1897) was complex and suggestive; it blended Pre-Raphaelite detail with Irish material in a richly patterned manner, which became even more complex and involved in the essays of *Ideas of Good and Evil* (1903) which show the influence of Wilde and, above all, Pater. The poems of *In the Seven Woods* (1904), however, record the effects of the passing of time — the beloved's hair has 'threads of grey' — and of the passing of hope — 'who would have thought/It all, and more than all, would come to naught/And that dear words meant nothing?' Yet in 'Red Hanrahan's Song about Ireland', he can still hymn Maud Gonne as 'Cathleen, the spirit of Ireland', in the romantically dramatic setting of Sligo:

> The old brown thorn-trees break in two high over
>   Cummen Strand
> Under a bitter black wind that blows from the left hand;
> Our courage breaks like an old tree in a black wind and dies,
> But we have hidden in our hearts the flame out of the eyes
> Of Cathleen, the daughter of Houlihan.

In 1896 Yeats, accompanied by Arthur Symons, had been staying with George Moore's friend Edward Martyn at Tulira Castle; on that visit to the west he met Lady Gregory, and visited the Aran islands — later that year recommending John Millington Synge, who was then living in Paris, to find his subject matter there. The group which was to set modern Irish drama in motion had now met and found they had ideals in common. The Irish Literary Theatre, with Moore, Martyn and Yeats as directors, was established. Yeats's *The Countess Cathleen* and Martyn's *The Heather Field* were staged in 1899. In 1902 Maud Gonne played in Yeats's *Cathleen ni Houlihan*, a play which had an electrifying effect upon its audience; in old age Yeats was to ask himself in 'The Man and the Echo':

> Did that play of mine send out
> Certain men the English shot?

The Irish National Dramatic Society replaced the Irish Literary Theatre, the new group containing the Fay brothers, and thus giving Yeats the gifted group of Irish actors and actresses he had wanted. Another aim which he shared with Lady Gregory was to bring the poetical tradition of the speech of the countryside to the city; out of this came his plays *The Pot of Broth* and *The Hour-Glass*. But when the Abbey Theatre was opened in 1904 Yeats was writing very different plays. *The King's Threshold* (1904), performed in 1903, founded on a middle Irish story of poets at the court of King Guaire in Galway, explored the aristocratic role of the poet prepared to enter into the world to assert the place of poetry in the life of the whole community.

Yeats himself was ready to enter very fully into another

world: though he spent much of the year in his rooms in Woburn Buildings in London and his summers at Coole Park, he immersed himself in 'theatre business, management of men' acting as manager of the Abbey Theatre in Dublin from 1904 to 1910. This was an unselfish task, of working for the realistic plays of younger dramatists, which proved more popular with the Abbey audiences and were so unlike his own continuing preoccupation with the heroic. In *On Baile's Strand* (1903) the hero Cuchulain unwittingly kills his own son. Into this verse-tragedy Yeats put the Fool and the Blind Man, who are shadows of Cuchulain and King Conchubar, and reflect the abstract ideas that were persecuting Yeats himself. These characters are in the play, yet out of it; they convey an increasing interest in extremes, oppositions, and the play's irony and its inexorability are impressive. *Deirdre* (1907) has great dignity in its treatment of the treachery of Conchubar which leads to Naoise's death and Deirdre's suicide; there is a sinister quality about the play's suspense, its imaginative intensity.

Irony became farce in *The Green Helmet* (1910), founded on an old Irish tale, *The Feast of Bricriu*; Yeats's capacity for the unusual had already irradiated *The Unicorn from the Stars* (1908) with its vision of the unicorns which will destroy the existing order. This subject — the replacement of one era by another — made *The Player Queen* (1922), originally a verse-tragedy, into a wild comedy. It has moments of very effective farce; but tragedy underlies its action; it is a play that works well on the stage.

Yeats soon found that to provide an Irish theatre and Irish plays for it did not lead automatically to popular success. Irish audiences swayed by nationalism and politically based puritanism did not appreciate his *The Countess Cathleen* when it was produced in 1899, and the adverse reception given to Synge's plays by a politically motivated section of the Abbey audience added to Yeats's disillusionment. His barren passion for Maud Gonne seemed so many wasted dreams once she married, yet he continued to celebrate her beauty and his love of it in poetry which he stripped bare of decoration. The poems of *The Green Helmet and Other Poems* (1910) refer directly to contemporary events, while those of *Responsibilities* (1914) are the antithesis of the

Twilight and its embroideries 'out of old mythologies'. He had faced the effect of a barren passion in the volume's 'Introductory Rhymes'. In his first autobiographical book *Reveries Over Childhood and Youth* (1915) he writes in a simpler prose though it provides a selective and carefully arranged backdrop to his life. His autobiographical writings show how little his poetry had been reflecting the activity of that life, though *Responsibilities* contains such masterly, timeless poems as 'The Cold Heaven'. He now writes poetry out of disappointment and despair with passionate rhetoric, deeply distressed by the philistinism which seemed to oppose his plans for creating a new cultural outlook in Ireland. The controversy over Sir Hugh Lane's offer of his pictures to Dublin produced savage poems such as 'To a Wealthy Man who promised a Second Subscription to the Dublin Municipal Gallery if it were proved the People wanted Pictures'. This poem contrasts the attitudes of Dublin's 'wealthy men' with the Italian rulers whom Yeats had come to think ideal patrons; he speaks with disdain about the people's capacity to understand or appreciate great art; and the poem reverberates with the excitement of his having seen the art which aristocratic taste and nerve had brought into being:

> What cared Duke Ercole, that bid
> His mummers to the market-place
> What th'onion-sellers thought or did
> So that his Plautus set the pace
> For the Italian comedies?
> And Guidobaldo, when he made
> That grammar school of courtesies
> Where wit and beauty learned their trade
> Upon Urbino's windy hill,
> Had sent no runners to and fro
> That he might learn the shepherds' will.

Yeats's visit to Italy in 1907 had reinforced his belief that the aristocrat was the ideal patron. In Dublin, however, there were patrons in plenty between 1900 and 1914 to buy the paintings of William Orpen (1878–1931) whose portraits and portrait groups were matched by his nudes and lively self-portraits. His portrait of George Moore in the National Portrait Gallery is particularly good. His senior, John Lavery (1856–1941), was also popular. (Both men were knighted for their work as war artists.) Lulled by the Edwardian peace Yeats ceased to take the Irish revolutionaries seriously, but once the Easter Rising occurred in 1916 he realised at once that the leaders who had been executed by firing squad were now martyrs:

> All changed, changed utterly:
> A terrible beauty is born.

Maud Gonne's husband John MacBride was one of the leaders shot: there ensued Yeats's renewed proposal of marriage to her, followed by the idea of marrying her daughter Iseult. Then, when she refused him in 1917, he married Georgie Hyde-Lees, whom he had known for some years. Through her automatic writing came the sanction for *A Vision*, published in 1926. This book provided him with metaphors for poetry and scaffolding for his ideas about history and human personality, based upon his deep knowledge of the occult. This was a period when his poetry burst into flower again, its style now flexible enough to convey the poet's own complex personality and its reaction to the very troubled times following the Easter Rising. His attitude to drama altered again and, significantly, his four *Plays for Dancers* (1921) were written for an audience quite unlike the Abbey's; influenced by Japanese Noh Drama he sought a ritualistic art aided by music and dancing, and the first of these plays was performed in Lady Cunard's drawing room: he could do without an orthodox theatre.

Yeats's own life had, in some senses, become more orthodox. A daughter and a son were born in 1919 and 1921; he now owned a home in Ireland, having bought at Ballylee (not far from Coole Park) an old Norman tower which he and his family occupied during the summer months up to 1929:

> A winding stair, a chamber arched with stone,
> A grey stone fireplace with an open hearth,
> A candle and written page.
> Il Penseroso's Platonist toiled on
> In some like chamber, shadowing forth
> How the daemonic rage
> Imagined everything.
> Benighted travellers
> From markets and from fairs
> Have seen his midnight candle glimmering.

He returned to live in Dublin when he became a senator of the Irish Free State in 1922; he won the Nobel Prize for Poetry in 1923. The former revolutionary turned sceptic now began to write his great poetry, filled with haunting questions on love, friendship, age, death, the pressures of politics and the problems of philosophy.

Out of *A Vision's* ideas came 'The Second Coming' with its horror at coming brutality, an antithetical age with anarchy annihilating innocence — a taut symbolic poem charged with meaning. The poems of *The Tower* (1928) include 'Sailing to Byzantium', 'The Tower', 'Meditations in Time of Civil War', 'Nineteen Hundred and Nineteen', 'Leda and the Swan', 'Among School Children' and 'All Souls' Night'.

'The Tower' revolves around the problem of old age, now the poet realises that he never had a more 'excited, passionate, fantastical imagination'. He is driven to abandon the muse, to become philosophical, content with argument and abstraction, but in the second section, where he contemplates the tower and the legends of its neighbourhood, he wonders whether all the old people of the place raged as he now does against age, and, prompted by thoughts of love gained and lost, in the third section rejects the idea of the philosophers:

> I mock Plotinus' thought
> And cry in Plato's teeth,
> Death and life were not
> Till man made up the whole,
> Made lock, stock and barrel
> Out of his bitter soul . . .

Thus the personal; but in 'Meditations in Time of Civil War' his thought expands to consider the general role of violence in the maintenance of greatness, then moves to describe the tower and its inhabitants. The poem is a masterly piece of compression; here, for instance, is civil war encapsulated:

> We are closed in, and the key is turned
> On our uncertainty, somewhere
> A man is killed, or a house burned,
> Yet no clear fact to be discerned

'Nineteen Hundred and Nineteen' records the realisation

that before the First World War, there had been a false lull, false hopes of amelioration. History, however, is remorseless:

> But is there any comfort to be found?
> Man is in love and loves what vanishes,
> What more is there to say?

'Among School Children' is the result of the 'sixty-year-old smiling public man' visiting a school, where his imagination shifts from the children to memories of Maud Gonne as she was in youth and in age, and shifts to age in general and the achievement of the great, until he questions the value of life and finally affirms it in a final stanza:

> Labour is blossoming or dancing where
> The body is not bruised to pleasure soul,
> Not beauty born out of its own despair,
> Nor blear-eyed wisdom out of midnight oil.
> O chestnut-tree, great-rooted blossomer,
> Are you the leaf, the blossom or the bole?

His prose became more flexible; it is eminently readable in, for instance, the Introduction to *The Words upon the Window-Pane* (1934) with its fusing of philosophy, history, biography and criticism. His autobiographical writings continued to stylise his experiences, just as the richly textured poems of *The Tower* and *The Winding Stair and Other Poems* (1933) present a pattern of impressive imagery. The image itself is dealt with in 'Byzantium' and the metaphysical poems of this volume have a superb confidence in their questioning, just as the poems celebrating Coole Park and its owners weigh up the achievement and the passing glory with a mixture of straightforwardness and symbolic suggestiveness:

> We were the last romantics — chose for theme
> Traditional sanctity and loveliness;
> Whatever's written in what poets name
> The book of the people; whatever most can bless
> The mind of man or elevate a rhyme;
> But all is changed, that high horse riderless,
> Though mounted in that saddle Homer rode
> Where the swan drifts upon a darkening flood.

Yeats had discovered his true intellectual inheritance in the nineteen-twenties, the Anglo-Irish writers of the eighteenth century, particularly Swift and Burke. He found in them sanction for direct speech, in the Senate, in his poetry and prose — notably in *Wheels and Butterflies* which contained his excellent, theatrically effective play on Swift, *The Words upon the Window-Pane*. And then there was the outspokenness of the Crazy Jane poems, in which sexuality provided a way to unity despite its Blakean contrarieties:

> 'Fair and foul are near of kin
> And fair needs foul', I cried.

Yeats no longer used the tower as a summer residence after 1929; he moved from the centre of Dublin in 1933 to a small house at the foot of the Dublin mountains, fulfilling dreams with 'a small old house, wife, daughter, son', though he had the creative energy, the remarkable old man's frenzy to remake himself:

> Till I am Timon and Lear
> Or that William Blake
> Who beat upon the wall
> Till truth obeyed his call.

Illness pressed in upon his last years; he continued to write plays — *The Herne's Egg* (1938) seemed 'the strangest and wildest thing' he had ever written, and *Purgatory* (1939) is a *tour de force*. His mind turned upon the possible ruin of civilisation in such fine poems as 'Lapis Lazuli' or 'The Gyres', where he courageously faced the threatened loss of all he valued in artistic, in human achievement. His own course, however, still ran between opposites; there are also poems of joy, of vivid praise, as he draws his friends a little larger than life. His defiance of death moved to an awareness that he could not know the outcome of it all, in 'The Man and the Echo', a poignant poem set in Sligo questioning the worth of his life:

> There is no release
> In a bodkin or disease,
> Nor can there be work so great
> As that which cleans man's dirty slate.
> While man can still his body keep

Wine or love drug him to sleep,
Waking he thanks the Lord that he
Has body and its stupidity,
But body gone he sleeps no more,
And till his intellect grows sure
That all's arranged in one clear view,
Pursues the thoughts that I pursue,
Then stands in judgement on his soul,
And, all work done, dismisses all
Out of intellect and sight
And sinks at last into the night.

ECHO

Into the night.

MAN

O Rocky Voice,
Shall we in that great night rejoice?
What do we know but that we face
One another in this place?

But there was no need to question the achievement when he
died in 1939, for in helping to bring a regenerated nation into
its strength he had also become the leading poet of his age.

III The Celtic Twilight

Yeats had exercised his influence from an early age. An inveterate maker and joiner of societies, he had begun with the
Hermetic Society in Dublin as a schoolboy, and by the time
he published *The Celtic Twilight* in 1893, he had been encouraging other Irish writers by example and precept for
several years, so much so that the term Celtic Twilight tended
to be attached to much Irish writing in the eighteen-nineties.
One of the difficulties facing him in his propaganda for the
literary revival he was calling into being was to find sufficiently outstanding talent, operating on a level with his own.

The kind of writing his elders were producing is exemplified
in the work of his father's friend and contemporary John
Todhunter (1839–1916), a Dublin-born and -educated doctor,
who moved to London in 1874, living at Bedford Park where
he was a friend of the Yeats family. Todhunter's classical
verse plays had some success, and he wrote melancholic,

technically accomplished lyrics on Irish subjects as well as a life of Patrick Sarsfield. His *Three Irish Bardic Tales* appeared in 1896, and some of his lyrics, notably 'Aghadoe', were anthologised.

Among his contemporaries Yeats had not met many obviously outstanding writers. When he compiled *A Book of Irish Verse* (1895) 'selected from modern writers' he was only able to include poems by T. W. Rolleston, Douglas Hyde, Rose Kavanagh, Katharine Tynan, AE, and Dora Sigerson. His later enthusiastic praise of Synge and Lady Gregory was genuine because he had found in them the kind of creative minds for which he had been looking.

Among the writers of the Twilight, T. W. Rolleston (1857–1920) was a strong supporter of the literary movement, as his editing of the *Dublin University Review* and his energetic secretaryship of the London Irish Literary Society demonstrated. He was primarily a learned man; his retelling of Irish tales in *The High Deeds of Finn* (1910) and his marrying of many myths to particular places in *Myths and Legends of the Celtic Race* (1911) are worth reading. His criticism was well expressed; the *Treasury of Irish Poetry* which he edited with Stopford Brooke in 1900 was a useful anthology. His own poem 'The Dead at Clonmacnoise', from the Irish of Angus O'Gillan, is a good anthology piece; the title poem in *Sea Spray, Verses and Translations* (1909) deals dashingly with his love of canoeing in the sea around the Irish east coast, but he was not an outstanding poet. Nor was his contemporary Jane Barlow (1857–1917), another learned writer, who wrote on Irish subjects without seemingly being affected by the literary revival. Her narrative poems proved popular, her *Bog-Land Studies* (1892) going through several editions; but these melodramatic stories verge too closely upon the sentimental and pathetic, their dialect has too stage-Irish a quality, and their metres are too mechanical to appeal to modern readers. Of her many rather humdrum, over-leisurely novels *Kerrigan's Quality* (1894) is perhaps the most compact in the architectonic control applied to its lugubrious story of the unhappy Kerrigan, who has returned, wealthy, from Australia to a countryside paralysed by the after-effects of famine and evictions.

Unlike Rolleston and Jane Barlow, however, Katharine

Tynan (1861–1931) at first seemed to have great potential as a poet, her early poetry admirable in its descriptive detail and technique in *Louise de la Vallière* (1885). Yeats was a close friend of hers in the late eighteen-eighties, frequently visiting her father's farm at Clondalkin outside Dublin and writing many letters to her from London about his work.

Though there was some good nature poetry in *The Wind in the Trees* (1898), Katharine Tynan's talent did not develop a lasting depth. In her early novels — she wrote over a hundred novels in all — she often expressed social protest, putting a strongly feminine point of view in her journalism to the fore. Later she turned to more conventional historical romance. After the death of her husband in 1919 she had to work hard and fast and this pressure probably explains why little of her large output now survives to justify the expectations her early poetry aroused. She was, however, a good minor poet, a respectable craftswoman, whose energy — conveyed convincingly in her four volumes of memoirs — remains most impressive.

Another prolific writer, though not on the scale of Katharine Tynan, was Alice Milligan (1866–1953). Born in Omagh, educated at King's College, London, she edited the *Shan Van Vocht* (1896-9) with Ethna Carbery in Belfast. In 1900 the Irish Literary Theatre produced her play on Oisin, *The Last Feast of the Fianna*; she wrote two other plays on Oisin. Her *Poems* were published in 1954, and are the work of a minor and uneven talent. Ethna Carbery (Anna Isabel Johnston, 1866–1902) also wrote many stories and much verse of an ephemeral kind (the poems are collected in *The Four Winds of Eirinn*, 1902; 1918); she married Seumas MacManus (1868?–1960) whose plays and stories are of an overdone stage-Irish kind. His *The Rocky Road to Dublin* (1938) is the autobiography of a limitedly talented writer, often sentimental in his patriotism.

Susan Mitchell (1866–1926), who was AE's devoted assistant editor on *The Irish Homestead* and *The Irish Statesman*, viewed the revival with amusement; her *Aids to the Immortality of Certain Persons in Dublin: Charitably Administered* (1908) conveys something of the atmosphere of the time with satiric wit; she also contributed to *Secret Springs of Dublin Song* (1918). Her contemporary Dora

Sigerson [Mrs Clement Shorter] (1866–1918), on the other hand, was suffused with fashionable melancholia in her fairy and folk poems and ballads. She was a friend of Yeats and Katharine Tynan, and wrote religious poetry with a touch of mysticism. Syntax and metre were not her strong points, but her patriotic romanticism appealed to many. She and her English husband felt her writing was insufficiently appreciated; she suggested that her gravestone should carry the legend 'a dead failure'.

Eva Gore-Booth (1870–1926), whose *Complete Poems* was published in 1929, wrote ten volumes of verse, 'The Little Waves of Breffny' becoming an anthology piece. The poems of Nora Hopper [Mrs Chesson] (1871–1906) were equally inspired by the Celtic Twilight. She wrote novels, and a libretto for *The Sea Swan*, an opera performed in Dublin in 1903. Her poems were misty in feeling, slight and delicate in their depiction of fairies and lamenting lovers. *Ballads in Prose* (1894) and *Under Quicken Boughs* (1896) probably contain the best work of an evanescent talent. Alice Furlong (*b.* 1875?) wrote many poems and stories, Irish in their context, her *Tales of Fairy Folks Queens and Heroes* (1907) also obviously influenced by the Twilight fashion. Though of a younger generation, Mary Devenport O'Neill (1879–1967; her husband Joseph O'Neill wrote novels) was also affected by it, especially in her plays. Her shorter poems in *Prometheus and Other Poems* (1929) are more effective.

One of the poets praised by AE, to Yeats's disgust since he saw them as echoing his own early 'Twilight poetry', was Seumas O'Sullivan (James Sullivan Starkey, 1879–1958) whose poetry is the epitome of the Celtic Twilight. Indeed his first volume was called *The Twilight People* (1905), and it echoed the kind of poetry Yeats had developed in the nineties and had now virtually left behind. *Verses: Sacred and Profane* (1908) were atmospherically melancholic and vague, though *The Earth-Lover and Other Verses* (1909) did deal with some subjects of street life. There is nationalistic feeling in *Requiem and Other Poems* (1917).

O'Sullivan's own gift to Ireland was his editing *The Dublin Magazine* which he founded in 1923 and edited till his death in 1958. In it he encouraged young writers as well as publishing the established. The magazine, elegantly produced, acted as a

valuable element in Irish cultural life, and its editing was
carried out with unselfish energy. O'Sullivan's volume of
Collected Poems was published in 1940; some of the essays
collected in *The Rose and the Bottle* (1946) reveal the
speculative and learned quality of his mind: his love of
Dublin was shared by his wife, the artist Estella Solomons,
whose etchings conveyed much of the city's historical heritage.

IV Douglas Hyde and AE

The difference between the poetry of the Celtic Twilight and
poetry nourished more directly upon Irish originals can be
traced back to the earlier outstanding interpreters and translators, Callanan, Mangan and Sir Samuel Ferguson and,
especially, after them, to Douglas Hyde. When Yeats had
proclaimed his purposes in 'To Ireland in the Coming Times',
included in *The Countess Kathleen* (1892), he was following
nineteenth-century writers who gave expression to Irish
literature and culture in English, but, never knowing any Irish
himself, his knowledge of the Irish legends had depended
upon the work of translators, just as his interest in the folklore of the west of Ireland had depended upon English
speakers. Many of the Celtic Twilight writers also had no
Irish; though Father Eugene O'Growney's (1863—99) *Simple
Lessons in Irish* (1894) proved popular, women writers would
have found it hard to obtain opportunities to study Irish
seriously.

The experience of Douglas Hyde (1860—1949), however,
was very different, and from his thirties to his middle-fifties
he exercised a profound influence upon the strand of Irish
intellectual life that centred upon the Irish language (we
catch glimpses of this enthusiastic interest in Irish in Joyce's
story 'The Dead' in *Dubliners*). Hyde grew up in a largely
Irish-speaking area of Roscommon, Frenchpark, where his
father was rector; he arrived at Trinity College dreaming in
Irish, possessing Irish texts as well as a stock of Irish songs
and stories, and filled with a strong desire to restore the
standing of Irish. Accordingly he joined the Society for the
Preservation of the Irish Language in 1877 and wrote many
poems in Irish for *The Irishman* and *The Shamrock*, using the

pseudonym *An Craoibhin Aoibhinn* (the Pleasant Little Branch). He contributed stories translated from the Irish to Yeats's *Fairy and Folk Tales of the Irish Peasantry* (1888), and poems in English to *Poems and Ballads of Young Ireland* (1888). His first book was *Leabhar Sgeulaigheachta* (1889), a collection of folk tales, rhymes and riddles.

In *Beside the Fire* (1890) he provided both English versions and the Irish originals, and in his translations he successfully used an Irish idiom translated fairly literally into English. His long preface dealt with the work of earlier collectors and assessed the significance of traditional Irish folklore.

At this time the whole matter of Celtic culture was being evaluated and appreciated outside Ireland. The antiquarianism of the late eighteenth century which had found expression in Bishop Percy, Gray, Chatterton and MacPherson had been succeeded by a European interest in Celtic, with Ernest Renan (1823-92) writing about the Celtic poetry of his native Brittany, Matthew Arnold lecturing *On the Study of Celtic Literature* (1867) with a sense of the imaginative energy of the Celtic peoples, and Marie Henri Arbois de Jubainville (1827–1910), the founder of the *Révue Celtique*, giving weight to the subject with his *Introduction à l'étude de la littérature Celtique* (1883), *Essai d'un catalogue de la littérature de l'Irlande* (1883), *Le cycle mythologique Irlandais et la mythologie Celtique* (1884) and *L'épopée Celtique en Irlande* (1892). German scholarship was also impressive; among these authorities were Rudolf Thurneysen (1857–1940), Heinrich Zimmer (1851–1910), Ernest Windisch (1844–1918), and Kuno Meyer (1958–1919), who founded the School of Irish Learning in Dublin in 1903 and the journal *Eriu* the next year. The best of his translations are contained in *The Voyage of Bran* (1895), *Four Old Irish Songs of Summer and Winter* (1903) and *Selections from Ancient Irish Poetry* (1911).

In Hyde's *Love Songs of Connacht* (1893) the prose paraphrases were more impressive than his poetic renderings, good though these generally were. His prose, however, conveyed the compact, tough nature of the Irish originals more effectively. Here, for instance, is the opening of his poetic version of 'The Brow of Nefin':

> Did I stand on the bald top of Nefin
> And my hundred-times loved one with me,
> We should nestle together as safe in
> Its shade as the birds on a tree.
>
> From your lips such a music is shaken,
> When you speak it awakens my pain,
> And my eyelids by sleep are forsaken,
> And I seek for my slumber in vain.

And here is his prose version of it:

> If I were to be on the Brow of Nefin and my hundred loves by my
> side, it is pleasantly we would sleep together like the little bird upon
> the bough. It is your melodious wordy little mouth that increased
> my pain, and a quiet sleep I cannot get until I shall die, alas!

Some of his verse translations are over-mannered and use
poetic diction excessively. But the vigour of, say, 'The Red
Man's Wife' or 'I shall not die for thee' counterbalance this.
His shorter pieces, 'I am Raftery', for instance, are effective
in their simplicity:

> I am Raftery the poet
> Full of hope and love,
> With eyes that have no light,
> With gentleness that has no misery.
>
> Going west upon my pilgrimage
> By the light of my heart,
> Feeble and tired,
> To the end of my road . . . .

His 'Though Riders be thrown' is a good rendering of the
epigram in Irish:

> Though riders be thrown in black disgrace,
> Yet I mount for the race of my life with pride,
> May I keep to the tracks, may I fall not back,
> And judge me, O Christ, as I ride my ride.

Hyde's ambitions, avowedly apolitical, were none the less
nationalist; they emerged clearly in 'The Necessity for De-
Anglicising Ireland', his Inaugural Lecture as President of the
National Literary Society in 1892. He was President of the

Gaelic League in 1915 when he made it clear at the annual conference at Dundalk that the league was becoming political against his advice: he thought a disservice had been done to it by the alteration of its constitution, when its aim was declared to be the establishment of a free Gaelic-speaking Ireland. He departed early from the conference, leaving word that he did not wish to be reconsidered for the presidency.

Hyde continued to publish. *The Story of Early Gaelic Literature* (1895) was succeeded by *A Literary History of Ireland* (1899; new edition 1967), *Songs ascribed to Raftery* (1903) which translated oral poems by Anthony Raftery (1784–1835) the blind Irish poet, and *Religious Songs of Connacht* (2 vols, 1906). A gifted amateur actor, he also wrote plays in Irish himself, his *Casadh an tSugain* (translated by Lady Gregory as *Twisting the Rope*) being performed very successfully in Dublin in 1901. He followed it with several other short plays in Irish, *The Poorhouse* being well translated by Lady Gregory as *The Workhouse Ward*. He collected more folklore in *Legends of Saints and Sinners* (1916) and *Mayo Stories told by Thomas Casey* (1939).

Hyde was Professor of Modern Irish at University College, Dublin from 1905 to 1932; he was the first President of Ireland, from 1939 to 1944. His poetry and translations as well as his successful use of an Irish idiom in English (it has been called an Anglo-Irish idiom by some critics), his capacity to write literary history, and his collecting of folklore were inspired by his passionate love of Irish and desire for a future in which an Irish-speaking people would preserve the language. His energy and organising powers, coupled with tactful and, despite his disclaimers, practical political skills, made his movement extraordinarily effective: though the Gaelic League did not go as he wanted it to, none the less he himself succeeded through his presidency of it in showing the language's capabilities and aiding those who spoke it to make their voices heard. Here is what he said in *Leabhar Sgeulaigheacta* (1889) in a note 'On the reasons for keeping alive the Irish Language', conveying his passionate enthusiasm in a flowing polemic which reminds us that George Moore called a speech of his volubility 'as extreme as a peasant's come to ask for a reduction of the rent', his Irish 'a torrent of dark muddied stuff . . . much like the porter which used to come up from Carmacus to be drunk by the peasants on mid-summer nights when a bonfire was lighted.'

> . . . what with the brutalized, sensual, unsympathetic gentry of the last century, the racing, blustering, drunken squireens, who usurped the places of the O'Connors, the O'Briens, the O'Donnells, the O'Cahans, the MacCarthys, our old and truly cultured nobility, who cherished hereditary poets and historians; what with the purblind, cringing pedagogues of the present century, whose habit it was to beat and threaten their pupils for talking Irish; what with the high-handed action of the authorities, who, with cool contempt of existing circumstances, continued to appoint English-speaking magistrates, petty-sessions clerks, and local officials among a people to whom they could not make themselves intelligible; what with the hostility of the Board of Education, who do not recognise the language of those baronies where no English is spoken, even to the extent of publishing school-books in it; what with this, and our long slavery as a nation, we assert that the Irish language has had no chance of showing its capabilities, or those who speak it of taking their own part, and making their voice heard.

Hyde's interest in the peasantry and his translations were to influence many younger poets who later turned away from the insubstantiality of much Celtic Twilight poetry. Another potent influence upon them was George Russell who was initially closely associated with Yeats. He had encouraged many of those who wrote of Ireland in the somewhat ideal-ising Celtic Twilight manner after Yeats had disowned it, though — no doubt after his own experiences of country life and belief in country people — he was to be equally encour-aging to those who wrote more realistically and directly about it. Russell, who wrote under the pen name AE (originally Aeon), was born in Portadown and studied painting at the Metropolitan School of Art in Dublin. There he met Yeats and his schoolfellow Charles Johnson, both deeply interested in Theosophy. AE began to experience waking dreams — an immortal self seeming to illuminate his mind from within while the visible world was like 'a tapestry blown and stirred by winds behind it'. He wrote verse about his visions, and then tried to paint the radiant supernatural beings of a golden age that had never passed from the world. He and Johnson discovered the Upanishads together; then he joined the Theosophists in 1889 or 1890, and found employ-ment at Pim's drapery store in Dublin while he continued to search for the primeval story of unfallen man. The pictures he painted on the walls of the Theosophical Lodge in Ely Place are Blake-like and reflect his preoccupation with the idea of opalescent light, of visitants from the spiritual world wavering into irridescent vapour which floated through infinite space. *Homeward Songs by the Way* (1894) shows how his thought prevailed over his style, for he could not always find adequate words to convey his mystical experiences, his 'yearning inexpressible'. 'Dawn' comes near them:

> Still as the holy of holies breathes the vast,
> Within its crystal depths the stars grow dim;
> Fire on the altar of the hills at last
> Burns on the shadowy ruin

This visionary vein continued in AE's second volume, *The Earth Breath and other poems* (1897) and *The Divine Vision and other poems* (1904), the best of them included in *Collected Poems* (1913). The best of his later work, in *The House of the Titans and other poems* (1934) and *Selected Poems* (1935), contains the same sense of wonder in 'A Mountain Tarn' where earth and spirit are united by light, while 'What Home' echoes the tradition of Vaughan's visionary poetry. Many of AE's poems, however, like many of his paintings, can be diffuse and imprecise, lacking in continuous craftsmanship, but his later poems gained clarity, possibly because of his need to write clear prose and his experience in achieving it in the *Irish Statesman*, where his maturity of mind is noticeable. His love poems moved from early melancholia to delight; his children and heroes remind us of Blake's poems, though his best poems are of landscape particularly when irradiated by light. He believed that light and darkness, like opposites of spirit and body, are to be reconciled.

His second volume of poetry had marked his increasing interest in Irish material, and in 1897 he became an organiser for the Irish Agricultural Organisation Society founded by Sir Horace Plunkett. This led him to blend his visionary dreaming with the practicalities of organising and running committees.

AE formed a friendship with George Moore, bringing him on a tour of the Boyne valley tumuli, finding him a Dublin house in Ely Place in 1901, and becoming known as one of Dublin's great talkers at Moore's Saturday nights. His interest in the Irish Literary Society developed into an ability to detect and encourage new literary talents. His circle of young writers included Padraic Colum, James Cousins, James Starkey (who wrote as Seumas O'Sullivan), Thomas Keohler, Susan Mitchell, and George Roberts. In 1904 he edited *New Songs* which included their work as well as poems by Eva Goore-Booth, Ella Young and Alice Milligan. He became friendly with Oliver St John Gogarty and helped the young James Joyce.

AE's play *Deirdre* was staged in 1902 with Yeats's *Cathleen ni Houlihan*, and he became a vice-president of the Irish National Theatre Society. His friendship with Yeats came under stress in 1904 when he allowed renegade members from the company to perform his *Deirdre* in the United States; the next year, however, it was AE who drew up a constitution for the Society, withdrawing from it himself along with most of the actors, who became paid employees. In 1905 he also joined with Yeats, Count and Countess Markievicz and others in setting up the United Arts Club as a meeting place for artists, intellectual and bohemian Dubliners. He then found a new role, as editor of the *Irish Homestead* (1905–23) and later as editor of the *Irish Statesman* (1923–30). He moved to Rathgar Avenue in 1906, presiding benignly over his Sunday 'At Homes'.

AE, his new friend James Stephens and their friend Stephen MacKenna (1872–1934), the journalist and translator of Plotinus, were among Dublin's most famous performers in a city of talkers. AE could be amusing and satiric, but fundamentally his view of Ireland's position was serious – he attacked, like Yeats, the employers in the Dublin strike and subsequent lockout of 1913; he foresaw, with 'a burden on the heart all the time', the likely result of violence, and the drift towards civil war. His journalism of the period which can be sampled in *Selections from the Contributions to the Irish Homestead* (2 vols, 1978) is excellent, and shows the evolution of the idea of a co-operative commonwealth. At least a third of *Co-operation and Nationality* (1912) was made up of journalistic writings; lively and clearly expressed though they were, AE thought them too hurriedly produced, and wrote in *The National Being* (1916) a more carefully constructed book, putting forward his own ideas for Ireland's future. His prose at its most imaginative appears in *The Interpreters* (1922) and *The Avatars: A Futurist Fantasy* (1933), though the latter displays a certain weariness of spirit as it attempts to recapture the romantic excitement with which he had prepared in 1896 for a great incarnation.

AE had reason for melancholia. His wife died in 1933, and he retired to England, where he himself died in 1935. But then his experience of political life had been disillusioning. His pamphlet *Thoughts for a Convention* (1917) shows the characteristic practical idealism be brought to the abortive convention of 1917–18. Always disliking the intransigent hard-liners of the North, he finally resigned when he realised the British government could not secure Ulster's agreement to the Convention's proposals, and that Irish control of the Irish customs was unlikely: he viewed the future of Ireland 'with the greatest foreboding', though his poem 'To the Memory of some I knew who are dead and who loved Ireland' conveys his hope that modern Ireland could avoid hatred by seeing itself as a nation of mixed identity with differing senses of duty. He supported the Treaty signed in 1921 and ratified in 1922, disliking the doctrinaire attitude of the anti-Treaty Republicans as much as that of the Ulstermen. In the *Irish Statesman* he showed his brilliance as a journalist and an educator. His articles, his reviews and his encouragement of others are still impressive to read. He had become a friend of Frank O'Connor and L. A. G. Strong; he viewed the work of Austin Clarke and F. R. Higgins with pleasure; and his ability to keep a fresh receptivity for new writers and particularly new poets is notable. Patrick Kavanagh was probably the last of the long line of poets he befriended. Throughout his life he had acted as a creative catalyst, an encourager of others, not always discriminatingly but generously and hopefully. His work at the *Irish Statesman* in providing a placid forum for sanity and support for the nascent Free State was indeed impressive. But he had come to realise that his dreams for the co-operative movement could not be realised as quickly as he had hoped, and that the spiritual rebirth of Ireland was a matter for the distant future.

V A new generation

Under the influence of Hyde and also of Russell, whose belief
in the primitive nature of the Irish country life, whose linking,
too, of the visionary experiences with nationalism had greatly
encouraged them, a young generation of poets turned from
mists and mythology to a simpler treatment of Irish subjects,
a more realistic portrayal of peasant life, an appreciation of
old ballads, and an altogether tougher poetry. These poets
included Joseph Campbell, Padraic Colum and James Stephens,
while Synge's *Poems* which appeared in 1909 and 1910 had
developed from the melancholy self-pity of his early *Vita
Vecchia* series not only to his love poems to Molly Algood
but also to such vigorous poems as the ballad 'Danny' (the
story of murder in Connaught) and the realism of 'On an
Island':

> You've plucked a curlew, drawn a hen,
> Washed the shirts of seven men,
> You've stuffed my pillow, stretched the sheet
> And filled the pan to wash your feet,
> You've cooped the pullets, wound the clock
> And rinsed the young men's drinking crock . . . .

Synge's 'The Passing of the Shee', written after looking at
one of AE's pictures, makes clear his difference from the
Twilight vision:

> Adieu Sweet Angus, Maeve and Fand
> Ye plumed and skinny Shee
> That poets played with hand in hand
> To learn their ecstasy.
>
> We'll search in Red Dan Sally's ditch,
> And drink in Tubber fair
> Or poach with Red Dan Philly's bitch
> The badger and the hare.

Campbell, too, though of an age with Seumas O'Sullivan,
in whose poetry the Twilight had glowed, was moving from
its spell, and writing with less 'Celtic' attitudes to poetry.
Born in Belfast in 1879, he first came to Dublin in 1902
where he published various articles and poems, and wrote
the words for Donegal folk songs collected by Herbert Hughes

in *Songs of Uladh* (1904). After a spell with the Ulster Literary Theatre Campbell worked in London but moved to a farm in Wicklow in 1911. By then he had published five volumes of verse, poems uneven in achievement but at their best simple in imagery, individual and highly compressed. His work in *Irishry* (1913) and *Earth of Cualann* (1917) is generally easier and less staccato, but Campbell's search for austerity, particularly in the later volume, while it echoed the Irish poetry he admired so much, also militated against any popular success. The character poems of *Irishry* were more obvious, and 'The Old Woman' where Campbell's terse restraint is at its best, has frequently appeared in anthologies.

Campbell was interned in the civil war and then, disillusioned with politics, moved to New York in 1925 where he worked to establish a centre of Irish studies, to develop cultural links between Ireland and America. He returned to Ireland in 1939, to live quietly in Wicklow until his death in 1944. Though but a minor and unduly neglected poet — revalued somewhat since Austin Clarke edited his poems in 1963 — his best work is elegant and precise, idiosyncratic and memorable.

From 1903 to 1909 when the Gaelic League's weekly paper *An Claidheamh Soluis* was edited by Patrick Pearse (1879–1916) the League was becoming more political. After a row when J. O. Hannay's authorship of the George A. Birmingham novels *The Seething Pot* (1905) and *Hyacinth* (1906) became known, Hannay described its leaders in 1907 as 'becoming cowardly and truckling to priest and politicans'. Pearse, however, turned his attention to running St Enda's School, became deeply involved in the Irish volunteers, joined the I. R. B., the Irish Republican Brotherhood, in 1913 and prepared himself for martyrdom. The last stanza of his poem 'Renunciation' puts this clearly:

> I have turned my face
> To this road before me,
> To the deed that I see
> And the death I shall die.

His patriotic lineage goes back to the classical sources; in his essay 'Ghosts' he quotes Wolfe Tone:

> I made speedily what was to me a great discovery though I might have found it in Swift and Molyneux that the influence of England was the radical vice of our government, and consequently that Ireland would never be free, prosperous or happy until she was independent, and that independence was unobtainable whilst the connection with England lasted.

He could, he said, have constructed the case for separation from Anglo-Irish political thinkers before Tone, but he chose instead the writings of Tone, Thomas Davis, Fintan Lawlor, John Mitchel and Parnell.

Pearse had published poems dealing with innocence and death in the *Claidheamh*, but his best poetry is contained in *Suantraidhe agus Goltraidhe* (1914) since his later poetry written in English was overweighted with a mixture of sentimentalism, as in 'The Mother', and politics, as in 'The Rebel'. 'The Fool' records his having squandered 'the splendid years that/the Lord God gave to my youth' but appeals to God to judge his motives, in an unorthodox harnessing of religion to his nationalism. His last poem 'The Wayfarer' reverts to his love of beauty, his adoration of Connacht, and has an appealing romantic simplicity about it.

Pearse could be naïve in his pursuit of chastity, and two poets who also took part in the 1916 Rising and were executed, his friends Thomas MacDonagh (1878–1916) and Joseph Mary Plunkett (1887–1916), on one occasion had to explain to him that 'Little Lad of the Tricks', the English version of his Irish poem 'A Mhic Bhig na gCleas', could be regarded as homosexual. MacDonagh wrote several plays between 1908 and 1915; his first volume of poetry, *Through the Ivory Gate* (1902), records his decision to leave the Holy Ghost order; other volumes followed but his best work is in *Lyrical Poems* (1913), notably 'John-John', 'The Yellow Bittern', based upon the Irish of Cathal Buidhe MacGiolla Ghunna, and 'The Man Upright'. His posthumous *Literature in Ireland* (1916) discusses the effect of the Irish language upon Anglo-Irish poetry and witnesses his deep interest in prosody. Another posthumous volume, Plunkett's *Poems* (1916) shows that Plunkett was more mystical than MacDonagh in his very romantic approach to poetry; though his diction was largely conventional he created many arresting lines. 'I See His Blood upon the Rose' is an example of how pleasing his work could be when he controlled its form.

Though Padraic Colum (1881–1972) published his early poems in the *United Irishman* (it was edited by Arthur Griffith (1871–1922) who had brought it into being to succeed his weekly review *Sinn Fein*, suppressed for its revolutionary tendencies), and though he had nationalist sympathies — he and his wife Mary taught at Pearse's School, St Enda's — they had left Ireland by 1914. Colum's poetry had none of Pearse's political content. He wrote about Irish country life with simplicity, his own warmhearted directness allowing him the born storyteller's licence. Some of his best poems are contained in his first volume *Wild Earth* (1907), but he wrote poetry continuously; even though very frail in his extreme old age he could recite it with a winning warmth of feeling, a bewitching quality that informs poems such as 'The Poor Scholar', 'Plougher' or 'The Ballad Singer' as they recapture images of people he knew as a child in the countryside. He had a good eye for detail and so his descriptive powers, as in 'The Book of Kells', for instance, were also very effective.

James Stephens (?1880–1950) was another poet to move towards the earthy in his translations from the Irish. His writing first appeared in the *United Irishman* in 1905 and after 1907 in *Sinn Fein*. In his memories of Dublin, Stephens stressed the poverty he knew:

> The Dublin I was born to was poor and Protestant and athletic. While very young I extended my range and entered a Dublin that was poor and Catholic and Gaelic — a very wonderworld. Then as a young writer I further extended to a Dublin that was poor and artistic and political. Then I made a Dublin for myself, my Dublin.

In this Dublin he earned his living as a clerk in various solicitors' offices, studied Irish under Griffith's influence, acted in the Theatre of Ireland group, became interested in Theosophy and Blake's ideas and imagery under AE's influence and had his first volume of poems, *Insurrections*, published in 1909.

Stephens at first wrote angry depictions of the city's slums — a subject to be treated by many writers, among them Oliver St John Gogarty, James Joyce and Sean O'Casey — showing a delight in using Browning's techniques. He was always open to influences, and Blake dominated a lot of his subsequent poetry. He had a capacity to illuminate women's points of view; 'The Red-Haired Man's Wife' is a good poem dealing with virtual warfare between the sexes, a theme continued in 'The Dancer', 'Nucleolus' and 'Fossils'. 'Slan Leath', however, conveys a promise of more gentle relationships, and Stephens had a capacity for wonder, notably about God in 'Bessie Bobtail'. This sensibility irradiated his *Seumas Beg* poems, which transmit childhood's experience of wonder and terror mingled.

In his middle period Stephens developed a musical quality in his verse. He was constantly experimenting technically, and his poems were designed to be spoken; they are more regular than their appearance on the page suggests. He could convey a simple empathic enjoyment, as in 'The Goat Paths' where, after precise description, he enters the poem:

> I would think until I found
> Something I can never find,
> Something lying on the ground,
> In the bottom of my mind.

In his translations from Irish in *Reincarnations* (1918) Stephens employed colloquial language effectively. He was impressed by David O'Bruadair (*c.* 1625—98), one of the last poets to be trained in the traditions of the poetic schools, by Egan O'Rahilly (1670—1726) who was probably educated at a bardic school, and by the blind folk poet Anthony Raftery (1784—1835). He used the Irish Texts Society's versions as a basis for his interpretative versions. Of his translations of O'Bruadair mention should be made of 'The Weavers', the often anthologised 'A glass of beer' and 'Skim Milk':

> . . . Once I had books, each book beyond compare,
> And now no book at all is left to me;
> Now I am spied and peeped on everywhere
> And this old head, stuffed with latinity,
> Rich with poet's store of grave and gay,
> Will not get me skim milk for half a day . . . .

Of his renderings of O'Rahilly's poems, which were based on Hyde's *Poems ascribed to Raftery*, perhaps 'The Coolin', 'Eileen, Diarmuid and Teig', a poem of exclamatory tenderness, and 'Egan O'Rahilly' are the best, the last giving the spirit of the Gaelic poet admirable concrete expression:

> Here in a distant place I hold my tongue;
> I am O'Rahilly!
>
> When I was young,
> Who now am young no more,
>
> I did not eat things picked up from the shore:
> The periwinkle and the tough dog-fish
> At even-tide have got into my dish.
>
> The great, where are they now! the great had said —
> This is not seemly! Bring to him instead
> That which serves his and serves our dignity —
> And that was done.
>
> I am O'Rahilly!
> Here in a distant place he holds his tongue,
> Who once said all his say, when he was young!

The Georgians seem to have had a sentimentalising effect on Stephens, and his mysticism and the particularly personal nature of his religious outlook made his later poems in *Kings and the Moon* (1938) too impersonal and static, though the earlier poems of *Theme and Variations* (1929) had contained clear contemplation of the transcience of beauty:

> Stars and the moon
> Are lost in the light of life,
> As the pure mind, withdrawn,
> Is lost in the light of God.

Poetry, however vigorous its attack, however multiple its subjects, is not what returns the reader to Stephens. His main achievement is to be found in *The Charwoman's Daughter* (1912) and *The Crock of Gold* (1912), which reflect the slum life of the city of Dublin and the countryside respectively. The first, originally inspired by Wilde's *A House of Pomegranates* (1891), explores the relationship between Mary Makebelieve and her mother the Charwoman. A mixture of romantic dreaming, realism and aphorism, the story examines Mary's attitudes to her suitors, the Policeman and the lodger, the latter sharing Stephens's own dislike of social injustice.

In *The Crock of Gold* Stephens blended several styles more successfully: there is an implicit parody of attitudes to the Celtic gods current among Irish writers, notably Yeats and AE, as well as some parody of Synge's loquaciously eloquent peasants through the dialogue of the tinker characters, when Stephens brings Angus Og, the young god, and Pan back to an Ireland divided between pastoral innocence and urban repression. The comedy of the story is based upon Caitlin's choice of marriage to Angus Og after her seduction by Pan. Like Caitlin, the Philosopher has to learn, has to be transformed under the influence of Angus Og; and the Thin Woman has to make a pilgrimage, has to forgive her enemies. The arrest of the Philosopher for alleged murder, based on the leprechaun's false evidence, and his subsequent return to prison after being rescued, lead to profound thoughts on the freedom of the mind. And there is a final apocalypse, when the fairies, no doubt echoing Yeats and AE, call the people away from the falsity of urban society to the country of the gods. It is a very able work, often unappreciated because its whimsy can verge on the sentimental; yet this is redeemed over and over again: by the narrator's skill demonstrated so clearly at the beginning of the book, by the comedy of the interplay between the Philosophers' logic and their wives' anger, by the honest curiosity of the children, by the sadness of the old woman's mumbling complaint when she has been driven away for playing with the puppy, and by the overall matter of factness:

> 'There's not much fun in being dead, sir,' said Meehawl.
> 'How do you know?' said the Philosopher.
> 'I know well enough,' replied Meehawl.

In *The Crock of Gold* Stephens created an idiosyncratic mixture of the apparently ephemeral and the profoundly serious, but in *The Demi-Gods* (1914) he wrote an unsuccessful story of three angels on earth. Here there is a simple outline for a complex cosmic vision, of a world with all its parts related. This is another case of opposites at work in love: in, for instance, disharmonies, in dialogue and in the reversals of the two pairs of lovers, who are finally united in what is again only apparently a picaresque story. The volume of *Irish Fairy*

Tales (1920) are excellent recapturings of the flavour of Gaelic storytelling, grotesque in fancy, yet dignified and powerful in their detailed description. There followed *Deirdre* (1923) and *In the Land of Youth* (1924) but these two were all Stephens completed of his plan to encompass the heroic nature of the *Tain* in five volumes: they are again imbued with his own highly comic sense, and with material recording his own emotional delight in countryside and animals.

In 1924 Stephens left Ireland for England, and his poetic inspiration seems to have dried up at about that time. It is difficult to capture in print the idiosyncracy of the man, inspired as it continued to be in his superb capacity for conversation, yet his radio talks published as *James, Seumas and Jacques* (1964) convey something of the nimble, darting quality of mind that made him an outstanding talker in a city where his roots were, where talk mattered and was a form of art.

Outrageous as well as occasionally serious conversation was a mark of Oliver St John Gogarty (1878–1957), who had an Elizabethan appetency for life: a racing cyclist in his youth, he later took up archery and aviation. A medical student at the Royal University for two years, he then moved to Trinity where he was influenced by the scholarship and wit of Robert Yelverton Tyrrell, John Pentland Mahaffy and Henry S. Macran. He spent a term at Oxford, then went to Vienna and became an ear, nose and throat surgeon in Dublin. He had a gift for parody and for composing entertaining bawdy verses as well as lyrics traditional in technique and polished in their elegance.

Gogarty's unpublished Aristophanic verses are still remembered in Dublin, and traces of their flippant impulse are visible in some of his published poems, in, say, the witty echoes of Keats's 'On first looking into Chapman's Homer' in the sonnet 'On first looking through Kraft Ebbing's *Psychopathia Sexualis*':

> Much have I travelled in those realms of old
> Where many a whore in hall-doors could be seen
> Of many a bonnie brothel or shebeen
> Which bawds connived at by policemen hold.
> I too have listened when the Quay was coaled
> But never did I taste the Pure obscene —

> Much less imagine that my past was clean —
> Till this Kraft Ebbing out his story told,
> Then felt I rather taken by surprise
> As on the evening when I met Macran
> And retrospective thoughts and doubts did rise,
> Was I quite normal when my life began
> With love that leans towards rural sympathies
> Potent behind a cart with Mary Ann?

The poem 'Ringsend' is another example of his capacity to shock unsophisticated Dublin readers with its blunt beginning:

> I will live in Ringsend
> With a red-headed whore
> And the fan light gone in
> Where it lights the hall-door;
> And listen each night
> For her querulous shout,
> As at last she streels in
> And the pubs empty out . . . .

Gogarty knew his Dublin slums, wrote plays, *Blight* (1917), *A Serious Thing* (1919) and *The Enchanted Trousers* (1919) that denounced the conditions under which people lived in them; he knew and loved the countryside; he joined Sinn Fein though he neither believed in nor practised violence; and he became a senator in the Irish Free State. His house at Renvyle was burnt down in the Troubles; he himself narrowly escaped being murdered by gunmen; and he had to practise — very successfully — in London for nearly a year. He attended Senate meetings regularly and returned to Dublin in 1924.

His life in Dublin was the subject of *As I was Going Down Sackville Street* (1937), a book that led to a libel action. This is a volume in the tradition of Moore's *Hail and Farewell*, and it conveys with brio the atmosphere of a more troubled Dublin than the one Moore knew. It was followed by *I Follow St Patrick* (1939) and *Tumbling in the Hay* (1939), which are probably his best prose works. He left for America in 1939 and wrote novels there, *Going Native* (1940), *Mad Grandeur* (1941) and *Mr Petunia* (1945), as well as another piece of autobiography *It Isn't That Time of Year at All* (1954). These lack the freshness and vitality of his earlier prose, as Gogarty himself seemed to lack the stimulating background of Dublin's talk and competitive malice. He should be read for his poetry, which appeared in *An Offering of Swans* (1923) — the title poem celebrating his famous escape from the gunmen who kidnapped him as a hostage in the Civil War in January 1923 and from whom he escaped by swimming the flooded Liffey — *Wild Apples* (1929), *Selected Poems* (1923) and *Collected Poems* (1950). Here is a rich profusion, poems celebrating the beauty of places in Ireland and digging into their history, as in the poems exploring the surroundings of Dublin and its heritage, 'Just One Glimpse' or 'Liffey Bridge', 'Fog Horns', 'High Tide at Malahide', 'Glenasmole' or elsewhere in 'New Bridge'; poems too, exploiting himself as a Horatian poet in poems to women; and poems expressing his own personality freely once he had balanced his knowledge of classical poetry with the romantic in his own make-up. His friendship with Yeats led, in the twenties and thirties, to a free exchange of ideas, even an echoing of words and phrases in poems, notably those linked with the myth of Leda. Gogarty could be Marvellian in 'Fresh Fields':

> I gaze and gaze when I behold
> The meadows springing green and gold.
> I gaze until my mind is naught
> But wonderful and wordless thought!
> Till, suddenly, surpassing wit.
> Spontaneous meadows spring in it;
> And I am but a glass between
> Un-walked-in meadows, gold and green.

He could capture the poignant moment in a poem such as 'Golden Stockings', written about his daughter playing in a field. To him poetry was ultimately a gesture; seriousness was to be worn lightly; his cavalier manner demanded that he should write with ease, even when summing up the worst of death as the loss of friends. 'Death may be very gentle' rises above classical cliché, but the achievement of simplicity in all his poems on death comes from the classical mastery of form, of architectonic control, varied metrics and cadences. Gogarty's wit is discursive, and blended with genuine sentiment.

Another writer of this idiosyncratic imagination was Gogarty's contemporary, Lord Dunsany (1878–1957) who came of a Norman family which arrived in Ireland in the twelfth century, he himself being the eighteenth baron. After Eton and Sandhurst he joined the Coldstream Guards, fought in the Boer War and returned to the family estate in Meath in 1904, and was to fight in France in the First World War. He blended his love of sport with writing, his first book *The Gods of Pegana* (1905) being rapidly followed by *Time and the Gods* (1906) and *The Sword of Welleran* (1908). Each collection showed improvement, Dunsany feeling that he was not so much inventing the gods of his tales as writing the history of lands that he had known in 'forgotten wanderings'. His imaginative capacity is impressive in its charting the effect of time on the world of phenomena; his often stylised, Biblical prose is very apt for creating the fabulous such as the cities, for instance, of Babbulkund and Perdondaris. All this mythologising is underpinned by his humorous appreciation of incongruity and a touch of the menacing. He worked closely with S. H. Sime, whose illustrations to his tales showed a similar undercurrent of the sinister and grotesque.

At Yeats's instigation he wrote *The Glittering Gate* (1909) for the Abbey; in it two dead burglars break into heaven and find it surprising. It is typical of many of Dunsany's subsequent plays — he had more than a dozen plays staged in London and New York as well as writing some for the Abbey and, later, others for radio; usually his plays deal with a simple problem in a striking setting without much action. *The Gods of the Mountain*, produced in 1911, is an example of beggars, who impersonate the gods of the mountain, caught between the doubts of the public and the vengeance of the gods.

Though Dunsany became friendly with Yeats, AE and Gogarty, and was a good patron to the poet Francis Ledwidge, he was a very independent, individualistic writer. No sharer in the aims of the Irish renaissance, he regarded genius as an infinite capacity for not taking pains, and he composed at high speed, sometimes dictating to his wife but usually standing at a desk and using a quill pen. He did not like writing about the familiar; one of his best collections of tales, *The Last Book of Wonder* (1914), shows his capacity to create black humour. Black horror characterises his play *A Night at an Inn* (1916), in which jewel thieves are destroyed by a jealous oriental god and priests in a play which is full of

1. *The marriage of Princess Aoife* [Eva, daughter of Dermot MacMurrough, King of Leinster] *and Strongbow*, by Daniel Maclise.

The Dr. S:P.D. the Poetical Works of M,D.C,C,XXXIV

2.   Frontispiece from Faulkner's edition of Swift's *Works*, volume II, Dublin, 1735.

3a. *The Irish House of Commons*, by Francis Wheatley. Henry Grattan addressing the Irish Parliament in Dublin on 19 April 1780, on the Repeal of Poyning's Law: 'That the people of Ireland are of right an independent nation and ought only to be bound by laws made by the King, Lords and Commons of Ireland'.

3b. *The Dublin Volunteers meeting on College Green*, by Francis Wheatley.

4.   *The Custom House, Dublin,* by James Malton.

5. *The Wake*, by Nathaniel Grogan.

6. *The Patron* [pattern], or *Festival of St Kevin at the Seven Churches, Glendalough*, by Joseph Peacock.

7. Tyrone Power as Connor O'Gorman in *The Groves of Blarney*, by Nicholas Crowley.

8. *The Ejectment*, an impression of the eviction of an Irish peasant family in the *Illustrated London News* (16 December 1848).

9a. George Bernard Shaw, by Gerald Karsh.

9b. W. B. Yeats and George Russell passing each
     other outside Yeats's house in Merrion Square, a
     cartoon by Mac [Isa MacNie].

10. The first page of the MS of W.B. Yeats's 'Byzantium'

*(handwritten) Jimmy, ale's looked [?] but ask the
[?] Quin is coming [?]. She'll
have brought the [?] [?] on her now,*   TS. ttt / 818

-(Widow Quin comes in hastily,with a jar of poteen under her

shawl:she stands for a moment in astonishment when she sees Mahon -

Widow Quin-(to Mahon)-

You didn't go far at all?

Mahon

I seen the coasting steamer passing,and I got t cramp in my leg,so

I said the devil go along with him and turned again.

Widow Quin

And where is it you're travelling now?

Mahon

I'm not ~~thinking it all~~, and it so droughty this day in the gleaming

sun.-(looking under her shawl)-(If it's the stuff you have)

(give me a supeen for the love of God, and I destroyed tramping

since Tuesday was a week.

Widow Quin *(treating him ostentatious) as a sick child,*

Sit down then by the fire and take your ease for a space.-(giving

him poteen)-May that be to your happiness and lenghth of life.

mahon

God increase you. -(drinks looking anto fire)--

Widow Quin-(going to men R.)--

Do you know what? That man's a raving maniac would scare the world.

Jimmy-(with druenken wisdom)-

I was well night thinking that.

11.   A page from a draft of J.M. Synge's *The Playboy of the Western World*.

Men and horses: east and west

12. *The Castletown Hunt with Tom Conolly 1768*, by Robert Healy

13. *The Finish of the Race*, by Jack B. Yeats.

14a. Coole Park, Lady Gregory's house in County Galway.

14b. A rehearsal in the old Abbey Theatre, Dublin.

15a.   James Joyce in 1902.

15b.   College Green (*c.* 1900) with the Bank of Ireland (formerly the Parliament building) on the left and the facade of Trinity College at the rear.

16a. Westmoreland Street, Dublin as it appeared about the period of Moore's *Hail and Farewell* and Joyce's *Dubliners* and *Ulysses*.

16b. A Dublin Slum Street in the late nineteenth century.

suspense but remorseless in the unfolding of inevitable vengeance.

Dunsany's sunnier moods are reflected in *If* (1921), a highly successful play despite several critics' attacks on its lack of intellectual content — a thing that did not worry him. *The Blessing of Pan* (1927) perhaps echoes some of his own life in the character of the good clergyman eventually overcome by Pan. The five volumes of tales of Mr Jorkens which began with *The Travel Tales of Mr Jorkens* (1931) and ended with *Jorkens borrows another whiskey* (1948) allowed Dunsany to tell incredible, fanciful stories set in exotic surroundings through the convincing good-humoured persona of a clubman, Jorkens, with his foil Terbut, a sceptical lawyer. It is hard to select among his novels, but *The Curse of the Wise Woman* (1935) is perhaps typical of them in its spontaneity; *My talks with Dean Spanley* (1936), however, is probably his funniest book, in which a bland churchman becomes a dog — or does he? His three autobiographical books (published in 1938, 1944, and 1945) are disappointing in that he left out the unpleasant parts of his life. There was a strong streak of perverse obstinacy in his often cranky character; he remained, in many ways, an Edwardian eccentric throughout.

'Your harper', as Gogarty described Francis Ledwidge in a letter to Lord Dunsany, was born at Slane in County Meath in 1887. A labourer from the age of twelve, he was warmly encouraged by Dunsany, to whom he sent some of his verses in 1912. He had been contributing poems to the *Drogheda Independent* and his friendship with Dunsany meant that he had access to the library at Dunsany Castle, and much helpful criticism. Dunsany introduced him to literary life in Dublin, remarking in a paper that 'He knows nothing about technique and far less about grammar, but he has the great ideas and conceptions of the poet, and sees the vast figures, the giant forces, and elemental powers, striving amongst the hills.' He selected fifty of Ledwidge's poems for *Songs of the Fields* (1915).

In the summer of 1913 Ellie Vaughey, with whom he was deeply in love, told him that their meetings must cease: her family owned land, he was merely a road-ganger. Like Yeats writing defeatist love poems to Maud Gonne such as 'The

Cloths of Heaven' with its wish for the heavens' embroidered cloths to lay under her feet and its realisation that he can only offer her his dreams — 'Tread softly because you tread on my dreams' — Ledwidge had only his songs to offer Ellie Vaughey. 'A Song' records the frustrating melancholy enforced on him by poverty, itself a spur to poetry:

> Had I but wealth of land and bleating flocks
> And barnfuls of the yellow harvest yield,
> And a large house with climbing hollyhocks,
> And servant maidens singing in the field,
> You'd love me; but I own no roaming herds,
> My only wealth is songs of love, for you,
> And now that you are lost I may pursue
> A sad life deep below the depth of words.

Hoping to improve his financial position, Ledwidge took a temporary post as secretary to a Labour Union, was founder of the Slane corps of the Irish Volunteers, and aimed to become a journalist. Then he enlisted in October 1914 in the Royal Inniskilling Fusiliers because, he said, the British army 'stood between Ireland and an enemy common to our civilisation'. Dunsany, who had joined the regiment in August, was annoyed, having hoped that Ledwidge would develop his poetry at home. Ellie Vaughey had married, but died suddenly in Manchester in 1915 and Ledwidge continued to mourn the death of their love in his poems. He survived Gallipoli, returned to Ireland after the 1916 Rising, writing a poem on the executed leader Thomas MacDonagh, which shows the influence of the Irish poetry he had begun to read in translation, which included MacDonagh's translation of 'The Yellow Bittern':

> He shall not hear the bittern cry
> In the wild sky, where he is lain,
> Nor voices of the sweeter birds
> Above the wailing of the rain.
>
> Nor shall he know when loud March blows
> Thro' slanting snows her fanfare shrill,
> Blowing to flame the gold cup
> Of many an upset daffodil . . . .

Ledwidge continued to mourn the death of his former

comrades in the volunteers. 'The Dead Kings' is a good example, with its Irish internal rhyming:

> All the dead kings came to me
> At Rosnaree where I was dreaming.
> A few stars glimmered through the morn,
> And down the thorn the dews were streaming.
>
> And every dead King had a story
> Of ancient glory, sweetly told.
> It was too early for the lark,
> But the starry dark had tints of gold.
>
> And one said: 'A loud tramp of men
> We'll hear again at Rosnaree.'
> A bomb burst near me where I lay.
> I woke, 'twas day in Picardy.

He himself was killed instantly by a shell in the third battle of Ypres on 31 July 1917. *Songs of Peace* was published posthumously and followed by Dunsany's selection of his *Last Songs* (1918). Ledwidge's *Collected Poems* (1974) have been edited by Alice Curtayne, whose excellent biography of the poet was published in 1972. The last poems show Ledwidge, always psychic, turning to religious meditations, to an interest in Irish literary and historical material: but he remains at his best in his short-lined fluid lyrics with their short words, their limpidity; like John Clare, he observed his local countryside with deep love of its detailed beauties.

In contrast, sophisticated urban themes and a fashionable consciousness of the ideas and techniques common to avant-garde writers, particularly during his period in Paris, shaped the modernist poems of Thomas McGreevy (1893–1967) who became Director of the National Gallery in Dublin from 1950 to 1964. A close friend of Jack Yeats, Joyce and Stephens, of Denis Devlin and Brian Coffey as well as Samuel Beckett, he moved from Paris to London in the nineteen-thirties, and wrote art criticism in *The Studio* as well as literary criticism. A volume of his poetry appeared in 1934, his *Collected Poems* in 1971. He could compress emotion tightly into poems which begin deceptively, as in 'Aodh Ruadh O Domhnaill' which has a cumulative effect similar to the near surrealism of his 'Homage to Hieronymus Bosch'.

VI Ancient and modern

Twice Round the Black Church (1962) describes Austin Clarke (1896–1974) growing up in the north side of Dublin, showing how he had the same kind of Catholic education and upbringing as Joyce. Sex was the major sin, and in Clarke's poetry warfare between flesh and spirit could often erupt into eroticism. His first work, *The Vengeance of Fionn* (1917), intensely over-applauded, attacked and defended on its appearance, differed from previous treatments of the Fenian cycle. Apart from being overloaded with adjectives, it was crammed with detail, some of it exuding a much more erotic sensibility than the love story of Diarmuid and Grainne had been given by previous writers. Clarke was impressed by the lectures of Douglas Hyde on Gaelic literature when he was an undergraduate at University College, Dublin, particularly liking Hyde's *Love Songs of Connacht*, but he was most influenced in his own treatment of the legends by a minor poet and playwright, Frederic Herbert French (1865–1923), who had treated the Deirdre story realistically in his *Deirdre Wed* (1907). The energy of this poem, to be found in French's *Collected Works* (1924), seemed 'a mad discordancy like pipes, drums, brasses' to Clarke, inspiring him in his attempts to recreate a pre-Christian Ireland innocent of Jansenist guilt.

Clarke's second use of Gaelic material, *The Sword of the West* (1921) is, however, more effective where it reflects a lyric liking for the countryside, and is uneven in accomplishment. (It had been preceded by *The Fires of Baal* (1921), an attempt — shades of Moore and Mangan! — at an Eastern tale.) *The Cattle Drive in Connaught* (1925) is Clarke's best approach to the energy he admired in French's poem. From its opening — the pillow talk between Maeve, boastfully insecure, greedy and sexually promiscuous, and her tough husband Ailill, to the fair held in celebration of the contest of wealth between them, there is an insistent earthy emphasis upon exuberant sensual vitality:

men

> Hammered the boards and laughing girls tucked up
> Red flannel petticoats around their frocks
> And footed to the reeds, as washerwomen,
> The high-step jig; the boys tripped from the drink
> And caught them into sixteen-handed reels

And grabbing hold of bolder wenches, big of bone,
With coarse red hair, shouting clapping
A gamey hand upon those buttocks loud
And shapely as a mare's, they danced them off
    their feet.

As far as the public was concerned Clarke came too late to
write about Gaelic legends: and privately there was not a full
committal on his part to the Gaelic epic; there was an evasive
element in his renderings; he seems to have disliked the
violence of the originals, to have chosen elements of an epic
rather than captured the whole of it. He explored a different
area of the past in the poems of *Pilgrimage* (1929), developing
his skill in assonance in the elaborate manner of Irish poetry,
cross-rhyming and vowel-rhyming, while delving into the
medieval monastic period, finding here material for exploiting
tension between the Church's disciplined asceticism and the
remnants of the pagan culture it seemed to have overthrown.
'Celibacy' puts the conflict clearly:

On pale knees in the dawn
Parting the straw that wrapped me,
She sank until I saw
The bright roots of her scalp.
She pulled me down to sleep
But I fled as the Baptist
To thistle and reed.

Clarke was no friend to asceticism, however much
Pilgrimage bravely celebrated Clonmacnoise and Cashel, the
chalices, the books of the holy school, the choirs, stained
glass, chasuble, wine cup and iron handbells. 'The Young
Woman of Beare' departs from the celebrated tenth-century
Irish poem 'The Old Woman of Beare' in which an old
woman laments her physical decay, Clarke's young woman
choosing sexual life in preference to the Church's rejection of
it.

Night and Morning (1938) carries the matter of *Pilgrimage*
far further, for in its twelve poems Clarke explores the gulf
between faith and reason ambiguously. 'The straying student'
may reflect the lure of reason:

They say I was sent back from Salamanca
And failed in logic, but I wrote her praise

Nine times upon a college wall in France.
She laid her hand at darkfall on my page
That I might read the heavens in a glance
And I knew every star the Moors have named.

With Riobeard O'Farachain (Robert Farren, *b.* 1909), a director of the Abbey Theatre from 1940, a composer of mainly religious poems also involved in writing for radio, whose *Selected Poems* (1951) contains some anthology pieces, Clarke formed the Dublin Verse-speaking Society in 1938 and the Lyric Theatre in 1944. Through these societies they maintained in Dublin a tradition of poetic drama on the radio, and in the Peacock and Abbey Theatres till the building burned down in 1951. Clarke's verse plays seem almost a professional exercise after the personal intensity of *Pilgrimage* and *Night and Morning*. Satire of modern Irish life, however, came to the surface in some of the plays such as *The Kiss: a light comedy in one act* (1942) and *The Viscount of Blarney* (1944), based on a Wexford folk tale. This interest in contemporary life concentrated on Dublin in *Ancient Lights* (1955) in a Joycean way. But Clarke's religious fears seemed absolved in the title poem, slightly reminiscent of Swift's 'A Description of a City Shower', where he shelters from the rain by the Protestant church. When writing of Dublin he was recreating the details of the Dublin of his youth and using it as a contrast to the Dublin of his later years, many aspects of which he disliked intensely. His compassionate rage overflows in 'Martha Blake at fifty-one': he attacks the ways of Irish Catholicism vigorously, with a fierce, burning sense of compassion as well in his 'Three poems about Children':

Has not a Bishop
declared that flame wrapped babes are spared
Our life-time of temptation

There were many targets, notably suburbia's spreading over his beloved County Dublin countryside; but Clarke's late flowering as a fully outspoken poet, whose pressing nouns into service as verbs, a sign of newfound if not always justified confidence, occurs in *Mnemosyne lay in Dust* (1966), a powerful, disturbing account of his stay as a young man in a

Dublin mental asylum. There followed a positive spate of poems in his last years, some of which are uneven in accomplishment often too private in symbolism, too tortuous in syntax, too self-indulgent in word play, some excessively elliptic in their compression. Some, however, express his satiric anger at local hypocrisy very effectively, as well as what Thomas Kinsella has called 'a cheerful sensuality'.

In his early concentration on Gaelic matter, in the conscience-ridden Catholicism of middle age, and in his late liberated mixture of satire and sensuality, of travel and talk, Austin Clarke is a supremely Irish poet. As a person, perhaps a prisoner, of his own time, he sees its problems in terms of a past when, he thought, there was a respect for man's dignity, his right to freedom and independence in the world of those old mythologies, whose uninhibited values he himself tried, increasingly, to maintain.

Two contemporaries of Austin Clarke's, F. R. Higgins and Monk Gibbon, have had opposite attitudes to poetry. Neither achieved lasting success in approaches which were based in the former's early work on the folk, in the latter's upon orthodox English verse technique. F[rederick] R[obert] Higgins (1896–1941), born in Mayo, was originally motivated by a desire to express folk emotion and racial memory. The poems of *Salt Air* (1924), *Island Blood* (1925) and *The Dark Breed* (1927) had rich sensuousness and an exuberance of invention, the gift for arresting language and imagery. In *Arable Holdings* (1933) he developed this imagery along with sound qualities, achieved often by assonance, though the often scanty meaning of the poems obviously mattered less to him than the lyric achievement. Higgins became a friend of Yeats in the nineteen-thirties, and was a director of the Abbey, writing *The Deuce of Jacks*, a play produced in 1935, on 'Zozimus' (Michael Moran, 1794–1846) the blind ballad singer. A last volume of verse *The Gap of Brightness* (1940) was more intellectual, more symbolist, but showed that Higgins's talent was, ultimately, thin. His reputation was built upon the projection of a rumbustious personality which is well captured in the portrait of him by Sean O'Sullivan (1906–64) in the Abbey.

By contrast, Monk Gibbon (*b*. 1896) seems almost wilfully archaic in his 'poetic' vocabulary, yet he can write well within conventional forms, and has composed economically controlled poems with a technical brio that gives them an arresting quality. He has written various prose works: *Mount Ida* (1948), an account of three love affairs, *The Masterpiece and the Man: Yeats as I knew him* (1959), a somewhat petulant book indicating the author's tendency to take himself very seriously, and *The Seals* (1935), an excellent piece of observation, a vivid description of a seal hunt in Donegal which remains in the mind for its simple and effective narrative.

Like Monk Gibbon, Patrick MacDonagh (1902–61) employed somewhat conventional language in *A Leaf in the Wind* (1929) and in his later more substantial volume *One Landscape Still* (1958), which contains some moving lyrics marked by a fine rhythmical control and variety. 'The Widow of Drynam' and 'One Landscape Still' are representative of his successful work.

The slender poetic talents of John Lyle Donaghy (1902–47) failed to match his abstruse ambitions, though *The Blackbird: songs of Inisfail* (1933) and *Into the Light, and Other Poems* (1934) have a few promising poems. His friend George Buchanan (*b*. 1904) has written poems in *Annotations* (1970) and *Inside Traffic* (1976) which are lively and tightly controlled. His autobiographical writing, fluent and evocative, is also well worth reading for its broad view of the current age, but his novel *Rose Forbes* (1950) ranges too widely. It is hard to characterise the fourteen volumes of poetry written by Ewart Milne (*b*. 1903), a Dubliner whose political attitudes to Ireland have changed over the years. His poetry, varied in style and range, lacks sufficient intensity.

Cecil Day-Lewis (1904–72), who was Poet Laureate from 1968–72, was born in Ireland in Ballintubber, County Laois, 'The House where I was born' being a precise evocation of the place. He spent youthful holidays in Monart near Enniscorthy in County Wexford, timeless days recorded in his autobiographical *The Buried Day* (1960). Unlike Louis MacNeice, three years his junior, who was to become with him one of the leading poets of the thirties, Day-Lewis was entirely bound up in English life. He became a schoolteacher after leaving Oxford, fashionably joined the Communist Party, then worked in the Ministry of Information in the war, later becoming a publisher and part-time academic poet.

His poetry has lost stature in recent years though some of his love poems will survive: those poems he wrote about Ireland, such as 'Fishguard to Rosslare' and 'Remembering Con Markievicz' are effective and ring true. His novel *Child of Misfortune* (1939) and some of the twenty detective stories he wrote as Nicholas Blake, especially *Thou Shell of Death* (1936) and *The Private Wound* (1958), are set in Ireland, and in the nineteen-fifties he began to cultivate a personal romanticism about Ireland and his Anglo-Irish background.

It would be hard to imagine more contrasting personalities than those of Day-Lewis and his contemporary Patrick Kavanagh (1904–67) who was born and lived in County Monaghan until 1939. He left school at twelve, and *The Green Fool* (1938) records with a light touch his growing up, his writing poetry after he left school. This activity made him feel somewhat set apart from his family and friends — his father was a small farmer who worked as a part-time cobbler — but he continued to write and to read modern literature. His early verse in *The Ploughman and Other Poems* (1936), sometimes clumsy in its rhyme, had a fine lyric quality, and, despite a slight sentimentality, a belief in a gay, imaginative God, well expressed in 'To a Blackbird':

> O pagan poet you
> and I are one
> In this — we lose our God
> at set of sun
>
> And we are kindred when
> The hill wind shakes
> Sweet song like blossoms on
> The calm green lakes
>
> We dream while Earth's sad children
> Go slowly by
> Pleading for our conversion
> With the Most High

Kavanagh thought a lot about the nature of poetry and the poet in these early poems, trying to avoid the unimportant which could impede the poet's detachment, could hinder the simplicity that was part of his comic, cosmic vision: it had all to be achieved without caring whether the poet seemed foolish or not.

In Kavanagh's progress from 'the simplicity of going away and the simplicity of return' (*Collected Pruse*, 1967, pp. 20—1) he went through a period of bitter ironic realism. 'The Great Hunger' is a sombre, powerful anti-pastoral poem about life on the land:

> Clay is the word and clay is the flesh
> Where the potato-gatherers like mechanical scarecrows move
> Along the side-fall of the hill — Maguire and his men.
> If we watch them an hour is there anything we can prove
> Of life as it is broken-backed over the Book
> of Death?

Maguire, sexually frustrated, married to fields and animals, sees the reproduction of the natural world; his was not a unique personal tragedy in the Ireland of Kavanagh's youth:

> . . . the peasant in his little acres is tied
> To a mother's womb by the wind-toughened navel-cord
> Like a goat tethered to the stump of a tree —
> He circles around and around wondering why it should be.

It is an over-dark, hopeless picture, and Kavanagh later thought that, though it had 'queer and terrible things' in it, it lacked 'the nobility and repose of poetry'. The poem does more than he thought. It creates a parish and presents the details of its life, focusing on the barren routines of its lonely bachelors with an ironic sympathy:

> He stands in the doorway of his house
> A ragged sculpture of the wind
> October creaks the rotted mattress
> The bedposts fall. No hope. No lust.
> The hungry fiend
> Screams the apocalypse of clay
> In every corner of this land.

The novel *Tarry Flynn* (1948) continues Kavanagh's 'authentic account' of rural Ireland with equal realism but less bitterness than *The Great Hunger* (1942), indeed with an unconvincing romantic conclusion, an escape from the grinding life of the small but secure farm. Kavanagh himself moved to Dublin in 1939, but the promised land, where literary life could be lived successfully turned into miasma, and he turned into an unsuccessful verse satirist, writing about literary life in the city out of deep disillusion. 'The Paddiad' and 'Who killed James Joyce?', however, remain in the mind, partly because they convey Kavanagh's envy disguised as contempt for those who had, unlike himself, gone through the educational treadmill:

> Who killed James Joyce?
> I said the commentator,
> I killed James Joyce
> For my graduation
>
> What weapon was used
> To slay mighty Ulysses?
> The Weapon that was used
> Was a Harvard thesis

While the satiric squibs savagely denounced what he saw around him in Dublin, the poems of *A Soul for Sale* (1947) indicate a sense of disappointment, even of personal failure. He was supporting himself by often bad-tempered journalism with occasional flashes of imaginative insight; out of this activity came his venture into publishing *Kavanagh's Weekly* which ran for some months in 1952.

That year was unfortunate for him. He lost a libel action against *The Leader* for an unflattering profile; he entered hospital suffering from lung cancer. The summer of 1955 he spent in Dublin, having lost his capacity for satire: 'I sat on the bank of the Grand Canal . . . and let the waters lap idly on the shores of my mind. My purpose in life was to have no purpose.' Out of this came a mixture of poems, some of them over-forced, over-written with little to say, but others with a fine sense of detachment coming from passive observation and sympathy. This was his 'rebirth', his return to simplicity, to the spirit of comedy. The sonnets of *Come Dance with Kitty Stobling and other poems* (1960) record it well. He had learned not to take himself too seriously, but to appreciate the gift of life with intensity and delight.

> O unworn world enrapture me, enrapture me in a web
> Of fabulous grass and eternal voices by a beech,
> Feed the gaping need of my senses, give me ad lib

To pray unconsciously with overflowing speech
For this soul needs to be honoured with a new dress woven
From green and blue things and arguments that cannot be proven

Kavanagh did not fit into country life, nor into the society of the city; the element of failure was there but, realising it, he submitted himself to God, knowing that he had not done what he had expected to, what he thought he might have been able to do. God refuses to take failure for an answer, he decided, and yet he wanted to 'Snatch out of time the passionate transitory', by naming things, by observing 'the passing gift of affection'. The essence of these last years was, Brendan Kennelly has suggested, the lack of mythology; he cites 'A Personal Problem', Kavanagh's supremely honest self-assessing and moving poem expressing his need for one:

To take something as a subject, indifferent
To personal affection, I have been considering
Some old saga without the person suffering
From the tiring years. But I can only
Tell of my problem without solving
Anything. If I could rewrite a famous tale
Or perhaps return to a midnight calving
This cow sacred on a Hindu scale —
So there it is my friends. What am I to do
With the void growing more awful every hour?
I lacked a classical discipline, I grew
Uncultivated and now the soil turns sour,
Needs to be revived by a power not my own,
Heroes enormous who do astounding deeds —
Out of this world. Only thus can I attune
To despair an illness like winter alone in Leeds

Three poets born in 1905, Brian Coffey, Bryan Guinness (Lord Moyne) and Padraic Fallon, show the various choices open to poets of their generation. Fallon (1905–74) was a poet who obviously did not feel inhibited from handling the material of Irish mythology. Born in Athenry, County Galway, he spent most of his life as a customs officer in Wexford. As a young man he was encouraged by AE and Seumas O'Sullivan, and wrote many poems both formal and informal in nature. Not all of them are included in his posthumous *Poems* (1974), an impressive volume which shows the influence of the techniques of Irish poetry, 'Painting of my Father' being particularly memorable. Fallon wrote many plays for radio, notably *Diarmuid and Grainne* and *The Vision of MacConglinne*. He has been highly praised for his presentation of Irish literature in lively English, for infusing the myths with a creative mixture of formality and simplicity, and for creating legendary characters larger than life with an inventive wit and an overflowing sense of fantasy.

Bryan Guinness, on the other hand, is orientated towards England in much of his work. His best collection of poems, *The Rose in the Tree* (1964), has a delicacy in its imagery, exemplified in '*By Loch Etive*'; he exercises a neat wit matched by metrical skill. He has also written plays, novels and books for children of which *The Story of Priscilla and the Prawn* (1960) is very good. His short stories are neat; the most interesting volume of them is *The Girl with The Flower* (1966).

The work of Fallon's contemporary Brian Coffey (*b*. 1905) has been influenced by European Catholicism and he has been determinedly avant-garde in expressing himself. Here is a passage from Section I of his long poem *Advent*, neo-Thomist in its intellectual structure, often subtle and witty in its expression:

> In the darkhouse They ask   'Who are you'
> Who are They and you say perhaps so to please
> 'I am Flea Ghost' and They say   Who are They
> 'Not ghostly but wit'   and you answer
> Are They Who   'You're funny today' and you turn
> to file-bank flick tabs enquire
> 'Do you like me' and They say 'Call again
> when you trust'   'We They say care'
>
> Take care you ponder   Care not to touch
> care not to touch   care not to touch
> What's avoided three times ain't there
>
> Under the hill I found the foiled people
> under the hill witted with witless endure
> under the hill give not take not

In *Leo* (1968) his wit was well matched by the illustrations of Geoffrey Prowse; the anger of, say, 'Positive Vetting' is impressive. Influenced by Claudel's poetry, and by the thought of Jacques Maritain, whose lecture courses he followed in the thirties, Coffey has translated French poetry incisively, notably Mallarmé's *Coup des Dés*, though his handling of Eluard and Neruda is also good. An intellectual astringency has probably put many readers off his occasionally over-surrealistic poems; they can be sampled in his *Selected Poems* (1971), and a special number in the *Irish University Review* (vol. 5, no. 1, spring 1975) devoted to his work.

Coffey was a close friend of Denis Devlin (1908–59), born in Glasgow but educated at Belvedere College and, after a year in a seminary, at University College, Dublin, where he met Coffey. They published a joint, very slim volume *Poems* (1930). After holding travelling scholarships Coffey became a lecturer in English but by 1935 had entered the Department of External Affairs, serving in various countries overseas, notably in the United States where he became friendly with Allen Tate and Robert Penn Warren, who edited his *Selected Poems* in 1963. Like Coffey, Devlin was influenced by French writers, notably Eluard; this appears very clearly in the fifteen poems of *Intercessions* (1937).

The title poem of *Lough Derg and other poems* (1946) is perhaps the best poem by which to judge his work; it contains his thought on the problem of modern man, seen through a deeply religious attitude centring on an Irish place of pilgrimage known to Europeans for many centuries:

> We pray to ourself. The metal moon, unspent
> Virgin eternity sleeping in the mind,
> Excites the form of prayer without content;
> Whitehorn lightens, delicate and blind,
> The negro mountain, and so, knelt on her sod,
> This woman beside me murmuring *My God! My God!*

Another poem, 'The Passion of Christ', conveys a modern sense of Sir Thomas Browne's *O Altitudo*, as well as Devlin's metaphysical sensibility. The third section of 'The Colours of Love' puts this neatly:

> It cannot well be said of love and death
> That love is better and that death is worse,
> Unless we buy death off with loving breath
> So he may rent his beauty with our purse.
>
> But is that beauty, is that beauty death?
> No, it's the mask by which we're drawn to him,
> It is with our consent death finds his breath;
> Love is death's beauty and annexes him.

Brian Coffey's edition of Devlin's *Collected Poems* (1964) and his critical edition of *The Heavenly Foreigner* (1967; originally published in *Poetry Ireland*, 1950) are useful because he clears up some of the difficulties readers can find in Devlin's complex intellectual attitudes and ideas which sometimes seem over-abstract.

From his European reading Devlin derived not a little of his approach; like Coffey, he is an intellectual's poet, but while decidedly ironic he did not bury his capacity for vision, nor his capacity to react sensitively to place, as in 'Ank' hor Vat' or 'Venus of the Salty Shell', nor indeed his capacity to write poems about human love in its many forms; witness the conclusion to the tightly compressed poem 'Renewal by her element':

> It is over now but once
> Our fees were nothing more,
> Each for use of the other
> In mortgage, than a glance.
>
> I knew the secret movements
> Of the blood under your throat
> And when we lay love-proven
> Whispering legends to sleep
> Braceleted in embrace
> Your hands pouring on me
> Fresh water of their caresses,
> Breasts, nests of my tenderness,
> All night was laced with praise.
>
> Now my image faded
> In the lucid fields
> Of your eyes. Never again
> Surprise for years, years.
>
> My landscape is grey rain
> Aslant on bent seas.

A precise particularity marked the early *Poems* (1938) of Sheila Wingfield, Viscountess Powerscourt (*b.* 1906) who developed with great sensitivity in *Beat, Drum, Beat, Heart* (1946) a long meditative poem about war and love. *Her Storms* (1978) is a selection of her poetry which reveals her liking for simplicity, for the factual.

In two contemporaries, both born in Belfast, we have

examples of poets who chose different ways of living: John Hewitt centred his verse on Northern Ireland; Louis MacNeice touched on Ireland but little until his later years when it seemed to offer a tentative escape into something more worthwhile than the contemporary civilisation of cities in which he had made his life.

John Hewitt (b. 1907), educated at Queen's University, Belfast, worked in the city's Museum and Art Gallery from 1930 to 1957, when he left to direct the Herbert Art Gallery and Museum in Coventry, returning to Belfast on his retirement in 1972. 'The Search' conveys his feelings at 'being a guest in the house' in England. His volume of *Collected Poems 1932–67* has been joined by two other volumes, *Out of my Time* (1974) and *Time Enough* (1976). A bare recital of the facts would not convey the nature of his commitment to the arts in Northern Ireland, but this might be deduced from the nature of his poetry, which conveys a staunch integrity not only in its detached recording of the countryside but also in its honest approach to the political, religious and social realities of the province. 'Parallels never meet' is a good example of this, where the poet, when 'Events in my native province now twist my heart, threatening any future I had planned', seeks to thrust it all back into a remote setting, drawing classical parallels, but in vain:

> Reality is of a coarser texture.
> The scene collapses, lath and canvas.
>
> But the heartbreak remains;
> the violence and the hate are palpable,
> the flames blacken and consume,
> the wounds weep real blood,
> and the future is not to be foretold.

Hewitt's poetry, technically accomplished, has a quiet strength about it which makes the reader aware of this maker's close links with his social region, his delight in and deep concern for it.

Though Louis MacNeice (1907–63) was educated at Marlborough College and Merton College, Oxford, his childhood in Ireland had a considerable effect upon him, his father being a clergyman who became Bishop of Down and

Connor and Dromore. MacNeice's classical education and the nine years he spent as a lecturer in classics at Birmingham University did not inhibit his use of slang and the colloquial in *Autumn Journal* (1939), a poem which conveys the thoughts and feelings of a particular but representative intellectual during the period of the Munich crisis. His poetry in the thirties delighted in the various nature of the visible world despite an awareness of its transience. 'The Sunlight on the Garden' captures this underlying melancholia:

> The sunlight on the garden
> Hardens and grows cold
> We cannot cage the minute
> Within its nets of gold,
> When all is told
> We cannot beg for pardon.

MacNeice also made several translations, including an elegant one of the *Agamemnon* of Aeschylus in 1936. In 1940 he joined the BBC features department: *Christopher Columbus* (1944) and *The Dark Tower and Other Radio Scripts* (1947) show how much thought he put into mastering a new form. Barbara Coulton has documented this work of his for radio in *Louis MacNeice in the BBC* (1980).

The MacNeice of 'Bagpipe Music' had, obviously, an ebullient and more sardonic creative energy than that of his fellow thirties poet Day-Lewis; the questioning behind his apparently left-wing poetry of the thirties moved in the wartime forties into an anxiety which contemplated the present through an awareness of the past. A visit to Ireland in 1939 produced the five poems of *The Closing Album* in one of which, 'Dublin', the receptivity of the city is stressed:

> She is not an Irish town
> And she is not English
> Historic with guns and vermin
> And of the old renown
> Of a fragment of Church latin
> Of an oratorical phrase . . .
>
> Fort of the Dane
> Garrison of the Saxon
> Augustan capital

Of a Gaelic nation,
Appropriating all
The alien brought . . . .

In the late fifties and sixties he seemed to develop a different attitude in his despairing dislike of his surroundings, his sharp awareness of the decline of the spirit, his detached reassessment of himself. The posthumously published poems of *The Burning Perch* (1963), for instance, show a recapturing of an earlier insouciant ease in the witty selection of words, even though this energy was sharpened by both a sombre consciousness of death and a need to grasp at the delight of the immediate present. In his Irish poems MacNeice's attitudes changed from a dislike of Ireland to a more discerning attitude; there was a sign of this in 'Among these turf-stacks', a realisation that there was 'no mass-production of neat thoughts' in Ireland; he recognised in the countryside's myths something which appealed deeply to him. He despised the present-day realities of Irish political life, yet there was something in him, too, he realised, which responded to that Irish background, something outside his experience of the modern urban life he had mirrored in all its ultimate emptiness.

The best poems of MacNeice's friend W. R. Rodgers (1909–69) are contained in *Europa and the Bull* (1952); they have an exuberant zest, notably in their treatment of sex, myth and religion. Rodgers's first volume *Awake! And Other Poems* (1941) had shown his interest in word play and in the technicalities of verse, as well as a capacity to record physical immediacy. A Belfast man educated at Queen's University and the Presbyterian Theological College, he acted as minister to Loughgall in County Antrim until 1946, when he moved to London and made some excellent BBC programmes, recording comment on writers of the literary revival, published as *Irish Literary Portraits* in 1972. His *Collected Poems* were published in 1971.

Valentin Iremonger (*b*. 1918) is a Dubliner who has served as Irish ambassador in several countries. He has written two volumes of poetry, *Reservations* (1950) and *Horan's Field and Other Reservations* (1972); these are somewhat lugubrious in tone, lacking in emotional vigour, as the title of the first volume suggests. Robert Greacen (*b*. 1920), who was born in

Londonderry and educated at Trinity College, wrote two
volumes of poetry in his twenties; then in 1975 *A Garland
for Captain Fox* appeared, freer in style than his earlier
poems which had been conventional in tone. Greacen's
Young Mr Gibbon (1980) continues the reflections of his
invented character Fox up to his death; this volume deepens
Greacen's ability to create character as well as to extend our
thoughts about actual people.

Contemporary Irish Poetry, the anthology that Iremonger
and Greacen collaborated in editing in 1949 shows that, on
the whole, the nineteen-forties marked the beginning of a
change in Irish poetry. By 1942 Kavanagh had written 'The
Great Hunger', though Austin Clarke was not to publish
Ancient Lights until 1955, and Kavanagh was not to have
what he called his 'poetic rebirth' till the nineteen-fifties. It
was clear that the poetic stage was now set for new plays and
new players. the work of poets who have grown up far
enough away from the period of 1891 to 1922 — the year of
Joyce's *Ulysses* and Yeats's *Later Poems* — to be utterly and
completely themselves. In addition to Seamus Heaney
(*b*. 1939), whose reputation is steadily and deservedly
increasing, they include, to name but a few, Alfred Austin
(*b*. 1925), Thomas Kinsella (*b*. 1929), Richard Murphy
(*b*. 1927), John Montague (*b*. 1929), Sean Lucy (*b*. 1929),
Brendan Kennelly (*b*. 1936), Michael Longley (*b*. 1941),
Derek Mahon (*b*. 1941) and Eavan Boland (*b*. 1945). In their
hands Irish poetry in English needs neither to be bound to
nor to be freed from English or Irish or even Anglo-Irish
traditions.

5
Modern fiction

I From George Moore to Brian Moore

MODERN Irish fiction can properly be said to begin with
George Moore. In his writings we find aestheticism, naturalism
and impressionism, an advanced exploration of new subject
matter, and constant experimentation with English style,
including a development of the stream of consciousness. He
exhibits confident control of the short story format, and is
adept at blending autobiography with fiction. His deployment
of historical imagination is flavoured by fantasy. His work is
irradiated by humour mingled with malice, and it contains a
skilful yoking together of talk and narrative.

From the nineties to the present day the variety of Anglo-
Irish fiction is large; it includes novels and stories written out
of the narrative art, the delight in dialogue, the big house
detachment, and the capacity to extract humour out of
absurd situations that Maria Edgeworth initiated, Somerville
and Ross developed and Elizabeth Bowen and Joyce Cary
continued. But, like Maria Edgeworth, Elizabeth Bowen and
Joyce Cary located only some of their fiction in Ireland: they
are part of that line of literature which spans both islands.

Joyce, however, concentrated upon Irish material and his
native city. He became a towering giant not only in the
history of Irish fiction but also in the history of the genre
itself. Though he has exerted such an innovative, infective
influence upon other novelists there are many other modern
writers who have added to the general distinction of Irish
fiction and often in very idiosyncratic ways. There is, for
instance, a particularly Irish attitude at work in the experimental work of Brian O'Nolan, the associative word play and
satire which enlivened his contributions to *The Irish Times*,
and in the grotesque exuberance of Mervyn Wall, reaching

well back into Irish literary traditions. An Irish penchant for fierce satire emerges in the writings of Eimar O'Duffy. The traditions within which some writers work do not go so far back. The tale of terror Brinsley MacNamara makes of life in a small community, and which Patrick Boyle brings up to date so horrifyingly in his short stories, are the Gothic strains of Maturin or Sheridan Le Fanu or Bram Stoker given new life. The romantic strain instituted by Lady Morgan has continued, too, in the work of popular romantic novelists such as Maurice Walsh and Donn Byrne, while there is always the melodramatic absurdity of Amanda M'Kittrick Ros for the *cognoscenti*. Irish humour in plenty exists, in the genteel rogue literature of Somerville and Ross's stories of Flurry Knox, the fun of George A. Birmingham's frolics, and the Ballygullion of Lynn Doyle, while, more recently, the light social comedy of Terence de Vere White has been balanced by the darker, sardonic views of W. J. White. Historical fiction, begun by Lady Morgan and Maturin, flourishes in the writings of, say, Francis Hackett, Liam O'Flaherty, Francis MacManus and Walter Macken, a particularly evocative writer.

The confessional exploration of his own youth in which George Moore indulged so exuberantly is continued more sensitively in the novels of Forrest Reid or in Michael Farrell's *Thy Tears Might Cease*, while Mary Lavin has skilfully brought a particular understanding of adolescence into her domestic stories and novels. And, of course, there is James Joyce with his portrayal of the artist's development from child into young man, shaped inexorably by his Catholic upbringing just as Joyce's own fiction is structurally moulded by his experience of Aristotle and Aquinas.

Catholicism in Ireland in the period before the First World War was treated tentatively by Canon Sheehan but much more forcibly and effectively by Gerald O'Donovan in novels surprisingly neglected by modern critics and readers. In our time Brian Moore continues to explore the subject, giving expression to the Catholicism of Belfast as no one else has, and in the process making himself one of the foremost novelists of his time.

Some years after the Irish Free State was established there came the Censorship, which for some decades, in addition to proscribing pornography, kept out of Ireland the work of many writers of international repute, and often banned the work of leading Irish writers. This led to considerable resentment, not least among novelists who had fought to bring the new Irish State into being. Both Frank O'Connor and Sean O'Faolain, for instance, found the repressive attitudes which prevailed in Irish life restrictive of artistic freedom. Austin Clarke's first novel, *The Bright Temptation* (1932) had seemed to Yeats 'a charming and humorous defiance of the Censorship and its ideals', and at one time three of Clarke's novels were banned by the Censorship board. Such Irish writers as Shaw, George Moore, Gogarty, Francis Hackett and Liam O'Flaherty also offended against the puritanical decorum of the censors who sought respectability for the new state, often achieving absurdity in their prohibitions which led to a suppression of discussion of many controversial matters. It was a period when, in the realistic fiction of Liam O'Flaherty, Sean O'Faolain and Frank O'Connor, a new kind of Irish sensibility expressed itself, finding in the discipline of the short story a suitable mould into which to put the kind of material that Griffin, the Banims and Carleton were handling earlier, though without the advantage of the forms and techniques which these more sophisticated modern writers deploy so effectively.

II George Moore

George Moore (1852–1933) set the scene for subsequent success in the short story; he brought cosmopolitan influences to bear upon Irish subject matter; and, like Joyce and Beckett after him, he had felt an impelling need to leave Ireland. He moved to Paris when he was twenty-one. A Catholic landlord, he came from Moore Hall, a 'big house' overlooking Lough Carra in County Mayo. In Paris he failed to become an artist, and when his Irish rents ceased to arrive he moved to England in 1880, having decided that he must try to earn his living by writing. He had educated himself in Paris, in its drawing rooms, studios and cafés. He knew the world of Parisian painters; he was friendly with Manet and Degas; and he knew the writers too. When he began to write novels his models were Balzac, Flaubert, Zola and Turgenev. At first he was concerned with social realism: *A Modern Lover* (1883; later revised and rewritten as *Lewis Seymour and Some Women*,

1917) was a naturalistic echo of Zola; *A Mummer's Wife* (1885), founded on experiences with a travelling theatre company and a mixture of the techniques of Balzac and Zola was rejected by the circulating libraries, but by *A Drama in Muslin* (1886) Moore was trying, somewhat unevenly, to find a style of his own and, fittingly, in a novel about Ireland.

This novel is full of contrasts. The background is sombre. Tenants, exasperated by evictions, are refusing to pay rents; landlords, alarmed by terrorism and the political threat to their way of living, are deeply disturbed. This is the period of the Land League, set up in 1879. Boycotting, shootings of landlords and agents had led to the Land Act of 1881. This met the principles established at the Tenant Right Convention of 1850, and brought in the three famous 'Fs': fair rents, fixity of tenure and free sale. This act was followed by the Land Acts of 1887, 1891 and 1903 which ultimately made Ireland a country of peasant proprietors. Moore realised clearly that the era of the Ascendancy was over: his contrasting pictures of wretched cabins and glittering salons showed why. And he examines the role of women in this society, his subject the history of a nation lying hidden, in his words, 'in social wrongs and domestic griefs'. This is the plight of the Muslin martyrs, the girls for whom marriage is the only answer, marriage pursued in the receptions and balls and parties, in the country houses in the west of Ireland and in the drawing rooms of Dublin during the season. The glitter and tinsel of the Viceregal Court contrasts with the big house. The aims of this society, Moore is saying, are frivolous. Although Moore himself plays omniscient narrator, at times the heroine, Alice Barton, criticises her society as she comes to understand it, and develops a strong compassion for others. Eventually she marries a man whom her family and friends think socially 'beneath' her, a doctor whose practical idealism matches her own. And they leave Ireland to work in London, their last experience symbolically that of seeing the horrors of an eviction.

Moore echoes Flaubert in the alternating scenes where the landlord and his agent argue with peasants in front of the house while Mrs Barton, Alice's mother, dismisses an army captain who is in her view an unsuitable suitor for her other daughter Olive. His style varied; he was still at the mercy of his exuberance, as the famous passage describing the dress-maker's shop shows with its musical parallels:

> Lengths of white silk clear as the notes of violins playing in a minor key, white poplin falling into folds statuesque as the bass of a fugue by Bach; yards of ruby velvets, rich as an air from Verdi played on the piano; tender green velvet, pastoral as hautboys heard beneath trees in a fair Arcadian vale; blue turquoise faille francaise fanciful as the tinkling of a guitar twanged by a Watteau shepherd; gold brocade, sumptuous as organ tones swelling through the jewelled twilight of a nave; scarves and trains of midnight blue profound as the harmonic snoring of a basson. . . .

Or there is the picture of the débutantes' shoulders seen in terms of different roses, reminding us of Moore's training as an artist, and of how well his critical views on art were put in *Modern Painting* (1893).

Moore himself realised the failings of *A Drama in Muslin*, but its effectiveness is undoubted. It should be read in conjunction with *Parnell and his Island* (1887) where Moore's awareness that his own landowning class were doomed is clear: the Irish-Americans would, he thought, repossess the land. This is a sardonic, Swiftian view of Irish poverty, lack of self-help, and brutalism; but even the fact that Moore saw it with pity as well as loathing has not made it popular in Ireland. At this time he felt a strong aversion for his country-men, as the autobiographical *Confessions of a Young Man* (1888) make clear. After several more novels (in *Spring Days* his questioning of English values is a forerunner of E. M. Forster's *Howard's End*; in *Vain Fortune* he is echoing Ibsen's queries) came *Esther Waters* (1894), his most English novel and the one by which he is now best known in England. This Balzacian story tells how an obsession with racehorses ruins servants as well as masters. Moore knew his subject — his father, who twice owned a racing-stable, had won large sums of money on the turf — and centred his story on the enduring heroism of Esther Waters, a kitchen-maid.

Moore fell in love with Mrs Craigie, an American heiress, with whom he collaborated in writing several plays. She dismissed him, and is portrayed in *Celibates* (1895) as Mildred Lawson; she also appears in 'Lui et Elles' in *Memoirs of My Dead Life* (1921) and as Henrietta Marr in *Single Strictness* (1922). Moore's biographer, Joseph Hone, relates the story of

how Moore told his friend Dujardin about his quarrel with
her in 1904:

'I was walking in the Green Park', he said, 'and I saw her in front of
me. I was blind with rage and I ran up behind her and kicked her.' At
first he related this story with some embarrassment, but when he
grew accustomed to his invention, with relish. The scene in the
Green Park was afterwards used in the sketch 'Lui et Elles' . . . where
a heartless woman on whose face he detected a mocking smile,
received the assault 'nearly in the centre of the backside, a little
to the right', and seems highly gratified to find that she has aroused
such a display of feeling. 'It was inevitable, I said, part of the world's
history, and I lost sight of all things but the track of my boot on the
black crêpe de Chine.'

There followed *Evelyn Innes* (1898), full of fashionable
feeling for Wagnerian operas.

Moore disapproved of the Boer War and Kiplingesque
imperialism; he disliked the conventional English theatre and
life in London; in 1900 he decided to join W. B. Yeats and
Edward Martyn (1859–1924) in their Irish Literary Theatre.
Martyn was also a Catholic landlord, with a home at Tulira
Castle, County Galway, and Moore was later to describe him
in *Hail and Farewell*. Martyn's Ibsenite play about Ireland,
The Heather Field, was the second play produced by the Irish
Literary Theatre; it was followed by *Maeve*. Then Moore,
who had moved to Dublin to hurl himself enthusiastically
into the creation of a new Irish literature, for which Yeats
had been working energetically since 1891, set himself a
political question of whether Ireland could be led by someone
outside the inarticulate mass of the people. He answered
it by taking over Martyn's play *The Tale of a Town*,
reworking it as *The Bending of the Bough*, and in this play,
produced in Dublin in 1900, put his view that the submerged
national will would emerge, using some temporary voice from
outside the people.

In 1901 Moore collaborated with Yeats in writing *Diarmuid
and Grania*. The problem here was what language was to be
used. Moore, like Yeats, knew no Irish, though he was inspired
by the ideals of the Gaelic League. He tells how he wrote the
play in French, which Lady Gregory translated into English,
which was in turn translated by Taidgh O'Donoghue into
Irish, which Lady Gregory then translated into English, to

which Yeats supplied style! Moore did not like Lady Gregory's own style, her use of an English that Yeats praised so warmly as like the living speech of the Galway peasants who thought in Irish, but he believed strongly that the new literature ought to come out of Irish. So he had the stories of *The Untilled Field* (1903) translated into and published in Irish first of all.

In these stories, the first modern exploration of the form to be undertaken in Ireland, Moore wrote in a very simple, level and direct style of the poverty-stricken parishes of Mayo, where recent ruined cottages marked one solution to the problem of life — emigration to the promised land of America. The struggle for existence based on an arranged marriage made for an austere and spiritually bleak existence on the small farms, occasionally relieved by drink or dancing, watched over, indeed controlled by the priests. Moore's strong anti-clerical feelings were tempered by kindness; he creates a pathetic figure in Father MacTurnan who suggests in a 'Letter to Rome' that the decline in the Catholic population could be arrested if priests abandoned celibacy, and who tries, with devastating results, in 'A play-house in the waste' to create an Oberammergau in the west of Ireland. Moore's compassion irradiates his treatment of women in the stories; there is a restraint and delicacy in his almost quizzical humour as well as in his insight into life in villages round Dublin as well as those in his native Mayo.

Moore said that he modelled *The Untilled Field* upon Turgenev, and there is a Russian quality in the contrast he draws between dream and reality. In *The Lake* (1905) he develops the idea of the inner dream, a self-questioning drama within the soul of a priest who has denounced one of his parishioners who was expecting an illegitimate baby. Father Gogarty becomes morally critical of himself and, after a breakdown, of his church; finally he leaves his parish, abandoning his clothes on the shore and swimming to a new life across the serene lake. His exploration of his consciousness has occurred on his walks, through the seasons, by the lake, through its woods; he is attuned to the moods of nature; and here Moore has created a style, the melodic line, which, in its apparent simplicity, builds up the picture of his character's inner consciousness:

He walked along the shore feeling like an instrument that had been tuned. His perception seemed to have been indefinitely increased, and it seemed to him as if he were in communion with the stones in the earth and the clouds in heaven; it seemed to him as if the past and the future had become one.

The moment was one of extraordinary sweetness, never might such a moment happen in his life again. The earth and sky were enfolding in one tender harmony of rose and blue, the blue shading down to grey, and the lake floated amid vague shores, vaguely as a dream floats through sleep. The swallows were flying high, quivering overhead in the blue air. There was a sense of security and persuasion and loveliness in the evening.

Moore's stay in Dublin produced his masterpiece of auto-biography, *Hail and Farewell* (1911–14), an account of his disillusionment with the Irish literary renaissance, and with Irish Catholicism. It hides its seriousness beneath a mask of comedy; Moore smiles at himself ironically. And he laughs at his friends and enemies as well as writing about them with a mixture of perception and sympathy, of mockery and malice. Edward Martyn he had attempted to portray in earlier novels, *A Mere Accident* (1887) and *Mike Fletcher* (1889); they shared an interest in Wagner, they travelled abroad together, but Martyn was not to come fully alive until the comedy of *Hail and Farewell*. He was a patron of several Irish artists, notably Sarah Purser and Vincent O'Brien; he continued his interest in the theatre after his ways and Yeats's parted: he left the Abbey in 1914, supporting the Irish Theatre, a brief venture in Dublin. AE (George Russell) is treated with respect and affection; he seems to Moore the most civilised figure in Dublin's literary world. And then there is Yeats, whose creative influence, Moore thought, formed the cultural movement: he is seen in his middle period of disillusionment, and so Moore could not foresee his later flowering, yet none the less he emerges as a man of determination.

There is, of course, a much richer context of personality even than that afforded by these three individualistic charac-ters. Moore uses anecdotes, nuances, situations, and reflections to illuminate the men and women of Dublin in a ruthless way. He is forthright, witty and provocative. Here, for instance, is his gossipy account of how Sir Thornley Stoker, a Dublin surgeon, acquired his antiques:

. . . on the trail of a Sheraton sideboard and Naylor has been asked
to keep it till an appendix should turn up. The Chinese Chippendale
mirror over the drawing-room chimney-piece originated in an unsuccessful operation for cancer; the Aubusson carpet in the back
drawing-room represents a hernia; the Renaissance bronze on the
landing a set of gall-stones; the King Cloisonné a floating kidney; the
Buhl cabinet his opinion on an enlarged liver; and Lady Stoker's
jewels a series of small operations performed over a term of years.

This series of reveries, varied and vigorous, is a writer's, an
artist's book. But Moore, by publicly pronouncing himself a
Protestant in 1903, by his view proclaimed so fiercely in
Hail and Farewell that Catholicism is opposed to art, by
thinking that he was an instrument to rid Ireland of priestcraft,
and by his own clear realisation that the Gaelic movement was
linked to a predominantly Catholic nationalism, had come to
the end of his Irish road.

In London again, ensconced in Ebury Street, he wrote *The
Brook Kerith* (1916), a prose epic which retells the New
Testament, in Joseph of Arimathea's account that Jesus did
not die on the cross but lives as a shepherd among the Essenes,
where Paul discovers him. Biblical rhythms and images enrich
the effective easy-moving narrative; it is flexible and dignified,
easy to read, and holds the reader's attention, subtle in its
humour, its use of trivia, which root it in a convincing reality.
From it Moore moved to eleventh-century life in the philosophical romance of *Héloïse and Abelard* (1921), in which
the ill-fated lovers move against a background of crowded
cities and convents, their intellectualism contrasting with the
earlier attitudes of minor characters, the whole a mixture of
movement and contemplation, a complex presentation of
human resolution.

There were many revisions of earlier works, in, for instance,
Celibate Lives (1927). Moore also wrote several plays in his
last years, some based on his novels. The very personal criticism
of *Avowals* (1919) was carried further in *Conversations in
Ebury Street* (1924), a work dictated to his secretary which
gave it the direct effect of talk. Moore died in 1933, with
twenty-one volumes of fiction, nine plays, two volumes of
verse, and eleven works of autobiography or essays to his
credit, as well as the many revisions. He affected the course
not only of fiction in English but also the style of its prose,

by his creation of a rich unhurried narrative, relying on rhythm and repetition to shape its often symbolic pattern. This style owed much to Moore's knowledge of art and music, and an ability — gained by sixty years of constant revision and experimentation — to incorporate his visual and aural delight into words.

III Ireland seen through different attitudes

While Moore experimented others used conventional methods to convey their views of Irish life. For instance, in 1889, the same year that Yeats emerged effectively as a poet, there was published an atmospheric, almost Gothic novel, *An Irish Cousin,* the first result of a remarkable collaboration by two Victorian maiden ladies, Edith Œnone Somerville (1858–1949) and 'Martin Ross', Violet Martin (1862–1915). The collaboration lasted for the rest of their lives and it continued, Edith Somerville believed, after Violet Martin died, through spiritualist communications. It is hard to discern the details of how this partnership worked, though *Irish Memories* (1917) gives an excellent account of its background. Edith, who had studied art in London and on the Continent and worked as a painter all her life, seems to have contributed more to their admirable descriptions of scenery and to the action of their novels and stories, whereas Violet supplied subtle, recondite adjectives, 'the more knife-edged slice of sarcasm', in Edith's words, 'and the more poetic feeling for words and a sense of style that seems to one flawless and unequalled.' By 1894 they had achieved their masterpiece *The Real Charlotte*.

This novel's dialogue, with all its social nuances, is subtle and lively, its narration skilled and varied, its action representative of Irish society as the world of the Ascendancy crumbled. Christopher Dysart is decent but weak, even decadent; he falls in love with Francie and learns how to cope with unrequited love. Lambert, his agent, also loves her and marries her when his first wife dies. Francie, high-spirited, vulgar, naïve and ultimately pathetic is pushed into the arms of the stupid, insensitive soldier, Hawkins, by Charlotte Mullen. Charlotte is an anti-heroine, ruthless, greedy and energetic in her acquisition of land and status. Her evil nature is constantly, cumulatively at work. Charlotte, ugly and squat, herself passionately loves Lambert and eventually, after Francie's death, through her stupid, dominating desire for revenge, loses him.

Somerville and Ross convey the complexity of this particular self-contained changing world, drawing it in sharp detail, and treating it with the consistent comic irony that can present guilt, suffering, and tragedy at a universal level of realism. And they set it superbly. Their descriptions of the Irish countryside are based upon lovingly minute observation of its detail as well as a sharp awareness of the effects of the ever-changing weather, the sweeping in of incessant rainstorms from the sea or the halcyon calm of a lake on some timeless summer day. They matched the scenery to the mood of their narration, no less in the cheerful energy of their hunting stories than in their occasional evocation of damp, Gothic gloom, and nowhere better than in *The Real Charlotte* do they use their settings as varied, emotive backdrops: symbolic, and deeply ironic — contrasting idyllic natural beauty with dissonant human behaviour.

Very different were the stories for which they gained and rightly retain popular praise: *Some Experiences of an Irish R. M.* (1899), *Further Experiences of an Irish R. M.* (1908) and *In Mr Knox's Country* (1915). Major Yeates, suddenly become a resident magistrate in south-west Ireland, finds both gentry and peasantry devious, and his attempts to understand and fit into a horse-centred and socially complex society give rise to a high-spirited, at times hilarious comedy of manners, packed with witty dialogue, the whole based upon close observation of and delight in eccentricity. The speech of these stories has been well described by F. S. L. Lyons as something not deliberately contrived, as in the writings of Lady Gregory or Synge, but flowing naturally out of the environment and recorded with the tender precision of the folklorist; he adds that 'What Somerville and Ross did have, of course, and what folk-lorists generally don't was a highly developed sense of the ridiculous and the ability to extract the maximum amusement out of the most mundane and trivial occasions. For that, surely, they do not need to be forgiven.' There has been a general tendency in Ireland to regard them as patronising, *de haut en bas*, but this is beginning to alter as their love of the country is realised, and their commitment to portraying the part of it they knew intimately, the crumbling society of the Anglo-Irish. The irony of their viewpoint is achieved in the comedy of manners of the Irish R. M. stories, where the narrator is often gulled. Somerville and Ross wrote with sympathy about country people; as well as enjoying their sense of humour they appreciated their simple wisdom and their sense of the sorrow of life in an entirely unsentimental way. They knew, as John Cronin has sensibly remarked, both the grave and the gay side of their worlds.

After Martin Ross died, *Mount Music* (1919) and *The Big House of Inver* (1925) continued the exploration of the decline and fall of the Ascendancy. *Mount Music* describes Ireland after the series of land acts culminating in the Wyndham Act of 1903 had changed land ownership, but it lacks the steely sureness of *The Real Charlotte*. *The Big House of Inver* — in many ways a modern version of Maria Edgeworth's *Castle Rackrent* — charts the decline of a family, the main events occurring in 1912. That was the year that Violet Martin had the idea of it all when she wrote to Edith Somerville to describe a visit she made to Tyrone House, near Galway, empty and derelict:

> on a long promontory by the sea, and there rioted three or four generations of X's, living with the countrywomen, occasionally marrying them, all illegitimate four times over . . . About one hundred and fifty years ago, a very grand Lady . . . married the head of the family and lived there, and was so corroded with pride that she would not allow her two daughters to associate with the neighbours of their own class. She lived to see them marry two of the men in the yard.

The letter ended: 'If we dared to write up that subject.' *The Big House of Inver* does that very thing, and it does it with panache. Shibby, a powerful character, and one convincingly possessed by hatred, dominates the novel's action, but that ghost-ridden action reaches right back into the past, as far as 1739. And yet there is excellent comedy woven throughout the sombre narration. Old John delights in his grand-daughter's having had her education in a French convent:

> I declare that to ye she's that cultured ye'd say she was born in a droign-room! Upon me soul ye would. And to hear her play the

p'yanna — Oh, 'twould delight a Turk! And as for French! — Honest
to God! she talks it as nice as easy as meself talks the English!

The social observation rested upon an acute awareness of
the minutiae of class, and a refusal to compromise with
nationalism despite the fact that the world Somerville and
Ross portrayed was passing. Their position was truly Anglo-
Irish, and *The Silver Fox* (1898) explores in no provincial
way the differences they saw between English, Irish and
Anglo-Irish. In constructing their pictures of a ramshackle,
carefree life beyond the Pale, where faded splendour shaded
into shameless shabbiness, they transcended their immediate
situations and subjects; theirs were novels of passion *and*
decay. However, they contemplated the actions and endlessly
idiosyncratic speech of all their characters with a fundamental
zest for living: cold yet compassionate in their detachment,
the paradox of their benign cynicism, they refined an intrinsi-
cally Irish sense of the comedy of existence.

In contrast the novels of Canon Sheehan (Patrick Augustine
Sheehan, 1852—1913) reflect some of the Catholic orthodoxy
of his day. Educated at St Colman's College, Fermoy and the
Maynooth seminary, subsequently a curate in England and
County Cork, he became parish priest at Doneraile in 1895.
That year his first novel, *Geoffrey Austin, Student*, was
published, but the first of his works likely to appeal to a
modern reader is *My New Curate* (1900) where he draws two
priests with masterly skill. The old priest tells the story of the
young zealous reformer brought up against inertia. The
Canon's own learning and intellect successfully inform these
portraits, but he is weaker when he turns to melodramatic
matters such as villains and heroines and their troubles. He
seems to have decided to observe and record rather than
interfere in public life and so *Luke Delmege* (1901) criticises
the ineffectiveness of Irish life and ends up indecisively,
Canon Sheehan's young priest having drawn a contrast
between English and Irish ideals. In general the novels mirror
Irish life with critical affection. *The Blindness of Dr Gray*
(1909), for instance, portrays, but not entirely successfully,
Jansenist legalistic rigidity in its main character, which proves
to be open to change, to perception of the force of love.

There is a great difference between either the urbanity of
Somerville and Ross or the gentleness of Canon Sheehan and

the vulgarity of Amanda M'Kittrick Ros (Anna Margaret M'Kittrick, 1860–1939) who arouses fierce feelings in admirers and detractors. Her novels are *Irene Iddesleigh* (1897) and *Delina Delaney* (1898); *Helen Huddleston* was unfinished but published with a final chapter by Jack Loudan in 1969. These novels are so absurd in their artificial coincidental content as in their bombastic, extravagant, alliterative style that they can be enjoyable — for a time. The result of a protracted legal battle over an inherited lime-kiln was that Mrs Ros carried her hatred of lawyers into her fiction and her poetry, *Poems of Puncture* (1913) and *Fumes of Formation* (1933). She also attacked critics savagely in her posthumously published works, with typical Rabelaisian gusto, direct rudeness and lavatorial crudity.

The vein of humour explored in the Irish R. M. stories of Somerville and Ross was also mined by (William) Percy French (1854–1920). Born in Roscommon, educated at Trinity College, he earned his livelihood as a civil engineer, but made his name internationally by his humorous stories — *The First Lord Liftinant and Other Tales* (1890) is still well worth reading — his sketches and, above all, his songs. Of these 'Phil the Fluter's Ball', 'Are ye Right There, Michael' (his song about the West Clare railway that led to a libel action with the railway's directors) or 'The Mountains of Mourne' are good examples of his continuing capacity to keep readers entertained.

In *Golden Apple* (1947), written at the age of eighty-two, George A. Birmingham quotes *Tristram Shandy* at a critical point, the farcical incident of Bert's proposal to Peggy. His lineage as a wit clearly derives from Sterne, and the same very pithy ironic humour runs throughout his work. George A. Birmingham was a pseudonym used by Rev. J. O. Hannay (1865–1950), whose varied life included being rector of Westport, County Mayo, where some of his novels are set. He also wrote several learned books under his own name; of these *The Wisdom of the Desert* (1904) is still very readable.

Spanish Gold (1908) is the best-known example of his light touch in fiction; it centres on the activities of a curate, the Reverend J. J. Meldon, a superbly comic character, possessed of an amiable and endearing realism. The local doctor, O'Grady, fulfils the same kind of role in *General John Regan*

(1913), a novel later staged by Charles Hawtrey with great success in London, but causing a fierce riot in Westport in 1914. It is still very funny, a comment that can be made about so many of George A. Birmingham novels, *Lalage's Lovers* (1911), for instance, *The Adventures of Dr Whitty* (1913) or *Send for Dr O'Grady* (1923). *The Grand Duchess* (1924) is particularly recommended. Birmingham's novels reflect the sanity of civilised humour; written to be read aloud, they respond to the test: they make people laugh. The best of his political novels is *The Red Hand of Ulster* (1912), which clearly analyses the intransigence of the political problem of the North, prophesying UDI on the part of the province. Birmingham blended high seriousness with his satiric treatment of Irish public life, and these political novels, based no doubt upon the experience gained when he played an effective part in the Gaelic League in its early days, are still worth reading for their sense of looming tragedy, as well as their admirable tolerance.

Following George A. Birmingham's example of placing humour firmly in the life of the countryside, Lynn Doyle (Leslie Alexander Montgomery, 1873–1961), a banker born in County Down, created the fictional village of Ballygullion as locale for his dialect stories: these are, however, less subtle than Birmingham's in their comedy and have at times a heavy-handedness about them. Doyle also wrote several plays for the Ulster Literary Theatre.

A northern contemporary of George A. Birmingham, born in South Fermanagh, Shan Bullock (1865–1935), a civil servant who worked in London, wrote an interesting auto-biography in *After Sixty Years* (1931). Like his novel *By Thrasna River* (1895) it deals with his early experiences, depicting what now seems a very remote Northern Ireland indeed. In addition to over a dozen novels (with generally unattractive characters) Bullock wrote poems and stories and several biographies, the best known being *Thomas Andrews, Shipbuilder* [of the *Titanic*] (1912).

Society seen from a working-class point of view was the subject of *The Ragged Trousered Philanthropists* (ed. Jessie Pope, 1914; ed. [and de-Bowdlerised] Frederick C. Ball, 1955) by Robert Tressell (Robert Noonan, 1870–1911). This picture of life in a resort town in 1903 was probably modelled on Hastings, where he lived from 1902–10; he was dying of tuberculosis as he wrote the book. In it he conveys the fears endemic in working-class life at the time, of unemployment, of ill-health, and of creditors; he does this through a sharp sense of satire, and an ability to present working-class attitudes — positive and negative — through vigorous dialogue in an entirely convincing way. His persuasive portrayal of his characters' differing attitudes, their humour and endurance has given his one work the status of being 'the' working-class novel of its time.

A novelist of considerable power, now slowly beginning to be reassessed and appreciated, Gerald O'Donovan (Jeremiah O'Donovan, 1871–1942), wrote about a period and an area of Irish history not often explored or indeed understood. A pupil at St Patrick's College, Maynooth, he was ordained in 1895, and worked in Loughrea from 1896. He was a modernist in his views, progressive in his attitudes to the improvement of social and economic conditions. He joined the Irish Agricultural Organisation Society; he brought artists, including Sarah Purser and Jack B. Yeats, to work on a new cathedral in Loughrea; and in 1901 he daringly invited actors and actresses to this western town. He was involved in the work of the Gaelic League, and he was a friend of writers as well as artists, musicians and actors. In 1904, however, as a result of difficulties with the new bishop of his diocese he left the priesthood, and went to Dublin, then to London. Readers of George Moore will probably recognise the progressive liberalism of O'Donovan in the story 'Fugitives' in *The Untilled Field* (1903) and in the situation of the priest in *The Lake* (1905).

O'Donovan wrote six novels, the best of them, *Father Ralph* (1913), dealing with situations similar to his own as a liberal priest whose work was checked by papal opposition to modernism. Papal views, expressed in *Ne Temere* decree, about marriage between Catholics and non-Catholics which have so affected the Protestant minority in Ireland are the subject of *Waiting* (1919). *Conquest* (1920) gives a good view of the cross-currents of life in early-twentieth-century Ireland. O'Donovan married in 1910, and formed a close friendship with Rose Macaulay (1889–1958) whom he met in 1918 and sketched in his last novel *The Holy Tree* (1922). By then O'Donovan, who became a publisher's reader after the First

World War, seemed to have exhausted his capacity for fiction; but what he wrote within nine creative years is valuable for its presentation of human beings facing and questioning abstractions and absolutes, and for the excellent, full picture that his novels give of a liberal, apparently progressive period.

The movement from realism to a freer, more imaginative, even poetic style that characterised George Moore's fiction, and was to be echoed in Joyce's development, is also to be found in the work of Forrest Reid (1875–1947). He wrote two effective, sensitive books in *Apostate* (1926), an auto-biography treating his life up to the period when he was apprenticed to the tea trade, and *Peter Waring* (1937), a novel about a boy's growing up in Northern Ireland, written with a precise elegance. It was a fresh version of *Following Darkness* (1912), where the adolescent's interest in art is over-introspective, and opposed by the hardness of an insensitive father.

Discontent with the commerical life of Belfast (Reid's father began as a trading shipowner, bankrupted himself, then became a manager of a firm) had triggered off *Apostate*, and Reid found the elegance of Cambridge to his liking after he gave up the tea trade for the university, where Lowes Dickinson and E. M. Forster admired his work. Moving among the Cambridge Hellenists strengthened his interest in male friendships, and when he returned to Belfast he wrote out of an ability to recreate boyhood understandingly, his capacity to create adults being less sensitively developed. Thus his trilogy about Tom Barber, *Uncle Stephen* (1931), *The Retreat* (1936) and *Young Tom* (1944) — the last awarded the James Tait Black Prize — deals particularly well with the discoveries and developments inherent in youthful dreaming.

Reid could also write in down-to-earth fashion, as his early novels *The Kingdom of Twilight* (1904) and *The Bracknels* (1911), with its harsh Belfast merchant, show convincingly; this capacity for creating the direct, even sordid details of Belfast life also surfaced in *At the Door of the Gate* (1915), where Reid portrayed Mrs Seawright and her family with sharp skill. He exibited insight as a critic, in his pioneering *W. B. Yeats: a critical study* (1915) and *Walter de la Mare: a critical study* (1929). Ultimately, however, he remains in the mind for Richard Jefferies-like evocations of youth and natural beauty, especially for his sensitive portrayals of adolescence arriving at the anxieties and alleviations of religion, sex and art.

IV James Joyce

The phenomenon of an urban Irish Catholic voice declaring *'non serviam'* in such a way that the medium of fiction was to be deeply affected by its example is, on the face of it, strange: yet the whole process through which Joyce came to write has a compelling logic about it. He was bound up intimately with Catholicism, but in him the often Jansenist Irish tradition collided head-on with a rival devotion, to artistic integrity and achievement: none the less, though the revolted against the Church, he remained steeped in Catholic thoughts and attitudes.

Joyce's development as a writer moved, rather as George Moore's had, from the naturalism of *Dubliners* (1914) through a more flexible aesthetic prose in *A Portrait of the Artist as a Young Man* (1916) to an interpretation of a city in *Ulysses* (1922) and then to the allusive impressionistic world of dreams in *Finnegan's Wake* (1939).

James Joyce (1882–1941) was born into a family always short of money and slipping socially: the Joyces could be described as being, like Shaw's family, 'downstarts'. It was a family deeply divided in attitudes to the Church. Joyce's mother was devout, his father an anti-clerical Parnellite; the pain of such splits is shown in the Christmas dinner in *A Portrait*. He went to the Jesuit school, Clongowes Wood College, then, when money ran out, to a Christian Brothers School before being given a place at Belvedere, another Jesuit school, in 1893. Though encouraged to enter the priesthood he decided against it, developing intellectual and aesthetic attitudes to literature as an undergraduate at University College, Dublin: he admired Ibsen greatly and began to study European languages and literatures.

After graduating in 1902 Joyce starved as a supposed medical student in Paris, then returned to Dublin to live in Gogarty's Martello tower. He taught in a school, met Nora Barnacle from Galway on 10 June 1904 and left Ireland permanently with her in October of that year. During the middle period of his life they lived at Pola, then Trieste, and in Zurich from 1915 to 1919, Joyce teaching in various Berlitz schools. A final phase of his exile began with the move to Paris in 1920, where *Ulysses* was published in 1922. Joyce, now freed from financial worries by a benefactor, wrote *Finnegan's Wake* which appeared from 1927 in fragments in *transition* and in book form under various titles. The Joyces spent a year near Vichy on the outbreak of the war, then moved to Zurich where Joyce died in 1941.

Before leaving Ireland in 1904 Joyce had finished the thirty-six poems of *Chamber Music* (1907): these slight conventional love poems remind us of Joyce's deep interest in music. Most of them have been set to music, some by Joyce himself. He had a fine tenor voice and grew up in a city where singing was part of social life; he was enthusiastic about Tom Moore, advising his son Giorgio to buy Moore's *Irish Melodies* and learn 'Fly not yet', 'Oh ye dead', 'Quick, we have but a second', 'The Time I lost in wooing', and 'Silent O Moyle'. Joyce's poem 'Gas from a Burner' shows his own attitude to Ireland after a brief return visit in 1912. The mockery of folklore and 'poets, sad, silly and solemn' in it is consistent with Joyce's lack of sympathy for the literary movement. In *Pomes Penyeach* (1927) he was more varied in theme, the poems on family relationships being the most interesting.

He had a reverence, however, for the continuity of culture; his own work is rooted in respect for past literary achievement. Thus he is influenced by French models in the stories of *Dubliners* (1914), in which he aimed to present Ireland's capital city as the centre of paralysis, drawing with 'a style of scrupulous meanness' childhood, adolescence, maturity and public life. These stories, of frustration, of sordid situations, capture Dublin speech in their subtle diction, for Joyce had a mimic's ear; they reflect his interest not only in realism but also in its opposite, what is sometimes summed up as modernism, an ordering of experience through symbolism, impressionism and even formalism. Joyce developed what he called epiphanies, as a means of showing forth reality; an economic concentration focusing upon a character or upon a moment of revelation. He combined a capacity to catch sentimentality with a cold irony, best seen perhaps in the story 'Ivy Day in the Committee Room' where both genuine and trite emotions about Parnell are exhibited. A sardonic onlooker's view pervades 'A Little Cloud' and 'Counterparts', but the last story, 'The Dead', moves away from the rest of the book. Apart from the social comedy so keenly observed in the clash between nationalist and European attitudes, Gabriel discovers that his wife, who comes from Galway, is not thinking of him but of Michael Furey, a youthful lover who died of love for her there. Gabriel is presented ironically as a complex character who feels superior to others, and sympathetically when he discovers his own ignorance. In the resolution of the story he becomes more aware of the complexities of all human life, and Joyce makes us aware, too, of some of the subtleties of Irish life, stressing once again that division marked by the Shannon between racial groups, between east and west:

> A few light taps upon the pane made him turn to the window. It had begun to snow again. He watched sleepily the flakes, silver and dark, falling obliquely against the lamplight. The time had come for him to set out on his journey westward. Yes, the newspapers were right: snow was general all over Ireland. It was falling on every part of the dark central plain, on the treeless hills, falling softly upon the Bog of Allen and, farther westward, softly falling into the dark mutinous Shannon waves. It was falling, too, upon every part of the lonely churchyard on the hill where Michael Furey lay buried. It lay thickly drifted on the crooked crosses and headstones, on the spears of the little gate, on the barren thorns. His soul swooned slowly as he heard the snow falling faintly through the universe and faintly falling, like the descent of their last end, upon all the living and the dead.

Stephen Hero (1944) is part of a longer manuscript in which Joyce had tried his hand at an autobiographical novel on an epic scale. What remains of this early attempt is realistically descriptive, with the narrator at times criticising the hero, though it is generally a book slanted to the hero's point of view, his rejection of Dublin. It has many excellent passages, such as the mockery of a country priest's sermon about the monkeys of Barbary, and some fine dialogue, but it was not what Joyce wanted. He cut, compressed, selected, and then wrote in *A Portrait of the Artist as a Young Man* (1916) a novel, a *bildungsroman* where the author is *not* Stephen Daedalus. Stephen's growth from about three to his graduation culminates in his decision to leave Ireland once he had formulated his aesthetic theory. He had rejected the literary movement's traditions in the famous diary entry of 14 April describing John Alphonsus Mulrennan's account of his meeting the old man in a mountain cabin (who said, 'Ah, there must be terrible queer creatures at the latter end of the world.'). Now he must 'go to encounter for the millionth time the reality of experience and to forge in the smithy of my soul the uncreated conscience of my race'. His aims are precise:

> I will not serve that in which I no longer believe whether it call itself my home, my fatherland or my church: and I will try to express myself in some mode of life or art as freely as I can and as wholly as I can, using for my defence the only arms I allow myself to use — silence, exile, and cunning.

What has led to this twentieth-century spiritual and intellectual crisis has been told with consummate skill. There is a gradual awakening of Stephen's consciousness from the first chapter with its Parnellite controversy and the atmospheric details of Clongowes Wood through the three chapters which show Stephen's struggling with decisions between body and soul — his precocious sexual encounters followed by his experience of a retreat (with the famous hell-fire sermon); there follows the rejection of the priesthood, and then comes the prose poem, the epiphany of Stephen's encounter with the girl on the seashore. Stephen has been experimenting with phrases: it was 'a day of dappled seaborne clouds'. In the final chapter there is a revealing discussion between Stephen and the English Dean centring on the word 'funnel' used by the Dean, and 'tundish' used by Stephen (and still used by so many other Irish people), who thinks 'The language in which we are speaking is his before it is mine . . . . His language, so familiar and so foreign will always be for me an acquired speech.' Finally Stephen realises that his true vocation is that of the artist, blending aesthetic experience with the logical ordering that he has learned from his Catholic upbringing: he describes himself in quasi-religious language as 'a priest of the eternal imagination, transmuting the daily bread of experience into the radiant body of everliving life'.

For Joyce, however, English was to a certain extent plastic:

he had to exert control over it and this he did with panache in *Ulysses*. This was preceded by *Exiles*, an Ibsenite problem play about marital infidelity set in the Dublin of 1912, which Joyce had revisited that year. The naturalism did not fuse with the somewhat sentimental autobiographical questioning about the nature of human communication; this, however, resulted in a detachment, an assertion of the individual's right to choose.

Ulysses, originally planned as a short story, looks at more than the individual; it shows us the sixteenth of June 1904 — eighteen hours in the lives of three main characters; we see their lives through their streams of consciousness; and there is a conscious structure of eighteen episodes — modelled upon and parodying episodes in Homer's *Odyssey* — that counterpoints the flux of human experience. And, of course, the novel is a comic satire, decidedly mock-heroic, with Leopold Bloom, a Jewish advertising salesman as a modern Odysseus; his wife Molly, unlike the faithful Penelope, is an adulteress, and Telemachus searching for a father is Stephen Daedalus, back from Paris, more mature now but still trying to come to terms with himself, aware of the difference between what he sees and what he feels. He finds Bloom, an ineffectual cuckold who is none the less kind, sympathetic, tolerant, and with a humorous mind, seen best when he feeds his cat, a typical passage of Joycean observation and stream of consciousness. His encounter in a pub with the Citizen, a fierce nationalist, echoes the Cyclops episode in the *Odyssey*, and ends after two journalistic parodies with a Biblical echo:

> When, lo, there came about them all a great brightness and they beheld the chariot wherein He stood ascend to heaven. And they beheld Him in the chariot, clothed upon in the glory of the brightness, having raiment as of the sun, fair as the moon and terrible that for awe they durst not look upon Him. And there came a voice out of heaven, calling: Elijah! Elijah! And he answered with a main cry: Abba! Adonai! And they beheld Him even Him, ben Bloom Elijah, amid clouds of angels ascend to the glory of the brightness at an angle of fortyfive degrees over Donohoe's in Little Green Street like a shot off a shovel.

The narrator of the passage begins his account of the flight in pure Dublinese, an example being the repetition of 'mister' in the slut's shout — 'Eh, mister! Your fly is open, mister!'

The parodies, notably in the hospital chapter, are admirably done; they supply additional variety to the novel which uses an omniscient narrator, dialogue and streams of conscious as well as subconscious thought in its complex pattern. Throughout, the realism blends with the fantastic, the surrealistic, as in the brothel scene, written in the form of a play. The first part of *Ulysses* deals mainly with Stephen, the second and largest with Bloom, while the third is Molly's famous soliloquy, a monologue which conveys through the stream of consciousness her somewhat jumbled circular way of thinking as she remembers her love affairs of the past, and rapidly gets over any guilty feelings about them.

After this realist novel of modern urban man which had taken seven years to compose came 'a history of the world', the comic paradoxical vista of *Finnegan's Wake*, of Man's fall and resurrection. The events centre on HCE, a Dublin publican and his family, especially his wife Anna Livia Plurabelle, their sons Shem and Shaun and Issy their daughter: the whole is at times an allegory of Joyce's family. To fathom the book requires devotion, and application to the numerous guidebooks which offer help through the complexities, the relativism, the cycles of the book, its vast learning, the mythology, the puns and allusions that stem from Joyce's self-confidence, allowing him to depict what may be merely HCE's dream, or his own, or a dream of humanity. It is a great piece of self-indulgence, 'that letter self-penned to one's other that never perfect ever planned', experimental certainly, synthetic in its language, but continuous in the aim of its creation. In T. S. Eliot's view Joyce's manipulation of a parallel between the contemporary and the antique was a way of controlling, of shaping contemporary history, otherwise a panorama of futility and anarchy. But in *Finnegan's Wake* Joyce's self-mockery does not entirely defend him from the charge that in his seventeen years of writing the book he gave way to 'toomuchness' and 'fartoomanyness'.

V Lesser talents

Conal O'Riordan (1874–1948), who used the pen name F. Norreys Connell, wrote short stories, plays and novels; he succeeded Synge on the Abbey Board but soon resigned.

Over a period of twenty years he created a novel cycle in twelve volumes, *Adam of Dublin: a romance of today* (1920) the best of them. *Judith Quinn* (1939) is typical of these uneven novels, which are often confused and confusing. A far better author was Alister McAllister (1877–1943), a graduate of the Royal University, then chief clerk of the National University from 1908–14, and a gifted painter, who wrote eight plays under the name Anthony P. Wharton, of which *Irene Wycherly* (1907) and *At the Barn* (1912) were very successful. As Wharton he wrote four novels – *The Man on the Hill* and *Evil Communications* (1926) are still eminently readable. As Lynn Brock he created Colonel Gore and gave him his head in the plots of thirteen novels in which sinister evil is exposed lurking beneath a smooth social surface.

In the same genre was Inspector French, invented by Freeman Wills Crofts (1879–1957), chief assistant engineer of the Belfast and Northern Counties Railway; but his realistic crime novels depend upon careful attention to detail, an insistence upon the slow logical gathering of information. A mixture of experience in the law, in wartime intelligence and in running his own detective bureau formed the foundation for Peter Cheyney's (Reginald Evelyn Peter Southouse Cheyney, 1896–1951) great success as a skilful writer of crime novels. Born in County Clare, he acted out the life of a 'clubland hero', but had the ingenuity to create Messrs Lemmy Caution and Slim Callaghan, and to write in an effective American style. *This Man is Dangerous* (1936) began his popularity, and *Ladies Won't Wait* (1951) is a good example of his Americanised writing.

Historical fiction was written by Joseph O'Neill (1878–1932), a graduate of Queen's College, Galway, who was Permanent Secretary of the Department of Education from 1923–44. *Wind from the North* (1934) blends eleventh- and twentieth-century life through the effect of an accident upon the hero; *Philip* (1940) evokes Jerusalem before the Crucifixion. Another author who moved into the past was Francis Hackett (1883–1962), born in Kilkenny. His second novel *The Green Lion* (1936) shows the effect of Parnell. Hackett's major work, however, was *Henry the Eighth* (1929), an exploration of how Henry made England into a modern nation state. Hackett examined authority further in *Francis the First*,

Gentleman of France (1935). He found the authority of the Irish Censorship Board distasteful; his novels convey his political views and his strong love of liberty.

Two novelists, Maurice Walsh (1879–1964) and Donn Byrne (Brian Oswald Donn Byrne 1889–1928), had a popular success in the twenties. Walsh, born in Kerry, served as a customs officer in Scotland, becoming an excise expert on whisky before transferring back to Ireland after 1922. Of his four novels *The Key Above the Door* (1926) and *The Small Dark Man* (1929) have an unsophisticated and agreeable tweediness about them. Set in Scotland and the south-west of Ireland, they convey appreciation of the scenery and country life with well-handled narrative and quiet romance. An excessive romanticism, however, overlays the narrative in Donn Byrne's novels *Hangman's House* (1925) and *The Power of the Dog* (1929). He was born in South Armagh and studied at Dublin, Paris and Leipzig; later he wrote short stories successfully for various American magazines.

While Maurice Walsh obviously enjoyed his life in Scotland and his returns to Kerry, Darrell Figgis (1882–1925) was more critical of modern Ireland. His best-known novel (originally published as written by 'Michael Ireland') is *The Return of the Hero* (1923), dealing with Oisin's return and reaction to Christianity; it is still worth reading (but did not endear him to an Irish public with its criticism of Ireland) though *The Children of Earth* (1918) has a more powerful, poetic force working through it. Figgis's life ended unhappily in suicide.

VI A middle state

The life of (Arthur) Joyce (Lunel) Cary (1888–1957) in constrast lay largely outside Ireland, though he was to write most evocatively about his youthful experience of it. Born in Londonderry, he was educated at an English school, then in France and Scotland where he studied art, and Oxford, where he entered Trinity College in 1909, to leave with a fourth-class degree. He served with the Red Cross in the first Balkan War of 1912–13, and later with the Nigerian regiment in the Cameroons campaign from 1915 to 1916. He had joined the Nigerian Political Service in 1913 and served as a magistrate and executive officer there until 1920 when he settled in Oxford. His period in Africa is reflected in his African novels *Aissa Saved* (1932), *An American Visitor* (1933), *The African Witch* (1936) and *Mister Johnson* (1939), and in the essays of *The Case for African Freedom and Other Writings in Africa* (ed. C. Fyfe, 1962). The novels deal with issues of freedom and religion; they convey convincingly turbulent violence, contrasts between local religion and Christianity, between tribalism and westernised society, and between colonialism's laws and local politics: but they are not designed as anthropological novels about Africa in the colonial period; they examine human beings in universal situations. The best of them is the tragi-comic *Mister Johnson* with its remorseless revolution of fortune's wheel; who better than an Anglo-Irishman to expose the clash of values between the dutiful, decent, English administrator and his exuberant, devoted, African servant with its inevitable tragic climax?

Cary turned to English subject matter in *Charley is my Darling* (1940), which described delinquency in the wartime evacuation of Cockney children to Cornwall and Devon. With *Herself Surprised* (1941), *To Be a Pilgrim* (1942), and *The Horse's Mouth* (1944), his first trilogy, Cary filled a larger canvas, employing his intense interest in art to animate the archetypally romantic, bohemian artist Gully Jimson and to evoke Sara Monday in the Blakean image of woman as sexual temptress, yet by instinct maternal. Against Jimson and his irrepressible creativity stands Thomas Wilsher with his traditional conservatism: these characters each dominate a novel (Jimson, *The Horse's Mouth*; Sara, *Herself Surprised*; and Wilsher, *To Be a Pilgrim*).

In *The Moonlight* (1946) Cary explores a clash of generations in a leisurely way; his next novel, *A Fearful Joy* (1949), moves faster, more impressionistically in its portrayal of Dick Bonser's effect upon Tabitha Basket. Cary's second trilogy, *Prisoner of Grace* (1952), *Except the Lord* (1953) and *Not Honour More* (1955), deals with political issues and the role of the creative individual in contemporary society. Cary rendered the shifting English social scene sensitively. He constantly captures the essence of that change — most notably, perhaps, in the circumstances of *To Be a Pilgrim*, where a threshing machine is at work among the former glories of the

Adam saloon decorated by Angelica Kaufman. His view was based on moral attitudes to life, on personal values partially formed by his early Irish background (as he tells us in part, and amusingly, in the preface to the Carfax edition of *Charley is my Darling*, describing his own youthful delinquencies in Donegal). He attempted to recapture the essence of being Anglo-Irish in some of *Castle Corner* (1938), which conveys somewhat unevenly the concerns of an Anglo-Irish family at the mercy of historical change. But a different change, that of paradoxically timeless childhood holidays, is caught surely in *A House of Children* (1941). This autobiographical book (which won the James Tait Black Prize), one of the great evocations of Irish scenery, is written out of a shrewd knowledge of and unsentimental sympathy for children, and written too in a luminous, limpid, evocative prose which shows us Donegal through an artist's eyes, with the steadfastness of Anglo-Irish affection for the changing landscape:

There is no more beautiful view in the world than that great lough, seventy square miles of salt water, from the mountains of Annish. We had heard my father call it beautiful, and so we enjoyed it with our minds as well as our feelings; keenly with both together. Wherever we went in Annish we were among the mountains and saw the lough or the ocean; often, from some high place, the whole Annish peninsula, between the two great loughs; and the Atlantic, high up in the sky, seeming like a mountain of water higher than the tallest of land. So, that my memories are full of enormous skies, as bright as water, in which clouds sailed bigger than any others; fleets of monsters moving in one vast school up from the horizon and over my head, a million miles up, as it seemed to me, and then down again over the far-off mountains of Derry. They seemed to follow a curving surface of air concentric with the curve of the Atlantic which I could see bending down on either hand, a bow, which, even as a child of three or four, I knew to be the actual shape of the earth . . . . I would feel suddenly the roundness and independence of the world beneath me. I would feel it like a ship under my feet moving through air just like a larger stiffer cloud, and this gave me an extraordinary exhilaration.
We travelled through this enormous and magnificent scene in tranquil happiness. . . . and the memory of bathing, shouting, tea, the blue smoke of picnic fires, was mixed with the dark evening clouds shaped like flying geese, the tall water stretching up to the top of the world, the mountains sinking into darkness like whales into the ocean and over all a sky so deep that the stars, faint green sparks, seemed lost in it and the very sense of it made the heart light and proud, like a bird.

Two other writers, C. S. Lewis and Elizabeth Bowen, spent much of their lives in England. Lewis (1898–1963), born in Belfast, spent a brief period at Campbell College there, and was an Oxford don until he was appointed to a chair at Cambridge in 1954. As an academic critic he will be remembered for the learning and evident enjoyment of an older world which informed such works as, say, *The Allegory of Love* (1936), a *Preface to Paradise Lost* (1942) and *English Literature in the Sixteenth Century, excluding drama* (1954) and *An Experiment in Criticism* (1961). His popular success as a plain man's theologian came with *The Problem of Pain* (1940) and the sharp wit of *The Screwtape Letters* (1942). But his Narnia series of stories for children displays yet another side of his character, a wish to blend the factual with the fictional. In his science fiction, particularly *Perelandria* (1943), his interest in myth emerges, to blend with his undoubted narrative art. This storytelling skill is also impressive in his discerning and alarming novel *That Hideous Strength: A Modern Fairy-Tale for Grown-ups* (1945). Lewis formed part of a group at Oxford called the Inklings which included his friend Tolkien; this met regularly to tell stories. There was a curious element of self-conscious heartiness, of adolescence almost, about this side of Lewis. Despite his Christianity, he does not seem to have shed or rather rounded his attitudes into a fully accepting humanity until he wrote *Surprised by Joy: The Shape of My Early Life* (1955), *Till we have Faces: a Myth Retold* (1956), a retelling of the story of Cupid and Psyche, and *A Grief Observed* (1961), an account of his reactions to his wife's death. He had emerged by the end of his life into a state where he could uninhibitedly face the full complexity of his character.

Quite unacademic, Elizabeth Bowen (1899–1973) belongs to the tradition of Maria Edgeworth and Somerville and Ross in her sense of social comedy and subtle awareness of social levels. She grew up in a big house, Bowen's Court, in the north-east of County Cork, virtually equidistant from Mitchelstown, Mallow and Fermoy. In *Bowen's Court* (1942; 1964) she told the story of the house and her family, of how she returned there in 1952, but after seven years found she simply could not manage to keep it on her own, sold it and it was then demolished.

Her first volume of stories, *Encounters*, appeared in 1923. She was always to write stories with the same intensity she gave to her novels; the best collection of them is probably *The Demon Lover and Other Stories* (1945). Her first novel *The Hotel* (1927) showed her capacity for creating atmospheric description; in it she displayed a range of characters very effectively, notably older, managing women. One of them in her next novel, *The Last September* (1929), breaks up a young girl's engagement to a young soldier. The girl is Anglo-Irish, and so is the social life centring on the big house in which she lives, Danielstown, soon to be burnt down. Here the round of tennis, dancing and dining continues despite the troubles, courtesy covering over the boiling pot of tensions, of conflicting Anglo-Irish loyalties in a doomed situation. After *Friends and Relations* (1931), *To the North* (1932) and *The House in Paris* (1935) came *The Death of the Heart* (1938) which dealt with innocence and experience, betrayal and awakening, refinement and vulgarity. It had itself a touch of snobbishness and vulgarity: the authoress was right to like it least of her novels.

Elizabeth Bowen was concerned not to make her fiction mere self-expression: a reader's recognition of the autobiographical elements would intrude the author's life too much into her art: for detachment and control — Yeats's 'Down *hysterica passio*' — and indeed a general Anglo-Irish coldness of passion were necessary. And yet the experience of life in London in the Blitz widened her range as a writer; the supernatural emerged, disturbingly, in her story 'The Demon Lover', while her own love affair with the Canadian Charles Ritchie may have lent some hectic excitement to her classic portrayal of wartime London in *The Heat of the Day* (1949), with its lively story of espionage and counter-espionage given an extra touch of the sinister by the complex Jamesian syntax she employed.

Elizabeth Bowen's unfinished autobiography *Pictures and Conversations* (1975) is more successful than her last three novels — *A World of Love* (1955) set in the decay of an Irish country house, where money is short and time as well, *The Little Girls* (1964) and *Eva Trout or Changing Scenes* (1969), where the authoress certainly takes the lid off life. The form of autobiography allowed her more scope to dwell in a leisurely way on her ideas. Indeed her continuation of nineteenth-century ways of writing about life in the twentieth century came from the timeless halcyon days of her Irish youth. Her strength as a writer of fiction derived from an unusual mixture of snobbish respectability and the *farouche*, a blending of high art and popular romance, though she possessed an ultimate simplicity which sanctioned her particular sense of comedy: fundamentally she believed in God and ghosts.

VII Irish-centred fiction

The writings of Brinsley MacNamara (John Weldon, 1890–1963) plunge us deep into the Free State of the twenties, a time when many authors found living in Ireland frustrating in the extreme as they were met by a repressive orthodoxy unsympathetic to artistic exploration and interpretation of life. MacNamara, son of a schoolmaster in Delvin, County Westmeath, became an Abbey actor, then lived in the United States from 1913 until he returned to Delvin in 1918: that year his powerful first novel, *The Valley of the Squinting Windows*, portrayed a midland village, warts and all. It caused a furore, the book was burned in Delvin, his father's school boycotted and the author forced into the exile of Dublin, becoming Registrar of the National Gallery there in 1922. *The Clanking of Chains* (1919) continued his ruthless examination of Irish village life. There followed *The Irishman* (1920) and *The Mirror in the Dusk* (1921) where a sense of tragedy swamps the comic touches of the earlier novels. His other novels, *The Various Lives of Marcus Igoe* (1929), *Return to Ebontheever* (1936) and *Michael Caravan* (1946), have various merits, the first being an engaging fantasy, the second an attack on orthodoxy, and the last a somewhat escapist view of the better side of life in the Irish countryside.

Brinsley MacNamara was a director of the Abbey in 1935; he resigned, curiously enough, at the staging of O'Casey's *The Silver Tassie*. His own nine plays include *The Glorious Uncertainty* (1923) and *Look at the Heffernans* (1926), both very successful 'Abbey' plays, but lacking the powerful bite of *Margaret Gillan* (1933), a play perhaps reflecting his own brooding nature; it is a bitter nonstop presentation of frustrated passion and revenge. The short stories of *Some Curious People* (1945) are mellower in their observation of human character.

The role of the countryman living in Ireland was clear in middle-nineteenth-century novels: the plight of the emigrant was not often treated before the writings of Patrick MacGill (1891–1963), who left school in Donegal at the age of twelve to become a farm labourer. He crossed to Scotland two years later and wrote several volumes of poetry dealing realistically with the life of navvies before his powerful Zola-esque novels *Children of the Dead End* (1914) and *The Rat Pit* (1915) depicted the potato-pickers' route from Donegal to Scotland. He fought in the British army in France and described the war in several of his novels, among them *The Amateur Army* (1915) and *The Great Push* (1916).

Another Donegal man, and near contemporary of MacGill's, who fought against the British army in the IRA, Peadar O'Donnell (*b.* 1893), wrote novels which also depict the hardships of migratory labourers or country people existing on the edge of starvation. *Storm* (1925), *Islanders* (1928), *Adrigoole* (1929) and *The Knife* (1930) are all realistic, convincing in their lively dialogue, and written out of a fierce compassion for the struggles and suffering of the poor. *Islanders* includes the heroic aspect of their life, and passages in *Adrigoole* achieve a tragic intensity.

The problems of the poor and near poor have been treated by several writers who used the Dublin slums as settings, among them Kenneth Sarr (under which name were written the novels and plays of Kenneth Shiels Reddin, 1895–1967), a district justice who was educated at Belvedere, Clongowes Wood, and St Enda's before attending University College, Dublin. *The Passing* (1924) is a slum tragedy in one act — Sarr's novels, in contrast, offer very full interpretations of Dublin life, *Somewhere to the Sea* (1936) centring on the troubled early nineteen-twenties.

The best work of Eimar O'Duffy (1893–1935) is to be found in his *King Goshawk and the Birds* (1926), the first volume of a trilogy which satirises modern life with savagely ironical invention. O'Duffy, born in Dublin and a graduate in dentistry of University College, Dublin, had been deeply involved in the revolutionary movement, but he became disillusioned by the 1916 Rising, out of which came *The Wasted Island* (1919), an informative, powerful and unduly neglected novel. O'Duffy could write well in several genres, with some satiric comedies as well as a good historical novel, *The Lion and the Fox* (1922), to his credit. *Printer's Errors* (1922) reveals a capacity for light-hearted satire, which illness and financial problems tended to suppress in O'Duffy after he left Ireland in 1925.

The often jaundiced views that Brinsley MacNamara put forward about Ireland at times find an echo in the writings of Liam O'Flaherty (*b.* 1896) who was born on Inishmore, the largest of the Aran islands. He learned Irish there as a child but was educated in Tipperary, Blackrock College and University College, Dublin. He organised a corps of Republican volunteers at Blackrock College, but left University College to join the Irish guards in 1915. He joined the Republicans in the civil war, then, having apparently shed his Catholicism, Communism and Republicanism, went to London to write.

His first novels are uneven in achievement. *Thy Neighbour's Wife* (1923) and *The Black Soul* (1924) — accepted by Edward Garnett, who gave him much help and encouragement — evoke their Aran background effectively, developing the split between the 'urbanised' people of Kilronan, the port of Inishmore, and the 'pagan' peasants of Bungowla, five miles away, wild and culturally remote. In Dublin O'Flaherty married Margaret Barrington (formerly wife of Professor Curtis the historian) who wrote stories and a novel *My Cousin Justin* (1939).

The Informer (1925) and *Mr Gilhooley* (1926) were written in Dublin. Despite crudities in technique, their powerful mixture of realism and romance, and their sense of immediacy caused many to think in the twenties and thirties that O'Flaherty should be regarded as on a par with Joyce and O'Casey. By 1927 O'Flaherty left Ireland, not to return till after the Second World War, having visited Russia and lived in England and America. The locale of *The House of Gold* (1929) moved to Galway and the rise and fall of a gombeen man there, but in *Skerrett* (1932) O'Flaherty returned to Aran for his subject matter. As Patrick Sheean has shown in *The Novels of Liam O'Flaherty* (1976) he utilised local material, the story of the eviction of a schoolmaster, David O'Callaghan, by the parish priest, Father Farragher, in 1914; O'Flaherty had himself been taught by O'Callaghan and served mass for Father Farragher. Skerrett the schoolmaster, after a period of success as a reformer, becomes a revolutionary and ends in a padded cell.

Many of O'Flaherty's characters are obsessed by self-discovery, and *Skerrett* was written during a period when O'Flaherty was occupied with self-discovery, mining an autobiographical vein in *Two Years* (1930), *I went to Russia* (1931) and the entertaining *Shame the Devil* (1934). In *A Tourist Guide to Ireland* (1929) he was occupied by the problems of what he perceived as a peasant population oppressed by priests, politicians and publicans. In 1937 came *Famine*, his best novel. In writing this story O'Flaherty drew on his knowledge of famines on Aran, on folklore and on historical accounts of the Great Famine; he presents this crucial period with a sharp sense of the pattern of family and community life that was destroyed not only by death but also by emigration. O'Flaherty's novels never again reached the achievement of *Famine*: but in the stricter confines of the short story he was often able to subdue his rebellious sense of frustration, to curb his verbal expressionistic exuberance, and to control his desire to impart views about man's predicament. There is a noticeable progress from violence towards compassion in the stories, of which he has written more than one hundred and fifty, more than half of them dealing with open-air subjects. In these, as in the novels and his Irish poems, he was expressing a desire for a simpler, less materialistic life than that which he often attacked with such verbal vitality in his fiction.

The questioning of Irish life that marked much of O'Flaherty's writing continued in the novels of Kate O'Brien (1897–1974). Educated in Limerick and at University College, Dublin, she made good use of her stay in Spain as a governess. She began to write there, using Spain as a background for several of her books. *Without my Cloak* (1931) was highly successful in its portrayal of three generations of an Irish family: it was followed by *The Anteroom* (1934), *Mary Lavelle* (1936), banned in Ireland, and *Pray for the Wanderer* (1938). *The Land of Spices* (1941) is perhaps the novel in which she best developed her theme of how women must fight to realise themselves; *As Music and Splendour* (1958) was her last treatment of the topic of the battle against the constraints of Irish Catholicism. She had a sharp eye for detail and her women characters were fully imagined if at times they seem over-emotional; her capacity to invest situations with intensity was balanced by an ability to hold the reader's attention through her excellent narrative art.

A feminist angle appeared in the nationalist propaganda writings of Dorothy Macardle (1899–1958), best known for *The Irish Republic* (1937), an account of the period from 1916 to 1923. Her imprisonment as a deeply involved Republican, her work with displaced children and a recurrent Irish interest in the supernatural inspired other works – for example, the novels *Uneasy Freehold* (*The Uninvited* in the US title, 1942) and *Dark Enchantment* (1953), which explore both the supernatural and women under stress.

The 1916 Rising deeply affected Michael Farrell (1899–1962), yet another of Dublin's engaging and volatile talkers. He was born in Carlow; as a medical student at University College, Dublin he became involved in the Troubles, was imprisoned, then worked in the Belgian Congo. He returned to his medical studies, this time at Trinity College, but eventually turned to making a film and working for Radio Eireann, while writing his novel *Thy Tears Might Cease* (1963). He finally became a very successful businessman.

Thy Tears Might Cease is Russian in scope; it was published posthumously through the efforts of Monk Gibbon, who cut Farrell's vast typescript ruthlessly; and it is, though uneven in tone, a moving evocation of the ease of life in Edwardian Ireland and the effect of the 1916 Rising upon the hero Martin Matthew Reilly. This is a *bildungsroman* conceived on spacious, nineteenth-century lines, and it contains some remarkable insights into Irish life, the description of the beginning of the 1916 Rising, and how people learned of it, being a most convincing achievement.

The character and beliefs of Sean O'Faolain (John Whelan, *b.* 1900) are well revealed in *Vive Moi* (1964), an engaging autobiography that tells of his childhood and student days in Cork, his time with the IRA, his period of schoolteaching, his postgraduate work at Cork and Harvard, followed by more teaching in Boston and England and his return to live in Dublin as a writer. He has written three novels, *A Nest of Simple Folk* (1933), *Bird Alone* (1936) and *Come Back to Erin* (1940), each of them concentrating on a main character whose idealism comes up against orthodoxy with devastating results. *Bird Alone* is the best of what are, ultimately, studies of frustration and stasis. O'Faolain's work includes forceful, often impressionistic biographies of Eamon de Valera, Constance Markievicz, Daniel O'Connell, Hugh O'Neill and Cardinal Newman, as well as travel books, a play, and literary criticism which includes an excellent book on *The Short Story* (1948) and *The Vanishing Hero, Studies in Novelists of the Twenties* (1956). He was founding editor of *The Bell* in 1940, a periodical he continued to edit for six years. He made *The Bell* an outspoken Irish platform for questioning, liberal and radical values in literature; he was succeeded by Peadar O'Donnell, who edited it from 1946 to 1954.

O'Faolain's impressive and varied merits are found at their best in his short stories. His first collection, *Midsummer Night Madness and Other Stories* (1932), was romantic, with a poetic delight in natural visual beauty and a Joycean repetition of words (notably 'and' and 'but'). In 'Fugue' the concentration is on emotion, and this attains an effective universality; the next volume, *A Purse of Coppers* (1937), shows developments in technique, implication and inference with the reader being guided in a subtle way. In *Teresa and Other Stories* (1948) O'Faolain conveys his sense of the often repressive climate of Irish Catholicism. In later stories, however, such as 'The Lovers of the Lake' and 'The Faithless Wife', he tells his stories not only with compassion but also with a sharply penetrating humour. He views the complexities of human relationships with a more ironic awareness, of the absurdity into which love can manoeuvre itself, for example, in stories such as 'In the Bosom of the Country'. He exhibits an understanding of loneliness and the role of consolation, as in 'Two of a Kind'; he understands, too, that illusion is a necessary part of life, but that it is at risk in a world where pressures of conformity, social, sexual and sectarian, threaten the individual's idiosyncrasies. As he develops his stories, individuality matters more and more.

O'Faolain is aware of the pressure of the past upon him

but he can evoke the present atmosphere of a street, a pub, a hotel, a bedroom or a landscape in speech which in his own words 'combines suggestion with compression'. In his later volumes he conveys a Chekhovian capacity for reflection in an easy, assured, conversational yet unobtrusive style; his range of subject matter is wider, more international, his characters more complex. He is mellower in his attitudes, while still catching the constraints and the realism of religion, in, say, 'Feed my Lambs' or 'Of Sanctity and Whiskey'. As well as being vulnerable his characters can have convincing vitality, a capacity to surprise the reader in what turns out to be a rational, an inevitable way, and yet is part of the para-doxical nature of life.

It is curious that the many novels of James Hanley (b. 1901) have not been given much critical attention, for at his best he writes in a most effective manner, blending fantasy and realism in studies of characters' inner minds made credible by a minute attention to details of background. Hanley's experiences in the Canadian navy in the First World War and as a merchant seaman obviously colour his novels about the life of sailors. Boy (1931) was the first of these; there followed several about the Fury family written between 1935 and 1958, centring on a seaman, Dennis Fury, and bleak in their picture of violence and inarticulacy. Three novels deal with warfare at sea: Hollow Sea (1938), The Ocean (1941) and Sailor's Song (1943), the last of them experimental in its use of language.

Though Francis Stuart (b. 1902) was born in Australia, he is of Irish stock and arrived in Ireland before he was a year old. Seventeen years later he married Maud Gonne's daughter Iseult; he was captured and interned during the civil war. Stuart, a quintessentially intense romantic, wrote poetry for some years, then turned to fiction with Women and God (1931), a novel which carried on investigating the subject his poems had explored, the connection between sexual and religious life. Pigeon Irish (1932) was better planned, and its romanticism set a pattern for the next nine novels he wrote before going to Berlin in 1940 to lecture at the University of Berlin. These novels portrayed characters who learn some spiritual insight, but at the cost of social isolation.

Stuart has written several novels since the war. These are

obviously closely based on personal experience but they and their successors remain too inturned and self-indulgent. However, in *Black List Section H* (1971) Stuart has finally written a novel within which he views his own experience of life with an objectivity indicated by the treatment of his main character as H. Again there is a feverish development, through the romanticism of youth and the genuine sufferings of middle age to a certain spiritual wisdom: in this case the development is convincing; here the novelist manages to relate the artist to society, to present characters and events with artistry and an impressive, controlled understanding of human values.

Eric Cross (*b*. 1903), an author with an inventive sense of humour, is best known for *The Tailor and Ansty* (1942); a *cause célèbre* when banned by the Censorship Board, this is a collection of pieces which centre on the conversation of the tailor, who lived in Gougane Barra in Cork. It contains a mixture of information about and comment on marriage customs, funerals and orgies inspired by them, the whole irradiated by a philosophical dislike of modern civilisation.

Another writer from Cork formed by fighting was Frank O'Connor (Michael Francis O'Donovan, 1903–66); he evokes with great sensitivity his own life up to the age of twenty in *An Only Child* (1964). Under the influence of Daniel Corkery he joined the volunteers, and fought with the Republicans in the civil war. After release from imprisonment he became a librarian and, encouraged by AE, contributed frequently to the *Irish Statesman*; he joined the board of the Abbey Theatre in 1935, resigning in 1939. *My Father's Son* (1967) describes this period of his life when he became a friend of Yeats and AE, and was embroiled in rows in the Abbey.

It was a fruitful decade for him, beginning with the civil war stories of *Guests of the Nation* (1931), the story which gives the volume its title, haunting in its account of how three Irish Republicans carry out an order to murder as a reprisal two English soldiers, hostages whom they have been guarding and with whom they have become friendly. In *Bones of Contention and Other Stories* (1936) O'Connor's narrator achieves what he deliberately sought, the sound of a man speaking conversationally to an audience. By *Crab Apple Jelly: Stories and Tales* (1944) O'Connor's criticism of Irish sexual puritanism was explicit. 'The Bridal Night', 'The Mad Lomasneys' and, particularly, 'The Long Road to Ummera' in this collection show O'Connor's capacity for holding the reader's attention, his narrative art having attained a controlled flexibility. His stories about children, 'First Confession' (1935), 'Babes in the Wood' (1947), 'The Drunkard' (1948), or 'My Oedipus Complex' (1950), for example, are deliberately simple, and none the less effective for that; among his adult characters priests, doctors or the old are given roles in which he explores how little men and women can exercise control over the circumstances of personal lives.

Though O'Connor is thought of mainly as a writer of short stories, the form for which he found appreciative audiences in American journals and on radio, he also wrote novels, *The Saint and Mary Kate* (1932) and *Dutch Interior* (1940), which capture the confinement felt by young people in Irish provincial life. He also wrote plays and poetry, some contained in *Three Old Brothers and Other Poems* (1930), in the nineteen-thirties, as well as a biography of Michael Collins. But he discovered a talent for translation as well, and his *Kings, Lords and Commons: An Anthology from the Irish* (1959) contains many excellent poems, notably Brian Merryman's 'The Midnight Court', banned in Ireland, as were *Dutch Interior* and the stories in the collections of *The Common Chord* (1948) and *Traveller's Samples* (1951). O'Connor's translation of 'The Midnight Court' successfully conveys the ebullient energy of the eighteenth-century Irish poet:

> Every night when I went to bed
> I'd a stocking of apples beneath my head;
> I fasted three canonical hours
> To try and come round the heavenly powers;
> I washed my shift where the stream ran deep
> To hear my lover's voice in sleep;
> Often I swept the woodstack bare,
> Burned bits of my frock, my nails, my hair,
> Up the chimney stuck the flail,
> Slept with a spade without avail;
> Hid my wool in the lime-kiln late
> And my distaff behind the churchyard gate; . . .
> But 'twas all no good and I'm broken-hearted
> For here I'm back at the place I started;

And this is the cause of all my tears
I am fast in the rope of the rushing years,
With age and need in lessening span,
And death beyond, and no hope of a man.

In *The Little Monasteries* (1963) O'Connor translated twenty poems, which have a sureness of touch, an economy of language that makes them direct and memorable. 'The Dead Lover', for instance, is masterly in its highly compressed account of how a mercenary leader elopes with the wife of another mercenary leader, is killed in battle and returns to keep his tryst. He regrets the past:

I am not the first in body's heat
Who found some outland woman sweet,
And though our parting tryst be drear
It was your love that brought me here.

It was for love alone I came,
Leaving my gentle wife in shame:
Had I but known what would befall
How gladly would I have shunned it all.

The poem ends, in a Yeatsian finality of phrase, as the ghost of the lover addresses the living woman:

Now my pierced body must descend
To torture where the fiends attend;
Worldly love is a foolish thing
Beside the worship of Heaven's king.

It is the blackbird! Once again
He calls at dawn to living men;
My voice, my face are of the dead.
Silence! What is there to be said?

In *Irish Miles* O'Connor was concerned that the new Ireland should not forget its heritage of buildings and sites, from pre-Christian sculptures to Georgian houses. He loved the land itself and could write evocatively about it. Then in 1951 he went to the New World to teach in American universities; he remarried in 1953; and he returned frequently to Ireland to recharge his literary batteries. He produced stimulating, unacademic criticism. *The Lonely Voice: A Study of the Short Story* (1963) gives a professional writer's view of his craft, and *The Backward Look: A Survey of Irish Literature* (1967) blends the poetic translator's view of writing in Irish with the civilised writer's spontaneous reactions to Irish writing in English. Here the nature of O'Connor as a critic is displayed at its best: blessedly intuitive and enthusiastic.

The literary qualities of Vivian Connell's (*b*. 1905) novels may be called in question for a certain brooding sexuality and modish intensity wrapped up in overwritten prose, but of their popular success there can be no doubt, *The Chinese Room* (1943) being probably the most typical and successful. Connell has also written plays and stories; his first appearance was in the *Irish Statesman*.

Sombre is the vision of Patrick Boyle (*b*. 1905) who has written in *Like Any Other Man* (1966) a penetratingly harsh study of Simpson, a bachelor bank manager, a strong man, a wencher betrayed by a visiting barmaid, Delia, who plays Delilah to Simpson's Sampson. The extravagantly tough writing is at times reminiscent of Liam O'Flaherty, the moral realism ultimately reductive, mock-heroic. Boyle's first collection of stories, *At Night All Cats Are Grey* (1965), shows him to be more effective in the shorter form because the necessary compression creates an explosive intensity. Betrayal is the great sin, the ultimate self-abuse: all around Boyle's characters are seas of hypocrisy, in which he often drowns them for their sins and crimes. Dublin suburbia gets its very effective thwacking in the stories of *All Looks Yellow to the Jaundiced Eye* (1969). The title story of *A View from Calvary* (1976) is a devastating account of moral cowardice in a small and cruel community.

A lighter treatment of foibles marks the satiric work of Mary Manning (*b*. 1906) in *The Last Chronicles of Ballyfungus* (1978): her earlier novels were *Mount Venus* (1938), a lively *roman à clef* about Dubliners, and *Lovely People* (1953), about Bostonians. The kind of urban sophistication to be found in Mary Manning's work also exists in the detective novels of 'Nigel Fitzgerald' (1906–197?), who wrote with wit — and a modern Gothic gusto — about the violent events he imagined occurring in rural areas of Ireland.

Michael McLaverty (*b*. 1907), born in Carrickmacross and educated at Queen's University, Belfast, became a teacher of mathematics and later a headmaster. He has viewed with sensitive understanding the people of Northern Ireland between the wars, notably in *Call My Brother Back* (1939; 1970), a novel which blends adolescence with the movement from country into city. McLaverty captures the dour atmosphere of the Ulster countryside well, using for the purpose a prose which is sometimes over-simple. His *Collected Short Stories* (1978) also show his capacity to create character convincingly.

Detail of observation rather than portrayal of character is to be found in *Shake Hands with the Devil* (1933), a realistic novel set in the time of the Black and Tans by Reardon Conner (*b*. 1907), the first of several powerfully written novels. *A Plain Tale from the Bogs* (1937) is a more directly autobiographical description of this troubled period, which repays reading more than his fiction.

Belfast has provided material for Janet MacNeill (*b*. 1907) who was born in Dublin and educated at St Andrews University. She has lived in Belfast since 1929 and written plays, novels and children's books. Her most effective novel, *The Maiden Dinosaur* (1964) is typical of its author's ruthless exploitation of the realities, shifts and compromises of the middle aged. Janet MacNeill writes about people leading very ordinary, very empty lives, for the ghosts of early disappointed passions crush the possibilities of emotionally rewarding marriages, of fulfilment in a world where the women, who are more interesting characters, could be dominated by the men, who might well be stronger, more vital. But the mediocre marriages settle into a pattern, a mixture of fantasy and minor rituals, and the hollow routines of modern suburbia precariously bridge over the deep void left by lack of any religious routines founded upon genuine belief.

The feeling of the Dublin streets was captured very effectively indeed in *Lift up your Gates* (1946; entitled *Liffey Lane*, 1947) an episodic novel centring on a teenage girl's paper round, written by Maura Laverty (1907–66), who was brought up in a Kildare village. Her earlier novel, *Never No More* (1942), had described village life in Kildare in a wandering way, while *No More than Human* (1944) was, like Kate O'Brien's work, built on experiences in Spain where she was a governess and journalist.

Kerry life is given more vigorous treatment in the work of Bryan MacMahon (*b.* 1909), first published in *The Bell*; his lively imagination is matched by exuberant energy in language, as his novel *The Honey Spike* (1967), based on a story of tinkers, shows. He is at his best in short stories where his sometimes intrusive tendency to over-elaboration is kept in check.

VIII Idiosyncratic innovators

Two civil servants, Mervyn Wall and Brian O'Nolan, have created, perhaps in reaction to the routine of bureaucracy, wildly imaginative worlds based in part upon medieval Irish literature, O'Nolan achieving in his fiction something akin to the novelty of Joyce or Samuel Beckett, though on a smaller scale, in his first two novels.

Mervyn Wall (Eugene Welply, *b.* 1908) was educated at Belvedere College and at University College, Dublin. He worked in the Irish civil service, then joined Radio Eireann before becoming secretary of the Irish Arts Council. He has written two very funny books, *The Unfortunate Fursey* (1946) and *The Return of Fursey* (1948). His hero is a medieval Irish monk, whose adventures with the Devil, witches, wizards, familiars, elementals and poltergeists are counterbalanced by the efforts of the Bishop of Cashel, the Abbot of Clonmacnoise and Father Furiosus. The matter-of-fact narrative, the convincing dialogue of these two books give Wall's fantasy both its suspense and humour. He has written other novels and two plays. Despite his imaginative inventiveness and effective, often deadpan humour, brooding discontent with modern Ireland colours all his writing; but his satiric expression reached its height in the final deal the Devil makes with the ecclesiastics in *The Unfortunate Fursey*.

An exuberant imagination, backed by a strong sense of satiric irony, a bilingual approach to language, a delight in words, and an immense capacity for fantasy ensured that the literary talent of Brian O'Nolan (1911—66) was exceptionally innovative. He wrote as Flann O'Brien and Myles na gCopaleen as well as using other pen names. Born in County Tyrone, he was educated at Blackrock College and University College, Dublin. He joined the Irish civil service in 1935 and retired from it in 1953. Out of sympathy with modern Ireland, he built a world of fantasy in his first experimental novel *At Swim-Two-Birds* (1939) where he used a medieval Irish tale in counterpoint to the life of a Dublin student: parody, a sharp ear for Dublin dialogue, a flair for pastiche, and a sense of the absurd make this novel at once a hilarious satire and modernist in its shifting Chinese-box-like views of experience. O'Brien's main target is the treatment of the Gaelic cultural inheritance which he thought was being generally sentimentalised, and handled with stupidity by the bureaucratic machine, but he also explored such literary forms as westerns and folk tales.

His next novel, *The Third Policeman*, completed in 1940, was not published until 1967: it is a disturbing work that examines, through the theories of de Selby, an eccentric intellectual, a state of fear, questions the value of the imagination, and leaves the reader uneasily aware of the emptiness O'Brien is presenting. *An Béal Bocht: nó, An Milleánach* (1941) is now available to those who do not know Irish in Patrick C. Power's translation *The Poor Mouth: A Bad Story about the Poor Life* (1973). This savage attack on the treatment and status of Gaelic Ireland is concentrated, effective, indeed devastating not only in its subject matter but also in its black humour. After *At Swim-Two-Birds* was reissued in 1960, there followed two more novels, *The Hard Life: an Exegesis of Squalor* (1961) and *The Dalkey Archive* (1964), but these lacked the fine originality of his earlier work. In *The Dalkey Archive* Joyce is made to renounce all his works except for *The Dubliners*: this develops the doubts about excessive imagination earlier shown in *The Third Policeman* through de Selby, who is now presented as evil.

After the early novels came the writing for *The Irish Times* of the Cruiskeen Lawn (Irish for full little jug) column, in which, as Myles na gCopaleen (Myles of the Ponies, a name taken from a character in Griffin's novel *The Collegians*), O'Nolan entertained and educated a large public from 1940 to 1966. Here is the rag-bag, the mixed grill element of *satura*, true satire, for the author ranged over the use and abuse of Irish and English, sometimes querulous, sometimes indulging himself happily in the puns which come as punch lines to the anecdotes attributed to Keats and Chapman, revelling in the range of Dublin conversation captured in the flat, banal, cynical, opinionatedly smug — and occasionally piercingly witty — talk of Your Man and the Brother. The column provided a suitable *métier* for Myles na gCopaleen's idiosyncratic castigation of cultural confusion or pretension, and through it runs an irresistible sense of humour, ranging from the deadpan to the free play of an exceptionally sharp associative mind.

IX Forties to eighties

Some Irish writers did not find the regime of the Censorship Board oppressive. Francis MacManus (1909–65), for instance, though he did write a novel *The Fire in the Dust* (1950) which attacked over-puritanical aspects of Irish Catholicism's attitudes to sex, obviously was able to write novels without feeling any need to challenge basic tenets of religious belief. A Kilkenny man, educated at University College, Dublin, who became features editor in Radio Eireann in 1948, he wrote a trilogy centring upon an eighteenth-century poet and schoolmaster, then set his second trilogy in his native Kilkenny, its second volume, *Flow on, Lovely River* (1941), a story of disappointed love, gaining greatly from MacManus's ability to match the events of the novel to this setting.

Sam Hanna Bell (*b*. 1909), though born in Glasgow of Irish parents, returned to Northern Ireland as a child; his novel *December Bride* (1951) captures the repressive and punitive nature of a northern rural community, though it has some comic moments to offset the toughness of the story of a servant who finally agrees to marry for the sake of her child. Bell, who has written a useful history of *The Theatre in Ulster* (1972), produced radio plays by Sam Thompson (1916–65), whose only published work *Over the Bridge* (1970) dramatised a labour dispute in terms of what might seem virtually inevitable, endemic religious bigotry, and was successfully staged in 1960.

Another writer to use a northern setting is Anthony C. West (*b*. 1910), born in County Down, who has written about the problems of adolescent and youthful love in an evocative, exuberant prose in *The Ferret Fancier* (1963). *As Towns with Fire* (1968) suffers from formlessness, though its account of wartime flying over Germany obviously gains from its author's own experiences in the RAF. An excellent war novel, *Bombadier* (1944), has been written by W. S. Gilbert (*b*. 1912) whose prose is admirable. *The Landslide* (1943) is marked by fantasy, and the unorthodoxy of *Ratman's Notebooks* (1968) has proved extremely successful.

Mary Lavin (*b*. 1912) believes that a writer distils the essence of his or her thought in a short story: she uses her stories as a way of looking closer into the human heart. She takes her readers into her confidence as she surveys her characters in a kindly yet detached fashion, with realistic compassion, selecting a particular moment of crisis as a means of crystalising life's significance for a particular person. Such moments of perception are exemplified in the story 'Love is for Lovers' in *Tales from Bective Bridge* (1942), her first collection.

Realisations of the differences between dream and reality are frequent in her stories, which deal mainly with domestic situations or with the pangs and problems of widowhood. She is also particularly good in treating adolescents attempting, often half-ashamedly, to assert their independence of their parents. Mary Lavin is obviously predominantly interested in the nature of character, and how people face problems — usually with resignation, with self-revealing speech. She relishes absurdity but she is compassionate in her understanding of human tragedy, notably the kind inflicted by stern provincial moralities, by the tyranny of a small society.

Though she herself prefers the form of the short story — good collections are *The Stories of Mary Lavin* in two volumes (1964; 1974) and the *Collected Stories* (1971) — she has written two impressive novels. *The House in Clew Street* (1945) portrays the loss of innocence, of how a boy growing up under the stuffy care of two aunts suddenly rebels and runs off with the servant girl. *Mary O'Grady* (1950) is a study of a Dublin suburban family and the growing-up of its children, evoking quietly but effectively the reader's sympathy and understanding. Narration is Mary Lavin's forte, though her stories do not demand action so much as revelation of character: she is not always even in her treatment and sometimes she can seem to lack architectonic control, and yet that is her strength, in that she is well aware that life has its irregularities, its untidinesses and its plethora of detail. Out of this comes a sureness, a lack of self-consciousness that make stories such as the title story in *The Becker Wives and other stories* (1946), or the title story in *Happiness and other stories* (1970), so completely memorable.

Mary Lavin's contemporary, Terence de Vere White (*b*. 1912), educated at Trinity College, had a legal career till the early nineteen-sixties when he embarked on a literary career, being literary editor of *The Irish Times* from 1962—77. His range is wide: biographies, an autobiography, histories, general studies — *Ireland* (1968), *Leinster* (1968) and *The Anglo-Irish* (1972) — as well as short stories and novels. The last are usually light comedies of manners, *Prenez Garde* (1961) being typical in its ironic treatment of its characters. *A Fretful Midge* (1959) gives a good autobiographical account of modern Ireland.

Walter Macken (1915—67), born in Galway, acted, directed and wrote plays for the Irish language theatre there, the *Taibhdhearc*; he became an Abbey actor, and was briefly the theatre's manager and artistic director in 1966. His plays in English are *Mungo's Mansion* (1946), *Vacant Possession* (1948), *Home is the Hero* (1953) and *Twilight of a Warrior* (1956). Macken is better known for his novels, neither innovative nor deep, but workmanlike and well written. *Rain on the Wind* (1950) presents the life of Claddagh fishermen sympathetically, and the first volume of a trilogy, *Seek the Fair Land* (1959), evokes Ireland in the Cromwellian period very effectively. *The Silent People* (1962), about the times of the Famine, is more persuasive than *The Scorching Wind* (1964) which carries the story up to the twentieth century.

Experience as a playground leader gave Olivia [Manning] Robertson (*b*. 1917) the material for *St Malachy's Court* (1946), a lively and sometimes surprising book about slum children. It was followed by *Miranda Speaks* (1953), a satiric novel. Recent writing by Benedict Kiely (*b*. 1919) has also been based upon observation, in his case of wide-ranging travel in Ireland. Kiely, born near Dromore in Tyrone, had a probationary period with the Jesuits, became severely ill and then decided to become a student at University College, Dublin. He has been a journalist and academic. His novels, which deal with sin, clerical life, and the achievement of maturity, are not as effective as his short stories. *A Journey to the Seven Streams: Seventeen Stories* (1963) shows him at ease as a natural storyteller rather than a controller of architectonics. The individual and the anecdote appeal to him, and he makes use of the Irish tradition to which his work adheres in its satire and comic exuberance, its lively language and elements of the fantastic.

A very different approach to the fantastic is to be found in the novels of Iris Murdoch (*b*. 1919), a Dublin-born teacher of philosophy at Oxford. She published a study of Sartre in 1953, and followed it with her first and probably her best novel *Under the Net* (1954), pleasantly picaresque, with a zany touch spiced by philosophical theory and inspired by Beckett's *Murphy*. It is funny and lively. Her next fiction, *The Flight from the Enchanter* (1956), explores freedom in a fantastical way, but *The Sandcastle* (1957) is less interesting in its portrayal of a boring schoolmaster in love, though *The Bell* (1958) moves to a more symbolic approach.

With *A Severed Head* (1961), also a funny novel, and *An Unofficial Rose* (1962) there is an increasing modishness in manipulation of plot and fashionable permissiveness. *The Unicorn* (1963) and *The Red and the Green* (1965) are set in Ireland, the former a messily melodramatic novel which fails to convey symbolic meaning, but the latter a more serious attempt to grapple with the divided loyalties created by the 1916 Rising. A slackly written novel, it fails to rise to the potential of its material. A quick comparison with, say, Michael Farrell's *Thy Tears Might Cease* reveals its superficiality. Later novels by Iris Murdoch have tended to create complex plots, groups of characters caught in the artificialities of life in the southern counties of England, and dominated by some influential person. The complex plots in these questions of identity are resolved in the simplest way — usually by violent and often unexpected deaths — and the characters are hardly worth the energy that must have gone into their creation. They remain, like some of Elizabeth Bowen's novels, clever but ultimately superficial.

James Plunkett (James Plunkett Kelly, *b*. 1920) grew up in Dublin, became a clerk in the Gas Company, then an official in the Workers' Union. He wrote stories published in *The Bell*, and his *Collected Short Stories* (1977) shows his range of subject matter and style. In the early stories collected in *The Trusting and the Maimed* (1955) he is interested in death, treating it from the perspectives of different ages; his later stories, more complex in construction, centre upon the stream of consciousness, notably 'Ferris Moore and the Earwig' which shows Plunkett's debt to Joyce as well as his own quizzical sensibility. Plunkett's novel *Strumpet City* (1969) — which obviously owes much to the techniques of modern American fiction — skilfully pulls together various separate skeins of Dublin society; its main drama comes from the strike of 1913; and it has shifted from Joyce's concept of Dublin's paralysis, so that the range of characters is treated not with scrupulous meanness but out of a more humane, balanced point of view than that of the youthful Joyce.

In the middle nineteen-fifties, Plunkett found, in his middle thirties, a stimulating *métier* in Radio Eireann, producing and writing plays for radio and after 1960 in Radio Telefis Eireann, for television. His interest in history expanded his subject matter, and perhaps because the nature of his new work proved satisfactorily stimulating, his novel *Farewell Companions* (1977) has a greater freedom, a more personal treatment of its characters. Though the novel is uneven in achievement, its readers cannot but respond to the lyrical sadness, which colours its five movements, its shift from the world of *Strumpet City* to a very different Ireland. Plunkett has an inclusive vision, an energy which overflows in rich detailed descriptions, yet he is following the pattern of Moore and Joyce, moving away from the restrictions of realism into a more personal, more imaginative, indeed more idiosyncratic presentation of the complexities of human existence.

Against the achievement of Plunkett, Paul Smith's (*b.* 1920) presentation of Dublin's slum life seems very flawed, strained and uneven. Pretentious verbosity, a non-stop insistence on violence and vulgarity mar *Esther's Altar* (1959; revised as *Come Trailing Blood*, 1977). Though *The Countrywoman* (1962) avoids the worst of these excesses, it is uneven; and *Annie* (1972; entitled *Summer Sang Me In*, 1975) returns back to the merely sensational again.

W. J. White (1920–80) who was educated at Middleton College, Cork, then read classics at Trinity College before a career as journalist culminated in his becoming Controller of

Television in Radio Telefis Eireann, wrote of the unpleasant side of new well-to-do Irish business and professional middle classes in his three novels, *One for the Road* (1956), *The Hard Man* (1958) and *The Devil You Know* (1962). These are marked by a merciless analysis, a professional, Waugh-like precision of satiric portraiture.

From the sophisticated rootlessness of White's Dublin to the social and religious rigidity of the Belfast of Brian Moore's (*b*. 1921) early novels about Belfast, *The Lonely Passion of Judith Hearne* (1955) and *The Feast of Lupercal* (1957), is a long journey, for Moore's Belfast is closer to rural society. Judith Hearne, the spinster, fails to conform to the mores, the modes expected by her community: she becomes a victim, she declines slowly into shabbiness, then rapidly into senility. The same element of failure is investigated, less successfully, in confusion between the sexual and spiritual in *The Feast of Lupercal*. *The Emperor of Ice-Cream* (1965) has as background the bombing of Belfast, as central figure a young Catholic growing up and eventually reaching a relationship with his bigoted father: the ending matters less than the portrayal of the boy's ineffectual adolescence and the war's precipitating him into manhood.

Moore left Ireland for Canada in 1948, then moved to the United States in 1959, living in the east for some years before shifting to California. Out of his different domiciles have come varied novels. *The Luck of Ginger Coffey* (1960), for instance, deals with an Irish immigrant in Montreal; it exhibits more sense of the comedy of life than the Belfast novels, but then its protagonist Ginger Coffey wins through his failures and is accepted by his new community. *An Answer from Limbo* (1962) describes the lack of community evident in the efficiency of New York. A Belfast emigrant writer's mother cannot accommodate herself to this new, efficient, godless society: the writer does adjust, at the cost of losing his links with his family, while his wife becomes frustrated and unfaithful. *I am Mary Dunne* (1968) builds upon Joyce's Molly Bloom soliloquy, and charts a woman's wanderings in search of herself, of her genuine identity. She is, of course, the women's liberationist who thinks that preferring her father's name, Dunne, to that of any of her various husbands may solve her crisis of identity, which is perhaps unsolvable in the fluidity of North American life. *Fergus* (1970) explores this modern society further, but, though as bitterly, less effectively.

In *Catholics* (1972) Moore returns to his obsessional investigation of Catholicism. Here is concern for a future where men have departed from old ideals and ideas, fear of the effect of the ecumenical movement, the loss of absolutes, the disappearance of ritual, indeed the loss of faith. Dramatic exploration of the tyranny of the provincially minded community in Ireland leads to investigation of the tyranny of the anonymous city in North America and then to the ultimate vacuum of a lack of religion. *The Great Victorian Collection* (1975) completes a phase in Moore's development where he is examining reality in a metaphysical way. *The Doctor's Wife* (1976) returns to simpler narrative, an account of a Belfast doctor's wife who embarks on a disastrous love affair but survives to live a lonely life in London, while *The Mangan Inheritance* (1979) returns us to Ireland, rooting the present yet again in the echoing, emotive past. Moore is one of the most effective novelists writing today.

A recent novel dealing with the Anglo-Irish, Molly Keane's *Good Behaviour* (1981), brings *Drama in Muslin* up to date, with the social gradations of *The Real Charlotte* somewhat simplified, the action set in a big house where an Anglo-Irish family fails to realise the nature of modern Ireland. Father a landlord, sleeping with a servant; mother a painter; governesses; son at public school, daughter virtually uneducated; horses, guns, hunt balls, race meetings and unpaid bills; the good behaviour that doesn't discuss sex, religion or money, all add up to black comedy set in elegant shabbiness. The truth behind the façade interests Molly Keane, who grew up in a 'rather serious' Anglo-Irish hunting, fishing and church-going family, concealing her literary interests from her sporting friends. As 'M.J. Farrell' she wrote four plays (the best-known is *Spring Meeting*, produced in 1938) and eleven novels — the first *Young Entry* (1928), the best probably *Devoted Ladies* (1934) and *Rising Tide* (1937). For all their sharp impish wit these were but rehearsals for *Good Behaviour*, in which she presents Anglo-Irish agonies — and absurdities — evoking, through an admirably detached account of fifty years of one family's disintegration, both gaiety and a profound sadness.

Modern drama

I Shaw to Beckett

SHAW, like Joyce and Yeats, dominates the genre in which his genius flourished: one in which the work of Synge, O'Casey and Beckett is to be found as well as many very good plays by other Irish authors, many of them written within the traditions established in the Abbey Theatre's repertoire. Shaw, whose first play was staged in 1892, expressed his own view of himself in *Shakes versus Shaw*, a brief puppet play staged at Malvern in 1949, making a comparison — which had often occurred to him earlier — between himself, an advanced thinker, and Shakespeare, less intelligent, though a superb poet.

If Wilde seems set firmly in the line of those Anglo-Irish dramatists who had begun to turn a sardonic eye on the foibles of fashionable life from the late seventeenth century onwards, making comedy of a classic kind out of it, Shaw, too, despite his apparently innovatory role, learned from this tradition and could write witty paradoxical plays of social comedy in a manner similar to that of Wilde. He could indeed also draw upon the melodramatic methods of Boucicault as well as many orthodox theatrical techniques, but his early affinities were with Ibsen. He saw Ibsen in *The Quintessence of Ibsenism* (1891; 1913) as a social iconoclast; and he was a useful model for Shaw the Fabian Socialist. Shaw, however, veered away from Ibsen's example. His own comedy is fundamentally serious, designed to put his ideas in challenging form in what is often a blending of moral allegory with fantasy. He could use parody skilfully; play devil's advocate almost too effectively; conceal burlesque beneath naturalism; blend rationalism with a sense of the ridiculous; and in all this cover a wide section of life. There remains the problem in weighing up his massive achievement of deciding how far the doctrine intrudes, how far the ideas may have dated and may overload even Shaw's vast capacity to entertain an audience while educating it.

Whereas Shaw found audiences and theatres in London, there was no theatre in nineteenth-century Ireland for those who wanted to create an 'Irish school of dramatic literature'. When Yeats, Lady Gregory and Edward Martyn made their plans for a national drama on a wet afternoon in County Galway in 1897 they knew little about theatre and had to enlist the aid of Martyn's cousin George Moore (who had been involved in the founding of the Independent Theatre in 1890–1, for which he had written *The Strike at Arlingford* (1893), an Ibsenite play) in staging their first two plays, Yeats's *The Countess Cathleen* and Martyn's *The Heather Field*. Each was typical of its author's aims: Yeats wanted poetic plays, which would appeal to Irish audiences through myth, reverie and symbolism, illuminating the history and indeed the mystic nature of the Irish people. Martyn, on the other hand, like Moore, was all for waking Ireland up with Ibsenite plays, dealing with ideas, with public and private problems.

After the Literary Theatre had staged several plays in 1900 and 1901 using English actors and actresses, and after Douglas Hyde had written *Casadh an t Sugain*, the first Irish play, which was received with acclaim, the National Dramatic Society, in effect run by the Fay brothers, produced AE's *Deirdre* and Yeats's explosively political play *Cathleen ni Houlihan* in 1902. It was now clear that there were Irish actors and actresses to act Irish plays. Albeit amateurs, the Fays knew about acting and about new developments in the theatre. The success of *Cathleen ni Houlihan* led to the formation in 1903 of the Irish National Theatre Society, which included the Fays, with Yeats putting forward his views about the need for simplicity in acting, simple scenery and, especially, beautiful speech.

There followed, thanks to the generosity of one of Yeats's English friends, Miss Annie Horniman (1860–1937), a fellow member of the Order of the Golden Dawn (Yeats's father painted her portrait in 1904), the creation of the Abbey Theatre in Dublin out of a former morgue and part of the

Mechanics' Institute in Abbey Street. And with the new theatre built, new playwrights appeared like mushrooms after a shower of rain. Lady Gregory had begun with an appealing play, *Twenty-Five,* in 1903, and the next year *Spreading the News* showed more clearly her superb craftsmanship, her elegant use of farce and the ironic vision that informed her later plays. In 1904 Yeats, who had been writing plays since his teens, imbued *On Baile's Strand* with the heroic qualities he found in the Cuchulain legend; he was to write several poetic plays, *Deirdre* (1906) being an example of his desire to capture the heroic gesture in the midst of despair. These plays, however, did not appeal to the Abbey audiences, whereas the realism Martyn had sought emerged in plays dealing realistically with Irish peasant life, typified by Padraic Colum's *Broken Soil* (1903) and William Boyle's *The Building Fund* (1905). It is possible that Douglas Hyde's various plays had set the tone for such writing. It contained qualities, good as well as bad, which have shaped so many subsequent 'Abbey' plays, about which the essential question was eventually alleged to be: Has it 'p.q.' (peasant quality)? These plays tended to fall into two groups: Ibsenite realism or broad farce.

Synge, however, treated the subject of Irish country people in a completely idiosyncratic way. His plays are impressive for their powerful poetic and idiomatic language, their violence, and their transmission of his delight in the wildness of the Irish peasantry, the richness of their nature. He knew his Ireland and loved it and the expression he gave it was strange and powerful. *The Playboy of the Western World* remains the great achievement of the Abbey's early years, although the patriotic nationalists were drawn to Yeats's hero Cuchulain rather than Synge's anti-hero Christy Mahon.

In 1910, the year after Synge's death, Yeats handed over the management of the theatre to Lennox Robinson, who was to write many accomplished and well-made plays, notably *Drama at Inish, The White Headed Boy* and *The Big House,* during his long association with the theatre. The 'Cork realists', particularly T. C. Murray, proved popular, and George Fitzmaurice wrote some excellent plays with a lively sense of fantasy but does not seem to have been encouraged by the Abbey. The realism of northern writers such as St John Ervine, Richard Rowley and Rutherford Mayne also contributed to the theatre's repertoire. Ervine's treatment of northern bigotry was matched by Brinsley MacNamara's of southern bitterness.

The Abbey Theatre, from which Miss Horniman, who had up to then been a most generous patron, withdrew her subsidy in 1910, was in a most difficult financial position for the ten years preceding 1924 when the Irish government decided to subsidise it.

As Synge's achievement dominated the early years of the Abbey, so in the nineteen-twenties it was Sean O'Casey who brought the language of the Dublin slums brilliantly on to the stage, in plays that were topical in their treatment of the fighting in Ireland between 1916 and 1922. *The Shadow of a Gunman* (1923) produced a new anti-hero. *Juno and the Paycock* (1924) was about the effects of outside events on life inside the teeming tenements: realism, farce, melodrama and irony contribute to its mixture of tragi-comedy. *The Plough and the Stars* (1926) was also a blending of powerful ingredients, grim but funny: it enraged nationalist sentiment with its questioning of the ideals behind the 1916 Rising. When O'Casey left for England his interest in realism waned and he turned to expressionism. But he seems to have lost a firm grasp on his material once he left, his experiments lacking the compact, convincing impact of his earlier work; and, though *Red Roses for Me* (1942) was a return to Dublin and its people, his later plays were written very much from the view of an exile. Yeats, who had turned to ideas taken from Nōh drama in his experimental *Four Plays for Dancers* (1921), now aimed at a small audience with plays, aided by music and dancing, which had no need for an orthodox theatre. Of these *Calvary* (1921) was somewhat static; but the theme was developed into a livelier play dealing with Yeats's view of history as antithetical, *The Resurrection* (1931), which exhibits a confident stagecraft, intense and economic, possibly owed to the general feeling of confidence writing *A Vision* had given him. He had shown the same superb dramatic skill in *The Words upon the Window-Pane* (1934), a play demanding an outstanding actress in the role of the medium who must also portray Swift's ghost. *Purgatory* (1938), the last of his plays to be acted in his lifetime, is a haunting story about a haunted house.

During the nineteen-thirties there was some experiment-ation in the Irish theatre. While the work of George Shiels, Louis D'Alton and Paul Vincent Carroll continued to a certain extent already established traditions in the Abbey, the Gate Theatre, under the imaginative guidance of Mícheál Mac-Liammóir and Hilton Edwards, had given Dublin a wide range of international drama, and had encouraged fresh talent. Lord Longford founded a new company known as Longford Productions which produced some interesting Irish work in its early seasons, though its later years concentrated upon work by English or European dramatists. The Gate staged Denis Johnston's *The Old Lady Says No*, an allusive, sceptical piece of work, contrasting Ireland's romantic past with the dingy reality of the present. Denis Johnston showed an intellectual depth and originality in this and his subsequent plays, though his very widely successful *The Moon in the Yellow River* smacks overmuch of the 'serious' Abbey play which it was originally intended to parody. This was also true of some of Paul Vincent Carroll's work, though *The White Steed*, which won the New York Drama Critics award for the best foreign play of 1939, was rejected by the Abbey. Indeed the theatre made some surprising rejections in the nineteen-twenties and thirties, the most notorious that of O'Casey's *The Silver Tassie*, which Yeats, Lennox Robinson and Lady Gregory (the last reluctantly) turned down because, as Yeats put it in his letter of rejection, O'Casey was ensnared by the greatness of the Great War which 'obtrudes itself upon the stage as so much wood that will not burn with the dramatic fire'. They thought O'Casey was unwise in deserting the themes and techniques of his earlier plays. When plays by others — for instance, Denis Johnston, T. C. Murray, and Robert Collis — were turned down by the Abbey, the Gate snapped them up. Not very many interesting new plays were staged by the Abbey in the nineteen-thirties and forties; (exceptions might include plays by Teresa Deevy, Seamus Byrne and Michael J. Molloy) and this may have been caused by not only the conservative taste of the audiences (who liked their old favourites — and the style of the Abbey actors playing them for laughs) but also a lack of enterprise on the part of the Board, over-keen on the one hand on giving the audience what it wanted and on the other of carrying out

Ernest Blythe's missionary feeling (when managing director from 1941—67) of what an Irish national theatre should be.

It is, perhaps, symptomatic of the decline that Beckett's *Waiting for Godot* was staged in a small experimental theatre in Dublin. With the work of Beckett — another Nobel prize-winner, like Yeats and Shaw — we are back to where we began, before the creation of the Abbey Theatre, with the situation of an Anglo-Irish author living outside Ireland and, in this case, often writing in French, yet shaped, just as much as Congreve or Farquhar, Wilde or Shaw, by his Dublin up-bringing. But we are back with a great difference to be noticed, the unusual nature of Beckett's outlook on life.

II George Bernard Shaw

The difficulties affecting so many Anglo-Irish writers recur in the youth of George Bernard Shaw (1856—1950): lack of financial stability recorded with that self-conscious combination of pride and self-mockery, the result of being in a middle state neither Irish nor English, and hence detached observers of the human scene. 'I was a downstart', wrote Shaw in 1921 in the preface of his first novel *Immaturity* (1879; first published 1930), 'and the son of a downstart'. He belonged, he went on, to 'the Shabby Genteel, the Poor Relations, the Gentlemen who are not Gentlemen'. Obviously intelligent and artistic, he grew up in a highly musical household in Dublin; he visited the National Gallery frequently; but he became a clerk in a land-agent's office at fifteen since the family was not well off. Though he had been promoted to cashier in the land-agent's by twenty he decided to leave Dublin in 1876: he had to sell his individuality in a larger market place since his business, he thought, could not be transacted in Dublin out of an experience confined to Ireland:

London was the literary centre for the English language, and for such artistic culture as the realm of the English language (in which I proposed to be king) could afford. There was no Gaelic League in those days, nor any sense that Ireland had in herself the seed of culture. Every Irishman who felt that his business in life was on the higher planes of the cultural professions felt that he must have a metropolitan domicile and an international culture: that is, he felt that his first business was to get out of Ireland. I had the same feeling.

He stayed with his mother and sister in London, and while he was with them his first five novels were all rejected by publishers.

Initially a shy man, Shaw taught himself to speak effectively; he served on the Parish Council of St Pancras; and he began to achieve fame as a music, art and drama critic in various London papers. His first play, *Widower's Houses* (begun in 1885), was produced in 1892, and from then on Shaw wrote a succession of plays, thirty of them full length, and over twenty other pieces. These plays were usually accompanied by lengthy prefaces, written in a lively, entertaining and challenging way. Shaw married a wealthy Irishwoman, Charlotte Payne-Townsend, in 1898; after a few years they settled at Ayot St Lawrence, a village north of London, where Shaw died in 1950 at the age of ninety-four, having survived his wife by seven years.

Shaw's comedy, marked by anticlimax, is a means of tolerating the tragedies of life; he differed from the writers of 'well-made' plays of his time in his ability to see individual characters as part of the general situation of their society: he portrayed the individual human feelings of his characters, balancing passion and intuition against ideas and systems. He blended high seriousness, the sense of social purpose he recognised in Ibsen with the scepticism of the comedy of manners that reached its apogee in Wilde. But whereas Wilde had been apolitical and amoral, Shaw became in 1884 a founder member of the Fabian Society: a convinced socialist, he believed that higher forms could overcome lower. And he was a more orthodox dramatist than he sometimes appeared to be in his own time. He would give the ordinary a twist of his own, reversing traditional roles, making an apparent hero a villain and vice versa. Of the three plays in *Plays Unpleasant* (1898), for instance, *Widower's Houses* has an exploiting slum landlord who is aimiable, *The Philanderer's* Ibsenite woman wants to be liberated, yet still to be treated as the weaker sex, and in *Mrs Warren's Profession* the genteel girl's mother turns out to be a successful brothel manageress not in the least inhibited in defending her role. At the time this play was regarded as daring in the extreme, for it questioned the basis of sexual morality, and dealt with matters not normally discussed openly. In *Plays Pleasant* (1898) Bluntschli of *Arms and the Man* is an anti-hero, an anti-romantic, a Swiss professional and highly practical mercenary while Sergius, the orthodoxly romantic hero, is shown to be a fool, for this is an anti-romantic comedy. Shaw remarked that he could no longer be satisfied with 'fictitious morals and fictitious good conduct, shedding fictitious glory on robbery, starvation, disease, crime, drink, war, cruelty, cupidity, and all the other commonplaces of civilisation which drive men to the theatre to make foolish pretences that such things are progress, science, morals, religion, patriotism, imperial supremacy, national greatness and all the other names the newspapers call them.' And so he probed into the nature of married love in *Candida*, into history in *The Man of Destiny* and, ironically yet humanly, into the age-old stylised comedy of romantic courtship in *You Never Can Tell*.

Three Plays for Puritans (1901) continued Shaw's challenging: the Caesar of *Caesar and Cleopatra* is an intellectually detached reformer, a great man like the Napoleon of *The Man of Destiny* partially because he has a sense of humour; Dick Dudgeon in *The Devil's Disciple* surprisingly finds his role as a minister, once he has been melodramatically saved from the hanging into which he had inexplicably placed himself, and the play itself inverts conventional morals; *Captain Brassbound's Conversion* mocks melodramas based on imperialist conventions, while showing the Captain's revolt as a pose.

Man and Superman (1901–3) reverses the Don Juan situation as woman becomes the pursuer; Don Juan is a sceptical socialist; and Shaw's theories of creative evolution, of the irresistible Life Force in action are, ultimately, inadequate — as he allows characters to remark in the play. But *John Bull's Other Island* (first produced in 1904; published in 1907) is one of Shaw's clearest reversals of accepted theatrical formulae and national stereotypes. In it Larry Doyle, successful like Shaw in England, is no stage Irishman but a bitter realist who sees Ireland's tragedy as caused by dreaming; the Englishman Tom Broadbent is the romantic dreamer of this play, and though his progressive plans for Ireland are seen as foolish his basic blundering decency is appreciated. The saint — and the traitor — are Ireland's achievement. Tension between opposites gives *John Bull's Other Island* a subtle balance;

apart from the obvious farcical episodes (which Shaw obviously enjoyed!) it is still funny, though Keegan the fool — or mystic prophet — is an impressive expression of despair, who does not, ultimately, answer the perennial problems. This was Shaw's first real commercial success, and in it he played the never-ending Anglo-Irish game of generalising about the very different characters of the English and the Irish, though he had a very serious purpose behind his jeering, a desire to educate his audiences. To the Irishman, he had written in 1895, 'there is nothing in the world quite so exquisitely comic as an Englishman's seriousness.'

Major Barbara (1905) attacks poverty as a crime, reconciles family discord, and contrasts idealism with the reality of wealth and power: it represents his devil's advocacy at its strongest, his diabolonian ethics harnessed to his desire to get things done, to have an efficient yet cultured society. *The Doctor's Dilemma* (produced in 1906) which Shaw labelled a tragedy is satirical in its comedy yet orthodox in its melodrama; like *Getting Married* (written 1908), it discusses social problems. Between 1909 and 1913 Shaw wrote *Misalliance, Fanny's First Play, Androcles and the Lion, Overruled* and *Pygmalion* and the short one-act plays *Press Cuttings* and *The Shewing-up of Blanco Posnet*. Of these *Androcles* shows the Roman persecutions as designed to stop the disruption threatened by Christian propaganda 'done as if it were a *revue* or a Christmas pantomime'; it is a play to be read in close conjunction with its preface, while on the stage it demonstrates Shaw's sureness and lightness of touch. *Pygmalion* studies the barriers of class; its comedy is lively, its ending in doubt. Did Eliza, Higgins's ultimately classless creation, have any place in society at all?

Heartbreak House (1919), thought to be one of Shaw's finest dramatic achievements, attacks the concepts of European society before the First World War; it explores broken love affairs and the divorce between power and pleasure which makes the occupants of 'Heartbreak House' drift before the storm of destruction that thunders down from the bombers at the end of the play. Yet it leaves awkward questions in the minds of an audience about its meaning — and its value.

Back to Methuselah (1921) was an over-optimistic, over-rational dream; in the preface to the play Shaw indicated his own difference from his predecessors. Wilde seemed the last of the line stretching from Molière, and Shaw asserted that from Congreve to Sheridan playwrights were all ashamed of their profession. He thought the possession of wit did not excuse the sterility caused by the 'lack of a positive religion': in his case he substituted, in this play, a dream of mature humans, just needing a longer time to achieve a full development of their intellects. In *Saint Joan* (1923), however, he showed how an individual can be ahead of contemporaries in protesting against those who interfere between the private person and God; he did this by balancing a more pessimistic, tragic concept of life with his levelling, demystifying comedy. In this he echoed some of the techniques of Shakespeare's history plays in a moving and effective portrayal of characters governed by the limitations of the thought and politics of their time.

Shaw's later plays show him open-minded about the possibilities of the future, seeing women's instinctive grip on life as more effective than men's theorising, their failure to face the failure of their plans resiliently. Invention, and the ability to write highly serious speeches and leaven them with wit marked his own ability to use comedy's 'terrible castigation' in a serious way, in a way, he thought, that marked it in modern times as a higher form of dramatic art than tragedy. His claim, though backed by the superb dramatic skills which make so many of his plays still challenging and pleasurable, has not been received without some reserve: he was perhaps more in the grip of the comedy of manners than he realised, and the characters he created, while designed to explore and educate, sometimes operate solely at comedy's depth, excluding deeper, more emotionally convincing realities of life.

III The earlier Abbey dramatists

When Yeats met Lady Gregory (1852–1932) at Coole Park for the first time in 1896 she was psychologically ready to join in the work of establishing an Irish literary theatre; and there began that fruitful literary collaboration, that close, lifelong friendship with Yeats. For nearly forty years she was to him, as he wrote to Mario Rossi after her death, his strength and conscience. Born Isabella Augusta Persse at Roxborough, County Galway, she came of big house stock, and married Sir William Gregory of the neighbouring estate of Coole Park; he was a cultured diplomat, a former governor of Ceylon, a traveller and scholar. Many years her senior, he died in 1892; encouraged by him and by Wilfrid Scawen Blunt, with whom she had a passionate affair which turned into a friendship lasting till his death, she had written a pamphlet in support of the Egyptian Arabi Bey in 1882. In the eighteen-nineties she wrote several pamphlets, edited Sir William's autobiography, made selections from his grandfather's correspondence, and developed a strong sense of nationalism. She also began to collect folktales and legends in Galway, and these appeared later in *A Book of Saints and Wonders* (1906), *The Kiltartan History Book* (1909), *The Kiltartan Wonder Book* (1910) and *Visions and Beliefs in the West of Ireland* (2 vols, 1920).

After meeting Yeats she helped Douglas Hyde to found a Kiltartan branch of the Gaelic League, and intensified her own efforts to learn Irish. The language into which Hyde translated Irish was given a more stylised form in many of her writings. Out of what she called her 'imperfect, stumbling' knowledge of Irish came three fine books. The first was *Cuchulain of Muirthemne* (1902), probably the best and most influential translation of the epic up to the recent one by Thomas Kinsella, *The Tain* (1969). Lady Gregory followed it with *Gods and Fighting Men* (1904) and *The Kiltartan Poetry Book, Translations from the Irish* (1919). These translations were intended for the common reader; following earlier translators she omitted what Standish J. O'Grady called 'the barbarism and very loose morality' of the originals. She succeeds in giving the legends vitality and conveying their idiom in a living prose, founded upon the English used by the people of Kiltartan, the village near Coole. Here is an example of it, recounting the third day of the tragic fight between Cuchulain and his friend Ferdiad for the ford:

So great was the fight, that the horses of the men of Ireland broke away in fright and shyness, with fury and madness, breaking their chains and their yokes, their ropes and their traces; and the women and the young lads and the children and the crazy and the followers of the men of Ireland broke out of the camp to the south-west.

They were using the edge of their swords through that time; and it was then Ferdiad found a time when Cuchulain was off his guard, and he gave him a stroke of the sword, and hid it in his body, and the ford was reddened with Cuchulain's blood, and Ferdiad kept on making great strokes at him. And Cuchulain could not bear with this, and he called to Laeg for the Gae Bulg, and it was sent down the stream to him, and he caught it with his foot. And when Ferdiad heard the name of the Gae Bulg, he made a stroke of his shield down to protect his body. But Cuchulain made a straight cast of the spear, the Gae Bulg, off the middle of his hand, over the rim of the shield, and it passed through his armour and went out through his body, so that its sharp end could be seen.

Lady Gregory was a highly successful populariser of legend and folklore, but she was more than that. An afternoon of talk at Duras House, Kinvara, in 1898, mentioned in her book *Our Irish Theatre* (1913; 1972), had led to the creation of the Irish Literary Theatre with Yeats, Martyn and Moore as its directors. By 1902 Martyn and Moore had dropped out of this movement. (Martyn, whose main interest was in music — he founded the Palestrina Choir in Dublin's pro-Cathedral — supported the Theatre of Ireland in 1906, and, eight years later founded the Irish Theatre which continued to stage, not very successfully, continental plays in translation as well as some Irish plays until 1920.) The Irish Literary Theatre was replaced by the Irish National Dramatic Society with Yeats as president. Now, instead of suggesting scenarios to Hyde, Lady Gregory became a skilled writer of one-act comedies in her own right, in response to the needs of the theatre. Her first play was produced in 1903, and in all she wrote forty plays, more than twenty of them original. She had a sense of construction, an ear for lively dialogue and, particularly, realistic comic situations. And she included a capacity for a certain zaniness in her invention. Excellent though her *Spreading the News* and her adaptation of several of Molière's comedies are, she also wrote effective folk-history plays and children's wonder plays. *The Rising of the Moon* (1907), *The Image* (1909), a three-act play about a defeated leader, and *The Deliverer* (1911), in part about Parnell, capture the sombre quality of political reality. *The Gaol Gate* (1906) is pure tragedy, and *Dervorgilla* (1907) with Dervorgilla's closing lament for the lasting trouble brought by her unfaithfulness devastating in its awareness of 'the swift, unflinching, terrible judgment of the young'.

Lady Gregory liked myth-making, and she liked mischief, but her fundamental desire was to be of realistic service to her own romantic, and idealistic, view of Ireland. She fought hard on behalf of Synge and O'Casey; she battled for the return of her nephew Hugh Lane's pictures from the Tate Gallery in London to Ireland (an unwitnessed codicil he added to his will just before his death in the *Lusitania* had left these impressionist pictures to Ireland). In her early days a Unionist in her politics, she later denounced Black and Tan atrocities, and then, as Yeats recorded in 'Beautiful Lofty Things', defied the gunmen of the Troubles:

> Yesterday he threatened my life
> I told him that nightly from six to seven I sat at this table
> The blinds drawn up . . . .

Her great work was to keep the Abbey viable, as a director and playreader, as a fund-raiser, and, ultimately, as a creator and defender of Irish art. At Coole Park she provided a centre for the meeting of many diverse men and women of genius; her posthumous autobiography *Seventy Years* (1974) and her book *Coole* (1971) convey something of her hospitable house and its surroundings, the ever-brimming lake and seven woods of Coole, a gracious setting for her generous spirit.

The language that O'Grady, Hyde and Lady Gregory had developed was carried to its ultimate in the work of John Millington Synge (1871–1909). Born into a closely-knit evangelical family of Protestant landowning stock, he was deeply affected in his teens by reading Darwin, and lost his religious belief. He spent much of his youth walking and cycling in the Dublin and Wicklow hills and mountains and he had an intense interest in natural history. At Trinity College he read Irish, but his main energies went into playing the violin, and he decided in 1891 that he would become a professional musician. He studied in Germany in 1893 and 1894. Then he moved to Paris in 1895 with the aim of becoming a writer; he spent part of each winter in Paris for seven years. While there he attended de Jubainville's lectures in old Irish and was impressed by Anatole Le Braz, the expert on Breton folk-life. His unreturned love for Cherry Matheson affected his early unpublished work (included in *Collected Works*, 1962–4): the fourteen poems of *Vita Vecchia* (1895–7), *Etude Morbide* (1899) and his first play *When the Moon has Set* (began 1900).

He met Yeats in 1896 and, possibly on his advice, visited the Aran islands in 1898, where an uncle of his had been Protestant incumbent in 1851; there he found the scenery and the Irish-speaking society stimulated his writing. The attraction of the west of Ireland affected painters too. Paul Henry (1876–1958) captured something of its impressive landscape in paintings, such as *Dawn, Killary Bay*, with an impressively atmospheric simplicity. The stoic quality of the people of the western seaboard has been interpreted by Sean Keating (*b.* 1889) in a romantic fashion, the romantic colouring echoed in more recent times by Daniel O'Neill (1920–74) in some evocative landscapes of Donegal. In the verbal description of *The Aran Islands* (written 1901, published 1907) Synge recorded detachedly yet compassionately the stark conditions of life which inform *Riders to the Sea* (1904). This one-act tragedy is short but effective in its use of suspense and recognition of simple symbols as well as an English based upon the language Synge had heard spoken in Ireland, and influenced by his knowledge of Gaelic syntax. In its elegaic way the play emphasises the endurance of the islanders, their continuous battle with the sea. And it does more than this in Maurya's final lamentation, with all its dignified stoical restraint, for her drowned sons:

Michael has a clean burial in the far north, by the grace of Almighty God. Bartley will have a fine coffin out of the white boards, and a deep grave surely . . . . What more can we want than that? . . . No man at all can be living for ever, and we must be satisfied.

In Wicklow, West Kerry and Connemara (1911), illustrated by drawings made by the artist Jack Butler Yeats (1871–1957), also shows us Synge moving through the scenery he loved. Out of Aran and Wicklow came [*In*] *The Shadow of the Glen* (1905), a play based upon a traditional, virtually international folk tale, which shows the lonely life of the glens. Nora, the wife of the old farmer who has feigned death, is finally ejected by him. And while the young farmer Michael

Darra is preoccupied with his sheep, the tramp, with what Nora calls 'a fine bit of talk', urges her to

> Come along with me now, lady of the house, and it's not my blather you'll be hearing only, but you'll be hearing the herons crying out over the black lakes, and you'll be hearing the grouse and the owls with them, and the larks and the big thrushes when the days are warm; and it's not from the like of them you'll be hearing a tale of getting old like Peggy Cavanagh, and losing the hair off you, and the light of your eyes, but it's fine songs you'll be hearing when the sun goes up, and there'll be no old fellow wheezing, the like of a sick sheep, close to your ear.

Synge next began to write *The Tinker's Wedding* (1908), and then involved himself in the work of the Irish National Theatre Company. After the Abbey Theatre opened in 1904, he became co-director with Yeats and Lady Gregory of the limited company which replaced the National Theatre in 1905. That year the production of *The Well of the Saints* bore witness to the darkly ironic side of his humour as he explored the contrast between the blind beggars' dreams and the physical reality that the gift of sight brings them, so cruelly destroying their illusions.

Two years later, in 1907, came his masterpiece, *The Playboy of the Western World*, that brilliant, robust mixture of comedy, farce and tragedy. In it Synge was celebrating the energy he found in peasant life, an emotional exuberance of word and deed, a violent expression of vitality, as Christy Mahon grows into the bold figure his imagination has created. This is mythologising that is tested out with the sudden appearance of Old Mahon, the father whom Christy is supposed to have murdered. The play is full of reversals, not least the fact that Christy is pursued by women; but then finally there is the reversal in which Pegeen loses the playboy hero whom she has, in part, created:

> Oh my grief, I've lost him surely. I've lost the only Playboy of the Western World.

The Playboy of the Western World infuriated nationalists who thought it a slur on Irishmen and Irish women. Synge pointed out that the play had several sides to it. He thought the Irish peasantry had a richness in them, an essential wildness, but the riots against it which began on the opening night continued, with Lady Gregory calling in the police on the second night. Yeats returned from Scotland to hold a famous public meeting in the Abbey to discuss the play, and to insist that it should continue to be performed.

A largely silent observer of life, Synge saw his Ireland in terms of romance, but also of realism; of Christianity, but also of residual paganism. He thought Ireland would have for a few years more an imagination 'fiery and magnificent and tender'. His work has a complexity hard to define, as he builds on folktale or anecdote with naturalism, but surprises his audience by his modification of the expectations aroused by his original material, with 'every speech as fully flavoured as a nut or apple'. His last unrevised play, *Deirdre of the Sorrows*, explores many issues: imbalances between youth and age (a reflection, perhaps of Irish marriage patterns in Conchubor's wish to marry Deirdre and perhaps also of Synge's own love for Molly Allgood); the endurance of love; the rival claims of love and life; the beauty of the countryside, and the life that pulsates through it. Synge's praise of life, characteristically expressed with careful craftsmanship, and his exploration of love, jealousy and frustration in this tragedy, carry with them a poignancy sharpened by his own intense awareness, at the age of thirty-five, that he had not long to live. He had Hodgkin's disease, and plans for his marriage to the young Abbey actress Maire O'Neill (Molly Allgood), then nineteen, were deferred after the spring of 1908. His often stormy relationship with her is hymned in poems such as 'Is it a month', 'The Meeting', and 'In Glenasmole', which celebrate their walks in the Dublin and Wicklow mountains. The poems, however, that also remain in the mind are the lively 'Beg-Innish' or those sombre reflections on the coming of death such as 'In Kerry', 'A Question' or 'End of the Book':

> I read about the Blaskets and Dunquin
> The Wicklow towns and fair days I've been in
> I read of Galway, Mayo, Aranmore,
> And men with kelp along a wintry shore.
> Then I remember that 'I' was I,
> And I'd a filthy job — to waste and die.

The illustrator of the 1911 volume of Synge's essays, the poet's brother Jack Yeats, matched its author in originality of mind. Beginning his career as an artist with black and white illustrations that contrive to capture the wild aspects of life in the west of Ireland in a very romantic way, he contributed to *Punch* for over thirty years under the name W. Bird, and edited *Broadsides* every month for seven years (1908–15). His painting, in watercolour up to about 1905, developed Irish subject matter in the late eighteen-nineties, leaving the strong simple outlines of his earlier work for a highly idiosyncratic and powerful, expressionist style in the nineteen-twenties. This allowed him to assemble his memories of the place that he regarded as his school — Sligo 'and the sky above it'.

Jack Yeats also wrote idiosyncratic drama of two kinds: plays for the miniature theatre intended to entertain neighbouring children, when he lived in Devonshire, with melodrama, pirates and circuses; and, later, plays for the 'Larger Theatre', several of which were produced, *La La Noo* (1942) being probably the best of them with its challenging of accepted orthodoxy. His novels are less effective in their intensely personal, original stream of consciousness, their quirky anarchic humour and philosophical questioning.

One effect of the row over Synge's *Playboy* in 1907 was that William Boyle (1853–1923) left the Abbey. At the time this seemed a serious blow since his plays had proved highly popular; he was one of the most popular of the Abbey's early dramatists, his best play *The Building Fund* (1905) being an effective study of avarice. He treated political trickery in a farcical way in *The Eloquent Dempsey* (1906) while in *The Mineral Workers* (1906) he exploited the contrast between Irish country conservatism and the modernism of the new world, getting good dramatic results from placing a returned Irish-American engineer full of modern ideas, eager to mine the land, up against the locals' resentment of change. Boyle's short stories in *A Kish of Brogues* (1899) had earlier shown his capacity to create character very convincingly; this ability was probably the main reason for the success of his early plays. He returned to the Abbey after an absence of five years, but the later plays, including *Family Failing* (1912) and *Nic* (1916), lacked the sharpness and energy of his former work.

The Abbey audiences obviously liked realism, and one

form of it, the 'cottage plays' which tended to stultify its later achievement, came largely from Cork. Lennox Robinson (1886–1958), the son of a clergyman, saw the Abbey players on tour in 1907 and the next year, when his first play *The Clancy Name* was produced, his long association with the Abbey began; he succeeded Yeats as manager in 1910 and became a lifelong director in 1923. There is a characteristic portrait of him in the theatre, painted by James Sleator (1889–1950), whose portraits of the dramatist Rutherford Mayne and the novelist Kate O'Brien are also excellent examples of his skill. He was a pupil of William Orpen (1878–1931), perhaps the most successful portrait painter of his time.

In *The Clancy Name* (1908) Lennox Robinson treated his subject ironically, and the play's realistic dialogue stresses the lack of sentiment in what is largely a melodramatic play. *Patriots* (1912) effectively explored the contrast between a revolutionary's expectations on returning from prison and the reality of the new style of negotiation. With *The White-headed Boy* (1920) Robinson found his *métier* in social comedy, following this excellent, well-constructed, convincing play, about a split in a family's attitudes where Denis Geoghegan has no wish to become a doctor, with *The White Blackbird* (produced 1925) and *The Far-Off Hills* (produced 1928). *The Lost Leader* (1918), drawing upon a supposition that Parnell was not dead, showed an attitude of experimental open-mindedness about Robinson, exploring now rather than didactic as he was in his early plays. His range of subject matter extended through society from cottage to big house and he had firm views to put in *The Big House* (produced 1928) and *Killycregs in Twilight* (produced 1937), both drawing attention to the nature and values of the Ascendancy. *Church Street* (produced 1934) and *Drama at Inish* (produced 1933) are both excellent well-made plays, the latter reflecting lightly upon the effect of heavy highbrow drama in an Irish seaside village.

He also wrote *Ireland's Abbey Theatre: A History 1899–1951* (1951), various early stories, and an autobiographical novel, *A Young Man from the South* (1917). At his best a professional dramatist of the highest skill, he wrote comedies with excellent dialogue, where situations develop with a convincing naturalness, the author's observation spiced with a pleasant sense of mischief.

The Clancy Name exerted a considerable influence upon another Cork dramatist, T. C. Murray (1873–1959), who wrote only one comedy *Wheel of Fortune* (1909, rewritten as *Sovereign Love*, for the Abbey, 1913). *Birthright*, Murray's first play to be produced by the Abbey in 1910, stemmed from its author's intimate knowledge of rural Irish life of which he has been a superb interpreter. In this tragedy the breakdown of a family is linked to love of the land. In *Maurice Harte* (1912) a final-year student at Maynooth finds he had no vocation for the priesthood, but the drama centres on his domineering mother's materialistic approach to the problem and its consequences. *The Briary Gap* (1917) presents a man wishing to delay for a month his marriage to a pregnant girl in order to get land from an uncle. The priest to whom she appeals is pitiless and the upshot is bitterness, a quality that informs many of Murray's plays, especially *Aftermath* (1922) and *Michaelmas Eve* (1932), another study of the effect on a family of the land and hunger of it. *Autumn Fire* (1924) dealt with the consequences of an older widower's marriage to a young girl, with whom his son falls in love. The damage done by the widower's frustrated daughter has an inexorable air to it, and the play moves through convincing coincidences to the climax with a sureness supplied by the subtle and sensitive dialogue. *The Pipe in the Fields* (1927) provides music as an escape from the daily common things of farm life: to an extent it is an escape from Murray's normally sombre subjects: domineering mothers, family strife, murder, insanity, land hunger, jealousy and hatred. Murray's Catholicism colours his presentation of suffering in the ordinary everyday life of rural communities: and that suffering seems likely to continue, for often the actions of the plays do not resolve it.

The characters in the plays of R. J. Ray (pseudonym of Robert Brophy, a journalist whose career as a dramatist extended from 1909–22) seem to have been in a more violent strain than those of Murray; the five unpublished plays dealt with gombeen men, informers, policemen, and murderers. There can be, however, no doubt of the merits of another Cork writer Daniel Corkery (1878–1964), three of whose one-act plays were published as *The Yellow Bittern and other plays* (1920). Corkery also wrote some excellent short stories, notably in *A Munster Twilight* (1916), and other fiction, *The Threshold of Quiet* (1917) being a quiet almost sentimental novel but one which explores several provincial lives convincingly, with sound psychological insight. His critical works, however, *The Hidden Ireland: a story of Gaelic Munster in the eighteenth century* (1924) and *Synge and Anglo-Irish Literature: a Study* (1931) are probably better known now, the former being based on his enthusiastic delight in Irish, the latter quite often bigoted, wrongheaded and limited, but none the less challenging in its vehement view that only national art is worthwhile, a view which allowed him to rule out such writers as Somerville and Ross from any Irish canon, only Synge being permitted in because his presentation of the peasantry chimed, though only in part, with Corkery's own.

The three major plays of Padraic Colum (1881–1972) had a strong influence on the Abbey dramatists. An early play, *The Saxon Shillin'*, was political propaganda, six other short plays were ineffective, but *Broken Soil* (produced in 1903, and revised as *The Fiddler's House* in 1907), *The Land* (1905) and *Thomas Muskerry* (1910) reflect the influence of Ibsen, and treat their subjects with a European realism based upon Colum's knowledge of the language spoken in the counties of Longford and Cavan where he grew up. 'You might say I had the advantage of the disadvantages that Yeats and others didn't have — I was born in a workhouse and knew common-speech from my birth, I always say I was born in a workhouse to make a romantic story; the fact is, my father was the master of a workhouse, which isn't quite so good, not being quite so bad.'

Broken Soil exhibits the differing pulls of a settled or an itinerant life on Conn Hourican who cannot settle on the land, for those who have 'the gift' of folk artistry must follow its call; *The Land* explores the conflict caused by materialism, as evinced in differing desires of the peasant: to work the land or to emigrate in search of travel and adventure. Ellen puts her sense of frustration clearly:

O, Matt what's the land after all? Do you ever think of America? The streets, the shops, the throngs?

Thomas Muskerry, centring on one worthy man's fall caused by the demanding greed of his relatives, shows the pettiness of small town life. Colum presented his characters realistically as rural Catholic peasants with a simple faith. Simplicity, however, could mar his sense of dramatic construction.

Colum and his wife Mary left Ireland in 1914 for the United States. There he developed a skill in writing for children, whom he treated as equals, his directness — and, in the best sense of the word, his simplicity — having great appeal. Colum's career as man of letters was based upon a natural versatility. He translated well; 'She moved through the fair' and 'The poor girl's meditation' are good examples of his skill. He recorded folklore with loving pleasure, *inter alia* in three volumes of Hawaiian material. He wrote good books for children, a biography of Arthur Griffith, *Ourselves Alone* (1959) and, with his wife, *Our Friend James Joyce* (1958), a conversational piece that matches her memories of the literary revival in *Life and the Dream* (1947). He created two novels, *Castle Conquer* (1923) and *The Flying Swans* (1957), the latter a much underrated work. His simplicity, spiced by delicate original humour and his incidental critical comments, made his writings in the sixties very effective.

Seumas O'Kelly (1875–1918), a journalist born in Loughrea, created a dramatically convincing character in *The Shuiler's Child* (1909), a vagabond woman who renounces her child, and in *The Bribe* (1914) he explored the effects of the election of an inefficient dispensary doctor. O'Kelly's novel *The Lady of Deerpark* (1917) shares the melodramatic quality of his plays, but it is, none the less, well-conceived and, at times, moving. He was at his best in the confines of the short story, particularly in the stories of *Waysiders* (1917), *The Golden Barque and the Weaver's Grave* (1919) and *Hillsiders* (1921). 'The Weaver's Grave' is most impressive; it is at once comic, simple, sensitively poetic and memorable.

Two years younger than Seumas O'Kelly, George Fitzmaurice (1878–1963), the son of a Protestant clergyman and a Catholic mother, lived a virtually recluse-like life as a clerk in the civil service. His first play produced by the Abbey (in 1907) was *The Country Dressmaker*, a broad comedy, the story of a dream destroyed. In this he explores the contrast between that dream and reality, bringing the experience of

America back into Ireland as Boyle had in *The Mineral Workers*. But in Fitzmaurice's play the pattern is different. The country dressmaker refuses a local suitor, hoping for the return of her lover from America. When he does come back after ten years he is a widower; her romantic illusions vanish and her final stoical acceptance of him is when 'the spring of life' in her is broken. This play was successful and has been revived, but many of Fitzmaurice's other plays were not produced during his lifetime. He moved from the realism of *The Country Dressmaker* to a portrayal of cynicism in *The Moonlighter*, which deals with the Land War, while in *The Magic Glasses* his sense of the fantastic is developed, with Jaymony Shanahan in his loft seeing visions through the glasses he bought from a pedlar woman, with Morgan Quille called in to cure him. This is a play where the grotesque erupts in violent ideas as well as language, the loft collapsing and Jaymony's throat being cut by the glasses. Pagan and Christian elements occur in the play, which depicts the destruction of illusion, just as they do in *The Dandy Dolls*, written between 1914 and 1916 and possibly influenced by Fitzmaurice's wartime experience. Here the wildness has become evil, with a nightmare quality about its fantasy as the priest fails to prevent Roger, the dreamer who wants to make a perfect doll, being carried off:

> . . . didn't I see Roger being carried away by the Hag and the Son of the Hag. Riding on two Spanish asses they were, holding him between them by a whisker each, and his whiskers were the length of six feet you'd think, and his nose was the length of six feet you'd think, and his eyes were the size of turnips bulging outside his head. Galloping like the wind they were, through the pass of the Barna mountains, sweeping him along with them, for ever and ever to their wonderful den in the heart of the Barna hills.

There is more than a little of the Gothic in Fitzmaurice's imagination, though he was also capable of satire, as *The Linnaun Shee* demonstrates in its mockery of Yeats's *Cathleen ni Houlihan*.

Fitzmaurice, obviously influenced by Synge, used a rhythmic, extravagant speech he based on the Kerry Irish he knew from his youth, fluid and just as inventive as Sean O'Casey's English prose was to be. The language was a means of exploring fantasies of the folk mind – probably at its best in *The Pie-Dish*, produced in 1908. *The Enchanted Land*, written in 1921, echoes the technique of the music halls that Fitzmaurice enjoyed so much. He failed to develop his talents; he was also writing at a bad time for the Abbey to use and shape them. Since his death and the publication of the plays by Dolmen Press in three volumes (vol I, 1967; vols II & III, 1969) his capacity to create fantasy has been appreciated and his inventiveness can be seen to balance the bitter quality of much of his work.

Bitterness also informed much of the work of St John Ervine (1883–1971), a Belfastman who moved to London at the turn of the century, and wrote four plays between 1911 and 1915, which portray the rugged nature of the northern Irish character. This is exemplified through the savage bigotry conveyed in *Mixed Marriage* (1911) with its portrayal of tense tribal warfare in the city streets, and the human tragedy of Protestant boy wanting to marry Catholic girl in a dogmatically divided society. His next play *The Magnanimous Lover* (1912) deals with hypocrisy; then came *The Orangeman* centring on the Twelfth of July, the anniversary of William of Orange's victory at the Battle of the Boyne, still celebrated by Orangemen with parades, notable for the bright banners of the Orange lodges, and the sound of shrill fifes and menacing Lambeg drums. *John Ferguson* (1915) is a melodramatic treatment of rape and reprisal, of religious belief and stoic endurance.

In 1915 Ervine became manager of the Abbey and, in contrast to Robinson's sometimes over-casual regime, his brief period of office proved a disaster. Before this debacle he had written a good novel about the 1798 Rebellion, *Mrs Martin's Man* (1914), but after serving in France and losing a leg in 1918, he turned to the composition of plays which suited the London stage, the best being *Mary Mary Quite Contrary* (1923), while *The First Mrs Fraser* was financially most successful in 1929. Among his other plays *Boyd's Shop* (1935), *William John Mawhinney* (1940) and *Friends and Relations* (1941) returned to Ulster, *Boyd's Shop* being another dramatically effective study of intolerance and the divisions between youth and age. Ervine's early realism presented a tragically, dogmatically divided Belfast focused on the tough unyielding nature of his male characters; his women, less powerful than those of the Cork realists, were stoic sufferers, enduring the harshness of their society. The early plays exude an abrasive vigour; the vitality of their dialogue will probably outlast Ervine's more successful middle period. Of his later work mention should be made of *Robert's Wife* (1937), and *The Christies* (1949). He wrote several biographies, of General Booth in 1934, of Oscar Wilde in 1951 and of Shaw in 1956, and up to 1939 he was an acerbic dramatic critic for the *Observer*.

Other plays dealing with Northern Ireland include *Thompson in Tir na nOg* (1918), by Gerald MacNamara (Harry Morrow, 1866–1938), one of the plays that continued to please audiences with its projection of an Orangeman into the Gaelic land of the young. MacNamara was an amateur actor involved in the Ulster Literary Theatre for which he wrote several other plays.

Another northern writer James H[enry] Cousins (1873–1956), born in Belfast, moved to Dublin in 1897 and there became part of the flickering Twilight. A friend of AE, he acted in the National Theatre Society, became a Theosophist and wrote many poems, *The Bell-Branch* (1908) and *Etain the Beloved and Other Poems* (1912) being typical of his early treatment of the Irish material — to which he returned in later life, with *The Hound of Uladh, Two Plays in Verse* (1942) written in India, where he lived from 1913. Many books of his were published in India, among them an autobiography written jointly with his wife *We Two Together* (1950). Both Yeats and Joyce tended to belittle him, though his play *The Racing Lug* (1902) was highly successful; slight as it may seem to a modern reader it was the kind of play that suited both actors and audience in the early days of the theatre movement.

There is a reversal of MacNamara's *Thompson in Tir na nOg* in *Apollo in Mourne* (1926) which puts the god among the peasants with rueful results. This play was written by Richard Rowley (Richard Williams, 1877–1947) who was also the author of some good dialect poems relating both to the country and Belfast, the latter monologues; his stories are set in the Mourne countryside.

Knowledge of the workings of the Land Commission gave substance to the serious realism of *Bridgehead*. It was the

best of several plays written by Rutherford Mayne (Samuel
Waddell, 1878–1967, brother of Helen Waddell). His cottage
plays for the Ulster Literary Theatre, included *The Drone*
(1908), a comedy, and *The Troth* (1909), an indictment of
bigotry and social injustice. These were followed later by two
plays produced by the Abbey, *Peter* (1930) and *Bridgehead*
(1934). The latter is an impressive play and was more successful than the other, which is a comedy about a young engineer-
ing student and based on his dream of failing and working in
a hotel instead.

IV O'Casey and the twenties

Sean O'Casey (1880–1964) grew up in Dublin, the last of
thirteen children in a poor Protestant family. His eyesight
was so troublesome that he attended school very irregularly,
but in his teens steeped himself in the Bible, Shakespeare and
Dion Boucicault. First employed at fourteen, he worked on
odd jobs as a labourer in his twenties, buying (and sometimes
stealing) books galore; he took great pleasure in the verbal
exuberance of the Elizabethan dramatists, and his reading
included Shelley, Ruskin, and Shaw among the reformers,
as well as Scott, Dickens and Balzac among the novelists.
An interest in religion, influenced by Dr Griffen, the Protestant rector of St Barnabas, was replaced by a devotion to
socialism inspired by the labour leader and orator James
Larkin (1876–1947) who came from Belfast to Dublin in
1908, founding the Irish Transport and General Workers
Union in 1909. At this stage of his life O'Casey was a compulsive joiner of clubs and organisations: he joined the Gaelic
League and learned Irish; he was secretary of about eight
organisations, including the Irish Citizen Army, a history of
which he wrote in 1919. Though active in the Dublin strike
of 1913, he did not, however, join in the 1916 Rising.

After four of his first plays had earlier been rejected by the
Abbey, *The Shadow of a Gunman* (originally entitled *On the
Run*) was accepted in 1922. When this was produced in 1923
it ran for three days; the final night filled the house for the
first time in the Abbey's history, and when *Juno and the
Paycock* was staged the following year it ran for two weeks,
the first time a play had run for a second week in the Abbey.

On receiving £25 in royalties O'Casey, then forty-four, decided to earn his living by writing. His work restored the theatre's flagging fortunes, but *The Plough and the Stars*, his next play to be produced in the Abbey, sparked off riots during its first week in 1926, though it was to prove a very successful part of the theatre's repertoire. Yeats defended *The Plough and the Stars* against the rowdy patriots who objected to its ironic portrayal of the Easter Rising just as he had earlier fought the mob for Synge's *Playboy*. 'You have disgraced yourselves again', he told the audience:

> Dublin has once more rocked the cradle of genius. From such a scene in this theatre went forth the fame of Synge. Equally the fame of O'Casey is born here tonight. This is his apotheosis.

Six weeks after this riot O'Casey went to London to receive the Hawthornden Prize for *Juno and the Paycock*; he lived in England for the rest of his life. His three Irish plays are set in the Dublin slums in the midst of violence. *The Plough and the Stars* has as its background the rising of the volunteers and the Irish Citizen Army against the British in Easter 1916; *The Shadow of a Gunman*, the guerrilla war (1917–21) between the Irish Republican Army and the British forces, and the campaign of counter-terror waged by the Black and Tans; and *Juno and the Paycock*, the civil war (1922–3) in the south between the Irish Free State forces and the anti-treaty Republicans.

This was new dramatic material, and in his handling of it O'Casey developed new dramatic forms and techniques; above all, he created a poetic ordering of his tragi-comic material and gave it expression in vital, arresting language. He was not the first Irish writer to treat slum life — earlier plays include A. P. Wilson's (*b. c.*1880–?) *The Slough* (1914), Alpha and Omega's (a pseudonym for Oliver St John Gogarty) *Blight* (1917) and Daniel Corkery's *The Labour Leader* (1920) — but he was the first to give it dramatic vitality in the way Synge had given dramatic expression to cottage life. O'Casey had a satiric sense that he shared with many of the Abbey dramatists: his satire is, like that of writers from other parts of Ireland, T. C. Murray, Padraic Colum and St John Ervine, for example, based on a sharp grasp of reality. While his comic sense derives from the mixture of character and idiosyncracy that he crowds together in the close contact of the slums, he sees the tragic effect that comes from ordinary people put under stress, cowardly and heroic both, a mixture of human selfishness and decency. Out of this come plays without strong plots: *The Shadow of a Gunman*, founded upon an autobiographical experience, is more a study of personalities; Davoren, the pseudo-poet and poltroon, and Shields, the former patriot, are two egotists. The former is admired by Minnie, the latter fails to realise that she is heroic in her hiding bombs to save Davoren, whom she thinks a gunman on the run. She is taken away by the auxiliaries who have found the bombs in her room, and as they leave the house with her they are attacked and Minnie herself is shot and killed.

Juno and the Paycock is a better-constructed play that contrasts masculine violence with the suffering endured by women. In the persons of the Paycock, the lying drunken irresponsible ineffective boaster 'Captain' Boyle, and his butty, the parasite Joxer Daly, O'Casey created a magnificent pair of comic characters, whose antics sharpen the contrast between them and Juno, Boyle's wife. She keeps the slum home together but has to endure the real horror of civil war when her guilt-ravaged son Johnny, crippled in earlier fighting, is dragged off to be shot for having betrayed a republican Commandant, Tancred; she has also to endure her pregnant daughter being deserted by her fiancé. The play turns on a wheel of fortune, Boyle thinking they have a legacy, until their world crashes, like the world outside their tenement, into a state of chaos, the 'tarrible state o' chassis' of the Captain's phrase. This chaos, fed by the abstractions and absolutes of the Patriots, is redeemed only by Juno's courage and her final lament over her son, not as stoical as Maurya's in Synge's *Riders to the Sea* though her plea to the Virgin is a universal cry of motherhood against the wasting of human life:

> What was the pain I suffered, Johnny, bringin' you into the world to carry you to your cradle, to the pains I'll suffer carryin' you out o' the world to bring you to your grave! Mother o' God, Mother o' God, have pity on us all! Blessed Virgin, where were you when me darlin' son was riddled with bullets, when me darlin' son was riddled with bullets? Sacred Heart o' Jesus, take away our hearts o' stone, and give us hearts o' flesh. Take away this murderin' hate, an' give us Thine own eternal love!

The Plough and the Stars develops the theme of *Juno and the Paycock*, for in it the effects of fanaticism are explored ruthlessly: masculine vanity and violence are contrasted with the bravery of the noncombatants, largely women; the patriotic orator's doctrinaire demand for bloodshed is balanced by Bessie Burgess's sacrifice when she dies protecting Nora; and poetic symbolism is blended with macabre realism.

The Abbey rejected O'Casey's first play written in England, *The Silver Tassie*, though Shaw praised C. B. Cochrane's production lavishly in *The Times* (26 November 1929). This was a play about man's capacity to distort religion, to behave inhumanly. Here we have comic realism, poetry, then the symbolism of the brutal reality of war, more comic realism, then the situation of a hero paralysed and deserted by his girl: an anti-war play obviously, and unlike the three Dublin plays loaded towards death and negativity.

Anglo-Irish writers, like prophets, are often not without honour save in their own country; and, reminding us of Swift's description of his return to Ireland as banishment, O'Casey chose a 'voluntary and settled exile' from his native land. He was turning to expressionism with *Within the Gates* (1933). Its stylised, symbolic approach, with its four seasons of the year, was pushed further in *The Star turns Red* (1940), a curious mixture of O'Casey's attempts to reconcile Marxism with Christianity. *Purple Dust* (1940) portrays two Englishmen in Ireland, and *Oakleaves and Lavender* (1948) treats Britain in 1941, again in an expressionist manner. These five plays suffer from what Yeats saw in *The Silver Tassie* as a divorce between O'Casey and his dramatic action: the dramatic action ought to burn up the author's opinions.

Vigorous writing surges through his six autobiographies — *I Knock at the Door* (1939); *Pictures in the Hallway* (1942); *Drums under the Windows* (1946); *Inish fallen Fare Thee Well* (1949); *Rose and Crown* (1952) and *Sunset and Evening Star* (1954). They chronicle his struggles as a suffering child and combative young man very successfully but the petty vexations spoil the effect of the later volumes. The first two volumes are books which use puns, parodies and literary echoes in rich profusion in prose which is often poetic. The autobiographies in their return to Dublin are parallel to the return, the very autobiographical return, in *Red Roses for Me* (1942). But

O'Casey could not recover the convincing tension of his early plays: the language of *Red Roses for Me* is too self-consciously literary, the profusion of verbal gymnastics overweening.

When O'Casey returned in his imagination to the actuality of the modern Ireland in which he did not live, the plays he wrote, *Cock-a-doodle Dandy* (1949), a rustic, exuberant piece of anti-puritanism in the form of fantasy, and *The Bishop's Bonfire* (1955), a satirical tragedy about the 'ferocious chastity' of modern Ireland, both lack conviction. In impulse O'Casey was akin to the Cork realists, but he tempered his darker view in *The Drums of Father Ned* (1959) where he celebrates the triumph of youth against age, in a mixture of Irish pagan mythology and Christianity, a theme given another twist in *Behind the Green Curtains* (1961), his last full-length play, which attacks contemporary bourgeois Irish intellectuals. These late plays are difficult to stage, though in them O'Casey was demonstrating his realisation that it was only through an Irish scene that his imagination could weave its way and create continuous action.

The Abbey was eager for the plays of George Shiels (1886–1949). He was born in Ballymoney, County Antrim, permanently disabled in Canada in 1913, and then lived in Ballymoney, finally settling at Carlough. The Ulster Theatre staged his first plays, but after *Bedmates* (1921) his plays pleased the Abbey audiences with their often broad comedy. *The New Gossoon* (1930) is, for instance, a good, well-constructed comedy, but Shiels could be very inconsistent in achievement; his play *Grogan and the Ferret* (1933), is a typical piece of stock Abbey comedy, written for, and often played to, an audience in search of easy laughter.

His later plays, however, are highly critical of contemporary Ireland. *The Rugged Path* (1940) deals with rural murder, the eventual giving of evidence (which would earlier have been 'informing'), the discharge of the murderer and the final disturbing hint that vengeance will be taken. *The Summit* (1941) supplies a possible solution to such situations. He continued to write plays with an increasingly satirical bite to them. *The Fort Field* (1942) centres on the bulldozing in the Second World War of a supposed fairy rath to make an aerodrome: yet another example of the conflict between romantic theory and the financially rewarding practice of the profit-seekers.

Whereas the plays of Shiels moved from the Ulster Theatre to the Abbey, John Coulter (*b*. 1888), a Belfast-born playwright, moved to Canada in the nineteen-thirties. He has written plays which present the apparently inevitable divisions of the northern province. These include *The Drums Are Out*, produced at the Abbey in 1948.

V The thirties onwards

The contribution of Micheál MacLiammóir (Alfred Willmore, 1899–1978) to Dublin's theatrical life was very great. In 1928 he founded the Gate Theatre with Hilton Edwards. This continued the work of the Dublin Drama League, founded by Yeats, Lennox Robinson, and James Stephens, under the auspices of the Abbey, to produce plays, largely by continental dramatists, not likely to be seen in Dublin in the ordinary course of events. At the Gate Theatre MacLiammóir acted brilliantly in a very wide range of parts indeed. He directed, produced, acted, designed costumes and sets, and wrote plays. His interpretation of *The Importance of Being Oscar* (1963), a one-man performance, was internationally successful, and his lively theatrical memoirs *All for Hecuba* (1961) and *Each Actor on his Ass* (1961) can be filled out by his autobiographical novel *Enter a Goldfish* (1977). The Gate Theatre complemented the Abbey's Irish plays, for its programme continued the traditions of Edward Martyn's earlier Irish Theatre, which had staged contemporary European drama, and the Dublin Drama League (1918–28) which had offered occasional productions of non-Irish plays of note. The Gate began its work in the Peacock Theatre (a small theatre with 102 seats, belonging to the Abbey and built in 1925 in an adjoining building) before moving to the Rotunda in 1930. The range of plays presented by the Gate Theatre has been very varied; though its programme has included the work of many Irish playwrights — Denis Johnston, Lord and Lady Longford, Mary Manning, Brian Friel, to name a few — it has sought to provide world drama, and it has done so with professional skill and distinctive taste, not least in its settings, where MacLiammóir, also an artist, had a considerable influence.

A new kind of satire began to emerge in the nineteen-thirties.

Louis D'Alton (1900–51), himself an actor running a touring company, an experience reflected in one of his novels *Rags and Sticks* (1938), wrote a play about James Clarence Mangan (published in *Two Irish Plays*, 1938) in addition to several rather obvious plays preaching the unimportance of money, of which *The Money Doesn't Matter* (1941) is typical. He has also contributed a very sharp discussion of modern Ireland in *This Other Eden* (1953). A similar strain of moralising runs through the much more effective work of Paul Vincent Carroll (1900–68), who came from County Louth, and from his early twenties to his late thirties was a schoolmaster in Glasgow. His first play *Things that are Caesar's* (1934) concentrates on the struggle between mediocre materialism and the growth of the individual human spirit. His next and best play, *Shadow and Substance* (1937), continues the theme, developing a struggle between a canon and a schoolmaster, with a saintly servant girl whose death makes both men less arrogant. *The White Steed* (1939) again explores a clash of characters with a puritanically severe priest opposed by a loving and gentle Canon. The role of the woman in this play, Nora Fintry, is to contribute to the resolution by bringing to bear a sense of human tolerance irradiated by a capacity for the simple enjoyment of life. Carroll was able to make both *Shadow and Substance* and *The White Steed* lively and effective well-made presentations on stage of his own belief in the capacity of character to change, in the force of love.

Didacticism, however, became obtrusive in his later plays, his irony giving way to a certain sentimentality, though his ability to write satiric dialogue was given its head in *The Devil came from Dublin* (1951) and, to a lesser degree, in *The Wayward Saint* (1955). Carroll also wrote plays for children and various film and television scripts.

Marrowbone Lane by Dr Robert Collis (*b.* 1900) continued the tradition of Oliver St John Gogarty in its very effective indictment of the appalling conditions of life in the Dublin slums; it could have been a tract, but as drama it has a powerful effect upon its audiences through its simple and stark story. Collis wrote an autobiography *The Silver Fleece* (1936); he was a younger brother of Maurice Collis (*b.* 1889) who retired from Burma to write several biographical studies, among them *Siamese White* (1934), *Cortés and Montezuma* (1954) and *Somerville and Ross* (1968).

A high-powered intelligence of a very individual order marks the writings of Denis Johnston (*b*. 1901) whose brilliantly clever first play *The Old Lady Says 'No!'* (1929), presented a sharply satiric view of the contrast between the romantic idealism of Robert Emmet and the reality of modern Irish life. The irony in this play, as in all Johnston's writing, is sharply intellectual, and there are allusive echoes throughout its episodic course, centred on an actor who is injured playing Robert Emmet in a romantic drama, and then imagines himself Emmet among modern Dubliners. Johnston, influenced by German expressionism, and by a mischievous desire to satirise the 'serious' plays favoured by the Abbey, followed it with *The Moon in the Yellow River* (1931) which revolves around the ultimate destruction of a power station. The tensions in this play are well created, but *A Bride for the Unicorn* was too episodic and too allusive. *Storm Song* satirised film making and the attitudes of its artists and technicians; *Blind Man's Buff* was a successful treatment of a murder trial and the machinery of the law. It was based on Toller's *The Blind Goddess* but Johnston later rewrote his part of it in *Strange Occurence on Ireland's Eye*.

The Dreaming Dust should be read in conjunction with Johnston's *In Search of Swift* (1959). The play shows actors discovering in Swift the seven deadly sins which they have been portraying in a masque; it has excellent scenes, and *The Golden Cuckoo*, which followed it, develops Johnston's sense of theatre further in a comic portrayal of the intrusion of the state upon the individual. His own attitudes to life emerge in *Nine Rivers from Jordan* (1953), graphic memoirs of his experiences as a war correspondent. He is an explorer of his own ideas, and has used his plays in different ways as means of analysing his own attitudes to those of others. *The Scythe and the Saint* (produced in the Abbey in 1958) is set in the heart of the Easter Rising and examines the nature of the attitudes held by characters who represent rebel leaders, Anglo-Irish, ordinary soldiers, ordinary people, intellectual observers. This play is ultimately analytic, expository: none the worse for that, but perhaps not ideal for popular dramatic success.

The early work of Lord Longford (1902–61) was produced by the Gate Theatre. He formed his own company, Longford Productions, in 1936 and staged plays at the Gate. He translated from Irish (notably Merryman's *The Midnight Court*), Greek, Spanish and French, and his own play on Swift, *Yahoo* (1933), and *Carmilla*, an adaptation of Sheridan La Fanu, both have good dramatic qualities.

Of the other dramatists born before 1922 mention should be made of Teresa Deevy (1903–63). Born in Waterford, she wrote plays in which the heroines are romantic young country girls at turning points in their lives, expressing themselves and their shifting moods in sudden turns of dialogue with all the uncertainty of adolescence. Seamus Byrne (1904–68) in *Design for a Headstone* (1956) and *Little City* (1970) dealt, respectively, with a prison strike and Dublin attitudes to abortion.

The main work of Donagh MacDonagh (1912–68) was *Happy as Larry* (1946), described as 'a ballad opera without music'. MacDonagh, a son of Thomas MacDonagh the 1916 leader, wrote various other ballad operas and poetic dramas as well as two volumes of verse, *The Hungry Grass* (1947) and *A Warning to Conquerors* (1968). A barrister who became a district justice, he was an excellent, lively broadcaster, a writer who wrote a play about tinkers, retold the Deirdre legend and had a deep interest in ballads. He was co-editor with Lennox Robinson of *The Oxford Book of Irish Verse* (1958).

MacDonagh's contemporary, John Boyd (*b*. 1912), educated at both Queen's University, Belfast, and Trinity College, Dublin, interprets the politico-sectarian strife with a full understanding of its roots and can capture the attitudes and speech of the region very skilfully, while Seamus de Burca (James Bourke, *b*. 1912) has written plays which show the influence of popular tradition and nineteenth-century melodramas. His father, who wrote several melodramas, was manager of the Queen's Theatre; his uncle was Peadar Kearney (1883–1942) who wrote 'The Soldier's Song', the Irish national anthem, sometime stage-manager of the Abbey; his cousin was Brendan Behan. Among de Burca's plays are *The Limpid River* (1956) and *The Boys and Girls are Gone* (originally *Margaret Nowlan*, when performed in 1950) written rather in the Boyle tradition, with its land hunger, made marriage and the tough widow woman, Margaret Nowlan, who reappears in *The Howards* (1960; originally *Mrs Howard's Husband*).

Complex plots and eccentric characters, intermittently overflowing eloquence and a general sense of the heritage of the Irish past as well as the depopulation of the west inform the plays of Michael J. Molloy (*b*. 1917). *The King of Friday's Men* (1953) is the best of them, though, like Molloy's earlier play *The Old Road* (1943), its plot is difficult, and its merits depend mainly upon a plethora of individual characters. Among a number of lesser dramatists, he is marked out by a lively energetic approach to playwriting.

VI Samuel Beckett

Educated at Portora Royal School, then Trinity College, Dublin, Samuel Beckett (*b*. 1906) was a lecturer at the École Normale Supérieure at Paris from 1929–30, then had a lectureship at Trinity College which he resigned in 1931, returning to live in Paris. He came from a well-to-do Dublin family; his relations with his mother were difficult and he was often painfully ill, perhaps because of the stresses imposed on him when he returned to Dublin. In Paris he was a close friend and admirer of Joyce, to whom he was introduced by Thomas McGreevy, and on whose *Finnegan's Wake* he wrote a piece in 1929. He is typical of many Irishmen in liking to live in France. This has been particularly true of painters from, say, the landscape painter Nathaniel Hone (1831–1917) who lived at Barbizon for twenty years, and the impressionist Roderic O'Conor (1961–1940) who found the landscape of Brittany engrossing and lived at Pont-Aven, to a most distinguished contemporary Irish painter Louis Le Brocquy (*b*. 1916) who lives in France and has in *Study in Reconstructed Head of S B* given his psychological impression of Beckett.

Beckett published *Whoroscope* (a poem) in 1930, *More Pricks than Kicks* (stories) in 1934, and *Echo's Bones and Other Precipitates* (poems) in 1935 before *Murphy* (his first novel) reputedly rejected by more than forty publishers, appeared in 1938. His second, less traditional novel *Watt*

(1953) was written during the war, in which Beckett worked for the French Resistance, living at Roussillon from 1942 to 1945. He received the *Croix de Guerre* in 1945. *Molloy* followed, written in French in 1951, and in English in 1958. The succeeding novel was *Malone Meurt* (1951; English translation *Malone Dies*, 1956) and the trilogy was completed with the novel *L'Innommable* (1953; English translation, *The Unnamable*, 1958).

In *Murphy* Beckett showed his capacity to build philosophical concepts — Cartesian and Newtonian — beneath the surface of a superbly comic novel. Murphy's mind is a hollow sphere; he searches after his own infinity; almost paradoxically he includes within his own microcosm — his mind a 'large sphere hermetically closed to The Universe without' — all that exists outside him; he wishes to reach nothingness. Beckett pursues rationalism, unlike the writers of the absurd: Murphy is split in two, a body and a mind; he needs no one. And yet he is loved by Celia the prostitute, and to his annoyance he, irrationally, loves her:

> 'At first I thought I had lost him because I could not take him as he was. Now I do not flatter myself.'
> A rest.
> 'I was a piece out of him that he could not go on without, no matter what I did.'
> A rest.
> 'He had to leave me to be what he was before he met me, only worse, or better, no matter what I did.'
> A long rest.
> 'I was the last exile.'
> A rest.
> 'The last, if we are lucky.'
> So love is wont to end, in protasis, if it be love.

Watt pushes philosophic content further: it is a novel about Watt's thought processes, his search for meaning in life. He acts as a servant to Mr Knott and then moves on, 'to the end of the line'. He is never able to free himself from twentieth-century man's tendency to want to see order in the universe. A logical positivist, he has failed to know anything beyond words; he has failed to impose rationality upon nothing, words cannot express it. Indeed human life is logically impossible: and yet it exists.

Beckett's next novels were written in French, possibly to escape from Joyce's example. *Molloy* is about Molloy's relations with his mother, who brought him into existence, into suffering, into a circumscribed freedom. Molloy ends up alone in a forest. Moran who is sent to find him fails to do so. The novel points to death, for life is exile from nothingness, and yet death does not supply an answer. Indeed some of the characters are not sure if they are dead or not. Malone in *Malone Dies* is dying, pondering the reason for suffering — a reason perhaps for life to exist. He wants to contemplate a timeless self; by creating several personalities he may be able to observe death. He is waiting, in effect, for nothing.

Death does not solve anything. The Unnamable in *L'Innommable* (1953; *The Unnamable*, 1958) reaches an absolute negative which he called Worm. Worm 'has nothing, is nothing', and yet time exists with words in it, and the Unnamable tries to use these words so as to discover, by some inconceivably remote chance, what he is.

Comment c'est (1961; *How It Is*, 1961) reduces words to the minimum necessary in an attempt to reach reality. This is a search for forms which will convey a vision of chaos. The 'I' of the novel realises he has a target, to reach Pim; he cannot talk, Pim has forgotten how to. There follows a process of torture to make Pim talk, and after Pim vanishes there is a vision of an endless sequence, a repetition of this torturing. There is no answer but nothing.

Though Beckett has carried experimentation in the novel far further than Joyce did, reversing the master's verbal exuberance into a plain, pared-down minimum, it was the Paris production in 1953 of his play *En Attendant Godot* (1952; English translation *Waiting for Godot*, 1954) that made him famous as an innovator, a dramatist who challenged audiences (not only those of intellectuals but also general audiences throughout the world) into thought. The tramps Vladimir and Estragon are waiting for Godot; the play is about man in time and how he is to cope with it. But who is Godot? Beckett thought that the play's success was caused by critics and audiences trying to extract allegorical or symbolical meanings from it. 'The key word in my plays', he said, 'is "perhaps".' *Waiting for Godot* is allusive, grotesque, circular, and utterly inconclusive.

Fin de Partie (1957; English translation *Endgame*, 1958) is more inhuman than *Godot*, Beckett has said, and the situation of the play is macabre. Hamm cannot walk; his parents, legless as the result of an accident, are in ashbins; only Clov the servant can walk, but he cannot sit down. He is bullied by Hamm, and, as the curtain falls, ready for the road he is watching Hamm. It is no longer the pain of waiting but of going.

Where has Beckett himself been going? His plays have dealt less and less in words. Mime attracts him, as in *Acte Sans Paroles* II (1957; English translation *Act Without Words*, 1958); and in *Happy Days* (1961) he has only two characters, one of them buried to the waist in Act I, to the neck in Act II. His own experience of illness has probably coloured his presentation of man and woman in distress, though he has been no invalid: he was a first-class cricketer as an undergraduate and he worked as a farm-labourer in France during the war. The narrative of *Company* compels us to picture a figure on his back in the dark whose senses leave him, though a voice in the dark tells of a past, and though not all that voice says can be verified, it is the quest for the self that runs through Beckett's work

> . . . finally you hear how words are coming to an end. With every inane word a little nearer to the last. And how the fable too. The fable of one with you in the dark. The fable of one fabling of one with you in the dark. And how better in the end labour lost and silence. And you as you always were. Alone.

Beckett is aware of certain facts: he has been born, is alive, will die, and must communicate. He does not know; he suffers; but he does not end in negativity. He is compassionate, modest, and, as the contents of the plays and novels show, highly inventive — and irreverent in a particularly Irish way.

Appendix 1
Books for children

IRISH books specifically written for children begin with Maria Edgeworth's well-known moral, educational stories which still appeal to children fortunate enough to have them read aloud to them. There is, however, more fantasy in the fairy stories of *Granny's Wonderful Chair and the Stories It Told* (1857) by Frances Brown (1816–79) the blind Donegal poet and novelist. Following Standish O'Grady's Irish stories came those of Ella Young (1865–1951). Born in County Antrim, she became an active Republican, learned Irish, and wrote *The Coming of Lugh* (1909) and *Celtic Wonder-Tales* (1910). Her later work *The Wonder Smith and His Son* (1927) and *The Unicorn with Silver Shoes* (1932) have a touch of pleasing fantasy about them. Another woman writer who produced stories for children was Winifred Letts (*b.* 1882), whose poems, in *Songs from Leinster* (1913) and *More Songs from Leinster* (1926), and an autobiography, *Knockmaroon* (1933), are worth reading. In more recent times Patricia Lynch (1900–72) wrote many very popular books for children, particularly her Turf-Cutter's Donkey Series which began in 1935, and the books about Brogeen the leprechaun, which began in 1947. Her writings, warmhearted and skilful, have been widely translated. *A Storyteller's Childhood* (1947) is a masterly rendering of her own youth. *The Singing Cave* (1959) by Eilis Dillon (*b.* 1920) is the best of this writer's work for children. She has also written a lively historical novel *Across the Bitter Sea* (1973) with a sequel *Blood Relations* (1977).

Appendix 2

Criticism and scholarship

A physician and pamphleteer, an eccentric, epigrammatic versifier, but, above all, a magnificent wandering scholar, James Henry (1798–1876) gave up medicine and applied himself to the study of Virgilian manuscripts in European libraries: the resulting five volumes of his *Aeneidea* were marked by vast learning and original comment.

There were several other nineteenth-century scholars who enhanced the reputation of Trinity College. They include Sir John Pentland Mahaffy (1839–1919), who was born of Irish parents in Switzerland, educated at home in Donegal, and then went on to a distinguished career in Trinity College, Dublin, of which he became Provost in 1914. *The Principles of The Art of Conversation* (1887) may give some idea of his own formidable powers as a talker. But Mahaffy was equally formidable as an author, with more than thirty books on classical, historical and philosophical subjects to his credit. The portrait by Sir William Orpen (1878–1931) shows a touch of arrogance but hardly conveys the kindly nature and honesty of the man who became a legend in his lifetime: the divergent opinions of his character can be understood by reading *Mahaffy: a biography of an Anglo-Irishman* (1971), by W. B. Stanford and R. B. McDowell.

A non-academic historian, William Hartpole Lecky (1838–1903) was educated at Trinity College, Dublin, travelled abroad and settled in London in 1871; he represented Dublin University at Westminster from 1895–1903, and was a liberal Unionist who opposed Home Rule. Five of the twelve volumes of his great *History of England in the Eighteenth Century* (1892) are devoted to Ireland because he wanted to refute Froude's calumnies against the Irish people. His first book was the anonymous *Leaders of Public Opinion in Ireland* (1861), followed by his *History of the Rise and Influence of*

Rationalism in Europe (2 vols, 1865) which established his reputation, and *History of European Morals from Augustus to Charlemagne* (2 vols, 1869). He has been characterised by James Auchmuty in his *Lecky* (1945) as 'almost the last in the great line of non-academic historians', and while Auchmuty points out that Lecky failed to understand the reality of nationalist emotions he rightly praises his principles of sanity and moderation, his love of justice and morality.

Two other classical scholars who wrote elegantly were Robert Yelverton Tyrrell and John Bagenal Bury. Tyrrell (1844–1914), born in Tipperary, became one of the greatest classical scholars of his day, holding the chairs of Latin (1870), Greek (1880) and Ancient History (1900) at Trinity College. His editions of classical authors include the massive Cicero's *Correspondence*; he was a wit as well as a scholar; he edited *Kottabos* (a journal publishing translations, parodies, lyrics and light verse, provided they were erudite and frivolous) and was a founder of the more solemn academic journal *Hermathena* in 1874. It still appears regularly. Bury (1861–1927), born in Monaghan, was educated at Foyle College, Londonderry and Trinity College, Dublin, where he held the chair of Modern History from 1893, and the chair of Greek from 1898; he then went to the chair of Modern History at Cambridge in 1902. Early in his life the *History of the Later Roman Empire* (1889) established his fame; he followed it with several other excellent books on Greek and Roman History.

In Irish scholarship P[atrick] W[eston] Joyce (1827–1914) combined a capacity for translation, for expertise in Irish place names and for writing general histories of Ireland that survived in schools until recently and provided a concise view of events. He wrote *English as we speak it in Ireland* (1910), to be compared with J. J. Hogan's *The English Language in Ireland* (1927).

More specialised in his interests was William J. Fitzpatrick (1830–95) who published much of the secret history of Ireland in books such as *The Sham Squire* (1866) and *Ireland before the Union* (1867).

It is hard to classify Joseph Holloway (1861–1944), an architect with a passion for the theatre whose vast diary records his daily life and gives details of performances in

Dublin theatres which he attended so assiduously. Four volumes selected from the 25 million words of the diary have been published by Robert Hogan and M. J. O'Neill (in 1967, 1968, 1969, and 1970) and are a valuable source of information. Like Holloway, W. J. Lawrence (1962–1940) came to dislike Yeats, and, particularly, Synge's *Playboy*; though his books deal with the Elizabethan stage, about which he had a deep and detailed knowledge, he wrote intelligent if often destructive cricitism of Irish drama for *The Stage*.

It is a relief to move among the less puritanical pages of Stephen Gwynn (1864–1950) who conveyed his enjoyment of Irish literature with an elegant ease, based upon knowledge and sound critical judgement. His *Irish Literature and Drama in the English Language* (1936), long a pioneering guide to the subject, may now seem simple, even superficial, but his books on Swift and Goldsmith are still eminently worth reading. Gwynn's public life as MP for Galway from 1906 to 1918 did not hinder his having a very large and varied output of writing, which is all pleasurable, be it autobiography, biography, criticism, fiction, poetry, books on fishing or guide books. He is a good guide, sharing his pleasures (and he had admirable taste) with his readers in an admirable way.

Another writer effective in communicating with his readers was the librarian and distinguished scientist Robert Lloyd Praeger (1865–1939) who in addition to *The Botanist in Ireland* (1934) and a very readable *Natural History of Ireland* (1950) wrote, in *The Way that I Went*, a lively account of his extensive travelling in Ireland.

John Eglinton (William Kirkpatrick Magee, 1868–1961) went to the High School, Dublin, where he was a contemporary of Yeats, who later thought him 'our one Irish critic'. Yeats selected *Some Essays and Passages by John Eglinton* for the Dun Emer Press, run by his sisters, to publish in 1905. A Theosophist, Eglinton became friendly with AE, and wrote transcendental essays under the influence of Emerson and Thoreau. His *Anglo-Irish Essays* appeared in 1917, and *A Memoir of AE* in 1937. Though he edited, with Fred Ryan, the twelve issues of *Dana* which contained work by many leading writers of the time during its brief run (between 1904–5), he was not regarded as sympathetic to the literary revival; his classical education led him to insist on literature having larger than national horizons. Inclusive in his taste, Robert Lynd (1879–1949), educated at Queen's College, Belfast, was a journalist who wrote graceful essays, very much part of the Edwardian period, which conveyed his appreciation of literature in a middle-brow manner.

With Joseph M[aunsel] Hone (1882–59) Irish biography came of age. A learned publisher, with a philosophical cast of mind, he wrote admirable lives of Bishop Berkeley and George Moore, and many subsequent writers have found his full, pioneering and shrewd life of W. B. Yeats (1942) a good starting point for their own work. Historical background for general readers is provided in Constantia Maxwell's (1886–1962) *Dublin under the Georges* (1936) and *Irish Town and Country under the Georges* (1940).

The Irish Literary Renaissance had its first historian in Ernest A. Boyd (1887–1946) who worked in the British Consular service and settled in New York in 1920. He began his account with Mangan and Ferguson, and blended history and trenchant criticism effectively throughout *Ireland's Literary Renaissance* (1920). Though this book gives the impression of having been written for readers with a knowledge of the literature rather than being designed as a text book for those with no knowledge of the background it still has much in it worth pondering; it was reissued in 1922. Another account also worth looking at is *The Irish Drama* (1929) by Andrew E. Malone (Laurence Patrick Byrne, 1888–1939) a journalist whose judgements are sensible, if excessively conservative.

Helen Waddell (1889–1965) was educated at Queen's University, Belfast, and later at Oxford. She produced *The Wandering Scholars* (1927), an account of the Goliards and translations from their work, a collection of *Medieval Latin Lyrics* (1933) and the novel *Peter Abelard* (1933) which, though obviously the work of a scholar rather than a novelist, remains a moving book best read in conjunction (and comparison) with George Moore's *Héloïse and Abelard* (1921), the work of a novelist rather than a scholar.

Arland Ussher (1899–1980), though born in London, was of Irish stock, was educated at Trinity College and knew Irish. Capable of deep philosophical thought, he developed a forte for making arresting generalisations, notably in *The Face and Mind of Ireland* (1949), a stimulating and often witty contemplation of the Irish character and the intellectual history that has been made by it. In *Three Great Irishmen* (1952) he applied his critical judgement to Shaw, Yeats and Joyce, making many profound comments which benefit from the highly original cast of his own mind, so much at its ease in the form of the speculative, provocative essay.

Among contemporary authors two, in particular, deserve praise. Originality of viewpoint is to be found in refreshing measure in the writings of Conor Cruise O'Brien (*b*. 1917), particularly in his *Maria Cross* (1952), subtle studies of modern Catholic writers, published under the pseudonym of Donat O'Donnell. He has written a book on Parnell, books on his own experiences in Katanga and about the United Nations, a play on the Congo, *Murderous Angels* (1968), and various studies of Ireland, past and present. He writes with discernment, wit and pungency. A notable discernment is also at work in *Dublin, 1660–1860*, a fine artistic, social and cultural history by Maurice James Craig (*b*. 1919), whose native Belfast was ironically apostrophised in 'Ballad to a Traditional Refrain', an anthology piece typical of his early poetry. Craig writes poetry and prose with a precision permeated by his particular sense of enjoyment; his *Life of the Volunteer Earl, James Caulfield, the first Earl of Charlemont* (1948) is informed by meticulous knowledge of the eighteenth-century background.

Select bibliography

THE following items deal specifically with general and particular aspects of Anglo-Irish literature; (for the history of Irish literature see Declan Kiberd, *A History of Literature in Irish*, a companion volume in the *Macmillan Histories of Literature*, 1982) there is, of course, coverage of many Anglo-Irish writers in such general works as the *Oxford History of English Literature*, the *Cambridge History of English Literature*, E. A. Baker's *History of the English Novel*, and Allardyce Nicoll's *English Drama 1900—1930*. The various volumes of *Great Writers of the English Language* and *Contemporary Writers of the English Language*, both edited by James Vinson, also provide useful critical and bibliographical information. Bibliographical information is also given in reference works such as the *Cambridge Bibliography of English Literature*; the annual Handlist of work in progress published by the Royal Irish Academy, Dublin, and in the bibliography published for IASAIL (the International Association for the Study of Anglo-Irish Literature) in the *Irish University Review*. A useful reference book for students is Maurice Harmon, *Select Bibliography for the Study of Anglo-Irish and its backgrounds* (Dublin: Wolfhound Press, 1977).

General

BOYD, ERNEST A.: *Ireland's Literary Renaissance* (Dublin: Maunsel, 1916; rev. edn, 1922; Dublin: Figgis, 1965).

BROWN, MALCOLM: *The Politics of Irish Literature: from Thomas Davis to W. B. Yeats* (London: Allen and Unwin, 1972).

COSTELLO, PETER: *The Heart Grown Brutal: The Irish Revolution in Literature from Parnell to the Death of Yeats, 1891—1939* (Dublin: Gill and Macmillan, 1977).

DUNN, DOUGLAS (ed): *Two Decades of Irish Writing* (Cheadle Hulme: Carcanet Press, 1975).

FALLIS, RICHARD: *The Irish Renaissance: An Introduction to Anglo-Irish Literature* (Syracuse: Syracuse University Press, 1977; Dublin: Gill and Macmillan, 1978).

GWYNN, STEPHEN: *Irish Literature and Drama in the English Language: A Short History* (London: Thomas Nelson & Sons, 1936).

HARMON, MAURICE: *Modern Irish Literature 1800—1967: A Reader's Guide* (Dublin: Dolmen, 1967).

HOGAN, ROBERT (ed. in chief): *The Macmillan Dictionary of Irish Literature* (London: Macmillan, 1979).

HOWARTH, HERBERT: *The Irish Writers, 1880–1960* (New York: Hill and Wang, 1959).

HYDE, DOUGLAS: *The Literary History of Ireland* (London: T. Fisher Unwin, 1899; new edn with Introduction by Brian Ó Cuív, London: Ernest Benn, 1967).

MACDONAGH, THOMAS: *Literature in Ireland: Studies Irish and Anglo-Irish* (Dublin: Talbot Press, 1916).

MARCUS, PHILIP L. : *Yeats and the Beginning of the Irish Renaissance* (Ithaca & London: Cornell University Press, 1970).

MARTIN, AUGUSTINE: *Anglo-Irish Literature* (Dublin: Dept. of Foreign Affairs, 1980).

MERCIER, VIVIAN: *The Irish Comic Tradition* (Oxford: Clarendon Press, 1962).

O'CONNOR, FRANK: *A Backward Look: A Survey of Irish Literature* (London: Macmillan, 1967).

RAFROIDI, PATRICK: *Irish Literature in English: The Romantic Period* (2 vols, Gerrards Cross: Colin Smythe, 1980).

SEYMOUR, ST JOHN D.: *Anglo-Irish Literature, 1200–1582* (Cambridge: Cambridge University Press, 1929).

USSHER, ARLAND: *The Face and Mind of Ireland* (London: Victor Gollancz, 1949).

Poetry

ALSPACH, RUSSELL K.: *Anglo-Irish Poetry from the English Invasion to 1798* (Philadelphia: University of Pennsylvania Press, 1943; 2nd rev. edn, 1960).

BROWN, TERENCE: *Northern Voices: Poets from Ulster* (Dublin: Gill and Macmillan, 1975).

FARREN, ROBERT: *The Course of Irish Verse* (London: Sheed & Ward, 1948).

LOFTUS, RICHARD: *Nationalism in Modern Irish Poetry* (Madison: University of Wisconsin Press, 1969).

LUCY, SEAN (ed): *Irish Poets in English* (Cork: Mercier Press, 1973).

O'DONOGHUE, DAVID JAMES: *The Poets of Ireland: a biographical dictionary with bibliographical particulars* (London: 1892; 2nd edn, Dublin: 1912).

POWER, PATRICK C.: *The Story of Anglo-Irish Poetry 1800–1922* (Cork: Mercier Press, 1967).

WELCH, ROBERT: *Irish Poetry from Moore to Yeats* (Gerrards Cross: Colin Smythe, 1980).

Drama

BELL, SAM HANNA: *The Theatre in Ulster: a survey of the dramatic movement in Ulster from 1902 to the present day* (Dublin: Gill and Macmillan, 1972).

CLARK, WILLIAM SMYTH: *The Early Irish Stage* (Oxford: Oxford University Press, 1955).

DUGGAN, D. C.: *The Stage Irishman: a history of the Irish play and stage characters from earliest times* (Dublin: Talbot Press, 1937).

ELLIS-FERMOR, UNA: *The Irish Dramatic Movement* (London: Methuen, 1939; 2nd edn, 1954).

GREGORY, LADY: *Our Irish Theatre* (New York & London: G. P. Putnam's Sons, 1914; 3rd edn enlarged, Gerrards Cross: Colin Smythe, 1972).

HOGAN, ROBERT: *After the Renaissance: a critical history of Irish Drama since 'The Plough and the Stars'* (Minneapolis: University of Minnesota Press, 1967; London: Macmillan, 1968).

MALONE, ANDREW E.: *The Irish Drama 1896—1928* (London: 1929; a continuation, with details of performances etc. is in MACNAMARA, BRINSLEY, *Abbey Plays 1899—1948, including the productions of the Irish Literary Theatre* (Dublin: Sign of the Three Candles, 1949)).

ROBINSON, LENNOX: *Ireland's Abbey Theatre: A History 1899—1951* (London: Sidgwick & Jackson, 1951).

Fiction

BROWN, STEPHEN JAMES: *Ireland in Fiction: a guide to Irish novels, tales, romances and folk lore* (Dublin and London: Maunsel, 1916).

CRONIN, JOHN: *The Anglo-Irish Novel, volume one: The Nineteenth Century* (Belfast: Appletree Press, 1980).

FLANAGAN, THOMAS: *The Irish Novelists, 1800—1850* (New York: Columbia University Press, 1959).

FOSTER, JOHN WILSON: *Forces and Themes in Ulster Fiction* (Dublin: Gill and Macmillan, 1974).

KIELY, BENEDICT: *Modern Irish Fiction — A Critique* (Dublin: Golden Eagle Books, 1950).

RAFROIDI, PATRICK AND TERENCE BROWN: *The Irish Short Story* (Gerrards Cross: Colin Smythe, 1979).

RAFROIDI, PATRICK AND MAURICE HARMON (eds): *The Irish Novel in our Time* (Lille: Presses Universitaire de Lille (C.E.R.I.U.L.), 1976).

ANTHOLOGIES

BROOKE, STOPFORD A., AND T. W. ROLLESTON (eds): *A Treasury of Irish Poetry in the English Tongue* (London: Smith, Elder & Co, 1900).

GREENE, DAVID H. (ed): *An Anthology of Irish Literature* (New York: Modern Library, 1954).

KENNELLY, BRENDAN (ed.): *The Penguin Book of Irish Verse* (Harmondsworth: Penguin Books, 1970).

LUCY, SÉAN (ed.): *Love Poems of the Irish* (Cork: Mercier Press, 1967).

MACDONAGH, DONAGH AND LENNOX ROBINSON (eds): *The Oxford Book of Irish Verse XVIIth Century—XXth Century* (Oxford: Clarendon Press, 1958).

MAHON, DEREK (ed.): *The Sphere Book of Modern Irish Poetry* (London: Sphere Books, 1972).

MERCIER, VIVIAN AND DAVID GREENE (eds): *1000 Years of Irish Poetry* (New York: Devin—Adair, 1953).

MONTAGUE, JOHN (ed.): *The Faber Book of Irish Verse* (London: Faber and Faber, 1974; 1978).

ROBINSON, LENNOX (ed.): *A Golden Treasury of Irish Verse* (London: Macmillan, 1925).

TAYLOR, GEOFFREY (ed.): *Irish Poets of the Nineteenth Century* (London: Routledge and Kegan Paul, 1951).

Background

THE ENGLISH LANGUAGE IN IRELAND

HOGAN, J. J.: *The English Language in Ireland* (Dublin: Educational Company of Ireland, 1927).

JOYCE, P. W. : *English as we speak it in Ireland* (London: Longmans; Dublin: M. H. Gill, 1910).

GEOGRAPHY AND LANDSCAPE

FREEMAN, T. W.: *Ireland: General and Regional Geography* (London: Methuen; New York: E. P. Dutton, 1950; 4th edn, London: Methuen, 1969).

MITCHELL, FRANK: *The Irish Landscape* (London: Collins, 1976).

GENERAL HISTORICAL BACKGROUND

BECKETT, J. C.: *A Short History of Ireland* (London: Hutchinson's University Library, 1952); *The Anglo-Irish Tradition* (London: Faber and Faber, 1976).

CRAIG, MAURICE JAMES: *Dublin 1660–1860* (Dublin: Allen Figgis, 1969).

CURTIS, EDMUND: *A History of Ireland* (London: Methuen, 1936).

INGLIS, BRIAN: *The Story of Ireland* (London: Faber and Faber, 1956; 2nd edn, 1965).

LYONS, F. S. L.: *Ireland since the Famine* (London: Weidenfeld and Nicholson, 1971; 2nd rev edn, London: Fontana, 1973); *Culture and Anarchy in Ireland* (Oxford: Clarendon Press, 1978).

MANSERGH, NICHOLAS: *The Irish Question 1840–1922* (London: Allen and Unwin, 1965; rev. edn, 1975).

MAXWELL, CONSTANTIA: *Dublin Under the Georges* (London: Harrap, 1936; new edn, 1937); *Country and Town in Ireland Under the Georges* (London: Harrap, 1940).

WHITE, TERENCE DE VERE: *The Anglo-Irish* (London: Gollancz, 1972).

ART

ARNOLD, BRUCE: *A Concise History of Irish Art* (London: Thames and Hudson, 1969; rev. edn, 1977).

CROOKSHANK, ANNE AND THE KNIGHT OF GLYN: *The Painters of Ireland c. 1600–1920* (London: Barrie and Jenkins, 1978).

BIOGRAPHICAL INFORMATION

BOYLAN, HENRY: *A Dictionary of Irish Biography* (Dublin: Gill and Macmillan, 1978).

CLEEVE, BRIAN: *Dictionary of Irish Writers: Fiction; Non-fiction* (Cork: Mercier Press, 1966; 1969 respectively).

CRONE, JOHN S.: *A Concise Dictionary of Irish Biography* (Dublin: Talbot Press, 1928).

SHARE, BERNARD: *Irish Lives: Biographies of Famous Irish Men and Women* (Dublin: Allen Figgis, 1971).

WEBB, ALFRED: *A Compendium of Irish Biography, comprising sketches of distinguished Irishmen* (Dublin: M. H. Gill, 1878).

LITERATURE IN IRISH

DILLON, MYLES: *Early Irish Literature* (Chicago: University of Chicago Press, 1948).

FLOWER, ROBIN: *The Irish Tradition* (Oxford: Clarendon Press, 1947).

KIBERD, DECLAN: *A History of Literature in Irish* (London: Macmillan, 1982).

MURPHY, GERALD: *Saga and Myth in Ancient Irish Literature* (Dublin: Colm O'Lochlainn, 1955).

O'SUILLEABHÁIN, S.: *A Handbook of Irish Folklore* (Dublin: Folklore of Ireland Society, 1942).

Chronological table
432–1980

Abbreviations: (D) = drama, (P) = prose, (V) = verse

DATE	AUTHOR AND TITLE	EVENT
432		Christianity brought to Ireland by St Patrick
795		Beginning of Viking raids
c.800		Book of Kells
1014		Decisive defeat of Danes in Battle of Clonstarf
1170		Strongbow arrives in Ireland
1366		Statutes of Kilkenny
1550		Humphrey Powell sets up first printing press in Ireland
1556		Plantation of Leix and Offaly
1577	Stanihurst, Richard (1547–1618): *Treatise containing a Plaine and Perfect Description of Ireland* (P.)	
1586		Plantation of Munster
1591		University of Dublin (Trinity College) founded
1596		Edmund Spenser, *A View of the Present State of Ireland*
1607		The Flight of the Earls
1608–9		Plantation of Ulster by English and Lowland Scots
1610	Barry, Lo/Lod/Lodwick (?James, b.?1591) *Ram Alley or Merry Tricks* (D.)	

DATE	AUTHOR AND TITLE	EVENT
1636		*Annals of Four Masters* (begun 1632) completed (trans. John O'Donovan (1809–61) 7 vols 1848–51)
1642	Denham, Sir John (1615–69): *Coopers Hill* (V.); *The Sophy* (D.)	
1649–50		Cromwell sacks Drogheda, Wexford and other towns
1652		Act for the Settlement of Ireland removes forfeiting landlords to Connaught
1654	Boyle, Roger, earl of Orrery (1621–79): *Parthenissa* (P.)	
1660		Thomas Southerne (*b.*)
1661	Boyle, Robert (1627–91): *The Sceptical Chymist* (P.); *Some considerations touching the Style of the Holy Scriptures* (P.)	
1665	Boyle, Roger, earl of Orrery: *Mustapha* (D.)	
1667		Jonathan Swift (*b.*)
1672		Richard Steele (*b.*)
1677	Tate, Nahum (1652–1715): *Poems* (V.)	George Farquhar (*b?*)
1684	Dillon, Wentworth, earl of Roscommon (1633–84) *Essay on Translated Verse* (V.) Southerne, Thomas (1660–1746): *The Disappointment or, The Mother in Fashion* (D.)	
1685		George Berkeley (*b.*)
1687	Tate, Nahum: [adaptation of] *King Lear* (D.); *The Sicilian Usurper* (D.)	

DATE	AUTHOR AND TITLE	EVENT
1690	Doggett, Thomas (*b.?* 1660–1721): *The Country Wake* (D.) Southerne, Thomas: *Sir Anthony Love* (D.)	William of Orange defeats James II at the Battle of the Boyne
1691	King, Archbishop William (1650–1729): *State of the Protestants of Ireland under the late King James's Government* (P.)	French army under St Ruth defeated at Augrim Treaty of Limerick negotiated by Sarsfield
1692	Congreve, William (1670–1729): *Incognita* (P.) Southerne, Thomas: *The Wife's Excuse* (D.)	Nahum Tate Poet Laureate
1693	Congreve, William: *The Old Batchelour* (D.)	
1694	Congreve, William: *The Double Dealer* (published 1695) (D.) Southerne, Thomas: *Isabella or the Fatal Marriage* (D.)	
1695	Congreve, William: *Love for Love* (D.)	Oath of Allegiance and Oath of Abjuration required by Westminster parliament Penal Acts passed by Dublin parliament
1696	Southerne, Thomas: *Oroonoko* (D.) Tate, Nahum and Nicholas Brady: trs *Psalms* [called the *New Version*] (V.)	Further Penal Acts passed by Dublin parliament
1698	Farquhar, George (1677–1707): *Love and a Bottle* (D.) Molyneux, William (1656–98): *The Case of Ireland being bound by Acts of Parliament in England, Stated*	
1699	Farquhar, George: *The Constant Couple, or a Trip to the Jubilee* (D.)	Export duty put on wool by Dublin parliament

DATE	AUTHOR AND TITLE	EVENT
	Philips, William: *St Stephen's Green; or the Generous Lovers* (D).	Irish prohibited by Westminster parliament from exporting wool except to some few English ports, and from only six Irish ports
1700	Congreve, William: *The Way of the World* (D.)	
	Tate, Nahum: *Panacea; a Poem on Tea* (V.)	
1701	Farquhar, George: *Sir Harry Wildair* (D.); *The Miscellanies* (P.)	
1702	Centlivre, Susannah (1670–1723): *The Beau's Duel* (D.)	
1704	Swift, Jonathan (1667–1745): *A Tale of a Tub* (P.); *The Battle of the Books* (P.)	
1706	Farquhar, George: *The Recruiting Officer* (D.)	
1707	Farquhar, George: *The Beaux' Stratagem* (D.)	George Farquhar (*b.*? 1677) (*d.*)
1709	Berkeley, George (1685–1753): *Essay towards a New Theory of Vision* (P.)	Richard Steele edits the *Tatler* (April 1709–Jan. 1711)
1710	Berkeley, George: *The Principles of Human Knowledge* (P.)	*The Examiner* (1710–12) started by Bolingbroke, Swift, Prior and others
1711	Swift, Jonathan: *Miscellanies* (containing *An Argument against abolishing Christianity*) (P.); *The Conduct of the Allies* (P.)	Richard Steele begins *Spectator* with Joseph Addison (it succeeds *Tatler*)
1713	Berkeley, George: *Three Dialogues between Hylas and Philonous* (P.)	Swift Dean of St Patrick's Swift, Pope, Congreve, Parnell and others form the Scriblerus Club

DATE	AUTHOR AND TITLE	EVENT
		Richard Steele (edits) *Guardian* (12 Mar–1 Oct.) (P.); *The Englishman* (6 Oct. 1713–11 Feb. 1714) (P.)
		Lawrence Sterne (*b.*)
1714	Centlivre, Susannah: *The Wonder: A Woman Keeps a Secret* (D.)	
1720	Swift, Jonathan: *A Proposal for the Universal Use of Irish Manufactures* (P.)	
1722	Parnell, Rev. Thomas: *Poems* (ed. Pope)	
	Steele, Richard: *The Conscious Lovers* (D.)	
1724	Swift, Jonathan: *Drapier's Letters* (P.)	
1726	Swift, Jonathan: *Cadenus and Vanessa* [written 1712] (V.); *Gulliver's Travels* (P.)	George Faulkner (?1698–1775) opens his printing and book-selling shop in Dublin
1728	Swift, Jonathan: *A Short View of the State of Ireland* (P.)	Oliver Goldsmith (*b.*)
1729	Swift, Jonathan: *A Modest Proposal* (P.)	Edmund Burke (*b.*)
		Sir Richard Steele (*b.*1672) (*d.*)
1731		Dublin Society founded by Thomas Prior (1682–1751) and friends
1732	Berkeley, George: *Alciphron* (P.)	
1735	Berkeley, George: *The Querist* I (II, 1736; III, 1737) (P.)	
	Swift, Jonathan: *Collected Works* (4 vols, Faulkner, Dublin; 6 vols, 1738; 8 vols, 1746)	
1739	Swift, Jonathan: *Verses on the Death of Dr Swift* [written 1731] (V.)	Hugh Kelly (*b.*)

DATE	AUTHOR AND TITLE	EVENT
1745		Jonathan Swift (*b.* 1667) (*d.*)
1746		Henry Grattan (*b.*)
		Thomas Southerne (*b.* 1660) (*d.*)
1748	Pilkington, Mrs Laetitia (1712–50): *Memoirs* (P.)	
1751		Richard Brinsley Sheridan (*b.*)
1753		George Berkeley, Bishop of Cloyne, (*b.* 1685) (*d.*)
1756	Burke, Edmund (1729–97): *A Vindication of Natural Society* (P.); *Philosophical Enquiry into the Origin of Our Ideas of the Sublime and the Beautiful* (P.)	
	Murphy, Arthur (1727–1805): *The Apprentice* (D.)	
1758	Swift, Jonathan: *The Four Last Years of the Queen* (P.)	
1759	Macklin, Charles (?1697–1797): *Love à la Mode* (D.)	British Museum (based on Sir Hans Sloane's collection) opened
1760	Goldsmith, Oliver (1728–74): *Letters from a Citizen of the World* (P.) [in the *Public Ledger* 24 January 1760 to 14 August 1761; collected 1762]	
	Sterne, Laurence (1713–68): *Tristram Shandy*, I–II [III-VI, 1761–2; VII-VIII, 1765; IX, 1767; collected 1767]	
1761	Bickerstaffe, Isaac (1733–?1808): *Love in a Village* (D.)	
	O'Keefe, John (1747–1833): *The She Gallant* (D.)	

DATE	AUTHOR AND TITLE	EVENT
	Sheridan, Frances (1724–66): *The Memoirs of Miss Sidney Biddulph* (P.)	
1762	Goldsmith, Oliver: *A Citizen of the World* (P.); *Life of Richard Nash* (P.)	
1764	Goldsmith, Oliver: *The Traveller* (V.)	
1766	Brooke, Henry (1703–83): *The Fool of Quality* (P.)	
	Goldsmith, Oliver: *The Vicar of Wakefield* (P.)	
1767	Bickerstaffe, Isaac (with Charles Dibdin): *Love in the City* (D.)	Maria Edgeworth (*b.*)
	Macklin, Charles: *The Irish Fine Lady* [orig. *The True Born Irishman: or the Irish Fine Lady* 1762] (D.)	
1768	Goldsmith, Oliver: *The Good Natur'd Man* (D.)	Laurence Sterne (*b.* 1713) (*d.*)
	Kelly, Hugh (1739–1777): *False Delicacy* (D.)	
	Sterne, Laurence: *A Sentimental Journey through France and Italy* (P.)	
1770	Burke, Edmund: *Thoughts on the Present Discontents* (P.)	
	Goldsmith, Oliver: *The Deserted Village* (V.); *Life of Thomas Parnell* (P.); *Life of Viscount Bolingbroke* (P.)	
1771	Goldsmith, Oliver: *History of England* (4 vols)	
1773	Goldsmith, Oliver: *She Stoops to Conquer* (D.); *On Sentimental Comedy* (P.)	
	Samuel Whyte (1733–1811): *The Shamrock* (V.)	

DATE	AUTHOR AND TITLE	EVENT
1774	Goldsmith, Oliver: *Retaliation* (V).; *Grecian History* (P.); *A History of Earth and Animated Nature* (P.) O'Halloran, Sylvester (1728–1807): *A General History of Ireland* (P.)	Oliver Goldsmith (*b*.1728) (*d*.)
1775	Burke, Edmund: *Speech on Conciliation with America* (P.) Sheridan, Richard Brinsley (1751–1816): *The Rivals* (D.); *The Duenna* (D.)	
1776		Sydney Owenson (Lady Morgan) (*b*.?)
1777	Sheridan, Richard Brinsley: *The School for Scandal* (D.)	Hugh Kelly (*b*. 1739) (*d*.)
1779	Sheridan, Richard Brinsley: *The Critic* (D.)	Thomas Moore (*b*.)
1780	Sheridan, Thomas (1719–88): *A General Dictionary of the English Language* (2 vols)	Arthur Young, *Tour in Ireland*
1781	Sheridan, Richard Brinsley: *A Trip to Scarborough* (D.)	The Custom House built (1781–91) designed by James Gandon
1782	Burke, Edmund: *Letter to a Peer of Ireland on Penal Laws* (P.)	Grattan's Parliament Charles Robert Maturin (*b*.)
1783	Sheridan, Richard Brinsley: *The School for Scandal* [1st English edn; play produced 1777] (D.)	
1784	Berkeley, George (*d*. 1753): *Collected Works* [contains *Commonplace Book*]	
1785	Burke, Edmund: *Speech on Nabob of Arcot's Debts* (P.)	Royal Irish Academy founded

DATE	AUTHOR AND TITLE	EVENT
1786	Walker, Joseph (1761–1810): *Historical Memoirs of the Irish Bards*	Sheridan's speech against Warren Hastings
1789	Brooke, Charlotte (?1740–93): *Reliques of Irish Poetry* (translations) Dermody, Thomas (1775–1802): *Poems* (V.)	
1790	Burke, Edmund: *Reflections on the French Revolution* (P.)	
1791		United Irishmen founded
1792	Burke, Edmund: *Letter to Sir Hercules Langrishe* (P.); *Speeches on Impeachment of Warren Hastings* (P.); *Collected Works* [concluded 1827]	Harp Festival in Belfast Engraved sets of James Malton's (*d.* 1803) views of Dublin (completed in 1791) published
1793		Penal Laws relaxed
1794		William Carleton (*b.*)
1795		Maynooth College founded Orange order founded Jeremiah Joseph Callanan (*b.*) Charles Darley (*b.*)
1796	Bunting, Edward (1773–1843): *General Collection of Ancient Irish Music* Burke, Edmund: 'Letter to a Noble Lord'; 'Letters I & II on a Regicide Peace' [Letter III, 1797; Letter IV in *Works* 1812] Edgeworth, Maria (1767–1849): *The Parent's Assistant, or Stories for Children*, pt I [completed 1800]	French invasion attempt (with Wolfe Tone) abandoned Michael Banim (*b.*)
1797	O'Keefe, John: *The Wicklow Gold Mines* (comic opera)	Samuel Lover (*b.*) Edmund Burke (*b.* 1729) (*d.*)

DATE	AUTHOR AND TITLE	EVENT
1798	Edgeworth, Maria: *Practical Education* (P.)	Revolution of United Irishmen John Banim (*b.*)
1800	Edgeworth, Maria: *Castle Rackrent* (P.) Moore, Thomas (1779–1852): *Odes of Anacreon* (V.)	Act of Union between Great Britain and Ireland
1801	Little, Thomas [Moore, Thomas] : *Poetical Works of the late Thomas Little* (V.)	
1802	Edgeworth, Maria, with R. L. Edgeworth, (1744–1817), *Essay on Irish Bulls* (P.)	First Christian Brothers School opened
1803	James Kenney (1780–1849): *Raising the Wind* (D.)	Robert Emmet's (*b.* 1778) rising and death Gerald Griffin (*b.*) James Clarence Mangan (*b.*)
1805	Owenson, Sydney [Lady Morgan] (?1776–1859): *The Novice of St Dominick* (P.); *Twelve Original Hibernian Melodies* (V.)	
1806	Morgan, Lady: *The Wild Irish Girl* (P.)	Charles Lever (*b.*)
1807	Dermody, Thomas (1775–1802): *The Harp of Erin* (V.) Maturin, Charles (1782–1824): *Montorio, or the Fatal Revenge* (P.) Moore, Thomas, *Irish Melodies* [1807–34; music by Sir John Stevenson] (V.)	
1808	Curran, John Philpott (1750–1817): *Speeches* (P.) Leadbeater, Mary (1758–1826): *Poems* (V.) Maturin, Charles: *The Wild Irish Boy* (P.)	

DATE	AUTHOR AND TITLE	EVENT
1809	Edgeworth, Maria: *Tales of Fashionable Life* [1st series: *Ennui, The Dun, Manoeuvering, Almeria*] (P.)	John Wilson Croker associated with founding of *The Quarterly Review*
1810		Samuel Ferguson (*b.*)
1812	Edgeworth, Maria: *Tales of Fashionable Life* [2nd series: *Vivian, The Absentee, Mme de Fleury, Emilie de Coulanges*] (P.) Maturin, Charles: *The Milesian Chief* (P.)	
1814	Edgeworth, Maria: *Patronage* (P.) Morgan, Lady: *O'Donnel, a National Tale* Sheil, Richard Lawlor (1791–1851): *Adelaide, or the Emigrants* (D.)	Sheridan Le Fanu (*b.*) Thomas Davis (*b.*)
1815	Moore, Thomas: *National Airs* [music by Sir John Stevenson]	Charles Bianconi (1786–1875) begins Bianconi car service in Ireland
1816	Maturin, Charles: *Bertram* (D.)	Richard Brinsley Sheridan (*b.* 1751) (*d.*)
1817	Edgeworth, Maria: *Harrington* (P.); *Ormond* (P.) Moore, Thomas: *Lalla Rookh* (V.)	
1818	Maturin, Charles: *Women, or Pour et Contre* (P.) Morgan, Lady: *Florence MacCarthy: an Irish Tale* (P.)	
1820	Edgeworth, Richard Lovell: *Memoirs* [completed by Maria Edgeworth] Maturin, Charles: *Melmoth the Wanderer* (P.)	Dion Boucicault (?*b.*)

DATE	AUTHOR AND TITLE	EVENT
1821		Theatre Royal, Dublin opened
1822	Darley, George (1795–1846): *Errors of Ecstasie* (V.) De Vere, Sir Aubrey (1788–1846): *Julian the Apostate* (V.) Grattan, Henry: *Speeches*	
1824	Maturin, Charles: *The Albigenses* (P.) Moore, Thomas: *Memoirs of Captain Rock* (P.)	William Allingham (*b.*) Rev. Charles R. Maturin (*b.* 1780) (*d.*)
1825	Banim, John (1798–1842) and Banim, Michael (1796–1874): *Tales of the O'Hara Family* (P.) Croker, Thomas Crofton (1798–1854): *Fairy Legends and Traditions of South Ireland* (P.)	
1826	Banim, John and Michael: *The Boyne Water, Tales of the O'Hara Family* (2nd series) [*The Nowlans* and *Peter of the Castle*]	Rev. Caesar Otway (1780–1842) founded the *Christian Examiner*
1827	Barrington, Sir Jonah (1760–1834): *Personal Sketches of his own time* [2 vols; 3rd vol. 1833] Griffin, Gerald (1803–40): *Holland-Tide; or, Munster Popular Tales* (P.); *Tales of the Munster Festivals* (P.) Morgan, Lady: *The O'Briens and the O'Flahertys* (P.)	
1828	Banim, Michael: *The Croppy. A Tale of 1798* (P.)	
1829	Griffin, Gerald: *The Collegians* (P.); *The Rivals, Tracy's Ambition* (P.)	Catholic Emancipation Jeremiah Joseph Callanan (*b.* 1795) (*d.*)

DATE	AUTHOR AND TITLE	EVENT
1830	Callanan, Jeremiah Joseph (d. 1829): *The Recluse of Inchidony* (V.) Carleton, William (1794–1869): *Traits and Stories of the Irish Peasantry* (1st series) [2nd, 1833; new edn 1843–4] (P.)	
1831	Banim, John and Michael: *The Ghost Hunter and His Family* (P.) Lover, Samuel (1797–1868): *Legends and Stories of Ireland* (P.)	Tithe war begins System of National Education introduced with English as sole medium of education
1832	Maxwell, William Hamilton (1792–1850): *Wild Sports of the West of Ireland* (P.)	*Dublin Penny Journal* begins
1833		*Dublin University Magazine* founded by Isaac Butt (1813–79) and five others
1834	Mahony, Francis Sylvester (1804–66): *Reliques of Father Prout* [Completed 1836, enlarged, 1860; 1876]	
1835	Darley, George: *Nepenthe* (V.) Griffin, Gerald: *Tales of my Neighbourhood* (P.)	
1837	Lever, Charles (1806–72): *Confessions of Harry Lorrequer* [begun in *Dublin University Magazine*, run till 1840; published as book 1839] (P.) Lover, Samuel: *Rory O'More (P.)*	Poor Law Relief Act
1839	Carleton, William: *Fardarougha, the Miser; or The Convicts of Lisnamora* (P.)	
1840		Gerald Griffin (b. 1803) (d.)

DATE	AUTHOR AND TITLE	EVENT
1841	Boucicault, Dion (1820–90): *London Assurance* (D.) Lever, Charles: *Charles O'Malley* (P.)	*Cork Examiner* founded by John Francis Maguire (1815–72)
1842	Griffin, Gerald (*d.* 1840): *Talis Qualis; or Tales of the Jury Room* (P.); *Gissipus* (D.) Lover, Samuel: *Handy Andy* (P.)	*The Nation* founded by Thomas Davis, John Blake Dillon and Gavan Duffy (1775–1847) Daniel O'Connell calls off monster meeting at Clontarf John Banim (*b.* 1798) (*d.*)
1844	Lever, Charles: *Tom Bourke of 'Ours'* (P.); *Arthur O'Leary* (P.)	
1845	Carleton, William: *Tales and Sketches illustrating the Character ... of the Irish Peasantry* (P.) Le Fanu, Sheridan (1814–73): *The Cock and Anchor: Being a Chronicle of Old Dublin City* (P.) Mangan, James Clarence (1803–49): *Anthologia Germanica* (V.)	The Great Famine begins Emily Lawless (*b.*) Thomas Davis (*b.* 1814) (*d.*)
1846	Davis, Thomas (*d.* 1845): *The Poems* (V.); *Literary and Historical Essays* (P.)	Standish James O'Grady (*b.*) Charles Darley (*b.* 1795) (*d.*)
1847	Carleton, William: *Valentine M'Clutchy, the Irish Agent; or Chronicles of the Castle Cumber Property* (P.); *The Black Prophet; a tale of the Irish Famine* (P.)	
1848	Carleton, William: *The Emigrants of Ahadarra: A Tale of Irish Life* (P.) De Vere, Aubrey (1814–1902): *English Misrule and Irish Misdeeds* (P.)	*United Irishman* founded by John Mitchel Rising of Young Irelanders

DATE	AUTHOR AND TITLE	EVENT
1849	Mangan, James Clarence: *The Poets and Poetry of Munster*	Maria Edgeworth (*b.* 1767) (*d.*)
		James Clarence Mangan (*b.* 1803) (*d.*)
1850	Allingham, William (1824– 89): *Poems* (V.)	Tenant League formed
1852	Carleton, William: *The Squanders of Castle Squander* (P.); *The Black Baronet* (P.)	George Moore (*b.*)
		Isabella Augusta Persse (Lady Gregory) (*b.*)
		Thomas Moore (*b.* 1779) (*d.*)
1854	Lever, Charles: *The Dodd Family Abroad* (P); *The Martins of Cro'Martin* (P.)	Catholic University of Ireland founded with J. H. (later Cardinal) Newman as rector
	Mitchel, John (1815–75): *Jail Journal* (P.)	Oscar Fingal O'Flahertie Wills Wilde (*b.*)
1856		George Bernard Shaw (*b.*)
	Browne, Frances (1816–79): *Granny's Wonderful Chair* (P.)	
1858		Fenian Movement founded
		Edith Somerville (*b.*)
1859		Edward Martyn (*b.*)
		Lady Morgan (*b.?* 1776) (*d.*)
1860	Boucicault, Dion: *Colleen Bawn* (D.)	Douglas Hyde (*b.*)
1861	Callanan, Jeremiah John: *Collected Poems*	Katharine Tynan (*b.*)
	O'Curry, Eugene (1796–1862): *Lectures and Manuscript Materials of Ancient Irish History* (P.)	
1862	De Vere, Aubrey: *Innisfail, a Lyrical Chronicle of Ireland* (V.)	Martin Ross (Violet Martin) (*b.*)
	Leadbeater, Mary: *The Leadbeater Papers*	
	Lever, Charles: *Barrington* (P.)	
1863	Le Fanu, Sheridan: *The House by the Churchyard* (P.)	

DATE	AUTHOR AND TITLE	EVENT
1864	Allingham, William: *Laurence Bloomfield in Ireland* (V.) Boucicault, Dion: *Arrah-na-Pogue* (D.) Le Fanu, Sheridan: *Uncle Silas* (P.)	
1865	Ferguson, Sir Samuel: *Lays of the Western Gael* (V.) Lever, Charles: *Sir Brook Fossbrooke* (P.)	George A. Birmingham (J. O. Hannay) (*b.*) William Butler Yeats (*b.*)
1867	Kennedy, Patrick (1801–73): *The Banks of the Boro* (V.)	Matthew Arnold, *On the Study of Celtic Literature* Fenian Rising Manchester Martyrs AE (George Russell) (*b.*)
1868		Samuel Lover (*b.* 1797) (*d.*)
1869	Kickham, Charles J. (1828–82): *Sally Cavanagh* (P.)	Disestablishment of Church of Ireland William Carleton (*b.* 1794) (*d.*)
1871		John Millington Synge (*b.*) Gerald O'Donovan (Jeremiah O'Donovan) (*b.*)
1872	Ferguson, Sir Samuel: *Congal, an Epic Poem in Five Books* (V.) Lever, Charles: *Lord Kilgobbin* (P.)	Charles Lever (*b.* 1806) (*d.*)
1873	O'Curry, Eugene: *Manners and Customs of the Ancient Irish* (P.)	Sheridan Le Fanu (*b.* 1814)(*d.*) T. C. Murray (*b.*)
1874	Boucicault, Dion: *The Shaugraun* (D.)	Michael Banim (*b.* 1796) (*d.*)
1875		Forrest Reid (*b.*)

DATE	AUTHOR AND TITLE	EVENT
1878	Lecky, William Hartpole: *History of England in the Eighteenth Century* [8 vols, concluded 1870] (P.) O'Grady, Standish James (1846–1928): *History of Ireland: Heroic Period* [2nd vol. 1880] (P.)	Oliver St John Gogarty (*b.*)
1879	Kickham, Charles J.: *Knocknagow: or, the Cabins of Tipperary* (P.)	Patrick Pearse (*b.*)
1880	Le Fanu, Sheridan (*d.* 1873): *The Purcell Papers* (P.)	Sean O'Casey (*b.*) James Stephens (*b.*)
1881	Wilde, Oscar 1854–1900): *Poems*	Royal University of Ireland established Padraic Colum (*b.*)
1882		The Gaelic League founded University College, Dublin founded Phoenix Park murders James Joyce (*b.*)
1883	Moore, George (1852–1933): *A Modern Lover* (P.) Shaw, George Bernard (1856–1950): *An Unsocial Socialist* (P.)	
1884	Davitt, Michael (1846–1906): *Leaves from a Prison Diary* (P.) Moore, George: *A Mummer's Wife* (P.)	Henri D'Arbois de Jubainville, *Le Cycle Mythologique Irlandais et la Mythologie Celtique* Gaelic Athletic Association formed
1885	Tynan, Katharine (1861–1931): *Louise de la Vallière* (V.)	

DATE	AUTHOR AND TITLE	EVENT
1886	Lawless, Emily (1845–1913): *Hurrish* (P.) Moore, George: *A Drama in Muslin* (P.) Yeats, William Butler (1865–1939): *Mosada* (V.)	Lennox Robinson (*b.*) Sir Samuel Ferguson (*b.* 1810) (*d.*)
1887	Wilde, Lady Jane Francesca [Speranza] (1826–96): *Ancient Legends, Mystic Charms and Superstitions of Ireland* (P.)	National Library of Ireland established
1888	Allingham, William: *Poetical Works* (V.) Moore, George: *Confessions of a Young Man* (P.) Wilde, Oscar: *The Happy Prince and Other Tales* (P.) Yeats, William Butler: *Fairy and Folk Tales of the Irish Peasantry* (P.); (ed.), *Poems and Ballads of Young Ireland* (V.)	Sir John Rhys, *Lectures on the Origin and Growth of Religion as illustrated by Celtic Heathendom* Joyce Cary (*b.*)
1889	Graves, A. P.: *Father O'Flynn and other lyrics* (V.) Hyde, Douglas (1860–1949): *Beside the Fire* (P.); *Leabhar Sgeulaigheacta* (P.) O'Grady, Standish James: *Red Hugh's Captivity* (P.) Somerville, [Edith Œnone, (1858–1949)] and Ross [Martin, Violet Florence (1862–1915)] *An Irish Cousin* (P.) Yeats, William Butler: *The Wanderings of Oisin* (V.)	William Allingham (*b.* 1824) (*d.*)
1890	Curtin, Jeremiah (1838–1906): *Folklore of Ireland* (P.) French, Percy (1854–1920): *The Lord Liftinant and Other Tales* (P.)	Charles Stewart Parnell's divorce case Brinsley MacNamara (John Weldon) (*b.*) Dion Boucicault (*b.*? 1820) (*d.*)

DATE	AUTHOR AND TITLE	EVENT
	Hyde, Douglas: *Beside the Fire: a Collection of Irish Gaelic Folk Stories* (P.)	
	Wilde, Lady: *Ancient Cures, Charms and Usages of Ireland* (P.)	
1891	Shaw, George Bernard: *The Quintessence of Ibsenism* (P.)	Charles Stewart Parnell (*b.* 1846) (*d.*)
	Wilde, Oscar: *Lord Arthur Savile's Crime and Other Stories* (P.); *A House of Pomegranates* (P.); *The Picture of Dorian Gray* (P.)	
	Yeats, William Butler: *John Sherman and Dhoya* (P.)	
1892	Barlow, Jane (1857–1917): *Bog-Land Studies* (V.)	
	Lawless, Emily: *Grania. The Story of an Island* (P.)	
	O'Grady, Standish James: *Finn and his Companions* (P.)	
	O'Grady, Standish Hayes (1832–1915): *Silva Gadelica* (2 vols) (P.)	
	Yeats, William Butler, *The Countess Kathleen* (D. & V.); (ed.), *Irish Fairy Tales* (P.)	
1893	Hyde, Douglas: *Love Songs of Connacht* (V.)	Gaelic League founded with Douglas Hyde as president
	Wilde, Oscar: *Lady Windermere's Fan* (D.) *Salomé* [in French] (D.)	
	Yeats, William Butler: *The Celtic Twilight* (P. & V.); (ed.), *Blake* [with E. J. Ellis]	
1894	AE (George Russell) (1867–1935): *Homeward, Songs by the Way* (V.)	Irish Agricultural Organisation Society founded by Sir Horace Plunkett (1854–1932)
	Barlow, Jane: *Kerrigan's Quality* (P.)	

DATE   AUTHOR AND TITLE   EVENT

Larminie, William (1849–1900): *West Irish Folk Tales* (P.)

Moore, George: *Esther Waters* (P.)

Somerville [Edith] and Ross [Martin, Violet] : *The Real Charlotte* (P.)

Wilde, Oscar: *A Woman of No Importance* (D.); *The Sphinx* (V.); *Salomé* [tr. by Lord Alfred Douglas] (D.)

Yeats, William Butler: *The Land of Heart's Desire* (D.)

1895   Bullock, Shan (1865–1935): *By Thrasna River* (P.)   *Irish Homestead* begins

Hyde, Douglas: *The Story of Early Gaelic Literature* (P.)

Moore, George: *Celibates* (P.)

1896   Austin Clarke (*b.*)

Liam O'Flaherty (*b.*)

1897   AE (George Russell): *The Earth Breath* (V.)   First Oireachtas held in Dublin

Ferguson, Sir Samuel: *Lays of the Red Branch* (V.)

O'Grady, Standish James: *The Flight of the Eagle* (P.)

Ros, Amanda M'Kittrick (Anna M'Kittrick, 1860–1939): *Irene Iddesleigh* (P.)

Sigerson, George (1836–1925): *Bards of the Gael and Gall* (V.)

Stoker, Bram (Abraham) (1847–1912): *Dracula* (P.)

Yeats, William Butler: *The Secret Rose* (P.); *The Tables of the Law* (P.); *The Adoration of the Magi* (P.)

DATE	AUTHOR AND TITLE	EVENT
1898	Shaw, George Bernard: *Plays Pleasant and Unpleasant* (D.)	
	Wilde, Oscar: *The Ballad of Reading Gaol* (V.)	County Councils set up
1899	Boyle, William (1853–1923): *A Kish of Brogues* (P.)	Eleanor Hull (1860–1935) founds Irish Texts Society
	Hyde, Douglas: *A Literary History of Ireland* (P.)	Kuno Meyer (1858–1919) *Stories and Songs from Irish MSS*
	Martyn, Edward (1859–1924): *The Heather Field* (D.)	
	Somerville, [Edith] and Ross [Violet Martin] : *Some Experiences of an Irish R.M.* [*Further Experiences . . .* 1908; *In Mr Knox's Country*, 1915]	*The United Irishman* founded by Arthur Griffith (1871–1922) Elizabeth Bowen (*b.*)
	Wilde, Oscar: *An Ideal Husband* (D.); *The Importance of Being Earnest* (D.)	
	Yeats, William Butler: *The Wind Among the Reeds* (V.)	
1900	Sheehan, Canon Patrick (1852–1913): *My New Curate* (P.)	Cumann na nGaedhael begun by Arthur Griffith
	Yeats, William Butler: *The Shadowy Waters* (D.)	*The Leader* begun by D. P. Moran (1871–1936)
		Paul Vincent Carroll (*b.*)
		Sean O'Faolain (*b.*)
		Oscar Wilde (*b.* 1854) (*d.*)
1901	Hyde, Douglas: *'The Necessity for de-Anglicising Ireland'*	Denis Johnston (*b.*)
	Shaw, George Bernard: *Three Plays for Puritans* (D.)	
1902	Gregory, Lady Isabella Augusta (1852– 1932): *Cuchulain of Muirthemne* (P.)	Cuala Press founded Maud Gonne plays in *Cathleen ni Houlihan*
1903	Gregory, Lady: *Poets and Dreamers: Translations from the Irish* (P.)	Wyndham Land Act Frank O'Connor (Michael Francis O'Donovan) (*b.*)
	Mangan, James Clarence (*d.* 1849) *Poems* (V.)	

DATE	AUTHOR AND TITLE	EVENT
	Moore, George: *The Untilled Field* (P.)	
	Shaw, George Bernard: *Man and Superman* (D.)	
	Yeats, William Butler: *Ideas of Good and Evil* (P.); *Where There is Nothing* (D.)	
1904	Gregory, Lady: *Gods and Fighting Men* (P.); *Spreading the News* (D.)	Abbey Theatre, Dublin opened
		The journal *Eriu* founded
	Synge, John Millington (1871–1909): *Riders to the Sea* (D.)	Irish Folk Song Society formed
		Patrick Kavanagh (*b.*)
	Yeats William Butler: *The King's Threshold* (D.); *The Hour Glass* (D.); *In the Seven Woods* (V.)	O'Duinnin [Dineen], Father Padraig (1860–1934): *Irish English Dictionary* (enlarged edn, 1927; 1934)
1905	Birmingham, George A. (Rev. J. O. Hannay, 1865–1950): *The Seething Pot* (P.)	Sinn Fein established
	Campbell, Joseph (1879–1944): *The Garden of the Bees* (V.)	
	Colum, Padraic: *The Land* (D.)	
	Lord Dunsany (Edward John Moreton Drax Plunkett, 1878–1957): *The Gods of Pegana* (P.)	
	Moore, George: *The Lake* (P.)	
	Moran, D. P. (1871–1936): *Tom O'Kelly* (P.); *The Philosophy of Irish Ireland* (P.)	
	O'Sullivan, Seumas (James Sullivan Starkey, 1879–1958): *The Twilight People* (V.)	
	Shaw, George Bernard: *Major Barbara* (D.)	
	Synge, John Millington *[In] the Shadow of the Glen* (D.); *The Well of the Saints* (D.)	
	Wilde, Oscar: *De Profundis* (P.)	
1906	Dunsany, Lord: *Time and the Gods* (P.)	*Sinn Fein* issued
		Samuel Beckett (*b.*)
	Hyde, Douglas: *Religious Songs of Connacht* (V.)	

DATE	AUTHOR AND TITLE	EVENT
	Alexander McAllister (1877–1943): *Irene Wycherly* (D.)	
1907	Colum, Padraic (1881–1972): *Wild Earth* (V.)	Riots at the Abbey Theatre over Synge's *Playboy*
	Gregory, Lady: *The Rising of the Moon* (D.)	Louis MacNeice (*b.*)
	Joyce, James (1882–1941): *Chamber Music* (V.)	
	Shaw, George Bernard: *John Bull's Other Island* [produced 1904] (D.)	
	Synge, John Millington: *The Playboy of the Western World* (D.) *The Aran Isles* (P.)	
	Yeats, William Butler: *Deirdre* (D.)	
1908	Birmingham, George A: *Spanish Gold* (P.)	National University of Ireland established
	Dunsany, Lord: *The Sword of Welleran* (P.)	Irish Transport and General Workers Union begun by James Larkin (1876–1947)
	Robinson, Lennox (1886–1958): *The Clancy Name* (D.)	Denis Devlin (*b.*)
	Synge, John Millington: *The Tinker's Wedding* (D.)	
	Yeats, William Butler: *Collected Works* (8 vols)	
1909	Gregory, Lady: *Seven Short Plays* (D.); *The Kiltartan Books* [completed 1912] (P.)	John Millington Synge (*b.* 1871) (*d.*)
	Stephens, James (?1880–1950): *Insurrections* (V.)	
1910	Colum, Padraic: *Thomas Muskerry* (D.)	
	Dunsany, Lord: *A Dreamer's Tales* (P.)	
	Synge, John Millington: *Deirdre of the Sorrows* (D.)	
	Yeats, William Butler: *Poems: 2nd Series. The Green Helmet and Other Poems* (V.)	

DATE	AUTHOR AND TITLE	EVENT
1911	Ervine, St John (1883–1971): *Mixed Marriage* (D.)	Kuno Meyer *Ancient Irish Poetry*
	Moore, George: *Hail and Farewell* [2nd and 3rd vols, 1912, 1914] (P.); *The Apostle* (D.)	Brian O'Nolan [Flann O'Brien, Myles na gCopaleen] (*b*).
	Robinson, Lennox (1886–1958): *Two Plays [Harvest and the Clancy Name]* (D.)	
	Shaw, George Bernard: *The Doctor's Dilemma* (D.); *Fanny's First Play* (D.)	
1912	Birmingham, George A.: *The Red Hand of Ulster* (P.)	Irish Labour Party begun by James Connolly (1869–1916) and James Larkin
	Campbell, Joseph: *Poems* (V.)	
	Murray, T. C. (1873–1959): *Maurice Harte* (D.)	Terence de Vere White (*b*.)
	O'Sullivan, Seumas: *Collected Poems* (V.)	
	Reid, Forrest (1873–1947): *Following Darkness* (rewritten as *Peter Waring*, 1937) (P.)	
	Shaw, George Bernard: *Pygmalion* (D.)	
	Stephens, James: *The Charwoman's Daughter* (P.); *The Crock of Gold* (P.)	
	Yeats, William Butler: *The Cutting of An Agate* (P.)	
1913	AE (George Russell) *Collected Poems* (V.)	Irish Volunteers formed
	Doyle, Lynn (Leslie Montgomery, 1873–1961): *Love and Land* (D.)	Dublin lock-out and strike
		Emily Lawless (*b*. 1845) (*d*.)
	Gregory, Lady: *New Comedies* (D.)	
1914	Fitzmaurice George (1878–1963): *Five Plays* (D.)	Gun running at Larne and Howth
	Joyce, James: *Dubliners* (P.)	
	Yeats, William Butler: *Responsibilities* (V.)	

DATE	AUTHOR AND TITLE	EVENT
1915	Byrne, Donn (1889–1928): *Stories Without Women* (P.)	*Lusitania* sunk by U-boat, Sir Hugh Lane among passengers lost
	Ervine, St John: *John Ferguson* (D.)	Walter Macken (*b.*)
	Yeats, William Butler: *Reveries over Childhood and Youth* (P.)	Martin Ross (Violet Martin, *b.* 1862) (*d.*)
1916	AE (George Russell): *The National Being* (P.)	1916 Rising. Among leaders were: Padraic Pearse (*b.* 1879) Thomas MacDonagh (*b.* 1878) Joseph Mary Plunkett (*b.*1887) Michael O'Hanrahan (*b.* 1877)
	Boyd, Ernest A. (1887–1946): *Ireland's Literary Renaissance* (P.)	
	Corkery, Daniel (1871–1964): *A Munster Twilight* (P.)	Sir Roger Casement (*b.* 1864) hanged
	Joyce, James: *A Portrait of the Artist as a Young Man* (P.)	
	Ledwidge, Francis (1887–1917): *Songs of the Fields* (V.)	
	MacDonagh, Thomas (1878–1916): *Literature in Ireland, Studies Irish and Anglo-Irish* (P.)	
	Moore, George: *The Brook Kerith* (P.)	
	Shaw, George Bernard: *Androcles and the Lion* (D.)	
1917	Clarke, Austin (1896–1974): *The Vengeance of Fionn* (V.)	
	Eglinton, John (W. K. Magee 1868–1961): *Anglo-Irish Essays* (P.)	
	MacKenna, Stephen (1872–1934): *Works of Plotinus* (completed 1930)	
	O'Kelly, Seumas (1875–1918): *The Lady of Deerpark* (P.)	
	Yeats, William Butler: *The Wild Swans at Coole* (V.)	
1918	AE (George Russell): *The Candle Of Vision* (P.)	
	Doyle, Lynn (Leslie Montgomery 1873–1961): *Ballygullion* (P.)	

DATE	AUTHOR AND TITLE	EVENT
	Joyce, James: *Exiles* (P.)	
	MacNamara, Brinsley (John Weldon 1890–1963): *The Valley of the Squinting Windows* (P.)	
	Robinson, Lennox: *The Lost Leader* (D.)	
	Stephens, James: *Reincarnations* (V.)	
	Yeats, William Butler: *Per Amica Silentia Lunae* (P.)	
1919	Ledwidge, Francis: *Complete Poems* (V.)	Anglo-Irish war (lasts till 1921)
	O'Kelly, Seamus: *The Golden Barque and the Weaver's Grave* (P.)	Dail Eireann meets for first time
		Benedict Kiely (*b.*)
	O'Donovan, Gerald (Jeremiah Donovan, 1871–1942): *Waiting* (P.)	Iris Murdoch (*b.*)
	Shaw, George Bernard: *Heartbreak House* (D.); *Great Catherine* (D.)	
1920	Corkery, Daniel: *The Hounds of Banba* (P.); *The Yellow Bittern* (D.)	Robert Greacen (*b.*)
		James Plunkett (*b.*)
	Crofts, Freeman Wills (1879–1957): *The Cask* (P.)	W. J. White (*b.*)
	Robinson, Lennox: *The White-headed Boy* (D.)	
	Yeats, William Butler: *Michael Robartes and the Dancer* (V.)	
1921	Moore, George: *Héloïse and Abelard* (P.)	The truce
	Shaw, George Bernard: *Back to Methuselah* (D.)	Brian Moore (*b.*)
	Yeats, William Butler: *Four Plays for Dancers* (V.)	
1922	[French, Percy (1854–1920)] *Chronicles and Poems of Percy French* (P. & V.)	*Dublin Opinion* begins, runs till 1968
	Joyce, James: *Ulysses* (P.)	Ratification of the Treaty
		Civil War (1922–3)

DATE	AUTHOR AND TITLE	EVENT
	Yeats, William Butler: *Later Poems* (V.); *The Player Queen* (D.)	
1923	Bowen, Elizabeth (1899–1973): *Encounters* (P.)	*Dublin Magazine* founded by Seumas O'Sullivan (James Sullivan Starkey)
	Ireland, Michael [Darrell Figgis (1882–1925)] : *The Return of the Hero* (P.)	*Irish Statesman* founded, edited by AE
	O'Casey, Sean (1880–1964): *The Shadow of a Gunman* (D.)	Irish Free State government led by W. T. Cosgrave (until 1932)
	O'Flaherty, Liam (*b*. 1896): *Thy Neighbour's Wife*	W. B. Yeats awarded Nobel Prize for Poetry
	Shaw, George Bernard: *Saint Joan* (D.)	
1924	Birmingham, George A.: *The Grand Duchess* (P.)	*Freeman's Journal* ceases, founded 1763
	Corkery, Daniel: *The Hidden Ireland* (P.); *Resurrection* (D.)	Edward Martyn (*b*. 1859) (*d*.)
	Moore, George: *Conversations in Ebury Street* (P.)	
	O'Casey, Sean: *Juno and the Paycock* (D.)	
	O'Flaherty, Liam: *Spring Sowing* (P.)	
1925	Brock, Lynn (Alister or Alexander McAllister, 1877–1943): *The Deductions of Colonel Gore* (P.)	
	Byrne, Donn: *Hangman's House* (P.)	
	Corkery, Daniel: *The Hidden Ireland* (P.) 2nd edn	
	Higgins F(rederick) R(obert) (1896–1941): *Island Blood* (V.)	
	O'Flaherty, Liam: *The Informer* (P.)	
	Somerville and Ross: *The Big House at Inver* (P.)	
	Yeats, William Butler: *A Vision* (P.)	

DATE	AUTHOR AND TITLE	EVENT
1926	Byrne, Donn: *Hangman's House* (P.)	Fianna Fail party established by Eamonn de Valera
	MacNamara, Brinsley: *Look at the Heffernans* (D.)	Radio Eireann begins broadcasting
	O'Casey, Sean: *The Plough and the Stars* (D.)	
	O'Duffy, Eimar (1893–1935): *King Goshawk and the Birds* (P.)	
	O'Flaherty, Liam: *Mr Gilhooley* (P.)	
	Reid, Forrest: *Apostate* (P.)	
	Walsh, Maurice (1879–1964): *The Key above the Door* (P.)	
1927	Byrne, Donn: *Brother Saul* (P.)	
	Higgins, F. R.: *The Dark Breed* (V.)	
	Joyce, James: *Pomes Penyeach* (V.)	
	Murray, T. C.: *The Pipe in the Fields* (D.)	
1928	Joyce, James: *Anna Livia Plurabelle* (P.)	Gate Theatre Dublin opened
	O'Donnell, Peadar (*b.* 1893): *Islanders* (P.)	Standish James O'Grady (*b.* 1846) (*d.*)
	Yeats, William Butler: *The Tower* (V.)	
1929	Bowen, Elizabeth: *The Last September* (P.)	Censorship of Publications Act
	Clarke, Austin: *Pilgrimage and Other Poems* (V.)	
	Hackett, Francis (1883–1962): *Henry the Eighth* (P.)	
	Johnston, Denis (*b.* 1901): *The Old Lady Says 'No!'* (D.)	
	MacNeice, Louis (1907–63): *Blind Fireworks* (V.)	
	O'Casey, Sean: *The Silver Tassie* (D.)	
	Yeats, William Butler: *The Winding Stair* (V.)	

DATE	AUTHOR AND TITLE	EVENT
1930	Coffey, Brian (*b*. 1905) with Devlin, Denis (1908–59): *Poems* (V.)	
	Ervine, St John: *The First Mrs Fraser* (D.)	
	Shaw, George Bernard: *The Apple Cart* (D.)	
1931	AE (George Russell): *Vale* (V.)	Katharine Tynan (*b*. 1861) (*d*.)
	Corkery, Daniel: *Synge and Anglo-Irish Literature* (P.)	
	Hanley, James (*b*. 1901): *Boy* (P.)	
	Johnston, Denis: *The Moon in the Yellow River* (D.)	
	O'Brien, Kate (1897–1974): *Without my Cloak* (P.)	
	O'Connor, Frank (Michael Francis O'Donovan, 1903–66): *Guests of the Nation* (P.)	
	Robinson, Lennox: *The Far-off Hills* (D.)	
1932	Bowen, Elizabeth: *To the North* (P.)	Fianna Fail party led by de Valera wins election, in power 1932–48
	Carroll, Paul Vincent (1900–68): *Things that are Caesar's* (D.) (stage)	Eucharistic congress, Dublin
	Cary, Joyce (1888–1957): *Aissa Saved* (P.)	Lady Gregory (*b*. 1852) (*d*.)
	Deevy, Teresa (1903–63): *Temporal Powers* (D.)	
	O'Connor, Frank: *The Saint and Mary Kate* (P.)	
	O'Donnell, Peadar: *The Gates Flew Open* (D.)	
	O'Faolain, Sean (*b*. 1900): *Midsummer Madness* (P.)	
	O'Flaherty, Liam: *The Puritan* (P.); *Skerrett* (P.)	
	Shaw, George Bernard: *Too True to be Good* (D.); *Adventures of a Black Girl in Search of God* (P.)	

DATE	AUTHOR AND TITLE	EVENT
	Stuart, Francis (b. 1902): *The Coloured Dome* (P.)	
	Yeats, William Butler: *Words for Music Perhaps* (V.)	
1933	AE (George Russell): *The Avatars* (P.)	George Moore (b. 1852) (d.)
	Conner, Reardon (b. 1907): *Shake Hands with the Devil* (P.)	O'Suilleabham Muiris (1904): *Fiche Blian ag Fa's* (trs as *Twenty Years A-growing*, 1933)
	O'Faolain, Sean: *A Nest of Simple Folk* (P.)	
	Robinson, Lennox: *Drama at Inish* (D.)	
	Starkie, Walter (1894–1976): *Raggle Taggle* (P.)	
	Yeats, William Butler: *Collected Poems* [2nd edn 1950; variorum edn 1957]; *The Winding Stair and Other Poems* (V.)	
1934	Beckett, Samuel (b. 1906): *More Pricks than Kicks* (P.)	
	Carroll, Paul Vincent: *Things that are Caesar's* (D.)	
	Lynch, Patricia (1900–72): *The Turf Cutter's Donkey* (P.)	
	MacManus, Francis (1909–65): *Stand and Give Challenge* (P.)	
	Mayne, Rutherford (Samuel Waddell 1878–1967): *Bridgehead* (D.)	
	Robinson, Lennox: *Killycregs in Twilight* (D.)	
	Yeats, William Butler: *The King of the Great Clock Tower* (V.); *Collected Plays* (new edn, 1952) (D.); *Wheels and Butterflies* (D.)	
1935	Deevy, Teresa: *The King of Spain's Daughter* (D.)	AE (George Russell) (b. 1867) (d.)
	Ervine, St John: *Boyd's Shop* (D.)	
	Gibbon, Monk (b. 1896): *The Seals* (P.)	

DATE	AUTHOR AND TITLE	EVENT
	MacNeice, Louis: *Poems* (V.)	
	Yeats, William Butler: *A Full Moon in March* (V.)	
1936	Cary, Joyce: *The African Witch* (P.)	IRA declared illegal
	Dunsany, Lord: *My Talks with Dean Spanley* (P.)	
	Hackett, Francis: *The Green Lion* (P.)	
	Kavanagh, Patrick (1904–61): *Ploughman and Other Poems* (V.)	
	Lewis, C. S.: *The Allegory of Love* (P.)	
	O'Brien, Kate: *Mary Lavelle* (P.)	
	O'Faolain, Sean: *Bird Alone* (P.)	
1937	Carroll, Paul Vincent: *Shadow and Substance* (D.)	New constitution
	Devlin, Denis: *Intercessions* (P.)	Douglas Hyde elected first President of Ireland
	Gogarty, Oliver St John (1878–1957): *As I was Going Down Sackville Street* (P.)	
	O'Flaherty, Liam: *Famine* (P.)	
1938	Beckett, Samuel: *Murphy* (P.)	Anglo-Irish agreement
	Bowen, Elizabeth: *The Death of the Heart* (P.)	
	Cary, Joyce: *Castle Corner* (P.)	
	Farrell, M.J. (Molly Keane): *Spring Meeting* (D.)	
	Kavanagh, Patrick: *The Green Fool* (P.)	
	McManus, Seamus (1868–1960): *The Rocky Road to Dublin* (P.)	
	Yeats, William Butler: *New Poems* (V.); *The Herne's Egg* (D.)	
1939	Carroll, Paul Vincent: *The White Steed* (D.)	William Butler Yeats (*b.* 1865) (*d.*)
	Cary, Joyce: *Mister Johnson* (P.)	

DATE	AUTHOR AND TITLE	EVENT
	Connell, F. Norreys (Conal O'Riordan): *Judith Quinn* (P.)	
	Joyce, James: *Finnegan's Wake* (P.)	
	McLaverty, Michael: *Call my brother back* (P.)	
	MacNeice, Louis: *Autumn Journal* (V.)	
	O'Brien, Flann (Brian O'Nolan, 1911–66): *At Swim-Two-Birds* (P.)	
	O'Casey, Sean: *I Knock at the Door 1880–1890* (P.)	
	Shaw, George Bernard: *In Good King Charles's Golden Days* (D.)	
	Yeats, William Butler: *Last Poems and Two Plays* (V. & D.)	
1940	Cary, Joyce: *Charley is my Darling* (P.)	*The Bell* begins
	D'Alton, Louis (1900–51): *The Spanish Soldier* (D.)	Lyric Theatre founded
	O'Casey, Sean: *The Star turns Red* (D.); *Purple Dust* (D.)	
	O'Connor, Frank: *Dutch Interior* (P.)	
	O'Sullivan, Seumas (James Sullivan Starkey): *Collected Poems* (V.)	
	Shiels, George (1886–1949): *The Rugged Path* (D.)	
1941	Cary, Joyce: *Herself Surprised* (P.); *A House of Children* (P.)	James Joyce (*b.* 1882) (*d.*)
	O'Brien, Flann (Brian O'Nolan): *An Béal Bocht* (tr. *The Poor Mouth*, 1973) (P.)	
	O'Brien, Kate: *The Land of Spices* (P.)	
	Stephens, James: *Collected Poems* (V.)	
1942	Bowen, Elizabeth: *Bowen's Court* (P.)	Gerald O'Donovan (*b.* 1871) (*d.*)

DATE   AUTHOR AND TITLE   EVENT

Connell, Vivian (*b*. 1905): *The Chinese Room* (P.)

Cross, Eric (*b*. 1903): *The Tailor and Ansty* (P.)

Kavanagh, Patrick: *The Great Hunger* (V.)

Lavin, Mary (*b*. 1912): *Tales from Bective Bridge* (P.)

Lewis, C. S.: *The Screwtape Letters* (P.)

O'Casey, Sean: *Red Roses for Me* (D.); *Pictures in the Hallway* (P.)

1943   Bell, Sam Hanna (*b*. 1909): *Summer Loanen and Other Stories* (P.)

Day-Lewis, Cecil: *Word over all* (V.)

O'Brien, Kate: *The Last of Summer* (P.)

Paul Vincent Carroll joins 'James Bridie' and others in founding Glasgow Citizens Theatre

1944   Cary, Joyce: *The Horse's Mouth* (P.)

Joyce, James: (*d*. 1941): *Stephen Hero* (P.)

MacNeice, Louis: *Springboard* (V.)

1945   Iremonger, Valentin (*b*. 1918): *Reservations* (V.)

Lavin, Mary: *The House in Clew Street* (P.)

1946   Bowen, Elizabeth: *The Demon Lover* (P.)

Devlin, Denis: *Lough Derg* (V.)

Kiely, Benedict (*b*. 1919): *Land Without Stars* (P.)

MacDonagh, Donagh: *Happy as Larry* (D.)

MacNeice, Louis: *The Dark Tower and other Radio Scripts* (D.)

Wall, Mervyn (Eugene Welply *b*. 1908): *The Unfortunate Fursey* (P.)

DATE	AUTHOR AND TITLE	EVENT
1947	MacDonagh, Donagh (1912– 68): *The Hungry Grass*	Forrest Reid (*b.* 1875) (*d.*)
1948	Bowen, Elizabeth: *Collected Edition* (1948–)	Fine Gael elected, John A. Costello Taoiseach
	Day-Lewis, Cecil: *Collected Poems 1929–36; Poems 1943–7* (V.)	
	Kavanagh, Patrick: *Tarry Flynn* (P.)	
	MacMahon, Bryan (*b.* 1909): *The Liontamer and Other Stories* (P.)	
	O'Flaherty, Liam: *Two lovely beasts* (P.)	
	Stuart, Francis: *A Pillar of Cloud* (P.)	
1949	Bowen, Elizabeth: *The Heat of the Day* (P.)	Douglas Hyde (*b.* 1860) (*d.*)
	Cary, Joyce: *A Fearful Joy* (P.)	Edith Somerville (*b.* 1858) (*d.*)
	Devlin, Denis: *Exile* (D.)	
	MacNeice, Louis: *Collected Poems 1925–48* (V.)	
	O'Casey, Sean: *Cockadoodle Dandy* (D.); *Inish fallen, Fare Thee Well* (P.)	
1950	Macken, Walter (1915–67): *Rain on the Wind* (P.)	George A. Birmingham (Rev. J. O. Hannay, *b.* 1865) (*d.*)
		George Bernard Shaw (*b.* 1856) (*d.*)
		James Stephens (*b.*?1880) (*d.*)
1951	Beckett, Samuel: *Molloy* (P.); *Malone meurt* (P.)	Fine Gael government resigns
	Gogarty, Oliver St John: *Collected Poems* (V.)	Abbey Theatre burned down
1952	Craig, Maurice James (*b.* 1919): *Dublin 1660–1860* (P.)	
	O'Connor, Frank: *The Stories of Frank O'Connor* (P.)	

DATE	AUTHOR AND TITLE	EVENT
1953	Beckett, Samuel: *En Attendant Godot* (D.); *L'Innommable* (P.)	Pike Theatre opened in Dublin
	Colum, Padraic: *Collected Poems* (V.)	
1954	Day-Lewis, Cecil: *Collected Poems* (V.)	
	MacNeice, Louis: *Autumn Sequel* (V.)	
	Murdoch, Iris (*b.* 1919): *Under the Net* (P.)	
	O'Casey, Sean: *Sunset and Evening Star* (P.)	
1955	Clarke, Austin: *Ancient Lights* (V.)	
	Moore, Brian (*b.* 1921): *The Lonely Passion of Judith Hearne* (P.)	
	Plunkett, James (*b.* 1920): *The Trusting and the Maimed* (P.)	
1956	Byrne, Seamus (1904–68): *Design for a Headstone* (D.)	
	O'Flaherty, Liam: *The Stories of Liam O'Flaherty* (P.)	
1957	Lynn, Doyle: *The Ballygullion Bus* (last collection of stories begun in 1908) (P.)	Fianna Fail elected (1957–63)
		Lantern Theatre, Dublin opens
		Joyce Cary (*b.* 1888) (*d.*)
		Oliver St John Gogarty (*b.* 1878) (*d.*)
1958	MacDonagh, Donagh, with Robinson, Lennox (eds): *Oxford Book of Irish Verse* (V.)	Lennox Robinson (*b.*1886) (*d.*)
	O'Brien, Kate: *As Music and Splendour* (P.)	
1959	Dillon, Eilis (*b.* 1920): *The Singing Cave* (P.)	de Valera president of Ireland
	Lavin, Mary: *Short Stories* (P.)	Denis Devlin (*b.* 1908) (*d.*)
	Macken, Walter: *Seek the Fair Land* (P.)	T. C. Murray (*b.* 1873) (*d.*)
	White, Terence de Vere (*b.* 1912): *A Fretful Midge* (P.)	

DATE	AUTHOR AND TITLE	EVENT
1960	Kavanagh, Patrick: *Come dance with Kitty Stobling* (V.) Moore, Brian: *The Luck of Ginger Coffey* (P.)	
1961	Clarke, Austin: *Later Poetry* (V.) MacNeice, Louis: *Solstices* (V.) Murdoch, Iris: *A Severed Head* (P.)	Television service begins
1963	Campbell, Joseph (*d.* 1944): *Poems of Joseph Campbell* (V.) Farrell, Michael (1899–1962): *Thy Tears Might Cease* (P.) Murdoch, Iris: *The Unicorn* (P.) West, Anthony C. (*b.* 1910): *The Ferret Fancier* (P.) White, W. J. (1920–80): *The Devil You Know* (P.)	Brinsley MacNamara (John Weldon) (*b.* 1890) (*d.*) Louis MacNeice (*b.* 1907) (*d.*)
1964	Devlin, Denis: *Collected Poems* (V.) Kavanagh, Patrick: *Collected Poems* (V.) O'Brien, Flann (Brian O'Nolan): *The Dalkey Archive* (P.) O'Connor, Frank: *An Only Child* (P.); *Collection Two* (P.) O'Faolain, Sean: *Vive Moi* (P.)	Sean O'Casey (*b.* 1880) (*d.*)
1965	MacNeice, Louis (*d.* 1963): *The Strings are False* (P.) Moore, Brian: *The Emperor of Ice Cream* (P.) Murdoch, Iris: *The Red and the Green* (P.)	
1966	Boyle, Patrick (*b.* 1905): *Like Any Other Man* (P.) Clarke, Austin: *Mnemosyne lay in dust* (V.) MacNeice, Louis: *Collected Poems* (V.)	New Abbey Theatre opens Frank O'Connor (*b.* 1903) (*d.*) Brian O'Nolan [Flann O'Brien, Myles na gCopaleen] (*b.* 1911) (*d.*)

DATE	AUTHOR AND TITLE	EVENT
1967	Holloway, Joseph (d. 1944): *Joseph Holloway's Abbey Theatre* (P.) Kavanagh, Patrick: *Collected Pruse* (P.) O'Brien, Flann (Brian O'Nolan, d. 1966): *The Third Policeman* (P.) O'Connor, Frank: *The Backward Look* (P.)	Patrick Kavanagh (b. 1904) (d.) Walter Macken (b. 1915) (d.)
1968	Hewitt, John (b. 1907): *Collected Poems* (V.) Moore, Brian: *I am Mary Dunne* (P.)	Cecil Day-Lewis Poet Laureate Civil Rights association demonstrating in Northern Ireland Paul Vincent Carroll (b. 1900) (d.)
1969	Fitzmaurice, George (d. 1963): *Plays* (D.) Plunkett, James: *Strumpet City* (P.)	Rioting in Northern Ireland Samuel Beckett receives Nobel Prize
1970	Beckett, Samuel: *Collected Works*, 16 vols	*Irish University Review* begins
1971	Coffey, Brian: *Selected Poems* (V.) Lavin, Mary: *Collected Stories* (P.) McGreevy, Thomas (1893–1967): *Collected Poems* (V.) Rodgers, W. R. (d. 1969): *Collected Poems* (V.) Stuart, Francis: *Black List Section H* (P.)	
1972	Ledwidge, Francis (d. 1917): *Collected Poems* (V.) Moore, Brian: *Catholics* (P.)	Cecil Day-Lewis (b. 1904) (d.) Padraic Colum (b. 1881) (d.)

DATE	AUTHOR AND TITLE	EVENT
1973		Ireland joins EEC Elizabeth Bowen (*b*. 1899) (*d*.)
1974	Clarke, Austin: *Collected Poems* (V.) Fallon, Padraic (1905—74): *Poems* (V.)	Austin Clarke (*b*. 1896) (*d*.) Padraic Fallon (*b*. 1905) (*d*.)
1975	Coffey, Brian: *Advent* (V.) Greacen, Robert (*b*. 1920): *A Garland for Captain Fox* (V.)	
1976	Boyle, Patrick: *A View from Calvary* (P.) O'Faolain, Sean: *Foreign Affairs* (P.) O'Flaherty, Liam: *The Pedlar's Revenge and Other Stories* (P.)	
1977	Plunkett, James: *Collected Short Stories; Farewell Companions* (P.)	
1979	Moore, Brian: *The Mangan Inheritance* (P.)	
1980	Greacen, Robert: *Young Mr. Gibbon* (V.)	
1981	Keane, Molly (*b* ?): *Good Behaviour* (P.)	

Index